COMMENTARY

ON THE

EPISTLES TO THE THESSALONIANS

COMMENTARY

ON THE GREEK TEXT

OF THE

EPISTLES OF PAUL TO THE

THESSALONIANS

JOHN EADIE, D.D., LL.D.

EDITED BY THE
REV. WILLIAM YOUNG, M.A.

WITH PREFACE BY THE REV. PROFESSOR CAIRNS, D.D.

Wipf & Stock
PUBLISHERS
Eugene, Oregon

Wipf and Stock Publishers
199 W 8th Ave, Suite 3
Eugene, OR 97401

A Commentary on the Greek Text of the Epistle of Paul to the Thessalonians
By Eadie, John
Copyright©1979 by Eadie, John
ISBN: 1-57910-166-6
Publication date 10/2/1998
Previously published by T & T Clark/Baker, 1979

𝔇𝔢𝔡𝔦𝔠𝔞𝔱𝔢𝔡,

BY KIND PERMISSION,

TO

THOMAS BIGGART, ESQ.,

OF DALRY,

BY THE AUTHOR'S WIDOW,

WITH GRATEFUL APPRECIATION OF HIS

PRACTICAL PROOF OF AFFECTION FOR HER HUSBAND'S MEMORY,

AND DEVOTION TO THE INTERESTS OF THE

UNITED PRESBYTERIAN CHURCH,

IN THE PURCHASE OF HER HUSBAND'S LIBRARY

FOR THE THEOLOGICAL HALL.

PREFACE

THE Lectures on First and Second Thessalonians here published were designed by their lamented author for the press; and they will be found to display in full measure his eminent qualities as an expositor. There is the same extensive and minute scholarship; the same originality of research and independence of judgment; the same penetration and sagacity in tracing the course of argument; and the same unfailing sympathy with the deepest thoughts and lessons of inspiration. Independently of his own understood purpose, these rare excellencies would have required the issue of what is likely to be his final contribution to exegetical literature. Nor is it without interest that a career of exposition, devoted to so many of Paul's epistles, returns upon itself to end with the first that bear his name.

The author's manuscript, which presents every mark of being complete, has been most carefully transcribed; and the quotations and references have been verified. Special thanks are due to the Rev. William Young, M.A., of Parkhead Church, Glasgow, who has kindly discharged the duties of editorship, and striven in every way to carry the work through the press, in as accurate a state as possible; and cordial acknowledgments are also made to the Rev. Professor Dickson, of the University of Glasgow, who has subjected the proof sheets to a final revision.

It is not doubted that this commentary will be welcomed by all lovers of sacred learning, and will tend to foster that exact study of the original Scriptures, the impulse given to which is perhaps the greatest of its author's many services to the church of Christ.

JOHN CAIRNS

NOTE BY THE EDITOR

WHILE it is certain that Dr. Eadie regarded the following work as ready for the press, it is much to be regretted that he did not live to give it those final touches which would have rendered it still more perfect and complete. It will be observed that there is no separate Introduction to the Second Epistle, though this will be found to some extent provided for in the Introduction to the First. In the manuscript, too, there are some indications that Dr. Eadie contemplated adding other two Essays to that on the "Man of Sin,"—one on the "Resurrection," and the other on the "Second Advent." With these exceptions, and that noted on page 96, the manuscript seems in every respect complete, and carefully arranged for publication. It is hoped that the work, though a posthumous one, will be found to have been well worth publishing; and that the state in which it is issued from the press will not do dishonour to so great and so dear a name.

9 ROSLEA DRIVE,
 October, 1877.

INTRODUCTION

I—The City of Thessalonica

THESSALONICA (Θεσσαλονίκη) was formerly called Therma (Θέρμη or Θέρμα), and the gulf on which it stood was named *Thermaicus Sinus*, on account of the hot salt springs which abounded in the vicinity. Two earlier legendary names have been handed down, Emathia and Halia.[1] The origin of the present name has been variously accounted for. According to Strabo,[2] Therma was rebuilt by Cassander, who added to it the population of three small towns near it, and called it Thessalonica, after his wife, a daughter of Philip. Stephen of Byzantium records, that Philip himself bestowed the new appellation in honour of a victory gained by him over the Thessalonians;[3] while in the *Etymologicum Magnum*[4] it is said that Philip gave the name in honour of his daughter whose mother had died in childbirth. Xerxes, according to Herodotus, paused at Therma, while his fleet cruised in the gulf, and his army lay at a short distance; and the town is mentioned by this early name twice at least in Greek history.[5] But the more ancient names have long passed out of view,

---

[1] Zonaras Hist. xii, 26; Steph. Byz., sub voce.
[2] Strabo, viii, p. 330.
[3] Θιττάλους νικήσας.
[4] τὸ παιδίον ἔδωκε Νίκῃ τρέφειν καὶ ἐκάλεσε Θεσσαλονίκην, ἡ γὰρ μήτηρ τοῦ παιδίου Νικασίπολις ἐκεκλῆτο.
[5] Herodotus, vii, 128; Thucydides, i, 61; Æschines de Falsa Leg.

while Thessalonica still survives in the corrupt forms Σαλονίκη, Saloniki. The city came first into eminence during the Macedonian period; and the new name, from whatever cause, may have been imposed by Philip, his own name being found in the neighbouring Philippi.

Thessalonica, rebuilt about B.C. 315, is first mentioned by Polybius and Livy as a great naval station.[1] When Macedonia was divided into four parts under Paulus Æmilius by the edicts of Amphipolis, it was made the capital of the second, or that part which lay between the Axius and the Strymon; and when, eighteen years afterwards, those four divisions were formed into one province, it became in course of time the metropolis.[2] At the period of the first Roman civil war it was occupied by the party of Pompey (Dion Cass., xli., 20), but during the second it sided with Antony and Octavius, and was on that account made an *urbs libera* (Appian, B. C., iv, 118). As a seaport on the inner bend or basin of the Thermaic Gulf,[3] and about half-way between the Hellespont and the Adriatic, Thessalonica grew into great importance. It shared largely in the commerce of the Ægean and the Levant, and in the inland traffic of the country, for behind it lay the great pass that led away to the Macedonian uplands, and it was closely connected with the large plain watered by the Axius. It was filled, according to Strabo, with a greater population than any other town in the region. Lucian makes a similar statement.[4] Theodoret also styles it πολυάνθρωπος.[5] Thessalonica has passed through many vicissitudes, but it is still the second city in European Turkey. With its history after apostolic times we have no immediate concern. It may, however, be noted that in the third century it was made a Roman colony, and it was the great bulwark of the empire during the Gothic inroads and the six Sclavonian wars. Theodosius executed by barbarian troops a terrible

---

[1] Polyb., xxxiii, 4, 4; Livy, xxxix, 27, xliv, 10.

[2] Strabo, who calls it Θεσσαλονικεία, says of it, ἣ νῦν μάλιστα τῶν ἄλλων εὐανδρεῖ (vii, 7, 4).

[3] Medio flexu litoris (Thermaici Sinus). Pliny, iv, 10. Strabo speaks of an isthmus εἰς τὸν Θερμαῖον διήκων μυχόν. Geog. viii, 1-3.

[4] Πόλεως τῶν ἐν Μακεδονίᾳ τῆς μεγίστης Θεσσαλονίκης. Asinus Aureus, 46.

[5] Hist. Eccles., v, 17.

massacre of thousands of its citizens as a punishment for the assassination of one of his generals; and for this atrocity he was obliged to do public penance at Milan under Ambrose, who, with a sublime and faithful audacity, refused the master of the world admission into the great Church; and only after eight months suspension, and a full confession in presence of the congregation, was he readmitted into church-fellowship on Christmas, 390 A.D. Thessalonica was three times taken—by the Saracens in 904, by Tancred and the Normans in 1185, and by the Turks under Amurath II, in 1430. Numerous and imposing monuments of its earlier greatness are still to be found in it. The old Roman road forms at the present day the main thoroughfare, and two of its arches may yet be seen. Fragments of columns abound, the sculptures and inscriptions of many of which indicate their varying ages, and the purposes of their original erection. The reader will find information on all points in Tafel (*Histor. Thessalon.*).

II—THE APOSTLE'S VISIT AND THE INTRODUCTION
OF THE GOSPEL

In the course of his second missionary journey the Apostle, along with Silas, and probably Timothy also, crossed over to Europe. "Loosing from Troas," touching at Samothrace, landing at Neapolis, he passed up to Philippi, where, as he says in this epistle, he had suffered and was shamefully entreated. In a Roman colony the majesty of the law was violated in his person; for, though he was a Roman citizen, he had been beaten with the lictor's rods—a punishment forbidden by the Porcian and Valerian statutes; and though he had not been convicted or even tried, the flagellation had been public, which was held to be an aggravation of the offence, and he had been also cast into prison. The terrified duumvirs, knowing at length what a crime they had committed, and what terrible vengeance would be inflicted on them, besought Paul and Silas to depart that the matter might be hushed up as speedily as possible. The apostle and his colleague having taken farewell of Lydia, at once left Philippi, as it presented no immediate prospect of usefulness. He travelled south and west, along the Egnatian road, thirty-three miles to Amphipolis, on the Strymonic gulf, but did not stay there, advanced thirty miles farther to Apollonia, and did not halt there either, but journeyed onwards other thirty-seven miles, and arrived at Thessalonica. This Macedonian capital had special attractions for him, as it had a large heathen and Jewish population, and could become a centre of missionary operations, as it was the chief station on the Egnatian road which connected Rome with the regions to the north of the Ægean. Cicero, who, when an exile, had found refuge in it, and had often tarried in it on his way to and from his Cilician province, describes it as *posita in gremio Romani imperii*. The Jews in it and its neighbourhood were so numerous as to have a synagogue; for the correct reading of Acts is, " where was the synagogue of the Jews" (Acts xvii, 1). Fully a third of the population is supposed to be Jewish at the present moment; the Jewish quarter being in the south-eastern section of the town. Allusions to the Thessalonian Jews as being numerous, and as forming an important section of the people, occur in several authors.

True to his heart's desire and prayer to God for Israel, the apostle commenced to labour in the synagogue. Though his special function was the apostolate for the Gentiles, he never forgot his own people, but, as his manner was, " went in unto them," and for three consecutive Sabbath days "preached to them." He and they had common ground " when he reasoned with them out of the Scriptures," the divine authority of which they acknowledged equally with himself. His reasonings were of course based on the Old Testament and had for their theme its central doctrine—the Messiah to come. His argument took two shapes—he " was opening," that is, he unfolded their sense, and "alleging," that is, he propounded or advanced the truth which the exposition had disclosed. The question at issue was —what is the idea of the Messiah as portrayed in the Old Testament, and has it been realized? Show from the law and the prophets what He was to be and then tell what Jesus was, depict what He was to do and then picture what Jesus did, and thus it could be proved how minutely the living person corresponded to the prophetic ideal. Now there was one point of transcendent moment in their national prophecies which the

Jewish people sadly misconceived—the suffering and death of the promised Messiah. The cross was a stumbling-block to them. They could not imagine that one who had been publicly executed could be the Messiah. So foreign was such a possibility to all their imaginations and hopes that they could not entertain it; and so certain were they that they were right, that they refused to examine it. The bare statement was to them its own refutation. The inspired preacher therefore took the right course and showed them that the promised Messiah was depicted specially and characteristically as a suffering Messiah—"opening and alleging that Christ must needs have suffered and risen again from the dead." So that if any one professing to be the Christ did not encounter agony and death, he must be an impostor; for only one who had died and risen again fits into prophetic fore-announcement and has a right to be regarded as Israel's hope and God's anointed servant. The burden of the apostle's teaching therefore was that in order to fulfil the Scriptures, the Christ must needs have suffered and have risen again from the dead; it being a plain consequence that one who had met with no suffering and hostility, but had been caressed on his triumphal car as he rode from victory to victory, could not be the Christ, for he did not embody in himself these old inspired predictions. The Christ promised was not only to teach many things but to endure many things, was to die while he conquered and rise from his tomb to universal empire. A grave lay between Him and His throne; for His kingdom was to be won by His blood. In short, the leading distinction of the Messiah to come was suffering and death. The first gospel in Eden dimly alluded to it. The typical dispensation had long foreshadowed it in the blood of its victims; the paschal lamb had pointed to the Lamb of God which taketh away the sin of the world—"Even Christ our passover sacrificed for us." Isaiah had described it with graphic minuteness; and in such a light the apostle accepted the fifty-third chapter of his oracles—"He was wounded for our transgressions and bruised for our iniquities"—"The Lord laid on Him the iniquity of us all"—"He is brought as a lamb to the slaughter"—"Cut off out of the land of the living"—"For the transgressions of my people was he stricken"—"It pleased the

Lord to bruise Him"—"His soul was made an offering for sin"—
"He hath poured out His soul unto death"—"He bare the sin
of many." The Psalmist had pictured Him as the great obla-
tion for man in man's nature—"a body hast Thou prepared Me."
Daniel had portrayed Messiah the Prince, not as clothed in
purple, but as one who "shall be cut off." The prophetic delineations of His conquest and kingdom presuppose his resurrection—"He rose again the third day according to the scriptures." His reward was a "portion with the great and the
dividing of the spoil with the strong." The second psalm depicts a conspiracy of the heathen and the people, Gentile and
Jew, kings and princes, Herod and Pontius Pilate, against Jesus
at His condemnation and death; and yet his enemies are overthrown, and He is installed as King upon God's holy Hill of
Zion. In being put to a death of shame and agony He
"abolished death," and the words were heard, "The Lord said
unto my Lord, Sit thou at my right hand until I make thine
enemies thy footstool." By such a chain of passages could the
apostle out of the Scriptures open and allege that the Messiah
to come was signally fore-pictured as a Messiah to suffer and
die and rise again from the dead. An unsuffering Christ such
as the nation dreamed of—warlike as David and glorious as
Solomon—could not be the promised Christ, for He wanted one
grand and prominent feature of similitude. Having shown that
the Messiah delineated in the Old Testament was to be noted
and known for His sufferings, the apostle then argued, "that
this one is the Christ—Jesus whom I preach unto you," or "that
Jesus whom I preach unto you is this Christ." This Jesus having
suffered and risen again has fulfilled the necessary conditions of
prophecy. The life and career of Jesus are in perfect harmony
with those prophecies which went before concerning Him.
The circumstances of that death had been foretold, and they
were quite peculiar. It was not to be the national mode of
execution by stoning, but by crucifixion—hanging on a tree, a
mode unauthorized by the law of Moses; for suspension from a
stake was only a posthumous degradation inflicted on some
criminals who had been already stoned to death. It was to be
preceded by treachery and an illegal condemnation—suborned
witnesses not even agreeing in their testimony. Despised and

rejected was He to be—"Not this man but Barabbas." Preparatory to His execution He was to be stripped of His clothes—"They part my raiment among them and cast lots upon my vesture," and so it was, as the evangelist tells us. He was to die and yet "not a bone of Him to be broken;" to be numbered with transgressors and yet to lie in a rich man's tomb. Not only was He to suffer openly at the hands of men, but there was to be an inner mysterious element in His agony—"He hath put Him to grief"—and so His mysterious complaint on the Cross was, "My God, my God, why hast thou forsaken me?" The conclusion to which the apostle in this way strove to bring them was that this Jesus is the Christ, surrounded by so great a cloud of witnesses; for His sufferings, in their character and purpose, in themselves and their adjuncts, were in close harmony with old prediction; the law and the prophets fulfilled in the agony of His Cross and humiliation of His sepulchre: the record of His last hours being simply prophecy read as history—Matthew relating what David had sung, and the difference between Isaiah and Luke being that between poetry and prose, between the portrait and the original. The nature and purpose of that death must have been also illustrated, as at Corinth (1 Cor. xv, 3). Thus, in the first epistle, it is assumed that they knew that He had died and gone down to the tomb, and thus delivered them from the wrath to come (1-10). The creed of believers, as he writes to the Thessalonians, is, "We believe that Jesus died and rose again." This death was not only an expiation, but a conquest of death and the obtainment of eternal life—" Them which sleep in Jesus will God bring with Him"—" Who died for us that, whether we wake or sleep, we should live together with Him" (ver. 10). These doctrines imply, of course, some statement of the nature of that sin and bondage from which the Christ came to free His people, and of that free forgiveness bestowed through faith on all believers.

As may be learned from the political charge brought against the apostle, he had also preached in Thessalonica the kingly power and prerogative of the Risen One—" another king, one Jesus"—that He has sole and supreme authority over men; that His laws are to be obeyed at all hazards; that loyalty to Him is to be in uniform ascendency; and that His claims on our suit and service are before those of every other master whatever be his human rank or position. For those who are ransomed by His blood consecrate to Him their lives. To Him all power is given in heaven and in earth, to Him who is Lord of all, crowned with glory and honour. To Him every knee shall bow, and every tongue confess. His church is His kingdom, and He is its one Sovereign Head. His people are "called to His kingdom and glory" as their blessed and ultimate inheritance.

When we pass from the brief records in the Acts to the Epistles, we may infer from many expressions in those epistles that another doctrine, which occupied some prominence in his preaching, was the second Advent.

The Thessalonians on being converted, not only as we are told, turned from idols, but waited for "His Son from heaven." On delivering a solemn charge connected with the Advent, he adjures "by the coming of our Lord Jesus Christ." In reference to some allied supplementary topics, he says, "Remember ye not that, while I was yet with you, I told you these things." The second Advent was the grand epoch to which the preacher ever pointed, and which he described as ever approaching. They had been taught to wait for His Son, the Saviour from heaven (1-10). They had been called to His kingdom and glory (ii, 12). His converts were "His crown and joy in the presence of our Lord Jesus Christ at His coming" (ii, 19). His prayer was and had been that they should be "perfect at the coming of our Lord Jesus with all His saints" (iii, 13). The connection of the dead believers with the second coming had been misunderstood by some, implying that the apostle had also touched upon it. "The Lord Himself shall descend from heaven with a shout, with the voice of the archangel and the trump of God." The period when the dead shall be raised, the living changed, and the church completed in numbers and in holiness, to be for ever with the Lord, yea, to live together with Him, is the grand hope and the true soul of all felicity (ver. 10). The suddenness of the second coming had also been dwelt upon—"Yourselves know perfectly that the day of the Lord cometh as a thief in the night;" and his final prayer is, "that their spirit and soul and body may be preserved blameless unto the coming of our Lord Jesus Christ." The recurrence of this thought so often in the first epistle, and the more full development of it in the second, are but an echo of his preaching on this momentous topic. Nay, so earnestly did he dwell upon it, that its supposed nearness seems to have induced not a few to forsake their ordinary habits of industry and threatened to break up their social life. There is earnest warning against the wrong impressions produced by his preaching on this point in the first epistle, by unwarranted oral and written repetitions of what was supposed to be his doctrine, as told in the second epistle—" That ye be not soon shaken in mind or be troubled, neither by spirit, nor by word, nor by letter as from us, as that the day of Christ is at hand," or rather " is arrived."

Such, as may be gathered from Acts and from the two epistles, were some of the doctrines preached by Paul at Thessalonica, and they were all closely connected. The Messiah predicted was to be a suffering Messiah, and such He was, but His sufferings terminated in His decease, for He rose again and He ascended to the Throne, " because He became obedient unto death." He reigns because He died, and from His throne He comes again to gather all His subjects, waking or sleeping, to Himself that they may live with Him for ever in blessed fellowship.

It is also evident from the tenor of the epistle that the apostle had very specially enjoined morality—abstinence from such sexual impurities as must have been too common in a maritime and commercial city like Thessalonica—" Ye know what commandments we gave you by the Lord Jesus" (iv, 2). "Abstain from every sort of evil." Brother-love had also been inculcated by him—" As touching brotherly love ye need not that I write unto you" (iv, 9). From whatever cause, there was, owing to the Apostle's visit, a perceptible tendency on the part of some, to leave honest industry and gad about in listless indolence, and the Apostle had studiously reprimanded it—"That ye study to be quiet, and to do your own business, and to work with your own hands as we commanded you." See Commentary under iv, 11, 12. More fully is this injunction given in the second epistle, iii, 6-13, as in verse 10— " For even when we were with you, this we commanded you, that if any would not work, neither should he eat." He had also exhorted them to "walk worthy of God who had called them."

And the style in which he had preached, and the general tenor of his conduct are apparent also from the two epistles. In the first half of the second chapter, the purity, simplicity, fidelity, and power of his preaching, and his own earnest, loving, and unselfish nature are specially declared by him to have been visible to all around him (ii, 10). Nay, he wrought with his own hands, because he would not be chargeable to them; and he was doing the same at Corinth, where he composed these letters (ii, 9). He wrought night and day—toiling by night, that he might have some leisure by day. The handicraft which he practised was probably the weaving of haircloth for tents. It is impossible for us to realize the apostle as a tradesman, dressed in a humble garb, and handling the implement of his calling, plying a shuttle or needle for daily bread—undistinguished in appearance from the operatives round about him, either at their work or at their meals. He who preached the unsearchable riches of Christ holds out his hands to accept the humble wages which his industry had earned. He who felt that in his highest function it was a small thing to be judged of man's judgment, must submit to have his work inspected and approved before he is paid for it. The world's greatest benefactor, next to its Saviour, might be found in a workshop—found there on deliberate purpose, a mechanic at Thessalonica, an orator at Athens. It must have been a very hard thing for him with so many interruptions to earn a scanty livelihood. He confesses it; but tells that his friends in Philippi had not forgotten him, and he joyfully records of them, "No church communicated with me concerning giving and receiving, but ye only, for even in Thessalonica ye sent once and again unto my necessity" (Phil. iv, 16). In fact, his whole demeanour in Thessalonica is laid bare by himself in earnest and continuous appeals to all who knew him. Thus: "Ye know what manner of men we were among you, for your sakes" (i, 5); "Yourselves, brethren, know our entrance in unto you, that it was not in vain: for even after that we had suffered before, and been shamefully entreated, as ye know, at

Philippi" (ii, 1, 2, 3); "Ye remember, brethren, our labour and travail" (ii, 9); "Neither at any time used we flattering words, as ye know, nor a cloke of covetousness" (ii, 5); "Ye know how we exhorted and comforted and charged every one of you" (ii, 11); "Ye are witnesses . . . how holily and justly and unblameably we behaved ourselves among you that believe" (ii, 10); "We told you before that we should suffer tribulation" (iii, 4); "As ye have received of us how ye ought to walk and please God" (iv, 1); "Ye know what commandments we gave you by the Lord Jesus" (iv, 2); "To work with your hands as we commanded you" (iv, 11); "Yourselves know how ye ought to follow us: for we behaved not ourselves disorderly among you" (2 Thess. iii, 7). If he wrought with his hands for six days, what an outflow of feeling on the seventh as he reasoned out of the Scriptures—opened and alleged, or spoke of the life of Christ within him, or the constraining love that lay upon him. His nature with all its softness and sympathies poured itself out at Thessalonica. He describes himself exhorting as a father, and he was gentle among them as a mother nursing her own child; nay, he adds in the fulness of his heart, being "affectionately desirous of you, we were willing to have imparted unto you, not the gospel of God only, but also our own souls, because ye became dear unto us." Yet while this affectionate fervour characterized the apostle, and all this yearning for the spiritual good of his converts filled his bosom, he was maintaining a heavy conflict. He had come from Philippi, where he had been scourged; and though he had borne it patiently, he must have felt it to be an unspeakable ignominy. The treatment was scandalous: $\pi\rho o\pi a\theta \acute{o}\nu\tau\epsilon\varsigma\ \kappa a\grave{\iota}\ \acute{\nu}\beta\rho\iota\sigma\theta\acute{\epsilon}\nu\tau\epsilon\varsigma$ (ii, 2). But his courage did not desert him, he was bold to speak the gospel $\grave{\epsilon}\nu\ \pi o\lambda\lambda\hat{\omega}\ \grave{a}\gamma\hat{\omega}\nu\iota$—in allusion to the dangers by which he was still surrounded. He refers to the Jews and their fanatical opposition to Christ and His followers. He must have foreseen the ominous gathering of the clouds which preceded the outbreak. Yet his heart never failed him, nor was his spirit soured by ingratitude and hostility. Though he had come to Thessalonica after persecution and subjection to personal outrage, he remained in it at his work though danger was thickening around him, and though he left the city when the storm burst, yet on his arrival at Berœa, he lost no time in beginning his work, but went at once into the synagogue of the Jews. But his Jewish antagonists from Thessalonica, disappointed of their prey, followed him, and as their exasperation appears to have deepened into ferocity, he was obliged to depart, his journey leading him to Athens by sea.

The results of the apostle's preaching in Thessalonica were varied. Not a few were converted, and the unbelieving Jews were enraged. The historian says, "some of the Jews," that is only a small number, "believed and consorted with Paul and Silas," or rather were allotted or granted by divine favour to Paul and Silas—for such is the meaning of the verb προσεκληρώθησαν (Winer, Harless, Meyer); " of the devout Greeks, a great multitude"—that is to say, of persons who were proselytes—persons who had forsaken polytheistic heathenism, and attached themselves to monotheistic Judaism. The insufficiently attested reading καὶ Ἑλλήνων would distinguish two parties—proselytes and heathen Greeks. "And of the chief women"— apparently also proselytes—"not a few"—ladies of high social rank, who from their position as proselytes, or anxious inquirers, were neither clouded with pagan darkness nor fettered with Jewish prejudices. This was the fruit of three Sabbaths' labours in the synagogue among Jews and proselytes of both sexes. But the apostle speaks of the Thessalonian church generally as turning "from idols to serve the living and true God"—an assertion which could be made of neither of the parties referred to. It is remarkable that in neither of the epistles does he quote the Scriptures of the Old Testament. The main purpose of the historian in the Acts is simply to record the offer of the gospel to the Jews, and how many of them rejected it and persecuted the preacher. He is silent as to any work of the apostle among the Gentile population, which, however, as appears from the epistle, was successful to a very great extent. In fact, the majority of the Thessalonian church appear to have been converted heathens. The apostle may either have laboured among them on other days than the Sabbath, when he went to the synagogue; or he may have for a brief period continued in the city and preached, after the synagogue had been shut to him. Still his residence at Thessalonica cannot be well extended beyond six or eight weeks, and such is the view of Wieseler. His evangelistic labours were abruptly terminated. The unbelieving Jews, jealous of the influence of those wonderful strangers, and unable to cope with them in argument—afraid too that the synagogue might be more and more deserted—associated themselves with "certain lewd fellows of the baser sort." These lewd fellows are called ἀγοραῖοι or market or Forum-loungers— a profligate rabble found in these Greek towns, and having a defined and well-known character, called dregs and mire by one old author, lying and perjured by another, like the lazzaroni of Naples to whom they have been compared. With these strange allies forward to any mischief, the Jews raised a mob, and set all the city on an uproar; assaulted the house of Jason, with whom the apostle lived, and who may have been a kinsman (Rom. xvi, 21), or may have wrought at the same occupation. The purpose of the assault was to bring Paul and Silas out to the people—εἰς τὸν δῆμον, the people in its corporate capacity—Thessalonica being a free city, with rulers who in the Forum tried causes in the presence of the people. Disappointed in not finding Paul and Silas, and resolved to accomplish their purpose in another way, they dragged Jason and certain brethren, who probably were at the moment in his house, before the rulers—ἐπὶ τοὺς πολιτάρχας. These rulers are called στρατηγοί at Philippi, it being a Roman colony; but here, in an *urbs libera* they were called 'politarchs;' and the title is still seen graven on one of the arches of the city along with the names of seven who held the office—three of them having the same names as those of Paul's Macedonian companions, Sopater, Gaius, Secundus. The charge laid against them was that "the men who have turned the world upside down have come hither also," with the same purpose of revolution—that, in short, they were rebels guilty of treason, having broken the Julian laws, disowning the authority of the Emperor, and setting up another king, one Jesus. No doubt this was a misconception of the apostle's doctrine, perhaps a wilful perversion of it: for we cannot acquiesce in Davidson's supposition, that the apostle preached a doctrine "which involved sensuous ideas respecting the nature of Christ's kingdom, which was to be in some sort an earthly one."[1] A clear distinct accusation of this nature could not have been treated with such lenience, nor is there any utterance of the apostle which can justify such an insinuation.

But the mob cared nothing about a religious question, and could not have been bribed to raise any disturbance about a Jewish dogma. A political accusation was therefore forged. The Jews, regarding their Messiah as a temporal sovereign, transferred their conceptions to the Christian doctrine of Christ's spiritual kingship, and charged the apostle with so holding and proclaiming it. Under a similar charge was He prosecuted Himself; the tablet on His cross bore the indictment, "Jesus of Nazareth, King of the Jews." On hearing such a charge involving such consequences, the people and the politarchs were alarmed—the Jews having been at that time banished from Rome by the Emperor Claudius as political disturbers;[2] and not entering into any judicial examination in the meantime, they took security of Jason and the others, and let them go. The ἱκανόν or bail taken from Jason could scarcely be that the apostle should appear; for he was sent away from the city that very night, and the money pledged in that case would be forfeited, for faith had not been kept. The pledge may have been, not that Jason should refuse Paul and Silas admission into his house, but that they should at once leave the city—Jason and his party being held bound for the preservation of the peace. Fines may have been exacted afterwards, for the Thessalonians had suffered like the churches in Judæa—and one feature of that suffering was "the spoiling of their goods." There was imminent danger of another and fiercer outbreak, and all hope of safety and usefulness being extinguished, the brethren immediately on the evening of the same day sent away Paul and Silas by night into Berœa, a town on the eastern slope of the Olympian range, and five miles

---

[1] Davidson's Introduction, vol. I., p. 26, 1868.
[2] Suetonius. Judæos impulsore Chresto assidue tumultuantes Roma expulit, Tib. Claud., xxv. See Lange on this. Wieseler and others identify this expulsion with the decree *De Mathematicis Italia pellendis* mentioned by Tacitus, Annal. ii, 32.

south-west of Thessalonica. The apostles, however, had a strong hope of returning after the popular fury had subsided. The phrase "by night" in verse 10 implies a suspicion of danger and ambush; for Jewish hostility was sly as well as vindictive, as wily in its methods as unscrupulous in its ends. Thus ended the apostle's brief visit to Thessalonica, but it has borne memorable fruit. The city in subsequent centuries was greatly instrumental in converting savage hordes of Sclavonians and Bulgarians; and, in times of warring heresies, it was called the 'orthodox city.' The legends of Demetrius—a martyr of the fourth century, and the patron saint of the city—have, however, superseded the fame of the apostle. The learned Eustathius was archbishop in 1185; and Theodore Gaza, who came to Italy after the fall of Constantinople, and contributed to the revival of letters in western Europe, belonged to Thessalonica.

III—Genuineness of the Epistle

The Church has been unanimous in holding the Pauline authorship up till a very recent period, and the objections of some German critics scarcely disturb the harmony. In the patristic writings little use is made of this epistle, and the reason is evident, for it is not distinctly doctrinal; it does not expose serious error; it does not vindicate either the apostle's office or defend the gospel which he proclaimed. It contains, save on one point, none of those profound arguments which are to be met with in the other epistles. It is a quiet and earnest letter written to encourage a people recently converted by the apostle, and exposed to such trial and persecution as might endanger their firmness and constancy. There is, therefore, little in it that could serve any of the polemical or practical ends which the early church writers had in view. The allusions in the Apostolic Fathers are few and faint. Some of the words and phrases, however, sound like an echo of several clauses in this epistle—though Lardner and Kirchhofer lay too much stress on them. Thus, in the Epistle of the Roman Clement to the Corinthians, "We ought in all things to give thanks unto Him," compared with 1 Thess. v, 18, there being some resemblance; but the second quotation usually given is quite indistinct, "let our whole body, therefore, be saved in Christ Jesus," compared with 1 Thess. v, 23. The quotations from the so-called Ignatian Epistles are as unsatisfactory. "Devote yourselves to unceasing prayers"—"Pray also for other men without ceasing," compared with 1 Thess. v, 17; but the distinctive epithet ἀδιαλείπτος—ως is wanting in the Syriac version of these epistles. The language of Polycarp is more decided as a reminiscence from this epistle—"making intercessions without ceasing for all," compared with v, 17; "abstaining from all iniquity," compared with v, 22.

But the allusions in succeeding writers are definite and conclusive. Irenaeus prefaces the quotation of v, 23, "and for this reason, the apostle explaining himself, has set forth the perfect and spiritual man of salvation, speaking thus in the First Epistle to the Thessalonians." Tertullian quotes i, 9-10 with the remark, "*haec tempora cum Thessalonicensibus disce;*" and, in quoting v, 1-2, says, "on that account the majesty of the Holy Spirit . . . suggests de temporibus autem et temporum spatiis, fratres, non est necessitas scribendi vobis, ipsi enim certissime scitis, quod dies Domini quasi fur nocte ita adveniet, quum dicent Pax, et tuta sunt omnia; tunc illis repentinus insistet interitus" (1 Thess. v, 1-3). Clement of Alexandria writes, "This the blessed Paul plainly signified, saying," the citation being ii, 8. Such allusions occur often in Origen, as when quoting ii, 14, "and Paul, in the First Epistle to the Thessalonians, says these things." Similar allusions occur in his treatise against Celsus. Eusebius placed the epistle among the ὁμολογούμενα. It is found in the Syriac Peshito version, in the old Latin version, and is named in the Muratorian fragment *ad Thessalonicenses sexta*. It was admitted into Marcion's canon as the fifth of the ten Pauline Epistles.

Against the genuineness of the epistle, Baur and Schrader threw out suspicions in 1835-36. Baur's first attack was in his *Die Pastoral-briefe;* but in his *Paulus*, 1845, he has formally argued the point, and ten years after he gave additional reasons in the *Theolog. Jahrb.*, p. ii, 1855. His theory, however, has met nothing but opposition, even

Hilgenfeld deserts him in defence of this epistle. Baur has been replied to by Koch, Grimm, Lange, Bleek, Reuss, Lünemann, Hofmann. It is needless to reply to an argument which has made no converts, and which Jowett and Davidson have so successfully exposed. A few sentences may suffice.

Baur's first objection, that the epistle is unimportant and devoid of doctrinal discussion, is easily met by affirming that the apostle did not discuss doctrines, save when they were challenged or misunderstood; and that, even in this epistle, there is one doctrine which occupies a prominent place, because the state of the Thessalonian Church required a full statement of it. The contents of the apostle's letters were suggested and moulded by the circumstances of the churches which he addressed, for they were not abstract or didactic treatises, but living communications made with immediate reference to wants, trials, errors, dangers, or inquiries, in the churches to which he writes. Though the apostle wrote for all times, he always wrote to meet some present exigency. Profound dogma, chains of lofty reasoning and illustrations of first principles, are not found in this epistle, for they were uncalled for; but it is full of those encouragements to the believers which they needed, since, as they were recent converts, their courage was sorely tried. It abounds also in practical counsels for Christians living in a heathen society so full of temptations; for it required no common caution, decision, fortitude, and self-denial, to walk worthy of God who had called them. Why should such an epistle be reckoned un-Pauline? It is surely Pauline wisdom and love to write to a church founded by himself in terms suited to its history and condition. That his epistles vary as the state of the churches differed is one great proof of his authorship; and that this epistle falls, in fulness and grandeur of material, behind those of the Romans, Corinthians, and Galatians, is no proof whatever that it did not come from his pen. Nor is the fact that the epistle contains so many historical appeals and reminiscences any objection to its Pauline authorship, since any one writing in the apostle's name might find such materials in the Acts of the Apostles. The reply is, that in the epistles there are allusions not found in

Acts, such as Timothy's coming to the apostle at Athens *(see under* iii, 2), and his labouring with his own hands for his support. Nor would any forger venture to characterize the Thessalonian Church as chiefly heathen, when the narrative in Acts might lead us to infer that the members were principally Jews and proselytes. The epistle, therefore, in its historical element is no mere expansion of the narrative in Acts. The apostle had recently been at Thessalonica, and the whole circumstances of his sojourn being fresh in his remembrance, he touches on several of them to show that they were cheering memories, and to assure them of the affectionate interest which he had still in them—ever in the hope not only that this relationship would not be disturbed, but also that their earlier spirituality and fruitfulness, their joy and patience—all the blessed results of their conversion, might remain with them. He appeals to their own knowledge of what they had been in heart and life when he was among them; and this is no aimless thing, for it is a virtual charge not to let their first impressions fade, but to continue steadfast, and to preserve what the prophet calls "the kindness of thy youth, the love of thine espousals" (Jer. ii, 2). Baur objects, too, that Paul, in chap. ii, holds up Jewish believers as a pattern, which he never elsewhere does. But the reader may compare Gal. i, 22-24. Nor is the reference to the Jews (ii, 14-16) so decidedly out of the apostle's style and manner as to wrest the authorship of the epistle from him. The apostle does certainly stigmatize the Jews with uncommon severity; but he is as unsparing against the Judaists in passages where Baur at once recognizes his hand. The description of the Jews is true, as the apostle had already felt at the Pisidian Antioch, at Iconium, at Lystra, Thessalonica, and Bercea. The apostle saw his own people ripening for judgment, and predicted it. In the clause "wrath has come upon them," $\dot{o}\rho\gamma\dot{\eta}$ does not, as Jowett supposes, mean judicial blindness, but divine punishment; and the declaration is no narrative of a past event. *See on the places.* In the Epistle to the Romans they are viewed under another aspect, that of pride and unbelief, and there is expressed a strong desire for their salvation. Another phrase at which Baur stumbles, "to speak to the Gentiles that they might be saved," has virtual parallels in Acts xiv, 1; xvi, 6-32; xviii, 8-9; 2 Cor. xi, 7.

The language employed to describe the Thessalonian Church, according to Baur, presupposes a longer time to have elapsed since its formation than the history warrants. How could they so soon be patterns to believers in Macedonia and Achaia, the report of their conversion being carried everywhere? How could the apostle say, after so short an interval, that he longed to visit them, &c.? We will not reply that the difficulty is lessened by assuming that the Second Epistle is really the First, and that thus we may elongate the interval. But there is nothing very startling in the language i, 7, 8, as Thessalonica was a great centre of maritime and commercial enterprise. Strangers visiting it from all parts of the country, would, on their return, spread the report of that great novelty which had taken place in the city, the wondrous revolution in belief and character which so many citizens had undergone at the bidding of two Hebrew strangers. Some six months might suffice for this circulation of news. The apostle longed to see them, for he had been forced to leave them abruptly, when the Christian community had not been fully consolidated. Baur wonders at members of the church becoming restless and indolent at so early a period; but the very earliness of the period makes it all the more likely as the result of a mighty change of creed and opinion, which seems to have bewildered them; not having had any long period of instruction, they had misunderstood the doctrine of the Second Advent. The paragraph on the relation to the Second Advent of those who died before it, on the resurrection of the dead, the change of the living, and the rapture of the saints, is surely not un-Pauline as Baur contends, but is in harmony with 1 Cor. xv, 52. Nor does the anxiety to which the apostle responds imply that a first generation of believers must have fallen asleep. On the other hand, though only one believer had died, or though none had died at all, each had the certainty of coming death; and it was therefore a natural question among a people who had enjoyed only a brief period of instruction, which on some points could be only fragmentary and partial, and which, being so foreign to all previous thoughts and associations, might not be fully comprehended without repeated illustration and argument. Further, if there are passages in this epistle like some in the other epistle, why should the resemblance be called imitation? and if a phrase without parallel occurs, why should it be styled un-Pauline? This hypercriticism of Baur is quite unsatisfactory, as it may be thought to serve either point, for or against any document. Unstudied resemblances are usual proofs of unity of authorship, and diction without parallel is usually regarded as a token of originality. Moreover, a forger writing after Paul's time would have called him by his official title of Apostle—and how could such make the dead apostle write, "we who are alive and remain unto the coming of the Lord"? Nor would any one, getting his only materials from the Acts, have ventured to say that Timothy was sent from Athens to Thessalonica, the statement of the Acts being, that Timothy and Silas having been left behind at Berœa, joined the apostle at Corinth. The two statements are not in conflict, but a forger would not have placed them in even apparent contradiction. See under iii, 1.

The reference to church officers[1] in v, 12 is objected to by Schrader, because, according to 1 Tim. iii, 6, no novices were to be invested with office, whereas all ordained to pastoral work in Thessalonica must have been in that category. There could not, his conclusion is, have been elders in that church when this epistle is ordinarily supposed to have been written. The objection may be met in various ways. It is not necessary to apply a general injunction given by Paul toward the end of his life, and when churches had been organized for years, to a special case occurring at a time so much earlier. The injunction in the Epistle to Timothy may have been based on experience. It was given to a fellow-labourer connected with a church long established, and where many matured believers could easily be found. In Crete all must have been novices, and no such counsel is given to Titus. The apostle did not himself always act on it (Acts xiv, 23). The neophyte in general was one not trained, one as yet devoid of practical adaptation to the work, on account of the recency of his conversion. But in Thessalonica there had been decided and

[1] Office-bearers. Davidson, page 449.

speedy spiritual advancement, nay, Jason may have been a believer of a date prior to the apostle's arrival. If the apostle set them apart himself, he must have had confidence in their general character; and if they were appointed after his departure, and before the writing of this letter, then the term novice would scarcely apply to his first converts. A church could not be permanently organized without an ordination of elders to preserve the order essential to edification. And the elders are named by no special title—as presbyters, overseers, or deacons —but by the general appellation of presidents.

IV —Time, Place, and Occasion of the Epistle

After the abrupt departure of the apostle from Thessalonica, he went to Berœa, and there leaving Silas and Timothy, he proceeded to Athens, his conductors being enjoined to send Timothy and Silas to him with all speed. After a brief period, he arrived at Corinth where he remained for a considerable time. Timothy rejoined him at Athens, but Silas seems to have sojourned some time longer at Berœa or elsewhere in the Macedonian province, for the absence of Timothy left the apostle "alone" at Athens. All the three were at Corinth when this epistle was written, their names being in the opening salutation. After the apostle had left Thessalonica, he yearned after his converts —his stay with them being so brief, and their external condition, their exposure to outrage, being so trying. The apostle made also two attempts to visit them in person; Satan, however, prevented him as he writes to them. But at Athens he could no longer forbear, and from that city, though he was to be left in solitude—Silas, if there, going perhaps on some other unrecorded mission—he despatched Timothy to visit the Thessalonians, to stablish and comfort them concerning their faith, and to present such truths and hopes as should animate them in the trying circumstances (iii, 1-5). Timothy accomplished his mission and came back to the apostle, now at Corinth (Acts xviii, 5), with a report which gladdened him (iii, 6); and the reception of such a report was the immediate occasion of the epistle. Some indeed, as Hug and Hemsen, suppose that Timothy was sent by Paul from Berœa to visit the Thessalonians;

but the supposition is distinctly opposed to the precise statement in iii, 1, 2, which speaks only of the mission of Timothy from Athens. This view is held by Theodoret, Hemming, Bullinger, and Aretius; and a modification of it is held by Calovius and Böttger, viz., that the epistle was written at Athens during a flying visit of the apostle, while his headquarters were at Corinth. The epistle was written during the earlier period of the apostle's residence in Corinth, probably A.D. 52, perhaps 53, so that it is the earliest of the extant Pauline epistles. Others, however, contend for a later date, but on very insufficient grounds. Wurm supposes a later visit to Athens, from the notion that 1 Thess. iii, 1, 2, 6, is opposed to Acts xvii, 15; xviii, 5: the argument being that, according to the epistle, Timothy and Silas were with Paul at Athens, while, according to Acts, they joined him at Corinth. But there is perfect harmony in the statements. In ii, 18 the apostle limits the plural to himself, and the following plurals must have a parallel limitation. Kochler places the epistle in date near the fall of Jerusalem from a misunderstanding of ii, 16; and Whiston assigns it to A.D. 67, or a little before the apostle's death, because it is seldom referred to in the "Apostolic Constitutions," and the persecutions referred to in the second chapter were such as happened under Nero. See Benson's reply. Schrader dates it at the period indicated in Acts xx, 2, but many allusions in the epistle would be totally inapplicable to such an hypothesis. The argument of Schrader, Böttger, and others is that i, 8, implies itinerant evangelistic labours on the part of the apostle in regions beyond Macedonia and Achaia. But the real meaning of the verse simply is, not that that missionary work had been extended, but that the reports of the success of the gospel in Thessalonica had travelled through the provinces and beyond them. Other arguments against the common view are incidentally referred to in our remarks on the genuineness of the epistle.

Grotius, and after him Baur, Ewald, Benson, and Davidson, invert the common order of the two epistles and assume the shorter one as the earlier—Grotius regarding the Man of Sin as the Emperor Caligula who attempted to have his statue erected in the temple, and, supposing that $\dot{\alpha}\pi'$ $\dot{\alpha}\rho\chi\hat{\eta}s$ (2

INTRODUCTION

Thess. ii, 13) refers to Jewish Christians who had come from Palestine, Jason being one of them, holds that to this party the epistle was written *altero anno Cajani principatus*. The theory chronologically and otherwise is wholly baseless. The arguments for a later date of the first epistle are taken from i, 8, as to the report of their conversion being circulated everywhere; from the injunction to submit to their church presidents, v, 12; and from their doubts about the connection of departed brethren with the Second Advent. These arguments adduced by Ewald and Davidson have been already referred to. It is alleged, however, that the so-called first epistle is to some extent a correction or fuller explanation of what had already been written in the so-called second one. The doctrine of the Advent had been misunderstood, and it is cleared up in 1 Thess. iv, 13. But the hypothesis is unnatural; for the result of the misapprehensions referred to might be indeed tremor, indolence, and dissatisfaction with present things; but there is nothing that can suggest the second point which the apostle takes up —the sorrow over the holy dead. Nothing is said in the so-called second epistle which could have given rise to such anxiety as the apostle describes and relieves.

Nor is there any real argument in the phrase—"The salutation of Paul with mine own hand, which is the token in every epistle, so I write." For the words do not assert that in the first epistle written by him he adopted a mark of authentication which was to characterize all his epistles; but the reference is to epistles circulated in his name (2 Thess. ii, 2), and his purpose is to guard against such fabrications. The allusion to such forgeries does not prove that he had not written a first epistle himself—it rather presupposes it, and that some one had imitated it. Ewald's admission that the second epistle had been preceded by an earlier one which is now lost is a needless conjecture. It is quite forced to take 2 Thess. i, 4, or iii, 2, as referring to what happened in Berœa—from which Ewald conjectures that he wrote the epistle.

In a word, the two epistles, regarded in the order usually assigned them, naturally fit in to one another. The second epistle is supplementary to the first, and the first sprang naturally out of the circumstances. It contains the fresh memories of his sojourn in Thessalonica; appeals to their own knowledge and experience; exhorts them to be steadfast under persecution, which, breaking out during his stay, had not yet subsided; comforts them under bereavement; and enforces many practical counsels. At the time of writing the second epistle the circumstances were different. His doctrine had been misunderstood as affirming the near approach of the Advent; nay, teaching had been given and letters published in his name which he had not authorized. In 2 Thess. ii, 15, there is an allusion to the previous letter. The exhortations to industry in the first epistle are general: "We beseech you;" but in the second the charge is more precise: "We command you." The germs of the evil may have been discerned by him during his personal ministry among them, but the mischief had ripened, and being absent during its growth, he writes, "We hear that there are among you some that walk disorderly." That evil warned against in the first epistle, and borne with too, was no longer to be tolerated; they were to withdraw themselves from the disorderly, and in no way to countenance them. In the first epistle his whole counsels presuppose that they may be accepted, but in the second he is afraid that direct disobedience may be manifested (iii, 14). The ordinary opinion as to the order of the two epistles has highest probability in its favour; the other may be plausible on some points, but rests on assumption and conjecture.

V —Contents of the Epistle

The contents of the epistle are simple, but full of interest. The details of his preaching and mode of life are given honestly and with the perfect assurance that the Thessalonians would sanction all his statements, and that every appeal would at once meet an affirmative response. The first part of the epistle is chiefly historical in outline. He touches on his entrance to them, and his success among them, their conversion, and its wonderful results. Then he reminds them how pure, humble, affectionate, and self-denying he had been among them as a preacher of Christianity, and what persecutions in consequence of their faith they had endured. He mentions also his own anxiety about them, his yearnings after them, and his repeated fruitless attempts to pay them a second visit. The mission of Timothy in his room, and the good report with which he had returned, increased his desire to see them, filled him with thankfulness for their steadfastness, and invited him to prayer for them. Next he warns them against impurity—a prominent sin of heathenism; and exhorts them to brotherly kindness and modesty. Now, he opens up the doctrine of the Second Advent: the certainty of the resurrection of the dead and its priority to the change which shall pass over the living, the period, however, being uncertain, and therefore laying believers under solemn obligation to watchfulness and preparation. The epistle concludes with detached counsels on social duties connected with church membership, and with an earnest prayer for them, and a desire to have an interest in their prayers. It closes with the benediction.

VI.—Works on the Epistles

The authors whose comments on the epistles are quoted or referred to are principally the following:—

The Greek Fathers—Chrysostom, Theodoret, Joannes Damascenus, Oecumenius, Theophylact, Theodore of Mopsuestia.

The Latin Writers—Jerome, Augustine, Pelagius, Ambrosiaster, Tertullian, Hilary, Primasius.

The Postills of Nicolas de Lyra belong to the fourteenth century.

Coming down to the period of the Reformation, we have the names of Erasmus, Luther, Calvin, Zwingli, Beza, with those of their followers, Hunnius, Camerarius, Hemming, Bullinger, Hyperius, Zanchius, Victorinus, Marloratus, Bugenhagen.

Partly of the same period, and partly later, we have—

Among the Catholics—Estius, Vatablus, a-Lapide, Justiniani, Harduin.

Among the Protestants of the Continent—Piscator, Cocceius, Crocius, Aretius, Clericus, Fromond, Cajetan, Grotius, Wetstein, Tarnovius, Er. Schmidius, Calixtus, Calovius, Bengel, Wolf, Schöttgen, Van Til, Musculus, Vorstius, Jaspis, Heumann,

Baumgarten, Koppe, Bolten, Rosenmüller, Michaelis, Balduin, Storr, Bouman, Reiche.

The following are the names of English expositors—Jewell, Cameron, Sclater, Hammond, Chandler, Whitby, Pierce, Benson, Macknight, Doddridge, Barnes.

The following collectors of annotations may also be named— Elsner, Kypke, Krebs, Loesner, Heinsius, Bos, Raphelius, Knatchbull.

The following may be more specially noted— Turretin (1739); Krause (1790); Tychsen (1823); Flatt (1829); Pelt (1830); Hemsen (1830); Schrader (1836); Hug (1847); Usteri (1833); Schott (1834); Bloomfield, *New Testament*, vol. II, 4th ed. (1841); Olshausen (1844); de Wette (1845); Baumgarten-Crusius (1848); Koch (1849); Peile (1849); Conybeare and Howson (1850); Hilgenfeld (1852); Jowett (1855); Ewald (1857); Bisping (1857); Wieseler (1859); Wordsworth's *New Testament*, p. III (1859); Webster and Wilkinson's *New Testament* (1861); Hofmann (1862); Alford's *New Testament*, vol. III, 4th ed. (1865); Ellicott, 3rd ed. (1866); Riggenbach, *Lange's Bibelwerk* (1867); Lünemann (Meyer) 1867; Lilly (1867).

Note

The Grammars referred to are those of—A. Buttmann, P. Buttmann, Matthiae, Kühner, Winer, Stuart, Green, Jelf, Madvig, Scheuerlein, Krüger, Schmalfeld, Schirlitz, Donaldson, Rost, Alt. In addition to these may be named Hartung's *Lehre von den Partikeln der griechischen Sprache*, 2 vols., Erlangen, 1832; and Bernhardy's *Wissenschaftliche Syntax der griechischen Sprache*, Berlin, 1829.

The Lexicons referred to are those of—Hesychius, Suidas, Suicer, Passow (Rost and Palm), Robinson, Pape, Wilke, Wahl, Bretschneider, and Liddell and Scott.

COMMENTARY

ON

FIRST THESSALONIANS

FIRST THESSALONIANS

CHAPTER I

(Ver. 1.) Παῦλος καὶ Σιλουανὸς καὶ Τιμόθεος—" Paul, and Silvanus, and Timotheus."

Silvanus, so named by the apostle here and elsewhere (2 Thess. i, 1; 2 Cor. i, 19); and also by Peter (1 Pet. v, 12); is called uniformly Σίλας Silas, in the Acts, as in xv, 22, 27, 34, 40. He is first mentioned in connection with the church in Jerusalem and the decrees of the convention, as "a chief man among the nation" (xv, 22), and as being "a prophet" (xv, 32). He became connected with Paul after he parted from Barnabas at Antioch, and he left that city along with him on his second missionary journey. Being the older man, of higher position as a prophet, and as somewhat earlier associated with the apostle, he is placed before Timothy, both by Luke and by Paul (Acts xvii, 14, 15; xviii, 5; 2 Thess. i, 1; 2 Cor. i, 19). That Timothy requested his name to be last, on account of his humility, is the suggestion of Chrysostom. Silas was probably his original or Aramaic name, and Silvanus its Hellenistic or Roman form. The possession of a double name was common—one of them sometimes Hellenic, or Roman, and sometimes only a contraction: Saul, Paul; Apollos, Apollo; Alexas, Alexander; Ktesis, Ktesias; Nymphas, Nymphodorus. For Timothy, see under Col. i, 1. These two names are naturally associated by the writer of this epistle with his own, not in any way to authenticate the letter (Piscator, Pelt), or as if one of them had written it at the apostle's dictation (Olshausen), but because they had laboured along with him in Thessalonica, and had co-operated in the founding of the church. He does not appropriate all the honours, as he had not monopolized the labours. Neither in this, nor in the Second Epistle to the Thessalonians, nor in that to the Philippians, does he name himself "apostle," or "servant," probably because no one in these churches had called his official prerogative in question. He had been so recently among them that he needed not to assume his distinctive title. This supposition is far more natural than that of Chrysostom and his followers—viz., that the official term is omitted because the Thessalonians had been recently instructed (διὰ τὸ νεοκατηχήτους εἶναι τοὺς ἄνδρας), and had not yet had experience of him. As unlikely is the notion of Cajetan and Pelt—in which Zwingli and Estius, so far asunder in so many things—agree that he withheld his title from regard to Silas *ne supra eum se extollere videretur* (Estius). But he specifies his apostleship in 1 Cor. i, 1, and in 2 Cor. i, 1, though he names Sosthenes with himself in the first case and Timothy in the second, as also in Col. i, 1. On this subject, and on the various ways in which Paul names himself in the epistolary addresses, see under Ephes. i, 1, and Philip. i, 1. The epistle is addressed—

τῇ ἐκκλησίᾳ τῶν Θεσσαλονικέων, "to the church of the Thessalonians,"—see Introduction. It may be noted that only in this epistle and in the second addressed to the same church does the apostle use this form of designation—the church of the population; in other places he writes to the church in the city, as 1 Cor. i, 2; 2 Cor. i, 1; Ephes. i, 1; Col. i, 2; Philip. i, 1; Rom. i, 7, and somewhat differently in Gal. i, 2, Galatia being a province. Compare the addresses prefixed to the letters to the seven churches in the Apocalypse. Why the apostle so varied, it is impossible to say. It could scarcely be that he writes "of the Thessalonians" and not "in Thessalonica," because he had laboured only for a brief period among them, and a church could scarcely be said to be planted among them (Wordsworth). But that a church existed among them the phrase certainly implies; and a church of the Thessalonians is surely a church in Thessalonica. In this early letter, the apostle had not settled down into the use of such introductory formulae as afterwards characterized his style.

The ἐκκλησία of the earlier epistles is changed in the later ones of the Roman imprisonment into the epithet denotive of character and consecration—τοῖς ἁγίοις—found in the address to the communities in Ephesus, Colosse, and Philippi. In the private letter to Philemon ἐκκλησία occurs, "the church in the house." But there is no ground for Jowett's conjecture that, as he does not here prefix his official title, probably the term apostle was not allowed to him with the same special meaning as to the twelve at Jerusalem, nor does his subsequent departure from the use of ἐκκλησία arise from the fact that he more and more invested the church on earth with the attributes of the church in heaven. Why then employ it in one of his last epistles—that to Philemon? That church is described as—

ἐν Θεῷ πατρὶ καὶ Κυρίῳ Ἰησοῦ Χριστῷ—"in God the Father and the Lord Jesus Christ." The full meaning is not belief. in God (Vatablus), nor is it simply connection with Him (Storr, Flatt, Pelt), nor is it existence through Him (Grotius), nor subjection to Him (Macknight), nor does ἐν mean *per Deum perductus ad finem*, but it is in union with the Father and Christ as the root and ground of their spiritual life and progress. It is not faith objectively which is adduced to characterize them, but this inner fellowship with Father and Son—"I in them and Thou in me—that they all may be one in us." "Mark," says Chrysostom, "ἐν applied to both Father and Son," as a common vinculum. The phrase is a kind of tertiary predicate (Donaldson, §§ 489, 490) specifying an additional element of spiritual condition. Chrysostom's remark is not without some force that the phrase specially marks out this ἐκκλησία—there being in the city πολλαὶ ἐκκλησίαι καὶ Ἰουδαϊκαὶ καὶ Ἑλληνικαί. The first part of the clause "in God the Father," according to De Wette and Lünemann, distinguishes them from heathen, and the second "in our Lord Jesus Christ" from Jewish assemblies. But the distinction cannot be strictly maintained, for the phrase "in God the Father" is in the apostle's view as truly and distinctively Christian as the other "in our Lord Jesus Christ." Jowett robs the phrase of all true significance by generalizing it, as when he says "that the actions, feelings, and words of men are in God and Christ," but that this "mode of expression is no longer in use among us." But it is not men generally, it is only believing men, whom the apostle describes as being in union with God and Christ; and the phrase as conveying a truth of primary significance and of conscious and blessed experience has not fallen into desuetude. There is no need to fill up the construction by supplying τῇ, as Chrysostom τῇ ἐν Θεῷ, or with others τῇ οὔσῃ (Winer, § 20, 2). As needless is the supplement proposed by Schott, χαίρειν λέγουσιν, for the full apostolic benediction immediately follows. Worse is the attempt of Koppe to unite the phrase with the χάρις καὶ εἰρήνη of the next part of the verse—χάρις ὑμῖν καὶ εἰρήνη, " grace and peace." For the salutation see Gal. i, 3; Eph. i, 2.

The concluding words, ἀπὸ Θεοῦ πατρὸς ἡμῶν καὶ Κυρίου Ἰησοῦ Χριστοῦ, are believed not to be genuine. They have certainly good authority as A D K L ℵ, but they are omitted in B F, in the Vulgate, and Syriac, and several of the Greek and Latin fathers, as by Chrysostom in his commentary, and in the Latin of Origen. The omission of the familiar words is striking and not easily accounted for, if they are genuine. Bouman and Reiche vindicate the genuineness very much on account of the similar wording of the previous clause; but possibly on that very account the usual formula was supplied by copyists from the other epistles.

(Ver. 2.) Εὐχαριστοῦμεν τῷ Θεῷ πάντοτε περὶ πάντων ὑμῶν, μνείαν ὑμῶν ποιούμενοι ἐπὶ τῶν προσευχῶν ἡμῶν—"We give thanks to God always concerning you all, making mention of you in our prayers."

The second ὑμῶν has good authority, though A B ℵ omit it, for many MSS., versions, minusculi, and fathers are in its favour. The ὑμῶν before μνείαν might induce the omission of ὑμῶν after it; similar variations occur in the text of Ephes. i, 16. The apostle begins in a spirit of devout thankfulness, so gladsome had been the good tidings brought to him from Thessalonica. The causes of his thankfulness he gradually unfolds: their election and the proofs and fruits of it; their hearty reception of the gospel, and its signal success among them, so visible in its living power; their exemplary stability in the midst of persecution ; and the profound impression made and diffused far and near by their conversion. In praising God for them, there is praise conferred upon themselves. As these manifestations dwell in his mind, he gives thanks, the grounds of them being joyously enumerated in sentences which, as Jowett says, "grow under his hand." Εὐχαριστοῦμεν occurs, as in Col. i, 3; Philip. i, 3; Phile. 4, and in the close parallels of Ephes. i, 16; 2 Tim. i, 3, and somewhat differently 2 Thess. i, 3; ii, 13; compare also Rev. i, 3. It is not natural in such a context to narrow the plural verb to the apostle himself, as is done by Pelt, Koch, and Jowett. The plural does sometimes mean himself only, as in ii, 18, where there is a corrective clause: probably this idea suggested the singular ποιούμενος in C¹, and the *faciens* in the Claromontane Latin. But the mention in the address of Silas and Timothy, who had been recently and personally interested in the Thessalonian Church, makes it very natural that they should be included with the apostle in the thanksgiving and the statement; 2 Cor. i, 19, warrants it. If in the address in Philippians, Philemon, and Corinthians, other persons besides the apostle are mentioned, and yet he says εὐχαριστῶ, we may infer that if after such names he says εὐχαριστοῦμεν, they are purposely included. The occurrence of the plural καρδίας (ii, 4) and ψυχὰς (ii, 8) corroborates our opinion. The Greek fathers do not formally pronounce on the point, though they speak of the apostle as giving thanks, he being the primary thanksgiver—a natural mode of reference in their interpretation, which, however, may not exclude the others mentioned in the first verse. Εὐχαριστεῖν belonging specially to the later Greek (Lobeck ad Phrynich., p. 18), occurs often in Polybius and after his time; but is also found in Demosthenes (*Pro Corona*, 257, p. 164, vol. I, *Opera* ed. Schaefer). The classic phrase was χάριν εἰδέναι; δοῦναι χάριν is to gratify, and the apostle has χάριν ἔχω in 1 Tim. i, 12; 2 Tim. i, 3; Phile. 4, according to one reading. The object of thanksgiving is He to whom all thanks are due for all spiritual change—for all spiritual grace. As the other epistles show (Col. i, 3; 2 Thess. i, 3; 2 Tim. i, 3), by τῷ Θεῷ God the Father is referred to, since He is the living and unwearied benefactor, " the Father of mercies and the God of all comfort." After mentioning Father and Son as sources of blessing in the opening benediction of his epistles, the apostle often and immediately turns himself to the Father with a special thanksgiving (2 Cor. i, 2-3; Ephes. i, 2-3; Col. i, 2-3). In Rom. i, 7-8; 1 Cor. i, 4; Philip. i, 3; 2 Thess. i, 3; 2 Tim. i, 3, the Father is simply named Θεός, as in this phrase; and in some of the verses where Father is not used, the apostle adds the equivalent μου—" my God," indicating that tender and confiding relation which the apostle instinctively felt in looking up to God, " whose I am, and whom I serve."

The thanksgiving was offered " concerning you all." Instead of περὶ, ὑπέρ is found in similar phrases, as in Rom. i, 8; Ephes. vi, 19; 1 Tim. ii, 1. See under Ephes. vi, 19, and Gal. i, 4. It is difficult to point out any substantial difference of sense between the two particles. See Ellicott on Philemon 7. To give thanks " about you " is apparently a wider or more comprehensive phrase than to give thanks " for you," and it is here so far emphatic from the position of πάντων, " all of you," the entire community, the fulness of the members deepening the thanksgiving which was at the same time πάντοτε, " always," continuous thanksgiving, there being no intrusion of perplexities about them. This adverb is not, with Koppe, to be diluted into πολλάκις, nor is the phrase to be explained away as if it only meant *non actu sed affectu*. From its position here the adverb is not connected with the verb, but is bound up with the participle, as in Philip. i, 4, Col. i, 3, the first connection being impossible, inasmuch as μνείαν ποιεῖσθαι περί τινος is not a Pauline formula. The parallel participial clause, μνείαν ὑμῶν ποιούμενοι ἐπὶ τῶν προσευχῶν ἡμῶν, " making mention of you in our prayers," is not a limiting assertion as in the alternative opinion of Jowett, and that of Baumgarten-Crusius, and Bisping, as if in effect the meaning were, " We give thanks so often as we make mention." But the sentence is modal, and describes not when, but how, the thanksgiving was offered; and that was by bearing them on his heart, and up before God in his earnest prayers (Rom. i, 9; Ephes. i, 16; Phile. 4). The phrase μνείαν ποιεῖσθαι does not signify to remember (Jowett, Koch, Ellicott), but to make mention of: " making mention of you in our prayers we always give thanks for you all." Such mention was made ἐπὶ τῶν προσευχῶν ἡμῶν, on occasion of my prayers. Ἐπὶ τῶν δείπνων (Diodorus Sic., iv, 3). For ἐπὶ see under Ephes. i, 16.

(Ver. 3.) ἀδιαλείπτως μνημονεύοντες—"without ceasing remembering." Not a few connect the participle with the preceding clause, as if it referred to ceaseless mention of them in his prayers (Balduin, Benson, Bengel, Ewald, Hofmann, Alford). Alford refers in proof to Rom. i, 9; but his admission that there the order is slightly different destroys the validity of the reference. That connection, too, would enfeeble the previous verse, by throwing in a statement at the end of it which yet really underlies it; but, taken with the present verse, it emphatically resumes and carries on the thought. The continuous and unexceptional thanksgiving found its utterance in his prayers, and was sustained in its fervour and continuity by unceasing remembrance. The participle may not be properly causal, or, as Ellicott says, "it may define the temporal concomitants," yet these temporal concomitants imply a reason; for, as he admits, the thanksgiving owed its persistence to the necessary continuance of the μνήμη. The clause is thus an explanatory aspect of the previous one, showing how natural this making mention of them was; for, as he had unfading memory of them, he could not but make mention of them, so that his thanksgiving for them was unbroken. The adverb is used only by Paul, and in reference to religious exercise (ii, 13; v, 17; Rom. i, 9). The participle is sometimes followed by an accusative (Matt. xvi, 9; Madvig, § 58); and sometimes by ὅτι, and other particles. It sometimes means *commemorantes* (Lünemann, after Beza and Cocceius); but here it signifies as in the Vulgate *memores*. The following genitive implies this latter sense, and, with the exception of Hebrews xi, 22, it is the uniform signification of the verb in the New Testament, as Gal. ii, 10; Col. iv, 18; Heb. xi, 13. Winer, § 30, 10 c.

ὑμῶν τοῦ ἔργου τῆς πίστεως, καὶ τοῦ κόπου τῆς ἀγάπης, καὶ τῆς ὑπομονῆς τῆς ἐλπίδος τοῦ Κυρίου ἡμῶν Ἰησοῦ Χριστοῦ—" your work of faith, and labour of love, and patience of hope." The genitive ὑμῶν is taken by some objectively, "remembering you," and ἕνεκα is supplied to the following genitives by Œcumenius,

Vatablus, Calvin, Zuingli, Hunnius, &c., but such a construction is clumsy and unwarranted. Winer, § 22, 7, 1. For the genitive pronoun, placed emphatically, is governed by all the three following nouns—$\xi\rho\gamma o\upsilon$, $\kappa\acute{o}\pi o\upsilon$, $\upsilon\pi o\mu o\nu\hat{\eta}s$—each of them emphatic and in turn governing another genitive. For the order, see v, 8; Col. i, 4.

"Work of faith" is a work springing out of faith (Koch, Schott, Jowett), or, rather, belonging to faith, and therefore characterizing it—your faith's work. It is not in contrast with $\lambda\acute{o}\gamma os$, as if signifying reality, *fidei veritas;* nor is it active, *eures thätigen Glaubens;* $\xi\rho\gamma o\upsilon$ is not pleonastic (Koppe and Rosenmüller); nor can the phrase be twisted to mean "faith wrought by God" (Calvin, Calovius, and Wolf); nor is it epexegetical, your work—to wit, that you believe (Hofmann); nor can the sense assigned by Chrysostom and his followers be sustained, which limits it too much to the endurance of suffering—$\epsilon\check{\iota}$ $\pi\iota\sigma\tau\epsilon\acute{\upsilon}\epsilon\iota s$ $\pi\acute{a}\nu\tau a$ $\pi\acute{a}\sigma\chi\epsilon$. Compare under Gal. v, 6. Their living faith was clothed upon with work; it was not a belief dead, barren, and alone. No principle of action is so powerful as genuine faith, and these believing Thessalonians were noted as active workers.

$\kappa a\grave{\iota}$ $\tau o\hat{\upsilon}$ $\kappa\acute{o}\pi o\upsilon$ $\tau\hat{\eta}s$ $\dot{a}\gamma\acute{a}\pi\eta s$, the force of $\dot{\upsilon}\mu\hat{\omega}\nu$ being still recognized, "your love's labour," the relation expressed by the genitive being, as in the previous clause, labour which belongs to your love and characterizes it. $K\acute{o}\pi os$ is earnest and toilsome service, into which the whole heart is thrown, travail of soul, often self-denial and exhaustion. $'A\gamma\acute{a}\pi\eta$ is not specially love towards Christ, as if the following words "our Lord Jesus Christ" belonged to it (a-Lapide); nor is it love to God or to God and our neighbours, but love to fellow-Christians, as in Col. i, 4, which is shown, not simply in overlooking errors and weaknesses (Theodoret), or in doing the work of a Christian pastor and teacher (De Wette), for such a meaning limits the reference in $\pi\acute{a}\nu\tau\omega\nu$ $\dot{\upsilon}\mu\hat{\omega}\nu$, which includes the entire community; nor does $\kappa\acute{o}\pi os$ expend itself merely in tending the sick or in caring for strangers, which is only one sphere of its operation (Acts xx, 35). The noun $\kappa\acute{o}\pi os$ comprises all the labour which belongs to Christian love. This love, the image of Christ's, is no ordinary attachment, resting on the slender basis of mere professional fellowship, but is embodied in travail, and busies itself in kindnesses of all shapes, in the doing of which it spares no pains and grudges no sacrifice (2 Thess. i, 3).

The third element of their character ever remembered by the apostle was—

καὶ τῆς ὑπομονῆς τῆς ἐλπίδος τοῦ Κυρίου ἡμῶν Ἰησοῦ Χριστοῦ —"and your patience of hope in our Lord Jesus Christ." The genitive ἐλπίδος, not that of origin (Schott, De Wette), indicates the same relation as the previous parallel one, "your hope's patience," and cannot signify the cause διὰ τὴν ἐλπίδα (Œcumenius). ὑπομονὴ is not, bearing up under evil, or the resigned endurance of it; but is perseverance or constancy, trials and sufferings being implied (Rom. ii, 4; xv, 4; Heb. xii, 1). Cicero well says, *perseverantia est in ratione bene considerata stabilis et perpetua permansio* (Koch).

The following personal genitives, τοῦ Κυρίου ἡμῶν Ἰησοῦ Χριστοῦ, do not belong to the previous clauses, or to "faith and love," as a-Lapide, Wordsworth, Olshausen, and Hofmann suppose, but under varying aspects, their special connection is with ἐλπίδος as its complement, the Lord Jesus Christ being its object (Philip. iii, 2, and i, 10). The hope of our Lord Jesus Christ is ever connected in this epistle with His second Advent, the hope of which He is the living centre and object, and which is realized when He comes again according to His promise. Their hope was no evanescent emotion, gleaming up fitfully and soon fading out again. It was calm and steady amidst trials and persecutions; it had, as ὑπομονὴ implies, a robust and noble persistence, in spite of what Theodoret calls τὰ προσπίπτοντα σκυθρωπά. The concluding phrase—

ἔμπροσθεν τοῦ Θεοῦ καὶ πατρὸς ἡμῶν—"before God and our Father," is used by the apostle in this epistle only.

(1) Vatablus, without any plausibility, joins the phrase to the words the Lord Jesus Christ, *qui nunc vultui Dei et patris nostri apparet*. (2) Some connect it with the previous clauses, as if it qualified them. Thus Theodoret, ἐπόπτης δὲ τούτων φησὶν ἐστιν ὁ τῶν ὅλων Θεός, and so Theophylact, and Œcumenius in an alternative explanation, with a-Lapide, Baumgarten-Crusius, Turretin, Wordsworth, and Jowett; while Doddridge apparently confines the connection to the last clause,

"the hope of our Lord Jesus Christ in the view of our God and Father." But in such a case, a connective article would have been necessary to give the phrase the power of an adjective, asserting the genuineness of these Christian graces. The exegesis, besides, is awkward and unnatural. (3) The phrase rather belongs to μνημονεύοντες, showing where the remembrance of these graces was experienced, "in the presence of God and our Father," in solemn prayer and in earnest thanksgiving. Compare Rom. iii, 20; xii, 17; 2 Cor. viii, 21, where ἐνώπιον is used. The phrase occurs often in the Septuagint, representing the Hebrew לִפְנֵי (Frankel, *Vorstudien zu der Sept.*, p. 159). For the formula Θεὸς καὶ πατήρ see under Ephes. i, 37; Gal. i, 4. These three graces are placed together by the apostle in natural order and development—faith, the spring of all spiritual excellence; love, allied to it and vitalized by it, for it worketh by love; and hope, based on that faith which is the substance of things hoped for, and stretching onward to the "glorious appearing" of Jesus Christ. Faith respects especially one's own salvation; love glows for the spiritual well-being of others; while the future, containing so much in reserve for us, is firmly grasped and realized by hope. When the apostle values these three graces, he sets them in a different order. Thus, in 1 Cor. xiii, 13, "Now abideth faith, hope, love, these three, but the greatest of them is love." Compare v, 8; Heb. v, 10-12; Col. i, 4, 5. Faith is child-like, hope is saint-like, but love is God-like.

(Ver. 4.) εἰδότες, ἀδελφοὶ ἠγαπημένοι ὑπὸ Θεοῦ, τὴν ἐκλογὴν ὑμῶν—"knowing (as we do), brethren beloved by God, your election," as in the margin of the English version. To apply this participle to the Thessalonians themselves mars the harmony of thought, the thanksgiving being founded on what the apostle knew of them, not on what they knew of themselves. Some, however, take the participle as a kind of nominative absolute, resolved into οἴδατε γάρ (Erasmus), or εἰδότες ἐστε (Theodoret, Homberg, and Baumgarten-Crusius). Grotius regards it as the beginning of a new sentence, stretching down to ἐγενήθητε in verse 6; Pelt attaches it to μνείαν ποιούμενοι, which is a needless narrowing of the connection.

VER. 4.]   FIRST EPISTLE TO THE THESSALONIANS   39

Εἰδότες, like μνημονεύοντες, belongs to the first and leading verb εὐχαριστοῦμεν, which is followed by three participles, the first defining the occasion on which the thanksgiving was offered, "making mention of you in our prayers," the second specifying its manner and the immediate prompting motive, "remembering your work of faith," and the third giving the ultimate grounds, "inasmuch as we know your election." The participle has a causal signification distinctly expressed in the Syriac. The translation of the Authorized Version—"your election of God," which is found also in Theophylact and Œcumenius, in Justiniani and Zanchius—is against the order of the Greek, and supposes an ellipse of the substantive verb (2 Thess. ii, 13; Rom. i, 7). The connection then of ὑπὸ Θεοῦ is not, knowing of God your election, nor your election of God, but beloved of God; not, however, as Estius is inclined to suppose, *continet ea pars, dilecti a Deo, causam sequentis,* electionem vestram. They were not only dear to the apostle and his colleagues, but he styles them in the highest sense, beloved by God, the objects of divine complacency, in silent contrast to the hatred and malignity of their persecutors. Compare 2 Chron. xx, 7; Ps. lx, 5, repeated in Ps. cviii, 6. Ἐκλογή is not election simply to external privilege (Whitby), but out of the world into eternal life by an eternal purpose, εἰς σωτηρίαν, and is not to be identified with that κλῆσις εἰς περιποίησιν δόξης (2 Thess. ii, 13-14), in which it realizes itself, or with regeneration (Pelt). God is ὁ καλῶν in the present, but He is also ὁ ἐκλεξάμενος always in the past. The grounds of his knowledge of their election are given by the apostle in the next paragraph, and they are historical in nature—his own experience of their changed character brightened by so many Christian graces. He did not profess to know the Eternal Will and Purpose in itself, or from having the pages of the Book of Life thrown open to him; but he came to a knowledge of it from its results so visibly brought out in them. See under Ephes. i, 4-11; Rom. viii, 29; 2 Thess. ii, 13; 2 Tim. i, 9; ii, 10. The next verse assigns the grounds on which the assertion begun with εἰδότες rested.

(Ver. 5.) ὅτι τὸ εὐαγγέλιον ἡμῶν οὐκ ἐγενήθη εἰς ὑμᾶς ἐν λόγῳ μόνον,—"because our gospel came not unto you in word only." For εἰς ὑμᾶς we have B K L ℵ and some of the Greek fathers; for πρὸς ὑμᾶς we have A C² D F, and also some of the Greek fathers. The words are so like in meaning that little stress can be laid on their quotation, so that the authorities being so nearly balanced, the reading is doubtful. There could not be any great temptation to change πρὸς into εἰς; though, as the context depicts not the mere arrival of the gospel to them, but the circumstances in which it came among them, εἰς might be changed into πρὸς or the words might appear so close in meaning that careless copyists might unconsciously exchange them. Some give ὅτι its demonstrative meaning "that," or to wit, *dass nämlich*. Ewald has *wie*, and some editors, as Lachmann and Tischendorf, prefix a comma, to show the expository connection and the grammatical dependence on εἰδότες. Thus Bengel, Schott, and Hofmann regard the following clauses as simply explanatory of the ἐκλογή, as pointing out its feature or wherein it consisted. But these verses do not describe election in any view, and are not in any real sense doctrinal, though they might apply to effectual calling. They refer to past historical facts, to certain elements of their history which assured the apostle of their election. His object is not to show what it was, but to adduce the grounds on which he and his colleagues were self-persuaded of it. The conjunction is therefore rightly rendered *quia* in the Vulgate and Claromontane, and in the Syriac by ܡܛܠ (Winer, § 53, 8).

The objective ὅτι thus introduces recognized facts in proof of the previous statement (De Wette, Koch, Lünemann, &c.). And he knew it on two grounds—first, a subjective ground, from the memory of his own consciousness in preaching; his own recollections of divine assistance poured in upon him as he proclaimed the truth—a token to him that he was not labouring in vain. Secondly, an objective ground, their immediate and cordial reception of the truth, "and ye became followers of us and of the Lord, having received the word in much affliction and in joy of the Holy Ghost."

The first ground is that "our gospel came not unto you in word only." "Our gospel" is the gospel which we preach and are known to preach, the genitive being vaguely that of possession or of instrumental origin. They had it, and by them it was published. The passive form ἐγενήθην, originally Doric, occurs often in this epistle in its middle sense, ἐγένετο. Its passive form has never the mere sense of εἶναι (Lobeck ad Phrynich., p. 108; Kühner ; Winer, § 13). It is therefore rightly rendered "came." It means that something has been brought about or has come to be "by divine grace," as Lünemann gives it. The word may not express this idea of itself, but it is really implied. If we adopt the reading εἰς ὑμᾶς, the meaning is simply *ad vos* as in the Vulgate, the Claromontane having *apud*, which is liker πρός and not unlike παρά with a dative. Fritzsche *in Marc.* vi, 3, p. 201-202 ; 1 Cor. ii, 3; 2 John, 12.

The gospel came not "in word only," ἐν denoting sphere, and not simply that the gospel was a mere word. The gospel was in the word, as οὐ μόνον implies, but it did not remain in it; it burst beyond it. Language was the vehicle of communication, but the message passed beyond the mere vehicle. It would have been a lifeless thing if it had been only ἐν λόγῳ as a kernel in an unopened husk; but vitality and power were in the truth so spoken—

ἀλλὰ καὶ ἐν δυνάμει καὶ ἐν Πνεύματι ἁγίῳ, καὶ ἐν πληροφορίᾳ πολλῇ—"but also in power and in the Holy Ghost, and in much assurance." Ἐν points again to the medium or manner in which the preaching was carried out. Now first these terms are subjective, or they characterize the emotions of the preachers, not those of the hearers (Koppe, Pelt), or of speakers and hearers both (Vorstius and Schott). How the hearers felt and acted under their preacher is told in the next verse; but this verse refers to the apostle's own remembrance of his preaching, what it was in his own consciousness, or when he was engaged in it, appealing in the next clause to themselves for the truth of his assertion—"As ye yourselves know what kind of persons we proved to be for your sakes." In short, the verse tells how the gospel came, or the manner of its advent, and not the results produced by it. It came ἐν δυνάμει, "in power," on the part of the preachers. Δύναμις does not mean here miraculous energy—as is supposed by the Greek fathers, followed by a-Lapide, Grotius, and Turretin. The plural is usually employed when such is the reference; but here, standing in contrast to ἐν λόγῳ, it denotes the mighty eloquence and the overwhelming force with which they preached (1 Cor. ii, 5), and not the external impression made by accompanying miracles. There had been an unusual outburst of mental and spiritual energy in the preaching; they had been carried beyond themselves; they argued, insisted, and urged. The second καὶ is not epexegetical, but in the phrase καὶ ἐν Πνεύματι ἁγίῳ it has an ascensive force, and the second clause says something fuller and higher than the first. They preached in the Holy Ghost; no wonder that such power was possessed by them and showed itself in their mighty utterances. The power was inwrought by the Holy Spirit, and could from its nature be ascribed only to Him. When Jowett explains the phrase as the inspiration of the speaker wrought by the hearer, the statement may not be a denial of the personality of the Divine Agent, but it reduces the result to that of ordinary human oratory in which no divine element is involved. It is slovenly and inaccurate to take the clauses as a hendiadys, ἐν δυνάμει Πνεύματος ἁγίου, as Calvin, Piscator, and Conybeare. On the want of the article with Πνεῦμα, see under Ephes. i, 17. The third conjunct characteristic of the preaching was—

καὶ ἐν πληροφορίᾳ πολλῇ—"and in much assurance." The repetition of καὶ and of ἐν gives a separate and distinct prominence to each of the three clauses in succession. Πληροφορία, "assured persuasion," is a noun found only in the New Testament and the ecclesiastical writers (Suicer, *sub voce;* Rom. iv, 21; xiv, 5; Col. ii, 2; Heb. vi, 11; x, 22). It does not mean certainty of the truth and of its divine original produced in the Thessalonians (Musculus, Macknight, Benson), nor fulness of spiritual gifts and instruction (a-Lapide, Turretin), nor fulfilment of the apostolical office, *ut plene apud eos officio satisfecisse non dubitaretur* (Estius). But the meaning is that they preached at once in the full persuasion of the truth of the gospel, and that, in presenting it at the moment, they were doing the Master's will. This inborn assurance, combined with the Spirit's inworking and the powerful utterance vouchsafed to them, were to them a token that there were in their audiences those whom they could soon recognize as God's elect, and these characteristics of their early labours in Thessalonica, showing that they were divinely owned and strengthened, are now adduced as one ground of their knowledge that those addressed in the epistle are the elect. Olshausen puts it somewhat dogmatically and sternly: "Paul means to show how from the way in which the Spirit operated in him at a certain place, he drew a conclusion as to the disposition of the persons there—where it manifested itself powerfully, there, he argued, there must be elect. Thus the Spirit suffered him not to travel through Bithynia because there were no elect there." But there were Christians in that province very soon afterwards (1 Pet. i, 1), and what then of their election? Was it a divine act subsequent to the interdict laid on the apostle as told in Acts xvi, 7?

And for the truth of what he had been writing he now appeals to themselves—

καθὼς οἴδατε οἷοι ἐγενήθημεν ἐν ὑμῖν δι' ὑμᾶς—"even as ye know what manner of men we were found to be among you for your sakes." The rendering of the Authorized Version "we were" does not give the full sense. Conybeare's translation is not correct, "behaved myself," nor yet is that of the Vulgate, *quales fuerimus*. The appeal is to themselves—to their own knowledge; it corresponded (καθώς) with the apostle's statement in the previous part of the verse. It witnessed that the gospel was preached to them "in power, and in the Holy Ghost, and in much assurance;" and these elements of character and labour proved what manner of men the apostle and his colleagues were really found to be. The first part of the verse describes the preaching, what it was, and this clause describes the preachers, what they were. As no one who had heard such preaching would forget it, every one would be eager to verify the apostle's statement from his own recollection.

The οἷοι ἐγενήθημεν therefore includes alone what we have just said, and to give it a reference to disinterestedness and self-support by manual labour, is going wholly astray from the text; and an appeal, as by Estius, Macknight, and Pelt, to ii, 7-9, is at this point wholly irrelevant. As remote from the apostle's immediate purpose is any allusion to dangers and persecutions—κινδύνους οὓς ὑπὲρ αὐτῶν ὑπέστησαν (Theodoret). Ἐν ὑμῖν is simply "among you," in your society; and δι' ὑμᾶς points to the final purpose of the whole procedure, which was prompted and fashioned from a regard to their eternal interests—καθὼς οἴδατε, the appeal is honest, and he felt that they would respond to it. It is no self-eulogy born of conceit—no flattering self-drawn picture—" ye yourselves know."

This, then, is the first or subjective portion of the grounds on which Paul and his colleagues knew the election of the Thessalonian believers. "Our transcendent energy, earnestness, and confidence—all inwrought by the Divine Spirit, and felt and manifested in our preaching—were proof to us that God was by us doing His work among you and marking you out to us as His own chosen ones."

To begin a new sentence, as Koppe does, with καθὼς οἴδατε, and to give it this meaning, *qualem me vidistis quum apud vos essem tales etiam apud vos nunc estis*, breaks the coherence, gives a past sense to οἴδατε, and a wrong meaning to ἐγενήθημεν, and would need οὕτως ὑμεῖς to be expressed in the next verse.

Now follows the objective ground of his knowledge of their election.

(Ver. 6.) καὶ ὑμεῖς μιμηταὶ ἡμῶν ἐγενήθητε καὶ τοῦ Κυρίου—"and ye on your part came to be followers of us and of the Lord." The connection is still unbroken, and hangs virtually on ὅτι beginning the fifth verse and signifying "for" or "because." Ὑμεῖς is emphatic and in contrast to ἡμῶν in the previous verse—our gospel on the one side—your reception of it on the other. The verb ἐγενήθητε has the same sense as in the previous verse—not ye were, but ye came to be (1 Cor. iv, 16; Ephes. v, 1). The additional idea *durch die Leitung Gottes* of Lünemann is a theological inference, for it does not lie in the words. The apostle brings out the result without touching the process, by his preference of this compound formula to the simpler verb μιμεῖσθαι. The first καὶ is copulative, and the second is rather climactic, not exactly corrective, as Bullinger, who says that we ought to be followers of the apostles, *eatenus quatenus illi Christi imitatores sunt*.

Their imitation of the apostle and his colleagues was, in its spirit and results, an imitation of Christ; for it was imitation of the apostles in their connection with Christ, in His truth and His life (1 Cor. iv, 16; xi. 1; Philip. iii, 17). Koppe destroys the cogency of the argument altogether, by holding that the points of imitation on the part of the Thessalonians were the power, the Holy Ghost, and the great confidence mentioned in the previous verse, as characterizing the preaching of Paul, Silas, and Timothy. But the point of imitation is plainly not the mere reception of the word, as that could not apply to ὁ λόγος, but the spirit and circumstances in which they received it—" in much affliction with joy of the Holy Ghost," as is now stated.

δεξάμενοι τὸν λόγον, ἐν θλίψει πολλῇ μετὰ χαρᾶς Πνεύματος ἁγίου. The participle seems to denote inner conscious acceptance (ii, 13), *amplexi estis* (Calvin), *excipientes* (Vulgate); and it is in the same tense or point of time with the verb— implying simultaneous action—ye became followers at the moment when, or in that, ye received the word. Ὁ λόγος is the gospel as preached (Luke viii, 13; Acts xvii, 11; Gal. vi, 6): τοῦ Κυρίου being added in verse 8. Other genitives are used in Ephes. i, 13; 2 Cor. ii, 17. The affliction in which they received it was great, as may be learned from Acts xvii, 5, 9, compared with ii, 14, and from iii, 2, 3. These afflictions seem to have continued after the violent outburst at the first preaching of the apostle. The Master had foretold tribulation to his followers, and the apostle had echoed the prediction during his residence in Thessalonica. The θλῖψις is therefore not that of the apostles, *praecones graviter affligebantur*, but that of the Thessalonians themselves. Compare iii, 7. They received the word, however, not only in affliction, but μετὰ χαρᾶς Πνεύματος ἁγίου, " with joy of the Holy Ghost," the genitive being that of origin, and as Ellicott calls it "originating agent" (Scheuerlein, § 17, 1). The phrase does not mean merely spiritual joy (Jowett), but joy inwrought by the Holy Spirit, and is therefore connected with the present conscious possession of spiritual blessings and hopes (Rom. xiv, 17; Gal. v, 22). See under Philip. iii, 1. This joy is no unnatural emotion, as if in stoical apathy they did not feel their sufferings, or pray that they should cease; but it is a grace of the Divine Spirit which exists independently of them, though it may be increased by means of them (Acts v, 41); the joy of living in Christ and of loving Him,—all that gladness of position and prospects which faith in the gospel brings, and which in Christ and his apostle coexisted with the endurance of great sufferings. The Lord "for the joy that was set before Him endured the cross, despising the shame," and His early servants passed through a similar experience of outer sufferings and inner gladness, so that they who, in receiving and holding the truth, are yet supported under affliction by the joy of the Holy Ghost, are followers both of the apostles and of the Divine Master. Now the circumstances of the Thessalonians in receiving the word which are so briefly described, were so striking and so Christlike, that they were typical—

(Ver. 7.) ὥστε γενέσθαι ὑμᾶς τύπους—"so that ye became an ensample." The reading is doubtful, the plural τύπους being found in A C F K L ℵ and many fathers; but the singular in B D 17, 67, in the Latin versions (Vulgate and Claromontane), as also in the Syriac and Coptic. The Syriac has ܠܐܣܐ. D³ and 49 have τύπος, conjectured by Mill to be a neuter form like πλοῦτος. It is more likely that τύπον should be changed into τύπους on account of the ὑμᾶς, than that the reverse should take place. The singular is accepted by Lachmann and Tischendorf, and is, moreover, grammatically correct, the believers being taken as a collective unity, *als ein Einheit-begriff* (Bernhardy, p. 58). Chrysostom in his exposition uses, in consecutive clauses, both the plural and singular form (Winer, § 27 ; Kühner, § 407).

They became an ensample. There is a binary process—first, they followed their preachers as a living pattern or example, μιμηταί, and then they became in turn an example, τύπος, a pattern for the imitation of other churches ; from being μιμηταί, they became τύπος.

πᾶσιν τοῖς πιστεύουσιν ἐν τῇ Μακεδονίᾳ καὶ ἐν τῇ Ἀχαΐᾳ—"to all the believers in Macedonia and in Achaia," the second ἐν having preponderant authority. The present participle with the article is used substantively, all idea of time being excluded. Compare Ephes. iv, 28; Matt. iv, 3; Gal. i, 23. Winer, § 45, 7. In his exposition Chrysostom virtually changes the tenses of the participle—ye became an ensample τοῖς ἤδη πιστεύουσι, "ye so shone that ye became instructors of them who received the gospel before you." Chrysostom is followed by Œcumenius and Theophylact, who has πιστεύσασι τύπος, and among many others by Pelt and Schott. But the Philippian Church was the only earlier church in Eastern Europe, as the apostle did not tarry at Amphipolis or Apollonia, and the language is scarcely applicable to it. Macedonia and Achaia, as two Roman provinces, are equivalent to northern and southern Greece, the entire territory. The Grecian churches could look upon the Thessalonians as a typical or representative community, whose example was worthy of universal imitation. But Theodoret's addition that the apostolic encomium is the more expressive, because the nations referred to were great and wise, ἐπὶ σοφίᾳ θαυμαζομένοις, is simply not in the text. The apostle now gives the foundation for the previous eulogistic statement.

(Ver. 8.) ἀφ' ὑμῶν γὰρ ἐξήχηται ὁ λόγος τοῦ Κυρίου—"for from you has sounded forth the word of the Lord." We cannot give ὑμῶν here a wider reference than the previous ὑμᾶς, so that Baumgarten-Crusius is wrong in including the Philippians under it. The natural sense of ἀφ' ὑμῶν is the local one, from you as the point of departure (1 Cor. xiv, 36). It cannot well mean ὑφ' ὑμῶν, by you, as the preachers of it (Rückert), nor δι' ὑμῶν, by your means as having saved our lives (Storr), nor are the two meanings to be combined as by Schott and Bloomfield. The "word of the Lord" is very plainly the gospel, as in the 6th verse, and not, as De Wette makes it, the fame of their reception of the gospel. Compare 2 Thess. iii, 1; and often and naturally in the Acts, as viii, 25; xiii, 48; xv, 35, 36; xvi, 32; xix, 10, 20. A word having the Lord for its origin, its centre, and its end; His life in its purity and sympathy; His death in its atoning fulness—told in man's language.

The verb ἐξήχηται (has been sounded out ὥσπερ σάλπιγγος λαμπρὸν ἠχούσης, Chrysostom) occurs only here in the New Testament, but it is found in the Septuagint (Joel iii, 14; Sirach xl, 13). The meaning is, that their conversion and its circumstances were so noted, that they carried the gospel through the province as if by the ringing peal of a trumpet. The rumour of what had happened at Thessalonica sped its way through Greece, and carried with it the gospel—sounded abroad loudly, fully, distinctly, the blessed message.

οὐ μόνον ἐν τῇ Μακεδονίᾳ καὶ Ἀχαΐᾳ—"not only in Macedonia and Achaia." Before Ἀχαΐᾳ, ἐν τῇ is inserted by C D F R L ℵ, 30

MSS., with the Vulgate and Claromontane Latin and the Syriac, and it is admitted by Lachmann, while A B and the majority of MSS. and some of the fathers omit it. It may have been repeated from the previous verse, as if again to mark Achaia as a distinct province, but the authority of MSS. in its favour is great. Lünemann asserts that ἐν τῇ is necessary, and must therefore be genuine; but, as Ellicott replies, the want of the ἐν τῇ is not only permissible, but grammatically exact, as Macedonia and Achaia are here regarded as a whole, and put in antithesis to all the rest of the world (Winer, § 19, 4). Between grammatical nicety on the one hand, and diplomatic authority on the other, the point cannot well be decided. The difference of reading involves a difference of meaning. οὐ μόνον . . . . ἀλλά being used, *ubi posterior notio ut major vel gravior vel latior in prioris notionis locum substituitur quidem sed prior non plane tollitur*: Kühner *ad Xenoph. Memor.* ii, 6, 2, p. 159. See examples in Stallbaum's Plato, vol. I, 210; *Phaedo*, 107 B; and in ninth excursus of Bremi *ad Isocr.*, p. 212.

ἀλλὰ ἐν παντὶ τόπῳ ἡ πίστις ὑμῶν ἡ πρὸς τὸν Θεὸν ἐξελήλυθεν —"but in every place your faith which is toward God has gone forth." The καὶ of the Received Text has no proper authority. The structure of these words is somewhat difficult. Were the sentence thus—"From you has sounded out the word of the Lord;" and were it to end thus, "not only in Macedonia and Achaia, but also in every place," it would appear natural and complete. But ἐν παντὶ τόπῳ, so far from concluding the clause, is connected with a new subject and predicate, "in every place your faith which is toward God has gone out." Some propose a transposition of οὐ μόνον, οὐ μόνον ἐξήχηται. Not only has the word of the Lord been sounded out in Macedonia and Achaia, but in every place your faith also has gone out. Such is the violent proposal of Beza, Piscator, Zanchius, Grotius, Rosenmüller, Storr, Schrader, Koppe, Schott, and others. It cannot be entertained for a moment, for it is tantamount to rewriting the verse.

Others, as Olshausen and De Wette, hold that the two subjects and their predicates are equivalent in meaning—the word of the Lord, the report of your faith in the Lord has sounded out, very much the same as, your faith Godward has gone out (Olshausen). Lünemann proposes to put a colon after Κυρίου, and begin a clause with οὐ μόνον, the sentence then being thus—"for from you has sounded out the word of the Lord." But this punctuation gives the clause a feeble and spiritless aspect, which is at the same time contradicted by the sonorous ἐξήχηται, while ἀλλὰ ἐν παντὶ τόπῳ stands in direct antithesis to οὐ μόνον ἐν τῇ Μ., and is, apparently, the natural and necessary complement of the sentence. It is probable that the apostle has mixed two constructions. In writing the sentence, the thought of a stronger climax came into his mind, and he puts a whole sentence in antithesis to οὐ μόνον ἐν τῇ Μακεδονίᾳ καὶ Ἀχαΐᾳ, instead of, as first intended, a merely local phrase, such as ἐν παντὶ τόπῳ, or, as he has said in Rom. i, 3, ἐν ὅλῳ τῷ κόσμῳ. The apostle, when he got to ἐν παντὶ τόπῳ, completing the comparison, felt that perhaps an explanatory statement was needed, and so losing sight of οὐ μόνον, he at once and without breaking the connection goes out into the additional statement, and, the first nominative also passing out of view, he inserts another and more directly personal one—ἡ πίστις ὑμῶν ἡ πρὸς τὸν θεόν. The phrase is made distinct by the repetition of the article—πρὸς being used also in Phile. 5 (Winer, § 50, 2). The πρὸς for the more common εἰς implies, perhaps, the change of creed and worship referred to in the next verse, before which their faith toward idols had vanished (Lünemann, Hofmann). For the verb used for the spread of a rumour, compare Matt. ix, 26; Mark i, 28. Observe, says Chrysostom, how he speaks of it as of a living thing, περὶ ἐμψύχου. The phrase ἐν παντὶ τόπῳ is a popular hyberbole, ἐν and not εἰς implying that the rumour was still in every place (Winer, § 50, 4 a). Chrysostom, however, warns, "let no one regard these words as hyberbolical, for Macedonians were not inferior in fame to the Romans" (John xii, 19; Rom. i, 8; Col. i, 6-23). Compare the use made of Ps. xix in Rom. x, 17, 12. The report of their conversion to Christianity had spread beyond Greece—was known and talked of everywhere. The words do not convey any impression that Paul in his travels beyond Macedonia and Achaia had met the report, and it is only conjecture to inquire how the report obtained such wide and speedy currency. Christian merchants might have carried it (De Wette, Zanchius, Grotius). Corinth, in which he was writing, was a great trading city, with a perpetual influx of strangers. Thessalonica was a centre of business, and the heathen merchants coming from it might repeat what would appear to them an unaccountable phenomenon. Wieseler supposes that Aquila and Priscilla had arrived at Corinth from Rome, and may have mentioned that the report was known in the metropolis itself. It is not necessary on this account, with Schrader and Baumgarten, to assign a longer existence to the Thessalonian church, as a few months might suffice to justify the apostle's statement.

The result was—

ὥστε μὴ χρείαν ἔχειν ἡμᾶς λαλεῖν τι—"so that we have no need to speak anything" that is, on this point, or of your faith; not, "anything of moment" (Koch), or "of the gospel" (Michaelis). Ἡμᾶς, standing after ἔχειν on highest authority, was put before the verb, perhaps for the sake of emphatic contrast with the following αὐτοί. What had happened in Thessalonica was so notorious everywhere, that any further description of it might well be spared, the reason being—

(Ver. 9.) Αὐτοὶ γὰρ περὶ ἡμῶν ἀπαγγέλλουσιν ὁποίαν εἴσοδον ἔσχομεν πρὸς ὑμᾶς—"For they (on their part) report concerning us what manner of entrance we had among you." The Received Text has ἔχομεν with no authority. By αὐτοί are understood the people alluded to in the previous verse, those not in Macedonia and Achaia, but in every place, and the construction is according to sense (Winer, § 22, 3; Matt. iv, 23; 2 Cor. ii, 12-13). We have no need to speak; they do it for us—the two pronouns in emphatic contrast. The persons comprised in περὶ ἡμῶν are Paul and his colleagues, not Paul and the Thessalonians (Bisping), and the emphatic position is in contrast to πρὸς ὑμᾶς, while their change of worship as the result of this entrance is told in the next clause. Εἴσοδος is not access to their heart, but simply and historically ingress (ii, 1; Acts xiii, 24; Heb. x, 19; 2 Peter i, 11. Rost and Palm *sub voce*). The kind of entrance, not *facilis* (Pelt), is explained in verse 5 by the apostle—his proclamation of the divine message in power and in the Holy Ghost and in much assurance—the external perils and persecutions not being excluded, though they are not put into prominence, as by Chrysostom, Œcumenius, and Theophylact. This clause then contains in brief what the general report was about the apostle and his fellow-labourers—that they had come and preached so mightily and obtained such a welcome, or perhaps in phrase nearer what might be the form of the report in the mouth of a wondering heathen—"The other day three Jewish strangers came to Thessalonica, two of whom bore the scars of a terrible scourging they had got north at Philippi ; they began to hold public meetings, and, so far from being opposed, they were tolerated, and the astounding doctrines which they taught with a superhuman earnestness made a deep and wide sensation through the city, which cannot be accounted for and which is not subsiding." The next clause tells what the universal report was about the Thessalonians themselves. They themselves are talking about us and they themselves are at the same time talking about you—

πῶς ἐπεστρέψατε πρὸς τὸν Θεὸν ἀπὸ τῶν εἰδώλων—"how ye turned from idols to God." Πῶς introduces an objective sentence, and though it may not involve εὐκόλως (Chrysostom), or *mit welcher Freudigkeit* (Lünemann), still all notion of manner is not to be excluded—mode as characterizing the fact. They could not report the fact without some detail of the circumstances, πῶς to some extent corresponding to the modal adjective ὁποίαν of the previous clause. The notion of return is not necessarily involved in the compound verb, ἐπιστρέφειν, for ὀπίσω and εἰς τὰ ὀπίσω are used with it. Compare Acts xiv, 15 ; xv, 19 ; Matt. xxiv, 18 ; Mark xiii, 16 : Luke xvii, 31 ; and see under Gal. iv, 9. But idolatry being apostasy from God, turning from idols may be regarded as a return to God. The idea of return to God in conversion, or from apostasy, is familiar to every reader of the Old Testament, and it underlies the epithets "living and true" applied to God, that these idols are dead and false (Heb. ii, 19). Idols are also called vanities (Deut. xxxii, 21 ; Ps. xxxi, 6 ; cvi, 28 ; cxv, 4 ; Jer. viii, 19 ; Acts xiv, 15 ; 1 Cor. viii, 4). See under Gal. iv, 8.

δουλεύειν Θεῷ ζῶντι καὶ ἀληθινῷ—"to serve the living and true God." On the absence of the article see Winer, § 19, 1. The infinitive is that of purpose, and needs neither the complement of εἰς τό nor of ὥστε (Winer, § 44, 1, and as in Ephes. i, 4; Col. i, 22). The Divine Being is called ζῶν in contrast with these dead inanities. He is Life and the source and substance of all life. He is also ἀληθινός, true or real; not ἀληθής, *verax*, but ἀληθινός, *verus*—this latter term becoming in old English *very*, as in the phrase of the Nicene creed, " very God of very God" (Θεὸν ἀληθινόν ἐκ Θεοῦ ἀληθινοῦ); or in Wycliffe's translation of John xv, 1, "I am the verri vine." Ἀληθής characterizes God ethically (John iii, 33; Rom. iii, 4) as He is true to Himself and all His promises, ἀψευδής (Titus i, 2); but ἀληθινός characterizes His essence—He is what He professes to be (John i, 9; xvii, 3). See the epithet with the same sense and a different reference, John vi, 32; Heb. viii, 2; ix, 24; Sept., Isaiah lxv, 16. Trench, *Synon.*, § 8. The clause by itself might describe a departure from heathenism ending simply in proselytism—the change of a heathen from polytheism to monotheism. But in this case it was more, it was specifically a Christian conversion.

(Ver. 10.) καὶ ἀναμένειν τὸν υἱὸν αὐτοῦ ἐκ τῶν οὐρανῶν—" and to wait for His Son from heaven," or "from the heavens," as the phrase is sometimes rendered in the English plural, but most frequently in the singular. The verb ἀναμένειν occurs only here in the New Testament: ἀπεκδέχεσθαι is used in 1 Cor. i, 7; Philip. iii, 20; and περιμένειν is similarly found in Acts i, 4. The ἀνα cannot give the additional sense of *with joy* (Flatt). Winer says it does not mean *rediturum exspectare* (Bengel), nor *avide exspectare*. Natura sua habet admixtam . . . patientiae et fiduciae notionem. (*De verborum cum praepositionibus compositorum usu. Particula*, iii). On the name "Son," see under Ephes. i, 3. The somewhat elliptical phrase, "to wait for His Son from heaven," implies that He is in heaven and that He is coming from it. He, in the fulness of humanity, has gone up to plead, to reign, to sympathize, to prepare a place, and He will return, according to promise, to complete His work, to raise His people, to invest them with spiritual bodies, and to confer on them the crown and totality of redemption. This distinctive Christian grace of hope is based on faith. There must be faith in Him as Saviour ere there can be the quiet and patient expectation of His advent. Compare Matt.

xvi, 27; xxvi, 64; Luke ix, 26; Acts i, 11; Rom. i, 7; 1 Cor. xi, 29.

ὃν ἤγειρεν ἐκ τῶν νεκρῶν—" whom He raised from the dead." The insertion of τῶν rests on preponderant authority both of MSS. and fathers, B D F L ℵ—its omission being due probably to the common form of the phrase without the article. The theology of Paul is, that the Father raised the Son from the dead, and this resurrection has an evidential connection with the Sonship and the completion of His earthly work (Rom. i, 4). See under Gal. i, 1. There could have been no faith, had He still been one of the νεκροί, but He comes as a living man, who has triumphed over death, and He is now ὁ ζῶν (Rev. i, 18). The apostle emphatically names Him—

Ἰησοῦν τὸν ῥυόμενον ἡμᾶς ἀπὸ τῆς ὀργῆς τῆς ἐρχομένης—" Jesus who delivered us from the coming wrath." The first participle is present, and is not on the one hand to be rendered as aorist (Vulgate *qui eripuit*—Grotius, Pelt, the English version: Tyndale, Cranmer, and the Genevan preserving the present) nor is it on the other hand to receive a future sense, as in the Claromontane Latin, *qui eripiet, res certo futura* (Schott; Bernhardy, p. 371). Christ redeemed us once, says Bengel, but He is always delivering us. "Jesus who is delivering us" gives the full force of the present tense, and by this work therefore He may be characterized. The combination of the article and participle may point Him out as our Deliverer. So Lünemann, Alford, Ellicott, Koch, and Conybeare; Winer, § 45, 7. Our deliverance was achieved by that act of self-sacrifice which placed Him among the dead, and He the risen Redeemer is ever applying its gifts and power. The present participle ἐρχομένης maintains its proper meaning—that wrath is coming, certainly coming, at the period of the judgment. But from it Christ delivers us, now, through faith in Him; and as the Deliverer is coming again from heaven believers wait for Him, that He may raise their bodies from the dead and confer upon them full and final blessedness. It is plain from this statement that these truths had occupied a prominent place in the Apostle's preaching at Thessalonica. He had preached Christ the Deliverer, a divine person, "the Son of God" who had given Himself for them and gone down to the dead, but who had been raised again—Christ who was now the Governor (Philip. iii, 20), and who was to be the Judge and Rewarder at His coming. These primary and prominent doctrines had been proclaimed to them "in power, in the Holy Ghost, and in much assurance," and their acceptance of them produced an immediate and correspondent revolution in their worship and life. Compare 1 Cor. xv, 34. See Introduction.

CHAPTER II

(Ver. 1.) Αὐτοὶ γὰρ οἴδατε, ἀδελφοὶ, τὴν εἴσοδον ἡμῶν τὴν πρὸς ὑμᾶς, ὅτι οὐ κενὴ γέγονεν—"For ye yourselves know, brethren, our entrance to you that it was not vain."

The γάρ is certainly something more than a mere particle of transition—*auch* as Krause, *ja* as Flatt and Pelt, "yea" as Conybeare, "nay" as Peile, or simply "and" as in the Syriac version, while others do not translate it at all. The connection is not so difficult as these exceptional senses given to γάρ would lead us to suppose. Bengel, Flatt, and Schott connect this verse with i, 5, 6; the intermediate verses being taken as forming a species of parenthesis. But such a connection is pointless and obscure. Grotius joins it to the 10th verse, and with this meaning, *merito illam spem vitae aeternae retinetis; vera enim sunt quae vobis annuntiavimus*. But the following verses are not doctrinal, they are merely historical in nature. They contain no direct proof of the statement put forward by Grotius. The phrase "ye yourselves" is in contrast to those beyond them— to the αὐτοὶ in i, 9, who told of the entrance of the apostle to them. This paragraph is thus connected with i, 9: "not only strangers in the province told about our entrance in to you; not only are such statements about your conversion current everywhere; but you yourselves know what our entering in to you was. We appeal not to such reports in universal circulation; we appeal now to yourselves, to your own personal knowledge." The paragraph down to the end of the twelfth verse is a detailed and confirmatory explanation of what is said in the first half of i, 9—"the kind of entrance in to you which we had," ὁποίαν εἴσοδον ἔσχομεν; and verses 13, 14, 15, 16, of this chapter in a similar way take up at length the second half of i, 9—their instantaneous reception of the gospel, πῶς ἐπεστρέψατε πρὸς τὸν Θεὸν ἀπὸ τῶν εἰδώλων, and the mighty change resulting from it which still endured in spite of persecution and suffering. The γὰρ thus introduces an explanatory vindication (Hartung, p. 463). The form of the sentence is common in Greek, in which, especially after οἶδα, there is an anticipation of the object—not, ye know that our entrance was not vain; but ye know our entrance—that it was not vain (Krüger, § 61, 6, 2; Bernhardy, p. 466; Luke xii, 24; Acts xvi, 3; 1 Cor. iii, 5; vii, 17; 2 Cor. xii, 7. See under Gal. i. 11.)

Αὐτοὶ expressed is emphatic—a direct appeal to themselves. "Brethren," a name of endearment. The epithet κενή has been variously taken; some give it an ethical sense — μάταια (Œcumenius), *mendax* (Grotius), *non inanis, sed plena virtutis* (Bengel, Schott), *vani honoris studio* (Rosenmüller), *non otiose* (Koppe). The apostle does not say εἰς κενόν, as in iii, 5; and the reference in the following verse is not to the fruit of his labours—for this idea does not come in till verse 13—but to the character of them. The following ἀλλὰ is in contrast to οὐ κενή and introduces an explanation: his entrance was not vain; it was, as already described, preceded by suffering, but it was characterized by boldness of utterance, παρρησία, by absence of deceit, of uncleanness, and of guile; by fidelity, by gentleness, and disinterested self-denying love, by continuous and affectionate industry; all these features of his ministry explain οὐ κενή. Chrysostom says, οὐ κενὴ τουτέστι, ὅτι οὐκ ἀνθρωπίνη οὐδὲ ἡ τυχοῦσα. Κενή refers then to the character of the entrance, not to the fruits; to its fulness of power and purpose and reality (Ellicott). This entering in was not empty or unsubstantial, but was marked by a living reality, by power, confidence, and spiritual manifestation. And that character remained (γέγονεν) Some, however, combine both ideas, the nature of the entrance with the results (a-Lapide, Pelt, Schott, De Wette, and Benson); but the second reference is against the context. Some of the Greek fathers suppose a special allusion to persecution and dangers; but these come into view first in the next verse, and are referred to also in i, 9, of which this is an expansion.

(Ver. 2.) Ἀλλὰ προπαθόντες καὶ ὑβρισθέντες, καθὼς οἴδατε, ἐν Φιλίπποις, ἐπαρρησιασάμεθα ἐν τῷ Θεῷ ἡμῶν λαλῆσαι πρὸς ὑμᾶς τὸ εὐαγγέλιον τοῦ Θεοῦ ἐν πολλῷ ἀγῶνι—"But after having suffered before and been injuriously treated, as ye know, at Philippi, we were confident in our God to speak unto you the gospel of God in much conflict." The καὶ of the Received Text after ἀλλὰ is a gloss without any authority. Ἀλλὰ is opposed to κενὴ (1 Cor. xv, 10); it was not vain; on the other hand its reality was manifested as follows. The participles might be taken as concessive if the καὶ had been genuine as Pelt supposes, "though we having suffered before" (Lünemann); but the simple temporal sense is more in harmony with the historical statement which follows. The reference is to the sufferings already endured, and described in Acts xvi. The participle προπαθόντες occurs only here in the New Testament, but is found in Herodotus, vii, 11; Thucydides, iii, 67; Plato, *Rep.*, ii, 376. The apostle adds καὶ ὑβρισθέντες, "and injuriously treated," the treatment expressed by the verb being insolent and wanton outrage such as the scourging to which, though a Roman citizen, he had been subjected, a punishment forbidden by the Porcian and Valerian laws (Matt. xxii, 6; Luke xviii, 32; Acts, xiv, 5; Trench, § 29).

If the first compound verb might have a medial sense like the simple one (Xenoph., *Memor.*, ii, 2, 5), the second verb in the clause effectually forbids it.

Καθὼς οἴδατε is repeated—they knew it well, as they had seen him immediately after the flagellation, and may have done on him such a work of kindness as did the jailer. The verb ἐπαρρησιασάμεθα means literally "we were bold of speech," as its composition indicates (De Wette, Ellicott). But the word signifies also to be confident (Job xxvii, 10; Ephes. iii, 12; vi, 20; 1 Tim. iii, 13; 1 John ii, 28; iii, 21).

The following λαλῆσαι would be somewhat tautological if we give ἐπαρρησιασάμεθα its original meaning, though that meaning may be admitted after all. That παρρησία was in our God, He being the sphere in which it existed, ἐπὶ being used in Acts, xiv, 13, to denote the ground (Ellicott); ἡμῶν indicates close relationship—God of our choice, our service, whose graces sustain, whose spirit cheers, whose presence is our reward. The infinitive λαλῆσαι may be either explanatory (Koch, Ellicott; Winer, § 44, 1); or it may be taken as the simple infinitive of object after the previous verb (Lünemann, Hofmann). The meaning, however, is not to be dwindled into μετὰ παρρησίας ἐλαλοῦμεν.

The genitive Θεοῦ is not that of object, but of origin—the gospel which is from God (Ellicott, Koch). It adds weight to the statement, and vindicates alike the πληροφορία of i, 5 and the παρρησία of this verse. He proclaimed the good news of God's grace, no earthborn scheme, no human speculation or conjecture as to the probabilities of the divine purpose in itself or its results.

He spoke this gospel ἐν πολλῷ ἀγῶνι as referring chiefly, if not solely, to outward circumstances, and not to inner care and sorrow (Fritzsche). The former is the view of the Greek fathers, and the subsequent verses confirm it. Compare Philip. i, 30; Col. i, 29. Some, as Schott, combine both ideas—our entrance was not vain, and our history shows it. After we had suffered indignity and cruelty for preaching the gospel at Philippi, we still had confidence to preach the same gospel to you in the midst of conflict. It was instigated by unbelieving Jews, "who took unto them certain lewd fellows of the baser sort and gathered a great company and set all the city in an uproar." Such confident persistence in spite of past sufferings, and in the midst of present perils among you, proves that our entrance was not vain, but full of honest, hearty, and unfearing energy. The conflict must have lasted some time, and its culmination is told in Acts xvii, 9.

(Ver. 3.) Ἡ γὰρ παράκλησις ἡμῶν οὐκ ἐκ πλάνης—"For our exhortation was not of error." Γὰρ explains and confirms. It does not knit the verse to the mere phrase, gospel of God (Flatt), nor simply to ἐπαρρησιασάμεθα (Olshausen, De Wette, Koch), nor yet to λαλῆσαι (Lünemann), but to the whole clause. We were bold to speak the gospel to you in much conflict, for our teaching has not its source in error; and ἐστιν, not ἦν, is to be supplied on this negative side of the statement, as is evident from λαλοῦμεν in verse 4 on its positive side. He is not telling simply what he did, but what his habit was. His preaching was characterized by none of those qualities, and therefore he was not backward or cowardly in it. He was so assured of the truth of the gospel and of the integrity of his own motives, that he proclaimed it everywhere and at all hazards. Παράκλησις is in effect what the Greek fathers render it—teaching, διδαχή; but specially it is rather persuasive than didactic instruction, hortatory rather than expository preaching. It does not mean here *consolatio* (Zuingli), nor is it *docendi ratio*, but rather what Bengel calls *totum praeconium evangelicum, passionum dulcedine tinctum*. It is the earnest practical preaching of the apostle bringing every motive to bear upon his audience, plying them with every argument, and working on them by every kind of appeal, in order to win them over to the gospel and to faith in Him who delivers from the wrath to come.

Πλάνη is probably not imposture (Erasmus, Calvin, Turretin), for the following ἐν δόλῳ has that meaning; nor *seducendi studium* (Grotius), *Verführungs-lust* (Baumgarten-Crusius). Lünemann renders it *Irrwahn*, "delusion," and so De Wette and Koch. We are not in error ourselves, neither self-duped, nor the dupes of others. Πλάνη, as Lünemann remarks, is opposed to ἀλήθεια either subjectively (1 John iv, 6) or objectively (Rom. i, 25). Compare Matt. xxvii, 6; Ephes. iv, 14 (Ellicott.)

οὐδὲ ἐξ ἀκαθαρσίας "nor of uncleanness," the genitive of origin, and the word is used in its widest sense—excluding impurity of all kinds in motive, relation, and act. Whatever could be deemed impurity in a public teacher—selfishness, lust of gain, insincerity, or craft of purpose—all is expressly denied or repudiated. The apostle may allude to charges which his enemies may have been in the habit of preferring against him, as in 2 Cor. xi, 8, where he rebuts a charge of pecuniary interest; and perhaps the same inference may be gathered from the counsels given to deacons (1 Tim. iii, 8) and bishops (Titus i, 7).

οὐδὲ ἐν δόλῳ—"nor in guile," the preposition marking the sphere in which the exhortation is denied to have taken place. Οὐδὲ has high diplomatic authority (A B C D F ℵ), though οὐτὲ occurs in the Greek fathers, and is preferred by Tischendorf in his 7th edition. Compare 2 Cor. ii, 17; iv, 2; xii, 16.

"We were not self-deceived or imposed upon; our exhortation was not of error, but of truth; it was not of impurity, but of disinterested and holy motive; nor was it carried on in or by means of guile, but in simplicity and godly sincerity. Truth and truthfulness, light and purity, openness and integrity characterized us."

(Ver. 4.) Ἀλλὰ καθὼς δεδοκιμάσμεθα ὑπὸ τοῦ Θεοῦ πιστευθῆναι τὸ εὐαγγέλιον, οὕτως λαλοῦμεν—"But according as we have been approved of God to be put in trust with the gospel even so we speak."

The καθὼς and οὕτως correspond—"according as"..."even so," the speaking being quite in harmony with the divine approval and the consequent trust. Καθὼς is therefore not causal *quoniam* (Flatt), nor "seeing that" (Conybeare), nor "inasmuch" (Peile). The verb δοκιμάζειν is to test as metal by fire (1 Cor. iii, 13; Ephes. v, 10; 1 Tim. iii, 10); then to distinguish or select after testing (Philip. i, 10); and then to approve what has been so tested (Rom. xiv, 22; 1 Cor. xvi, 3). The second and third meanings insensibly blend, so that the rendering "have been thought fit" represents the general meaning (ἀξιοῦν, 2 Thess. i, 11), and it does not much differ from ἐκλέγεσθαι. Any idea of innate fitness in the men themselves must be discarded. Theophylact puts Chrysostom's notion into briefer phrase—"He would not have chosen us if he had known us to be unworthy." Nor is the idea of Œcumenius more tenable "that God foresaw their fidelity to Himself, and so chose them"—ἡμᾶς μηδὲν πρὸς δόξαν λαλεῖν ἀνθρώπων μέλλοντας (1 Tim. i, 12). Better is an explanatory clause of Theodoret—ἀντὶ τοῦ ἐπειδὴ ἔδοξεν αὐτῷ καὶ ἐδοκίμασε πιστεῦσαι ἡμῖν.

The phrase πιστευθῆναι τὸ εὐαγγέλιον is the leading thought, that for which the δοκιμασία prepares (Winer, § 44, 1). For the idiom by which the passive verb retains the accusative of the thing, see Winer, § 32, 5. Compare 1 Cor. ix, 17; Gal. ii. 7; 1 Tim. i, 11; Titus i, 3.

Our work as preachers is in unison with the divine approval and choice of us. Οὕτως λαλοῦμεν, "so we speak," our speaking has been and is still thus characterized, now at Corinth, then in Thessalonica. And the proposition is still further explained—

οὐχ ὡς ἀνθρώποις ἀρέσκοντες, ἀλλὰ Θεῷ τῷ δοκιμάζοντι τὰς καρδίας ἡμῶν—"not as pleasing men, but God which trieth our hearts."

Ὡς does not look back to οὕτως, but characterizes the action or the actors engaged in it as persons who are not pleasing men. The present participle has its widest sense. Laying ourselves out, presenting as our work and aim not to please men. See under Gal. i. 10; Stallbaum, *Protag.*, p. 56; Scheuerlein, p. 313.

Their life's labour did not lie in pleasing men: they were too faithful to their trust, too noble in purpose to be men-pleasers. They had none of that mixed motive, astute self-adaptation and versatility of address, discovered in men-pleasing. Their aim in preaching was to please God, to gain his approval by cordially and unfeignedly doing His work because it was His work and they bore His commission (2 Cor. v, 9). They wrought so as to please Him in this special aspect—

ἀλλὰ Θεῷ τῷ δοκιμάζοντι τὰς καρδίας ἡμῶν—"but God that proveth our hearts." The τῷ before Θεῷ in the Received Text has good authority; but B C D¹ ℵ omit it, and it may have been inserted, as it often occurs before a noun when so followed by an article and adjective or participle. The participle making a kind of paronomasia, has its literal meaning, and ἡμῶν is not to be generalized (Pelt and Koch), as in some general statements (Ps. vii, 10; Rom. viii, 27), but it has the same reference as the leading nominative ἡμεῖς—Paul, Silas, and Timotheus—as is also indicated by the plural καρδίας. It is in vain to appear other than we are in motive or work before Him who tests not only outer actions, but knows and tries the heart (Acts i, 24; xv, 8; Rom. viii, 27.) There is in the clause a tacit appeal to God for the truth of what is uttered, as there is a direct and formal appeal in the end of the following verse.

(Ver. 5.) Οὔτε γάρ ποτε ἐν λόγῳ κολακείας ἐγενήθημεν, καθὼς οἴδατε—"For neither at any time used we speech of flattery, as ye know," that is, in pleasing men. This is a further assertion, probably expounding what is meant by οὐδὲ ἐν δόλῳ. The verb, as already said, means to come to be, to turn out to be, and here, as followed by ἐν, "found to be in" or "to take part in" or "to have our being in" (Hofmann); or it denotes characterizing habit, *in aliqua re versari*. Jelf, § 622. Compare Herod. ii, 82, οἱ ἐν ποιήσει γενόμενοι; Plato, *Phaedo*, p. 59 a, ἐν φιλοσοφίᾳ εἶναι; 2 Cor. iii, 7, 8. See Kypke *in loc*. As Ellicott remarks, "When the Greek fathers render the phrase by the simple verb ἐκολακεύσαμεν, they do not express this full idiom, and fail to mark the entrance into and existence in the given thing or condition."

Λόγος κολακείας is speech of flattery—the genitive not being that of origin (Schott), but that of quality or contents (2 Cor. vi, 7). Heinsius, Hammond, and Pelt wrongly take λόγος in the sense of *crimen* or imputation; for the opinion of others does not come into the vindication. Nor do the two words stand for the simple ἐν κολακείᾳ, as Pelt takes them, resting on the likeness of use in λόγος to בְּ. Κολακεία occurs only here. It is described by Theophrastus, *Char*. 2, and the κόλαξ is characterized in Aristotle, *Nicom. Eth.*, iv, 12. The appeal suddenly interjected is made directly again to themselves, καθὼς οἴδατε; and their knowledge was so complete and continuous as to cover the declaration—ποτέ, at any time.

οὔτε ἐν προφάσει πλεονεξίας—" nor in a cloke of covetousness" (ἐγενήθημεν). The Vulgate and Claromontane render wrongly *in occasione avaritiae*. It is not *species* (Wolf), nor *accusatio* (Heinsius, Ewald, and Hammond), nor is it used for the simple πλεονεξία, as Koppe, Rosenmüller, Loesner, nor *Scheinwerk* (Hofmann). Πρόφασις is *pretext*—that which is put forward to mask the real feeling, motive, or act—as the act of the sailors who wished to escape from the ship under the pretext of preparing to let go an anchor (Acts xxvii, 30). See under Philip. i, 18.

Πλεονεξίας, genitive of object, is that to conceal which the πρόφασις is intended—*praetextu specioso quo tegeremus avaritiam* (Bengel), *neque usi sumus praetextibus ad velandam avaritiam* (Grotius). This is more natural than to take πλεονεξίας as containing the motive of the πρόφασις

(Beza, Schott, Olshausen). Πλεονεξία is avarice or covetousness, the desire to have more and yet more (Trench).

Θεὸς μάρτυς—"God is our witness." They knew the character of the apostle's preaching, and could bear witness to it, but God too was witness (Rom. i, 9; Philip. i, 8). The remark of the Greek fathers is just in one aspect. In what features of his work they could judge, he appeals to their own knowledge; in what lay beyond their inspection, he appeals to God. He used not speech of flattery—of that they could judge; he put forward no pretext to veil a πλεονεξία, which might be hidden from them in his heart, and he makes appeal to God.

(Ver. 6.) Οὔτε ζητοῦντες ἐξ ἀνθρώπων δόξαν, οὔτε ἀφ' ὑμῶν οὔτε ἀπ' ἄλλων—"neither seeking of men glory, neither of you, nor of others"—still a negative description of his ministerial work, repeating more fully and pointedly what he had said in verse 4, "not as pleasing men." Glory from men, the apostle did not covet; he knew it in its fickle worthlessness.

Ζητοῦντες depends still on ἐγενήθημεν. The emphasis lies on ἀνθρώπων—the sense being, not as Chrysostom explains, "not that they did not obtain glory, that were to reproach them, but that they did not seek it." Œcumenius puts it more correctly—"they sought not glory of men; but the glory that is from God they both sought and received." The difference if any between ἐκ and ἀπὸ has been explained variously. The notion of Ellicott after Koch is scarcely probable, that the two prepositions are synonymous—especially when we regard the apostle's distinctive use of them even in an accumulated form. The examples given by Winer, § 50, 2, will not bear out such an exegesis here; nor can the common distinction be adopted, as by Schott and Olshausen, that ἐκ marks the primary source and ἀπὸ the secondary or intermediate, for the clause describes a uniformity of source, with this difference, that the first general relation is separated in the next clause, into two special ones. See under Gal. i, 1; Winer, § 50, 6. But as Lünemann suggests, after Bouman, δόξα ἐξ ἀνθρώπων *universe est ἀνθρωπίνη quae humanam originem habet, ex hominibus exsistit; δόξα ἀφ' ὑμῶν quae singulatim a vobis, vestro ab ore manat ac proficiscitur.* Alford thus expresses it, "ἐκ belongs more to the abstract ground of the δόξα, ἀπὸ to the concrete object from which it was in each case to accrue." 'Ἐκ, we may say, is used with the more general, ἀπὸ with the more specialized sources. They were not seeking glory from men in any aspect, neither from you when we were with you, nor from any others among whom we happen to be labouring. Human glory is never, and in no sphere of our work, an object of ambition. And this—

δυνάμενοι ἐν βάρει εἶναι, ὡς Χριστοῦ ἀπόστολοι—"when we might have been of weight as Christ's apostles." The participle is concessive and subordinate to ζητοῦντες. It is not natural to begin a new sentence with this clause, supplying ἦμεν, as Flatt; or making the clause a protasis to ἐγενήθημεν in the following verse, as Calvin and Koppe; or connecting it, as Hofmann, with verse 8; or, with Schöttgen and Griesbach, marking it as a parenthesis.

Two very different interpretations have been given of ἐν βάρει εἶναι. The first which has been suggested by πλεονεξία is adopted by the Vulgate, *oneri esse*, and by our English version, "when we might have been burdensome to you," in the matter of our temporal support—that is, we might have demanded carnal things in return for spiritual things, but we did not, for we earned our sustenance by our manual labour. So Wycliffe, "whanne we mygten haue bène in charge." A good deal may be said on behalf of this view, which is supported by Theodoret, Estius, Beza, Grotius, Turretin, Koppe, Flatt, Ewald, Hofmann, Webster and Wilkinson, and virtually Jowett. Similar phraseology is used by the apostle of ministerial support, ἐπιβαρῆσαι in verse 9, and in 2 Thess. iii, 8; καταβαρεῖν, 2 Cor. xii, 16. Similarly too the simple verb βαρεῖσθαι occurs in 1 Tim. v, 16, in reference to the support of widows by the church, and we have ἀβαρῆ ἐμαυτὸν ἐτήρησα in 2 Cor. xi, 9. But the exegesis cannot be fully sustained. (1) For why, had such been the meaning, did not the apostle use the actual verb which he had employed in verse 9, instead of this idiomatic phrase? (2) If the clause be a disclaimer of πλεονεξία, it contains an admission that the gratification of it was possible, under the plea of ministerial support—a degradation of office which the apostle would certainly not suppose for himself and his colleagues. (3) The apostle has passed from a disclaimer of πλεονεξία to a new and different subject, the non-reception of human honour—"neither of men sought we glory, neither of you nor of others." (4) This clause of the verse must, from the participial connection δυνάμενοι, be in immediate harmony with the preceding one, and is meant to tell how in some way human honour might have been secured—that is, we do not seek honour, though we might have stood upon our dignity as Christ's apostles—the English margin having also "used authority." (5) βάρος has the sense of dignity or authority. The Claromontane Latin has *in gravitate*. In Diodorus Siculus, iv, 61, occurs the phrase διὰ τὸ βάρος τῆς πόλεως; xvi, 8, τῶν δ' Ὀλυνθίων βαρεῖαν πόλιν. . . . διὰ τὸ βάρος καὶ τὸ ἀξίωμα τῆς πόλεως; in Polybius, iv, 32, 7, πρὸς τὸ βάρος τὸ τῶν Λακεδαιμονίων; xxx, 15, 1, καὶ τὸ βάρος τῆς τῶν Ἀργείων πόλεως—Suidas *sub voce*. Compare the phrase in 2 Cor. iv, 17,—βάρος δόξης, opposed to ἐλαφρὸν τῆς θλίψεως. Such in general seems to be the meaning of the term here. The apostles did not seek glory from men, "from you or from others," though they could have been of weight—could have pressed their claims and official importance, or demanded honourable recognition as Christ's apostles. (6) The contrast of the following verses supports this view—we could have been ἐν βάρει, but were not; on the contrary, so far from being ἐν βάρει we were gentle among you; so far from our insisting on the honour due to the apostolic office, we were ἤπιοι among you. This is the view of Chrysostom, Ambrosiaster, Calvin, Hunnius, Pelt, Schott, Olshausen, De Wette, Koch, Bisping, Lünemann, Baumgarten-Crusius. Chrysostom explains, "not seeking honour nor boasting ourselves, nor requiring attendance of guards. And yet, even if we had done this, we had done nothing out of character; for if persons sent by mere earthly kings are in honour, much more might we be." Œcumenius and Theophylact give both interpretations. Piscator, Heinsius, and Hammond understand the phrases of church censures, *severitas apostolica: se quum severitatem exercere apostolicam posset lenem fuisse*. Compare 1 Cor. iv, 21. But the notion is not vindicated in any way by the context.

The last clause ὡς Χριστοῦ ἀπόστολοι does not mean as other apostles (Grotius, Pelt), but as Christ's apostles, there being stress on Χριστοῦ, genitive of possession, and ἀπόστολοι is not to be confined to Paul, for the term includes his colleagues. See under Ephes. i, 1; iv, 2; and for the plural ἀπόστολοι, Gal. i, 17.

(Ver. 7.) ἀλλ' ἐγενήθημεν ἤπιοι ἐν μέσῳ ὑμῶν—"but we were (were found to be) gentle in the midst of you." The readings ἤπιοι and νήπιοι are nearly balanced in regard to authority—the last having perhaps the higher, B C¹ D¹ F ℵ, the Latin and Coptic versions, and several of the fathers—ἤπιοι having A C² D³ K L ℵ³, and the majority of manuscripts. But the ν may have come from the last letter of the previous word. Νήπιος also is the more familiar term, and may for either reason have been inserted; but its use here destroys the figure—we were first as "children," then "as a nurse." The negative description is continued down to ἀλλά, which introduces a strong contrast to the entire preceding verse, and not merely to the previous clause (Heinsius, Turretin), and begins the positive account of their deportment. The term ἤπιος, "mild," occurs only twice in the New Testament—here and in 2 Tim. ii, 24, connected probably with ἔπω, εἰπεῖν. It occurs in classic writers with some frequency, and is applied in a variety of ways to persons and things. Thus it is opposed to τὰ μάλιστα θυμῷ χρώμενον in Pausanias, (Eliac., ii, 18, 2, p. 434, vol. II, ed. Schubart); applied to a God ἠπιώτατος θεῶν (Euripides, Bacchae, 861); to a father (Odyssey, ii, 47); to a ruler and father (Herodian, iv, 1); to Cyrus, in contrast to Cambyses (Herodotus, iii, 89), ἠπιώτατος ὁ ἐν λόγοις πραότατος καὶ ἥσυχος; we have also ἤπια φάρμακα (Iliad, iv, 218). Etymologicum Mag., sub voce; Tittmann, Synon., p. 140, &c. So far from seeking human glory, so far from insisting on official standing and prerogative, and exacting recognition and service, we were "gentle in the midst of you"; "we were each of us as one of yourselves;" and so Œcumenius adds, οὐκ τὴν ἀνωτέρω λαβόντες τάξιν. Our deportment was mild, quiet, unassuming, and affectionate.

ὡς ἐὰν τροφὸς θάλπῃ τὰ ἑαυτῆς τέκνα—"as a nurse cherishes her own children." The fuller ἐάν has the authority of B C D

F א³. 'Ως is a particle of comparison, *tanquam si;* and the verb, akin to θάλλω, θῆλυς, denotes fostering warmth as applied to a bird (Deut. xxii, 6; Job xxxix, 14; Ephes. v, 29.; Josephus, viii, 14, 3). Τροφὸς, occurring only here in the New Testament, is a suckling mother or nurse, and is used in a figure, as here, often by Philo—of which several examples are given in Loesner's *Observat.*, p. 337; Gen. xxxv, 8. The nursing mother warms and fosters her own offspring, ἑαυτῆς— the offspring which she recognizes as her own, and loves and cherishes with all that maternal fondness and tenderness which has passed into a proverb (Is. xlix, 15.) The particle ἐάν with the present subjunctive betokens something which may have already taken place, or usually should have taken place, or something still continued (Winer, § 42, 3, *b*, β. See Peile's note).

(Ver. 8.) Οὕτως ὁμειρόμενοι ὑμῶν, εὐδοκοῦμεν—"so yearning after you, we were willing to impart to you." The οὕτως corresponds to the clause beginning with ὡς, which is at once illustratively connected with what goes before, and also stands as protasis to this verse—"we were gentle among you as a nurse—so .... we." The participle is read in the common text ἱμειρόμενοι, but our text is supported by A B C D F K L א, 30 cursives, and several of the fathers, and though the word is not found in the usual lexicons, it occurs in old glossaries, in Job iii, 21 (Codd. A B), in Ps. lxii, 1 (Symmachus), but the MSS. vary as to the spelling. Hesychius explains it ὁμείρονται, ἐπιθυμοῦσιν. Photius in his lexicon gives it as compounded of ὁμοῦ ἡρμόσθαι (p. 331, ed. Porson). Theophylact supposes it to be ὁμοῦ εἴρειν. It is, however, against this conjecture that the verb governs the genitive. Μείρεσθαι occurs in Nicander, *Ther.*, 402. If this be the original form the prefix is added for euphony or strength, as δύρεσθαι and ὀδύρεσθαι; or if it be, according to Rost and Palm, for the sake of the metre, then ὁμείρομαι is a different form found in the later stage of the language (Winer, § 16). Fritzsche supposes that the ι and the ο were used as suited the writer's taste. Εὐδοκοῦμεν is not present (Grotius, Pelt), but is in the imperfect—*cupide volebamus* (Vulgate)—the imperfect, like the aorist in the New Testament, without the augment, though some codices have it (Winer, § 12, 3). The verb has in it the idea of willing purpose, not bare resolve, but generous desire, spontaneous and hearty impulse. See under Ephes. i, 5.

μεταδοῦναι ὑμῖν οὐ μόνον τὸ εὐαγγέλιον τοῦ Θεοῦ ἀλλὰ καὶ τὰς ἑαυτῶν ψυχὰς—"to impart not only the gospel of God but also our own souls." There is a species of zeugma in the clause, as μεταδοῦναι does not strictly agree with the last words (Kühner, § 853). This verb, like verbs of participation, is often followed by a genitive and with the dative of person, but here by an accusative and dative, as the last clause does not admit of a partitive notion—we were willing not only to share the gospel with you, but to give you our own souls or lives—ἑαυτῶν with the first person (Winer, § 22, 5). They proved this by their cheerful and undaunted endurance of danger and toil: they carried their lives in their hands and would have given them up, when they so lovingly persisted in preaching the gospel to them.

διότι ἀγαπητοὶ ἡμῖν ἐγενήθητε—"because ye became dear to us," "because ye grew to be dearly beloved to us," the verb retaining its usual meaning, as in i, 5. The reading γεγένησθε has little authority. They had listened to and accepted the good tidings immediately and intelligently and decidedly, and became followers of us and of the Lord, were not swayed off by persecution, but so steadfastly adhered to their profession, that they were everywhere spoken of. Becoming so dear to Paul and his colleagues, these devoted men cherished them like a nurse fostering her own children, did not lord it over them, but were gentle, affectionate, and self-imparting; and not only with enthusiastic fondness had they preached to them the blessed gospel, but they would have willingly died a martyr's death for them, had such a proof of heroic attachment been necessary. Bengel's notion is foreign to the meaning, *anima nostra cupiebat quasi immeare in animam vestram.*

(Ver. 9.) μνημονεύετε γάρ, ἀδελφοί, τὸν κόπον ἡμῶν καὶ τὸν μόχθον—"for ye remember, brethren, our toil and travail." The apostle appeals again to themselves—to their recollection of his ardent and self-sacrificing labours. The connection indicated by γὰρ has been looked at in various ways. Lünemann and Alford connect the clause directly with the previous one, "because ye became so dear to us," but this connection is limited to a mere angle of the thought. Nor is it better to select an earlier clause, δυνάμενοι ἐν βάρει εἶναι, or ἐγενήθημεν ἤπιοι, for in either the reason alleged would be irrelevant. The chief thought of the previous verse is—" we were willing to impart to you our own souls," urged by the subordinate thought, "for ye grew to be dear to us," and the present verse brings proof of it—a proof, that is, of actual hard labour, willingly undergone, and accompanied at the same time with peril. They gave up their lives to daily and nightly drudgery, which wholly absorbed all their physical powers, and they would have given their lives in the highest sense, if there had been a necessity for the sacrifice. The verb μνημονεύετε followed by a genitive in i, 3, is here followed by an accusative, the meaning, perhaps, being—ye bear in mind, or ye keep in remembrance (Matt. xvi, 9; Rev. xviii, 5). Κόπος and μόχθος, used together in 2 Thess. iii, 8, and in 2 Cor. xi, 27, do not essentially differ in sense. Grotius, however, distinguishes them thus— κόπον *in ferendo*, μόχθον *in agendo*. Ellicott says that the first word marks the toil on the side of the suffering it involves, and the latter on the side of the magnitude of the obstacles it has to overcome. Beza affirms that "the second term means something more severe than the first." But it is better, perhaps, to say that the repetition is meant to intensify the meaning, for μόχθος occurs in the New Testament only in connection with κόπος—the phrase being a terse and familiar idiom. Comp. Sept., Num. xxxiii, 11; Wisdom x, 10. It will therefore denote toil even to weariness, labour even to utter exhaustion, comprising alike the work which he did as our apostle and the fatigue endured by the effort to support himself by manual industry. It is wrong, however, in Balduin to make a distinction between the terms by understanding the first *de spirituali labore*, and the second *de manuario labore scenopegiae*. The apostle adds—

νυκτὸς καὶ ἡμέρας ἐργαζόμενοι, πρὸς τὸ μὴ ἐπιβαρῆσαί τινα ὑμῶν, ἐκηρύξαμεν εἰς ὑμᾶς τὸ εὐαγγέλιον τοῦ Θεοῦ—" night and day working, in order not to burden any one of you, we preached unto you the gospel of God."

Γάρ in the common text, after νυκτός, is rightly rejected as a correction. The genitives are emphatically placed, and the apostle always places νυκτός first (Acts xx, 31; 1 Thess. iii, 10;

2 Tim. i, 3; 1 Tim. v, 5). Night may stand first, as the Jews reckoned from sunset to sunset—the evening preceding the morning, as we speak yet of a fortnight; or the order may depend on some suggestion of the apostle's own mind, the most striking part of the expression being put first, the period of common rest becoming to him one of heavy toil. The order is reversed in Luke xviii, 7; Acts ix, 24; and five times in the Apocalypse, for Hebrew יוֹם לַיְלָה (Jer. viii, 23; xvi, 13; xxxiii, 25). It may be remarked that Luke places νύκτα first when he uses the accusative, but ἡμέρας first when he uses the genitive. The temporal genitive is explained by Donaldson (§ 451) as "out of," "within the limit of;" and examples of this and of other formulæ, with varying order, may be seen in Lobeck's *Paralip.*, p. 62. The participle ἐργαζόμενοι here refers to manual labour (Acts xviii, 3; 1 Cor. ix, 6; 2 Thess. iii, 10; Xenoph., *Mem.*, i, 2, 57). In 1 Cor. iv, 12, ταῖς ἰδίαις χερσίν is added. Compare Ephes. iv, 28. This continuous physical toil was carried on πρός—with this end in view (Winer, § 44, 6). The verb ἐπιβαρεῖν is used only tropically in the New Testament (2 Cor. ii, 5; 2 Thess. iii, 8). See Appian, *B. C.*, 4, 15. That we might not overburden any of you, by claiming temporal support from you, we supported ourselves by unremitting labour. Εἰς ὑμᾶς is neither among you nor *in vobis* (Vulgate), but unto you. Εἰς implies the direction of the preaching (Mark xiii, 10; Luke xxiv, 47; 1 Peter i, 25), the ἐργαζόμενοι being parallel in time to the ἐκηρύξαμεν—all the while they were preaching they were winning wages by daily and nightly toil. It is beyond proof in Balduin, Pelagius, and Aretius to make νυκτός the period of working, and ἡμέρας that of preaching. For we have no means of making such a distinction, as probably teaching and working might alternate at shorter intervals, as opportunity offered or necessity required. No anxious inquirers would be put off during the day because the apostle was at work, and the work laid aside for such a purpose would be resumed during the watches of the night; or disciples like Nicodemus might visit him during the night, and the toil so interrupted would be taken up during the day. Why the apostle gave up his claim for pastoral maintenance, and lived and wrought in this independent spirit in Thessalonica, we do

not know; but the probability is, that he was anxious that he might not be misinterpreted or the purity of his motives challenged, and that he might not be likened to a selfish and grasping sophist to whom hire was everything, and therefore he would take nothing in compensation, but toiled to support himself, that the gospel without hindrance, and in an unselfish and disinterested form, might win its way among the Gentiles. Chrysostom supposes that the Thessalonians were poor, and that the apostle compassionated their poverty. We read, however, of "honourable women not a few" among the converts, and the abstinence of the apostle from support is to be ascribed to a higher motive (Jowett; Philip. iv, 15).

The apostle abruptly, and without any connecting particle, now solemnly summarizes what he had previously said in detached clauses about the behaviour of himself and his colleagues at Thessalonica.

(Ver. 10.) Ὑμεῖς μάρτυρες καὶ ὁ Θεός—"Ye are witnesses and God is witness." Much they could judge of, and on such points he appeals to them; much they could not judge of, and on such points lying beyond their cognizance he appeals to God. He submits himself unconditionally to their judgment and to that of God, and has no doubts of the decision which would be given by them and ratified by Him who trieth the heart.

ὡς ὁσίως καὶ δικαίως καὶ ἀμέμπτως ὑμῖν τοῖς πιστεύουσιν ἐγενήθημεν—"how holily, and righteously, and unblameably we behaved ourselves in the judgment of you who believe." The apostle does not employ adjectives, for he is not bringing out the elements of his own personal character, but is describing his deportment or dealing toward believers (Luke i, 75; Ephes. iv, 24; Titus i, 8; Josephus, *Antiq.*, vi, 5, 5).

The accumulation of epithets intensifies the meaning. The three words are not to be taken as adjectives (Schott), but they are a species of secondary predicates (Donaldson, § 436; Winer, § 54, 2). The epithets are to be distinguished at the same time, though not perhaps with decided discrimination of meaning. The first two adverbs assert with a positive aspect, and the third puts forward a negative statement. The first epithet, ὁσίως, is defined in Plato, περὶ δὲ θεοὺς ὅσια (*Gorg.*, 57, A. B.), and so in Polybius, τὰ πρὸς τοὺς ἀνθρώπους δίκαια

Ver. 10.] FIRST EPISTLE TO THE THESSALONIANS 71

καὶ τὰ πρὸς θεοὺς ὅσια (*Hist.*, xxiii, 10 ; Rost and Palm *sub voce*). It stands thirty times in the Septuagint for the Hebrew חָסִיד, and ἅγιος stands a hundred times for קָדוֹשׁ, and the two are never exchanged. Perhaps this meaning may not be thoroughly sustained in the New Testament; yet compare 1 Tim. ii, 8; Heb. vii, 26, where purity in its divine aspects is referred to. The second term, δικαίως, "righteously," means in all conscientiousness and integrity, with special reference to man. The apostle has called God as well as themselves to witness, and the ordinary classic reference of ὁσίως may therefore be admitted (Tittmann's *Synon.*, p. 25), while δικαίως has a deeper range of meaning than the classical quotations intimate, and does not merely characterize elements of human relationship (Trench). Holiness in the New Testament is not restricted to divine relation, but enters into the second table of the law; and righteousness, though occupied with the duties of the second table, has its root and life in piety. The third epithet, ἀμέμπτως, is "blamelessly"—if holily and righteously, then blamelessly. It is too restricted in Olshausen to make this adverb the negative iteration of the positive δικαίως, and too vague in Flacius to refer it to other graces, as *castitas, sobrietas*. It is a rhetorical weakness in Turretin and Bengel to restrict this third epithet to the apostle and his colleagues—the first having allusion to God, the second to the people, and the third to themselves. Ὑμῖν is not specially connected with ἀμέμπτως, as Œcumenius—τοῖς γὰρ ἀπίστοις οὐκ ἄμεμπτος—nor is it probably the dative of interest (Ellicott), nor is the sense "toward you" (De Wette). Œcumenius and Theophylact make it the dative of opinion (Bernhardy, p. 337); and so Koch, Lünemann and Alford: Hofmann finds a contrast in the participle to the time when they first believed; the Vulgate has *qui credidistis*.

The apostle's appeal was to the believing Thessalonians, to them, and to God; and it was on account of their being believers in God that he so confidently summoned them to witness on his behalf. The τοῖς πιστεύουσιν is not pointless, as Jowett supposes; it forms, in fact, the very point of the appeal. Whatever impressions unbelievers formed of us, you who believe concur in our description of our holy, righteous, and blameless conduct. When they wrought at a secular occupation, fellow-workmen might form varying estimates of their character; but those who had profited through their preaching were better qualified to understand and judge them, and that because they believed. "How could we act otherwise to believers?" οὐ γὰρ ἄμεμπτοι πᾶσιν ὤφθημεν. Still closer and more individualizing appeal—

(Ver. 11.) καθάπερ οἴδατε, "even as ye know." Καθώς is the term commonly employed; καθά occurs only once (Matt. xxvii, 10); in the word before us it is strengthened by περ, and is perhaps employed because καθώς immediately follows.

They had conducted themselves holily, righteously, and unblameably, and all this in accordance with the universal and the individual experience of the Thessalonian believers :—

ὡς ἕνα ἕκαστον ὑμῶν, ὡς πατὴρ τέκνα ἑαυτοῦ, παρακαλοῦντες ὑμᾶς καὶ παραμυθούμενοι—" how every one of you, as a father his own children, we were exhorting you and encouraging you." There are two accusatives—first, ἕνα ἕκαστον, and then ὑμᾶς—both governed by the participles; "every one of you" placed emphatically, "each one of you," individualized, and "you" collectively or in the mass, not a mere pleonasm. Εἷς ἕκαστος is found in Plato, *Soph.*, 223 D; *Protag.*, 332 C; Luke iv, 40; xvi, 5; Acts ii, 3, 6; 1 Cor. xii, 18; Ephes. v, 7, corresponding to the Latin *unus quisque, ita ut nemo excludatur* (Pelt). The two participles may either be a broken construction—modal clauses—with a finite verb omitted; "ye know how we did so —exhorting you" D(e Wette, Ellicott). This is a common form of idiomatic construction with the apostle. The simpler way, however, is to supply ἐγενήθημεν, which has been already employed (Lünemann, Alford, Hofmann). Other resolutions of the difficulty have been proposed. Beza, Grotius, and Flatt propose ἦμεν, which is not in the context. Schrader, Ewald, and Riggenbach make καθάπερ οἴδατε a parenthesis, and connect the participles with ἐγενήθημεν in ver. 10, an awkward connection. Others, perplexed with the double accusative ἕνα ἕκαστον, ὑμᾶς, propose to connect ὑμᾶς alone with the participles, and supply a finite verb to ἕνα ἕκαστον. Thus, Vatablus, Er. Schmid, Ostermann propose ἠγαπήσαμεν. Whitby and others propose that, or ἐθάλψαμεν from ver. 7. Pelt introduces οὐκ ἀφήκαμεν; and Schott prefers a verb in which is *notio curandi sive tractandi sive educandi*.

The three participles are closely connected in sense and in relation with the following εἰς—

παρακαλοῦντες ὑμᾶς καὶ παραμυθούμενοι καὶ μαρτυρόμενοι— "exhorting you and encouraging and adjuring you." The Received Text has μαρτυρούμενοι, with D¹F, and most manuscripts, but the other reading has in its favour B D³ K L ℵ. A omits καὶ μαρτυρόμενοι altogether. The first is the more general, appealing to you by every argument and motive; the second is suggested by the peril and persecutions around them, on account of which they needed to be animated and consoled (v, 14; John xi, 19, 31; Philip. ii, 1; Plato, *Leg.*, ii, 666; the Syriac has ܡܠܟ ܗܘ ܕܩܪܐܟܘܢ); and the third is of special strength, laying charge on them as if in presence of witnesses, solemnly adjuring them to walk worthy of God (Gal. v, 3; Ephes. iv, 17; Polybius xiii, 8, 6; Thucydides, vi, 30; viii, 53; Raphel. *in loc.*) As the three participles are connected with εἰς τὸ περιπατεῖν as the purpose, it is wrong to give any of them a special supplement, such as Chrysostom and Theophylact give to the first, πρὸς τὸ φέρειν πάντα, or such as Œcumenius and De Wette give to the second, to meet trials bravely, πειρασμοῖς (1 Cor. xiv, 3). This work of the apostle was directed to every one of them, to each individual by himself and for himself, and also to the mass of believers; so that Chrysostom exclaims, βαβαὶ ἐν τοσούτῳ πλήθει μηδένα παραλιπεῖν, μὴ μικρὸν μὴ μέγαν, μὴ πλούσιον μὴ πένητα.

And the whole of this comprehensive and yet individualizing pastoral work has as its model a father toward his children. It was earnest and faithful, the yearning importunity of a father's heart, and the fresh, familiar loving counsels breathed from a father's lips. Compare verse 7; Ὥς τε πατὴρ ᾧ παιδί *Odyss.*, i, 308.

(Ver. 12.) καὶ μαρτυρόμενοι εἰς τὸ περιπατεῖν ὑμᾶς ἀξίως τοῦ Θεοῦ τοῦ καλοῦντος ὑμᾶς εἰς τὴν ἑαυτοῦ βασιλείαν καὶ δόξαν —"and testifying that ye should walk worthily of God, who is calling you into His own kingdom and glory." The present περιπατεῖν has preponderant authority over the common reading of the aorist περιπατῆσαι, and the καλέσαντος of the

Received Text has only in its favour A ℵ and eight manuscripts, the Vulgate (*qui vocavit*), and some of the fathers.

Εἰς τὸ with the infinitive denotes the purpose of all their exhorting, encouraging, and attesting (Winer, § 44, 6), and does not indicate merely direction or subject (Lünemann, Bisping; 1 Cor. ix, 12; 2 Cor. iv, 4).

The adverb ἀξίως is similarly used with the genitive (Rom. xvi, 2; Ephes. iv, 1; Philip. i, 27; Col. i, 10; 3 John 6; Demosth., *Olynth.*, i, 5, 2; Thucyd., iii, 39, 5). For the divine κλῆσις, see under Gal. i, 6. The present participle indicates the call as ever present, while it is reaching to the future. The call is ever ascribed to God, whatever be the instrumentality; εἰς points to that into which they are being called (Matt. xviii, 9; xix, 17; John iii, 5), "His own kingdom and glory," the article τὴν being common to both nouns, though omitted before the second one, on account of the pronoun ἑαυτοῦ (Winer, § 19, 4). The Syriac reads ܠܡܠܟܘܬܗ ܘܠܫܘܒܚܗ. His kingdom and glory is not His glorious kingdom, βασιλεία ἔνδοξος (Koppe, Olshausen). Βασιλεία τοῦ Θεοῦ is the kingdom which God sets up in His grace and which is founded in the merit and mediation of His Son, into which believers enter now by a second birth, and which reaches its full and final development at the Second Advent. His glory is His own perfection and happiness which He confers upon His people, His own image reimpressed on the hearts of those who have been made meet for beholding Him and enjoying fellowship with Him (Rom. v, 2; viii, 13; 2 Cor. iii, 7. See under Ephes. v, 5; Col. i, 13). Βασιλεία τοῦ Θεοῦ is not the kingdom in its earthly aspect, glory being its heavenly form (Baumgarten-Crusius). To walk worthily of God, who is calling us to His kingdom and glory, is to have one's whole course of life preserved in harmony with God's gracious work upon the soul, and with the high and hallowed destiny with which that work is lovingly connected, and into which it is ever ripening. And such being the propriety and necessity of this "worthy" walk, the apostle and his fellow-labourers laid themselves out in exhorting, encouraging, and conjuring the Thessalonian believers—all of them as a body, each of them by himself—to maintain it (1 Peter v, 10).

(Ver. 13.) Καὶ διὰ τοῦτο—" and on this account " the καὶ is omitted in D F K L and in the Latin fathers; but is found in A B, in the Syriac and Coptic Versions, and it is inserted by Tischendorf and Lachmann. The authority for καὶ is thus good, but it may have been added for the sake of connection.

καὶ ἡμεῖς εὐχαριστοῦμεν τῷ Θεῷ ἀδιαλείπτως—" and for this cause we also thank God without ceasing." See under i, 2, 3. The reference in διὰ τοῦτο has been debated. (1) Jowett refers it to the verses both before and after—an admitted tautology. (2) Pelt and Bloomfield connect it thus, *quoniam tam felici successu apud vos evangelium praedicavimus*—another form of tautology: we preached with great success, and we thank God because ye received our preaching. (3) Schott and De Wette join the clause to εἰς τὸ περιπατεῖν, and as connected with the result; the former putting it thus, *quum haec opera in animis vestris ad vitam divina invitatione dignam impellendis minime frustra fuerit collocata. . . . ego vicissim cum sociis Deo gratias ago assiduas.* But this connection also is not free from tautology, even though Schott places καὶ ἡμεῖς in direct contrast to ὑμᾶς of the previous verse; and then εἰς τὸ περιπατεῖν is the purpose, not result of the exhortation for which thanks might be rendered. The latter connects the word with the purpose, that purpose being one of high moment; but of that momentousness, as Lünemann remarks, the context says nothing. (4) Another view is adopted by Auberlen, Balduin, Zanchius, Olshausen, Bisping, and Alford. They join διὰ τοῦτο to the immediately preceding clause—who hath called you to His kingdom and glory; as God is thus calling you, we thank God that ye understood and followed the divine call. But not only, as Ellicott objects, is διὰ τοῦτο thus joined to a mere appended clause, an objection by no means insuperable, but the chief statements of the previous verse are in this way overlooked. These statements as to the apostle's zeal and assiduity occupy a special prominence, so much so that appeal is made both to God and to themselves for the truth of them. (5) Ellicott and others connect διὰ τοῦτο with the previous verses, the reference being to the zeal and earnestness with which the apostle and his colleagues laboured, and the thanksgiving being that in a similar spirit they had received the gospel so proclaimed to them.

The apostle says καὶ ἡμεῖς. Some, as Koch and De Wette, join the καὶ to the previous διὰ τοῦτο—" for this cause also," as in the Authorized Version. But such a connection is uncommon, though Lünemann's objection to it, that such a sense would require διὰ καὶ τοῦτο, cannot be borne out—the insertion of καὶ between the preposition and the noun being very uncommon (Hartung, vol. I, 143). But if the καὶ naturally belongs to ἡμεῖς, who are the persons referred to by it? Some, as Lünemann, give this sense, we also, *i.e.*, we and all true Christians, which is too vague; while Alford brings in, all who believe in Macedonia and Achaia, " we and they give thanks "; but the reference is both too special and too remote, Auberlen carrying the reference back to verse 1, and Ewald apparently to the commencement of the epistle. So that we regard the ἡμεῖς as simply in contrast to the ὑμᾶς of the previous verses—we too, as well as you, thank God for these spiritual blessings, we too thank him; *non solum vos propter hanc vocationem debetis agere gratias, sed etiam nos* (Zanchius, Balduin, Ellicott), καὶ insinuating a slight contrast in the connection. See under Philip. i, 3; Col. i, 12.

ὅτι παραλαβόντες λόγον ἀκοῆς παρ' ἡμῶν τοῦ Θεοῦ, ἐδέξασθε οὐ λόγον ἀνθρώπων—"that having received from us the word of preaching—itself of God—ye accepted not the word of men." Ὅτι introduces the contents and reason of the thanksgiving. The participle παραλαβόντες is temporal, describing the act which was necessarily connected with ἐδέξασθε, and prior to it, or all but coincident in time with it. The two verbs are not synonymous (Baumgarten-Crusius), as the Vulgate in its repetition of *accipere* would imply, or as the English Version, which renders both words by the same term, "receive." The verbs have been thus distinguished—the first as being more objective in its nature, and the second more subjective; the first describing the reception of the truth as external matter of fact, and the second the inner acceptance of it as matter of faith. Bengel distinguishes thus, παραλαμβάνω *dicit simplicem acceptionem*, δέχομαι *connotat prolubium in accipiendo*. See under Gal. i, 9, 12. Compare Luke viii, 13; Acts viii, 14; xi, 1;

xvii, 11; 1 Cor. ii, 14; xi, 23: xiii, 1; 2 Cor. viii, 17; Col. ii, 6; Raphelius *in loc.*; Thucyd., i, 95. In the first act described they received it as a divine message orally conveyed to them.

λόγον ἀκοῆς παρ' ἡμῶν. Λόγος is the doctrine or the gospel, and ἀκοῆς is used in the passive sense which it has so often in the New Testament (John xii, 38; Rom. x, 16; Heb. iv, 2. See under Gal. iii, 2).

'Ακοῆς may virtually be the genitive of apposition (Ellicott), or it may be the characterizing genitive, the word distinguished as being heard, not read, nor the result of mental discovery. It was preached, and they on listening received it.

The notion of Theophylact adopted by Pelt is overstrained: the word of hearing is κήρυγμα ὡς διὰ τοῦ ἀκουσθῆναι πιστευόμενον—*verbum quod audiendo creditur.*

'Ακοή may mean actively, the hearing; or passively, that which is heard. 'Ακοή πίστεως may mean the hearing or reception of that doctrine of which faith is a distinctive principle; or, in a passive sense, that which is heard of faith, that report or message which holds out faith as its prominent and characteristic element. This passive sense is perhaps uniform in the Septuagint.

The connection of παρ' ἡμῶν has been variously taken, as the phrase may be joined either immediately to ἀκοῆς (Schott, Olshausen, Lünemann, Hofmann, Bisping, Pelt), or to the participle παραλαβόντες (Turretin, De Wette, Koch, Baumgarten-Crusius, Auberlen, Ellicott). The first construction is admissible, as in John i, 41, and as (Lünemann) substantives and adjectives retain the force of the verbs from which they are derived. It is no objection to the second connection that παρ' ἡμῶν is separated by some words—the accusative of object—from the participle; for it is a form of syntax by no means uncommon, and such a sense would not necessitate the order παραλαβόντες παρ' ἡμῶν λόγον. Such is the connection indicated by the Vulgate *accepistis a nobis*, and so the Syriac ܡܢܢ ܩܒܠܬܘܢ.

Nor in this case is ἀκοῆς superfluous, as is alleged by Lünemann; for not only does it characterize the mode of conveyance as an oral communication, παρὰ denoting the more immediate source, but it forms a contrast to the following τοῦ

Θεοῦ—from us the word of hearing, but that word in its ultimate origin from God—we preaching it, you hearing it, but God the giver of it. Compare iv, 1; Gal. i, 12; 2 Thess. iii, 6.

This λόγος ἀκοῆς is at the same time τοῦ Θεοῦ, "of God," the genitive of origin, as the contrast in the following ἀνθρώπων plainly indicates. It is not the genitive of possession, nor of object (Vatablus, Hunnius, Balduin, Grotius). Gal. ii, 9; 2 Peter iii, 1; Heb. vi, 1. The τοῦ Θεοῦ, appended abnormally and on purpose, qualifies the preceding clause, λόγον ἀκοῆς παρ' ἡμῶν, its human source near and immediate to them, as contrasted with its true divine origin. Chandler needlessly supplies περὶ before τοῦ Θεοῦ.

ἐδέξασθε οὐ λόγον ἀνθρώπων, ἀλλ' (καθώς ἐστιν ἀληθῶς) λόγον Θεοῦ—"ye accepted not the word of men, but, as it is in truth, the word of God." The difference between this verb and the previous participle has been already referred to, it being the inner reception by faith which is now being described. The genitive ἀνθρώπων is again that of origin. The English version inserts a supplemental "as," and Pelt says *ante λόγον vero quasi ὡς supplendum esse, res ipsa docet*. But the *res ipsa* teaches the opposite. Were the apostle's thankfulness based not only on the fact that the Thessalonians had accepted the message, not from man but from God, but also on their estimate or appreciation of this difference, and their consequent mode of acceptance, then "as" might be more naturally interpolated. But it is superfluous, for the apostle simply states the fact of their acceptance, saying nothing about its manner (Kühner, § 560). The parenthetical clause also states the apostle's opinion—they accepted not the words of men, but the word of God, which it really is, ἀληθῶς (Matt. xiv, 33; John i, 48). As a message spoken to them and heard by them, it was a word from men; but when they accepted it, they accepted it in its divine character, the word of God. Men were but the instruments, God was the primary author and origin. To accept a human word is ordinary credence; to accept a divine word is saving faith, accompanied in them that believe with joy in the Holy Ghost. The first part of the process, the hearing and comprehension of the message, may exist without the second; but the second, the belief, ever implies the first (Rom. xi, 14).

ὃς καὶ ἐνεργεῖται ἐν ὑμῖν τοῖς πιστεύουσιν—" which worketh also in you who believe." The Vulgate (by its *verbum Dei qui*), a-Lapide, Bengel, Koppe, Auberlen, take Θεοῦ as the antecedent. Peile apparently understands by λόγος the Son of God (John i, 1). Whitby, with the same antecedent, thinks the reference is to the primitive gifts or χαρίσματα, called ἐνεργήματα (1 Cor. xii, 6, 10), a far-fetched and groundless explanation. But the reference to λόγος is decidedly to be preferred. (1) For the "word" is the special theme, and their acceptance of it the special ground of the apostle's continuous thanksgiving. (2) Θεός is never used in the New Testament with ἐνεργεῖσθαι, but uniformly with the active (1 Cor. xii, 6; Gal. ii, 3; iii, 5; Ephes. i, 2; Philip. ii, 13). (3) Καί points to the same conclusion—the word of God which also, in accordance with, or because of, its divine origin, worketh in you. So the Claromontane Latin (*quod operatur*), and the Syriac (ܗܘ), Theophylact, Œcumenius, and very many expositors.

Ἐνεργεῖται is not to be taken as passive (Estius, Hammond, Schott, Bloomfield), but as a kind of dynamic middle, evolving energy out of itself (Krüger, § 52, 8), and is usually spoken of things (Winer, § 38, 6). The ascensive καί does not belong to the relative (De Wette, Koch), but to the verb (Klotz, *Devarius*, vol. II, p. 606). That working is experienced—

ἐν ὑμῖν πιστεύουσιν—"in you who believe." The Latin versions erroneously have the past tense, *qui credidistis*. The meaning is not temporal, *ex quo tempore religionem suscepistis* (Koppe), for that would require the past tense; nor is it causal, *quum susceperitis* (Pelt); nor is it *propterea quod fidem habetis*, for, as Ellicott remarks, that would necessitate the omission of the article (Donaldson, § 492). Faith was the present characteristic of those to whom the apostle wrote, and only in them did this working manifest itself, and not in those who heard merely, or gave but an outer credence to the word in its human medium and aspect. The word shows its power through the believing acceptance of it as an enlightening, elevating, guiding, sanctifying, comforting, and formative principle (2 Tim. iii, 15).

(Ver. 14.) Ὑμεῖς γὰρ μιμηταὶ ἐγενήθητε, ἀδελφοί, τῶν ἐκκλησιῶν τοῦ Θεοῦ τῶν οὐσῶν ἐν τῇ Ἰουδαίᾳ ἐν Χριστῷ Ἰησοῦ

—" For ye became followers, brethren, of the churches of God which are in Judaea, in Christ Jesus."

Γὰρ gives a proof and illustration of the preceding clause, "which worketh in you that believe," ὑμεῖς corresponding to the previous ὑμῖν. The divine word made its power to be felt in their believing hearts; for through it they imitated the Judaean churches in patience and constancy under persecution. Other references are remote and pointless. Olshausen supposes the allusion to be to their faith, *i.e.*, ye are believers because ye imitated the churches in Judaea; but their faith is viewed not in itself but in connection with the ἐνέργεια of the divine word. Flatt, again, groundlessly refers the γὰρ to ἐδέξασθε— that ye received it willingly, is proved by your adherence to it in spite of suffering. So Œcumenius. But the proof of the ἐνέργεια lay in this, that they had become followers—imitators —not in intention, but in fact. As the Judaean churches felt and acted, so they felt and acted. See under i, 6.

The pointed meaning of the noun is diluted, however, in Pelt's explanation, μιμηταὶ *hic non tam ii sunt, qui sponte imitantur, quam potius quibus simile quid contingit*. The phrase τῶν οὐσῶν describes the churches as existing at that moment in Judaea. See under Gal. i, 22; and under 1 Thess. i, 1. They were in Judaea as their locality, the sphere of their outer existence, but they were in Christ Jesus as their sphere of inner life and spiritual blessing; in Him, in union with Him, and in fellowship with Him, the source of their vitality and strength. See under Gal. i, 22. The churches in Judaea which had been so oppressed and persecuted had set an example of patience and faith which the Thessalonian Church had followed, as they received the word "in much affliction, with joy of the Holy Ghost." The apostle proceeds to explain the similarity of position—

ὅτι τὰ αὐτὰ ἐπάθετε καὶ ὑμεῖς ὑπὸ τῶν ἰδίων συμφυλετῶν, καθὼς καὶ αὐτοὶ ὑπὸ τῶν Ἰουδαίων—" for ye also suffered the same things of your own countrymen, even as they also did from the Jews."

Ταυτά is a form of reading which is without authority, and some few codices of no great value have ἀπό for ὑπό in both clauses where it occurs: ὑπό being found after neuter verbs used as passives and indicating the efficient cause. Compare παθεῖν ἀπό (Matt. xvi. 21). Winer, § 47; Ellendt, *Lex. Soph.*, *sub voce*, II, p. 880. The phrase τὰ αὐτά is emphatic in position, "the same things" in suffering warranting the use of μιμηταί.

Συμφυλέτης (*contribulis*, Vulgate) is defined by Hesychius as ὁμοεθνής. Herodian remarks that the word φυλέτης, like some others, was used ἄνευ τῆς σύν, since they indicated a continuous relation, while other terms, like συμπότης, are used with it, as indicating a temporary connection. See the note in Phrynichus, ed. Lobeck, 471. The compound word is found only here in the New Testament, though it occurs in Isocrates (263 A), where, however, some codices read the simple noun (p. 540, vol. III, *Orat. Attici*, ed. Dobson). It belongs to the decaying stage of the language, which was marked by a frequent use of compounds, as Thiersch says, *id commune linguarum a prisco vigore degenerantium, ut verba cum praepositionibus composita invalescant loco verborum simplicium* (*De Pent.*, p. 83). Their own fellow-countrymen are plainly not Jews (a-Lapide, Hammond), nor Jews and Gentiles (Calvin, Piscator, Bengel), but heathens, for they are here placed in direct contrast to the Jews; and as the Thessalonian Church was made up chiefly of heathen (i, 9), and as the emphatic term ἰδίων implies, "their own fellow-countrymen" must refer to them (Matt. ix, 1; John i, 11). The statement is verified in Acts xvii, 5-9.

καθὼς καὶ αὐτοὶ ὑπὸ τῶν Ἰουδαίων—"even as they also from the Jews." The phrase καθὼς καὶ αὐτοί forms an imperfect apodosis; τὰ αὐτὰ ἅ or ἅπερ, as Alford remarks, would have been grammatically more exact. Compare Philip. i, 30. But the inaccuracy is not uncommon, a comparative adverbial sentence standing for an adjectival one: τὸν αὐτὸν τρόπον, ὥσπερ...οὕτω καί (Demosth., *Phil.*, p. 34, vol. I, ed. Schaefer); εἰς τὸ αὐτὸ σχῆμα, ὥσπερ (Xenoph., *Anab.*, i, 10, 10; Plato, *Phaedo*, p. 86 A; Kühner, § 830, 2; Lobeck ad Phrynich., p. 426). In καὶ αὐτοί there is a reciprocal reference to the previous καὶ ὑμεῖς (Ephes. v, 23), the double καί giving it prominence. Αὐτοί is not Paul and his colleagues (Erasmus, Musculus, Er. Schmid), which would altogether destroy the point of the comparison; but αὐτοὶ is construed according to sense, the antecedent being τῶν ἐκκλησιῶν ἐν τῇ Ἰουδαίᾳ, the believers in Palestine (Winer, § 22, 3). See especially Gal. i, 22, 23. That the Judaean churches suffered no little persecution from their fanatical unbelieving brethren, is plain from several sections of the Acts. The apostle Paul at an earlier period of his life had himself a prominent hand in it. They who stoned Stephen "laid down their clothes at a young man's feet whose name was Saul." "Saul yet breathing out threatenings and slaughter against the disciples of the Lord." "Saul made havock of the church, and entering into every house, and haling men and women, he committed them to prison." "I have heard by many of this man, how much evil he has done to thy saints at Jerusalem," was the reply of Ananias. He himself says, "Many of the saints did I shut up in prison, and when they were put to death I gave my voice against them." "I punished them oft in every synagogue, and compelled them to blaspheme, being exceedingly mad against them." Saul was but a prominent and resolute associate or leader of the persecuting Jews, not doing the work of ferocity and blood single-handed, but having hosts of coadjutors and sympathizers in the Sanhedrim and among the popular masses. Many must have felt as he felt, though they might not have his daring and enthusiasm, and their malignant hostility did not cease with his conversion. The martyrdom of Stephen led to a more general onslaught, which scattered abroad the disciples. Herod slew James and imprisoned Peter, because he saw it "pleased the Jews." The apostle himself was in danger from the Jewish mob; and forty of them banded together, and bound themselves under a curse to kill him, as a representative of Christian zeal and enterprise. Compare Acts viii, ix, xi, xii, &c. These indications of feeling prove the profound enmity which the Jews cherished toward believers in Christ among them. Paul was only an intensified type of them, and their conduct toward him indicates their hatred of all who, though in humbler position and in a narrower sphere, held his doctrines and stood by them. In Thessalonica the unbelieving leaders took to them that excitable and profligate rabble which in such towns lounge about the market place, and with these worthless allies easily creating a tumult, assaulted the house of Jason, with whom the apostle was living, hoping to find Paul and Silas, and bring them before the people in their corporate capacity (εἰς τὸν δῆμον). Disappointed in not getting the apostles into their grasp, they dragged Jason before the rulers, ἐπὶ τοὺς πολιτάρχας—Thessalonica being a free city, and not a Roman colony governed by στρατηγοί. The charge against the strangers was that they had broken the Julian laws and disowned the authority of the emperor, saying that there is another king, one Jesus. Jason was admitted to bail, security for the peace being taken from him. Perhaps he was bound over not to accommodate the apostles any longer. A fine may have been exacted too—something amounting to spoiling of goods—and this was one way of resemblance to the churches of Judaea, who endured similar wrong (Heb. x, 32-34). The first outbreak at Thessalonica did not exhaust the heathen animosity, and wrongs of various kinds must have been inflicted on the Christian brotherhood. What had happened to the Judaean churches had happened to them, as the apostle so fully intimates.

The reason why the apostle here breaks out so strongly upon the Jews lies in the context. As he thought of the churches in Judaea and their native persecutors, this complaint was wrung from him. Olshausen's remark is far-fetched, that the apostle "in this diatribe wished to draw the attention of the Thessalonians to the intrigues of those men with whom the Judaizing Christians stood quite on a level, as if it were to be foreseen that they would not leave this church undisturbed either." But Judaizing is no way referred to in the context; the enemies are unbelieving Jews, and it would be premature to censure the Jews on account of the possibility of a future form of hostility. Calvin's remark, which is virtually accepted by Auberlen, though he points out some blunders in it, is ingenious, but quite foreign to the course of thought. "The apostle," he says, "introduces this topic because this difficulty might occur—if this be the true religion, why do the Jews, who are the sacred people of God, oppose it with such inveterate hostility? To remove the stumbling block he asserts first, that they had this in common with the Judaean churches; and, secondly, that the Jews are determined enemies of God and of all sound doctrine." The statement does not solve the difficulty which he proposes, it only reasserts the fact contained in it. Hofmann's suggestion is similar in its remoteness from the context—that the object of the apostle was to free the Thessalonians from the error that the gospel was a mere Jewish thing; for their heathen neighbours might suppose that their conversion was but falling into the net of Jewish error. But the Jews "which believed not" were the instigators of the first outbreak at Thessalonica, and they were from their position the persecutors of the Judaean churches—the earliest in origin and the earliest in suffering. At the moment of his writing, too, the apostle in Corinth was in intense conflict with the Jewish population "who opposed themselves and blasphemed," so that he was obliged to say to them, "your blood be on your own heads! I am clean: from henceforth I will go unto the Gentiles." At this period the Jews in Corinth, whose number may have been increased because of their banishment from Rome, made insurrection with one accord against Paul and brought him to Gallio's judgment-seat. One need not wonder that the apostle, so circumstanced at the moment of his writing, and remembering what had happened at Thessalonica, opened his mind on the subject. His own position and recollections, their experience and his own, naturally led him to portray some unlovely elements of Jewish character.

(Ver. 15.) τῶν καὶ τὸν Κύριον ἀποκτεινάντων Ἰησοῦν καὶ τοὺς προφήτας, καὶ ἡμᾶς ἐκδιωξάντων—"who killed both the Lord Jesus (or, Jesus the Lord) and the prophets, and drave out us:" marginal rendering, "chased us out."

The ἰδίους of the Received Text before προφήτας has not great authority, and was probably suggested by ἰδίων in the previous verse. Tertullian affirms that it wasMarcion who interpolated it into the text: *licet " suos" adjectio sit haeretici* (*Adver. Mar.*, v, 15, p. 318-19, vol. II, *Op.*, ed. Oehler). De Wette suggests that it may have been dropped on account of the repetition (Reiche). The καὶ is not to be joined to the participle—who both killed the Lord Jesus and also persecuted us—*qui ut et Dominum occiderunt . . . ita et nos* (Erasmus,

Vatablus). Nor is καὶ ascensive, *ipsum Dominum*, as in the Claromontane, for such a climactic beginning enfeebles the remainder. Lünemann, De Wette, and Auberlen assign it to τῶν, *welche auch*, who also, impelled by the same spirit, or, who besides persecuting the Judaean churches, killed—a meaning not very different from the first given. This connection is not required, and the position of καὶ . . . καὶ indicates a different arrangement. The one καὶ is correlative to the other in the enunciation, "who killed both the Lord Jesus and the prophets," both objects being presented in one simultaneous predication (Winer, § 53, 4; Donaldson's *Cratylus*, § 189, 195). Still, τὸν Κύριον, emphatic from its position, and separated from the human name Ἰησοῦν, points out the notoriety or heinousness of the deed, which is described by the aorist as an act in the indefinite past. Jesus the Lord, as Alford suggests, is the proper translation.

καὶ τοὺς προφήτας—or, adopting ἰδίους, "their own prophets." Chrysostom brings out this emphasis—whose books even they carry about, ὧν καὶ τὰ τεύχη περιφέρουσι. De Wette and Koch join προφήτας to ἐκδιωξάντων, but without reason. The majority of expositors naturally connect it with the previous ἀποκτεινάντων. De Wette's objection that all the prophets were not killed is met by a similar statement that all the prophets were not persecuted. The phrase is used in a popular sense. The Jewish nation, by an act of its high court in which the people acquiesced, put to death the Son of God, but it was only the culmination of many previous similar acts, as is portrayed in the parable, Matt. xxi, 34, 39. Compare Jer ii, 30; Matt. v. 12; xxiii, 31-37; Luke xiii, 33, 34; Acts vii, 51, 52. Chrysostom brings forward the second statement to destroy the excuse of ignorance on the part of the Jews, for they could not but know their own prophets, and yet they put to death those messengers who came to them in God's name. The apostle adds—

καὶ ἡμᾶς ἐκδιωξάντων—"and drave us out." The ἐκ is not without force in the verb (Koppe and De Wette), and it does not so much strengthen the meaning (Lünemann) as retain a sublocal signification (Luke xi, 49; and in the Sept., Deut. vi, 19; 1 Chron. viii, 13; xii, 15; Ps. cxix, 157; Dan. iv, 22, 29,

30; Joel ii, 20;—Thucyd., i, 24). The ἡμᾶς, as found in the context, is naturally Paul, Silas, and Timothy—the ἡμεῖς throughout the previous verses. To restrict the reference to Paul (with Calvin) is wrong; and to stretch it so as to include all the apostles (with Lünemann and Ellicott, Pelt and Schott) is true in fact, but not warranted by the immediate narrative before us. Does the apostle mean "drave us out" of Palestine or out of Jewish society? or is it not simply out of the city in which dwelt those whom he was addressing. and who were aware of his expulsion? (Acts xvii, 5.)

καὶ Θεῷ μὴ ἀρεσκόντων—" and please not God," not *non placuerunt*, as the Claromontane—for, though the preceding participles are aorists referring to past acts, this is present marking out a continued condition (Winer, § 45, 1). Nor is the sense *placere non quaerentium* (Bengel and others), or *Gott nicht zu Gefallen leben* (Hofmann). See under Gal. i, 10. Lünemann makes it a meiosis for θεοστυγεῖς. The subjective μὴ is not to be unduly pressed, as it is the usual combination with participles in the New Testament, and the shade of subjectivity is to be found in the aspect under which facts are presented by the writer and regarded by the reader (Winer, § 55, 5; Hermann ad Viger., No. 267, p. ii, p. 640, Londini, 1824; Gayler, p. 274). What they did to the Son of God, to the prophets, and to the apostles representing Jesus, was of such a nature that it brought them into this position—they were not pleasing Him, and therefore a terrible penalty was to fall upon them. Still further they are characterized as—

καὶ πᾶσιν ἀνθρώποις ἐναντίων—"and are contrary to all men." It is natural at first sight to find in this clause a description of the sullen and anti-social elements of character ascribed to the Jewish race. Such is the view of Grotius, Turretin, Olshausen, De Wette, Baumgarten-Crusius, Koch, Jowett, &c. They were regarded as haughty and heartless bigots, who looked down with insolence and scorn on all other nations. The Gentiles repaid their hatred with indignant and contemptuous disdain. Haman in his day when he wished to destroy the Jews impeached them as a "strange people, whose laws are diverse from all people" (Esther iii, 8). Tacitus writes, "*Moyses quo sibi in posterum gentem firmaret, novos ritus contrariosque ceteris mortalibus indidit, . . . Profana illic omnia quae apud nos sacra; cetera instituta sinistra foeda, pravitate valuere . . . apud ipsos fides obstinata, sed adversus omnes alios hostile odium* (*Hist.*, v, 4, 5). Diodorus Siculus records, . . . καὶ νόμιμα παντελῶς ἐξηλλαγμένα . . . Μωϋσέως νομοθετήσαντος τὰ μισάνθρωπα καὶ παράνομα ἔθη τοῖς Ἰουδαίοις (*Excerpta* Photii, xxxiv, 1). Josephus *Cont. Apion*, ii, 11. The sneer of Horace is

> . . . *Memini bene, sed meliore*
> *Tempore dicam; hodie tricesima sabbata: vin' tu*
> *Curtis Judaeis oppedere? Nulla mihi, inquam,*
> *Religio est* (Lib. i, Sat. ix, 70).

Juvenal's account is—

> *Quidam sortiti metuentem sabbata patrem,*
> *Nil praeter nubes, et coeli numen adorant;*
> *Nec distare putant humana carne suillam* (Sat xiv. 96).

He complains too,

> *Nunc sacri fontis nemus, et delubra locantur*
> *Judaeis, quorum cophinus, foenumque supellex* (Sat. iii, 12).

Martial deals out scornful vituperation (iv, 4; vii, 30, 35, 82; Statius, *Silvae*, i, 14, 72). But the isolation enjoined on the Jew by the Mosaic institutes, his fierce hostility to other nations, intensified by disasters, persecution, and gross idolatries, cannot be the reference of the apostle. For, first, much of this spirit of particularism originated in and was cherished by their monotheism and by their observance of their national statutes; and this opposedness to all men, in so far as it did not deepen into morose malignity, the apostle could not condemn. See the tract *Aboda Sara* in the Talmud (Milman, II, p. 460). Secondly, the apostle observed "the customs" and great feasts himself, and, as a consistent though enlightened Jew, he was in this state of separation from polytheism, with its impurities, and from the characteristic elements of heathen society. Thirdly, the clause is to be taken in a more pointed and specific sense, for it is explained by the following assertion or rather identified with it, κωλυόντων ἡμᾶς τοῖς ἔθνεσιν λαλῆσαι. No additional fact is brought out by it, as no καὶ connects the two clauses as it does the previous ones; so that the anarthrous κωλυόντων explains the ἐναντίων. They are contrary to all men in that they are hindering us from speaking to the Gentiles (Donaldson, § 492). This obstruction of the apostle in preaching to other races was on the part of the Jews a special manifestation of contrariness to all men—the result of a selfish and haughty exclusiveness. Such is the view of the Greek fathers. Thus Chrysostom, "if we ought to speak to the world and they forbid us, they are the common enemies of the world."

(Ver. 16.) κωλυόντων ἡμᾶς τοῖς ἔθνεσιν λαλῆσαι ἵνα σωθῶσιν—"hindering," or "in that they are hindering us to speak to the Gentiles, that they may be saved."

Pelt, De Wette, Schott, and Koch find in the verb what does not belong to it—the idea of endeavour, *conatus*. They were not simply striving to hinder, but, as the participle expresses it, they were outwardly hindering so far as they were able, though they could not stop it altogether. The pronoun has the same reference as in the previous verses. Τοῖς ἔθνεσιν, the same in meaning with "all men" of the previous verse, or non-Jewish men, has the stress, as it was not preaching, but preaching to the heathen—preaching under this special aspect and to this special class, which they prevented. Compare Acts xi, 3; xiii, 45; xvii, 5; xviii, 6; xxii, 22; xxvi, 21. See the Martyrdom of Polycarp, xii, xiii, xiv.

The λαλῆσαι ἵνα σωθῶσιν forms one combined idea, the last words giving virtually an objective case to λαλῆσαι, and defining it as speaking the gospel; salvation being the end, the gospel must be the means. To give λαλῆσαι the meaning of *docere* (Koppe, Flatt) is as wrong as it is needless to supply τὸν λόγον. The conjunction ἵνα is telic, but the end merges so far into result or object. See under Ephes. i, 17. Not instruction nor social betterment, but salvation was the object of the apostle's labours and preaching; and the speaking which does not effect this falls short of its true and mighty purpose.

εἰς τὸ ἀναπληρῶσαι αὐτῶν τὰς ἁμαρτίας πάντοτε—"to fill up their sins at all times." Εἰς τὸ (see verse 12). The clause, connected closely with the whole accusation, and not merely with κωλυόντων (Hofmann), denotes the final purpose or object. Not that they had this purpose in definite view and strove to realize it: τουτέστι ᾔδεισαν ὅτι ἁμαρτάνουσι καὶ ἡμάρτανον (Œcumenius). The purpose of God accomplished itself in their continuous perversity. They acted freely and from selfish motive when with wicked hands they crucified the Son of God, and yet they were unconsciously carrying out the divine purpose: "Him being delivered up by the determinate counsel and foreknowledge of God, with wicked hands they put to death." Acting from conscious impulse and wicked resolve, they were unconscious actors in the great drama. Their sin was filling, but was not filled up (ἀναπληρῶσαι being more than the simple verb) till that awful period when they slew Jesus, and in the same spirit drove out His servants (Matt. xxiii, 32). Compare Gen. xv, 16; 2 Macc. vi, 14. It is best to preserve the temporal sense of πάντοτε, which, as the last word of the clause, has a special moment on it, and not to give it the meaning of παντελῶς (Olshausen, Bretschneider); 2 Cor. ix, 8. At all times in their history, ἐπὶ τῶν προφητῶν, when they killed God's messengers to them, they were filling up their sin, though it was far from reaching its fulness; but νῦν ἐπὶ τοῦ Χριστοῦ καὶ ἐφ' ἡμῶν—in Christ's time and ours, by putting Him to death and chasing out His apostles, the measure of their iniquity was at length filled up.

ἔφθασεν δὲ ἐπ' αὐτοὺς ἡ ὀργὴ εἰς τέλος—" but the wrath is come on them to the utmost."

The reading ἔφθασεν has preponderant authority over ἔφθακεν, a probable emendation of the more idiomatic aorist; and τοῦ Θεοῦ added to ὀργή in D F, the Latin versions and fathers, and the Gothic version, gives the true sense, but the reading is unsupported by diplomatic authority. Δέ points to the contrast between their past disobedience to God and hostility to man's highest interest, on the one hand (ἀναπληρῶσαι πάντοτε); and their certain and awful punishment on the other. It is not *enim* (Vulgate followed by Luther and Beza), but *autem*, as in the Claromontane. By ἡ ὀργή, the wrath is characterized in its prominence and terribleness, either as merited or predestined and foretold (Chrysostom). The noun does not mean punishment (Lapide, Schott, De Wette, Ewald), but wrath, the opposite of χάρις. In φθάνειν the idea of anticipation is not to be thought of, for it has this meaning in later Greek only when followed by an accusative of person, as in iv, 15.

It signifies "to come to," "to reach to," with εἰς τι (Rom. ix, 31; Philip. iii, 16), or ἐπί τινα (Matt. xii, 28; Luke xi, 20), or ἄχρι τινός (2 Cor. x, 14). The construction with εἰς occurs in Dan. ii, 17, 18; with ἐπί in Dan. iv, 21; Xenophon, *Cyr.*, v, 4, 9. The meaning of the verb therefore is not *poena divina Judaeos vel citius quam exspectaverint, vel omnino praeter opinionem eorum superveniente*, for the verb is not *praevenit*, as the Claromontane, Beza, Schott, Pelt. See Fritzsche *ad Rom.* ix, 31. The aorist is idiomatic and cannot stand for the present (Grotius, Pelt), nor yet is it used as a prophetic term (Koppe), nor does it mark of itself the certainty of the event. It has its proper sense, which cannot be wholly transferred into English. The apostle places himself close by the divine purpose which foreappointed that wrath in the indefinite past, and he uses the aorist, identifying that divine purpose with its fulfilment. The wrath reached them at the past period when they had filled up their sins; the aorist does not say that it is over, for its most awful manifestations were still to come. Εἰς τέλος does not mean *penitus, ganz und gar* (Koch, Hofmann), as if it were τελέως; nor is it *postremo* (Wahl), or *tandem* (Bengel). In this sense it occurs by itself in Herodotus, i, 30; Æschylus, *Prom.*, 665. Nor is the meaning, to the end of the Jews, *i.e.*, to their final destruction (De Wette, Ewald, Peile) in contrast to Jer. iv, 27; v, 10. In that case αὐτῶν would need to be supplied, and De Wette's quotation of ἕως εἰς τέλος, from 2 Chron. xxxi, 1, is not to the point. Nor does the phrase qualify ἡ ὀργή, wrath which shall continue to its end, or to the end of the world. Thus the Greek fathers Œcumenius and Theophylact explain εἰς τέλος as ἄχρι τέλους, an inadmissible explanation. This defining connection would require the repetition of the article before εἰς τέλος. Grotius, Flatt, Olshausen, refer to the full magnitude of the divine chastisement—the wrath will work on to its full manifestation. The phrase εἰς τέλος is connected with the verb and by its usual construction; it had reached its end and would exhaust itself in palpable infliction. The coming miseries of the Jewish people are plainly alluded to in this verse: the destruction of their capital and their dispersion; the slaughter of myriads and the subjection of many others to servitude, blood, bonds, and long and weary exile. Because the iniquity ot the Amorites was not full in Abraham's time, four hundred years passed away before the promise was realized; but when it grew and ripened into fulness, they were dispossessed. So now by the time that the iniquities of the Jews had culminated to their fulness, the anger of God reached them to its end or utmost.

(Ver. 17.) Ἡμεῖς δὲ, ἀδελφοί, ἀπορφανισθέντες ἀφ' ὑμῶν πρὸς καιρὸν ὥρας, προσώπῳ οὐ καρδίᾳ—"But we, brethren, being be-' reaved in separation from you for the space of an hour, in face not in heart." The three verses 14, 15, 16, are a species of digression, though the first of them naturally springs out of verse 13. One illustration of the efficacy of the word in them was given by their patient endurance of sufferings inflicted on them, specially by the Jews, against whom, when so referred to, the apostle is at once led to bring these awful charges. Δὲ now resumes the ἡμεῖς of verse 15 under a somewhat different aspect, and the apostle places himself at the same time in contrast with the Jewish persecutors. "We, on the other hand" (Klotz, *Devarius*, vol. II, p. 353; Winer, § 53, 7, *b*).

Ἀδελφοί, his usual term of affectionate address. According to De Wette, Koch, Hofmann, ἡμεῖς is in contrast to the ὑμεῖς of verse 14, but this connection is rendered exceedingly doubtful by the structure and course of thought in the verses. Nor is there any ground for the idea of Calvin, followed by Hunnius, Piscator, Vorstius, and Benson, and more recently acquiesced in by Pelt, Hofmann, and Auberlen, that the verse is an apology for the apostle's absence, lest they should think that he had deserted them while so momentous a crisis demanded his presence. " It is not the part of a father to desert his children in the midst of such distresses." But the apostle was forced to leave Thessalonica, as the city and church well knew, and needed not therefore to offer any explanation of his involuntary absence (Acts xvii, 9, 19). He had said that he thanked God unceasingly for their willing reception of the divine word, and he now expresses his profound interest in them and his yearning once more to visit them. Those feelings he would have uttered immediately after the record of his thanksgiving, but his mind was taken off in an allusion to the

Jews, their great sins for ages, and their accumulated penalty. He keenly felt his enforced separation from them, though he does not need to make any excuse for it. This state of heart is described by a very expressive participle, ἀπορφανισθέντες, *desolati* (Vulgate). Ὀρφανός is defined by Hesychius ὁ γονέων ἐστερημένος καὶ τέκνων. Thus it is properly a child bereaved of its parents, a word often occurring; reversely, it is also followed by a genitive of parents bereaved of their children—ὀρφανὸς παιδός (Euripides, *Hecuba*, 150); ὀρφανοὶ γενεᾶς (Pindar, *Olym.*, ix, 92). It is employed in the sense of "bereaved," in reference to relationship still more remote—ὀρφανὸς ἑταίρων (Plato, *Leg.*, v, 130, D); and then in a sense more tropical, τῶν φιλτάτων κτημάτων ὀρφανὸν (Plato, *Phaedo*, p. 239, E); ὀρφανοὶ ὕβριος (Pindar, *Isthm.*, 4, 14); ὀρφανὸς ἐπιστήμης (Plato, *Alcib.*, ii, p. 147). The verb is similarly employed with its ordinary natural sense, to make, or to be made an orphan; or, more generally, to bereave, as γλῶσσαν ὀρφανίζει (Pindar, *Pyth.*, 504); ζωᾶς, ὕπνου (*Antholog.*, 7, 483, 2). The bereavement of some one or some thing, the being reft from one, clings to the passive verb through all its modes of use, with the pain and loss consequent on a forced or violent separation. The compound verb of the text is found in the *Choephorae* of Æschylus, 249, Τοὺς δ' ἀπωρφανισμένους νῆστις πιέζει λιμός—"on them (the brood of the parent eagle killed in the folds and coils of a terrible serpent) bereaved is hungry famine pressing." The ἀφ' in composition with the verb, followed also by ἀπὸ before the pronoun ὑμῶν, expresses strongly the idea of separation (Winer, § 47). The idea of local severance as the source or concomitant of bereavement is thus expressed by the participle, implying his deep attachment to them and his strong desire to be among them again. It is not in good taste to press the figure, and ἀδελφοὶ also forbids it. Thus Œcumenius, Ὀρφανοὶ καταλειφθέντες ἀφ' ὑμῶν, and the Syriac ܝܬܡܐ ܡܢܟܘܢ, Chrysostom explains, "as children after an untimely bereavement are in great regret for their parents, so really do we feel." But this reverses the meaning and application of the words. This orphaning separation had been πρὸς καιρὸν ὥρας—"for the season of an hour" only, when that strong desire filled his heart. The temporal participle expresses a time before that of the verb. When we had been bereaved and separated only for a briefest period, we were the more abundantly longing to see you again. Πρὸς καιρὸν ὥρας belongs to the participle, and expresses a very brief space of time, more vividly and distinctly than πρὸς καιρὸν or πρὸς ὥραν, of which phrases it is made up. Compare 2 Cor. vii, 8; Gal. ii, 5; Luke viii, 13. *Horae momentum* occurs in Latin (Horace, *Sat.* I, i, 7, 8; Pliny, *Hist. Nat.*, vii, 52). Πρὸς means " motion " toward a point of time which is before the subject (Donaldson's *New Cratylus*, § 177), as in the phrase πρὸς ἑσπέραν (Luke xxiv, 29; Bernhardy, p. 564). It has been usually explained as denoting the time during which anything lasts (Luke viii, 13; Heb. xii, 11; James iv, 14). It does not mean *subito et quasi horae momento ereptus* (Turretin, Balduin). Nor is the meaning that the time of separation would be very short, and that still he hoped soon to return (Flatt, De Wette, Koch), for the use of the past participle and its connection with the following past verb disallow it. The general sense then is that the separation was immediately followed by an intense desire of reunion. The severance was, however, προσώπῳ οὐ καρδίᾳ, " in face, not in heart," the dative of relation to—neither instrumental nor modal—limiting the separation to this special point or element (Donaldson, § 458; Winer, § 31, 6; 2 Cor. i, 12; Gal. i, 22; Col. ii, 5). While the severance was only in person, his heart was ever knitted to them in indissoluble bonds. And he adds—

περισσοτέρως ἐσπουδάσαμεν τὸ πρόσωπον ὑμῶν ἰδεῖν ἐν πολλῇ ἐπιθυμίᾳ—" we were the more abundantly zealous to see your face with great desire." The comparative περισσοτέρως, a form very rare in classic Greek, occasions some difficulty. It can scarcely be a species of strong positive; nor, more abundantly than usual, that is, very abundantly (Turretin, Pelt, Conybeare, Olshausen). But this comparative seems always to retain its proper signification in the apostle's usage (Winer, § 35, 4). Fromond and Hofmann interpolate this idea, which is not in the context, that he longed to see them the more, on account of the danger to which, as new converts, they were exposed. Nor is the notion of Calvin to be fully accepted, that it was the separation which intensified his regret; nor the similar one of Winer, that the bereavement made his regret stronger than it would have been, but for the Christian affection by which they were united (§ 35, 4). Two other interpretations are at opposite poles; that on the one hand of the Greek fathers, that his longing for them was more than was to be expected from persons so recently separated, ἥ ὡς εἰκὸς ἤν τοὺς πρὸς ὥραν ἀπολειφθέντας. But regrets and longings are all the keener soon after the separation. On the other hand the view of Lünemann, adopted by Alford, is that the regrets were the more bitter just on account of the very recency of the bereavement, the comparative referring to πρὸς καιρὸν ὥρας; or, as Schott had given it, *ea ipsa de causa, quod temporis intervallo haud ita longo ab amicis Thessal. sejunctus fuerat.* This statement would imply that the apostle was conscious that mere lapse of time would diminish his love for his converts and his interest in them. But the apostle would surely not base the greater abundance of his zeal either on the more or fewer weeks of the interval. The reference then seems to be to οὐ καρδίᾳ—to the fact that the separation was one only of person, not of heart; and on account of this unbroken affection, the desire to see them again was the more ardent. Lünemann objects that if the separation had been in heart there would have been no σπουδάζειν at all. Granted; but that does not hinder the apostle from saying that his unbroken oneness of heart with them, in spite of his personal absence, made him all the more desirous to revisit them; had there been less of love, there would have been proportionately less endeavour to be present again with them. So Musculus, Zanchius, De Wette, Baumgarten-Crusius, Koch, Ellicott. But as ἀπορφανισθέντες is also closely connected with καρδίᾳ, the violent mode of the severance might mingle itself with his thoughts and help to intensify the desire again to see those from whom he had been so rudely torn away. The ἐσπουδάσαμεν implies that he had put forth actual effort to return to them—had taken measures to bring it about. The more abundant endeavour was—

τὸ πρόσωπον ὑμῶν ἰδεῖν—"to see your face," not simply yourselves (Schott), but yourselves in person "face to face" (iii, 10; Col. ii, 1). Compare 2 John 12; 3 John 14.

The last clause ἐν πολλῇ ἐπιθυμίᾳ, "with much desire," points to the sphere in which the action of the verb showed itself. In no listless spirit did he make the endeavour to reach them; the desire to return to them was little less than a passion. The noun is generally used in a bad sense, sometimes with a qualifying epithet or genitive attached to it, and is usually translated lust or concupiscence. It bears a good sense here, as in Luke xxii, 15; Philip. i, 23; Sept., Ps. cii, 5; Prov. x, 24.

(Ver. 18.) Διότι ἠθελήσαμεν ἐλθεῖν πρὸς ὑμᾶς, ἐγὼ μὲν Παῦλος, καὶ ἅπαξ καὶ δίς—" Wherefore we wished to come to you—even I, Paul—both once and twice." The διό of the Received Text, which is also read by some of the Greek fathers, has insufficient authority, διότι being found in A B D¹ F ℵ. " Wherefore," that is, because we so longed to see your face, ἠθελήσαμεν being parallel to ἐσπουδάσαμεν. It has been remarked that the apostle does not use ἠβουλήθημεν, as the latter would indicate merely disposition (Tittmann, *Synon.*, p. 124). It is, however, to be borne in mind, as Ellicott cautions, that θέλω is used by the apostle far more frequently than βούλομαι, in the proportion, indeed, of seven to one, the latter occurring oftenest in the Acts of the Apostles. The apostle singles out himself, the μὲν *solitarium* giving prominence to ἐγώ by the sudden severance of himself from the others (Hartung, vol. II, p. 413; A. Buttmann, p. 313). On the word itself, see Donaldson's *Cratylus*, § 154. The contrast is not so strong as Chrysostom makes it. Grotius, laying stress on the contrast of the suppressed δὲ, joins ἐγὼ μὲν Παῦλος to the next clause καὶ ἅπαξ καὶ δίς, I, Paul, once and again; and brings out this sense, that Paul made the effort to revisit them more than once, Silas and Timothy only once. So Cocceius, Rosenmüller, Conybeare, Hofmann, and the text of Lachmann and Tischendorf. But the ἐγὼ μὲν Παῦλος is parenthetic, and for a moment distinguishes the apostle from his colleagues, we—I, Paul—a special reference to himself, alone in the midst of his trials and labours. The period so referred to may have been that after his hasty departure from Beroea by himself, Timothy and Silas remaining behind him, and while he was for some time in Athens alone waiting for them to rejoin him. The phrase καὶ ἅπαξ καὶ δίς is precise, and means, on two several occasions, literally "both once and a second time," καὶ...καὶ giving this distinct enumeration, and the clause is not to be taken in a general way, as if it meant only several times (Turretin, Koppe, Pelt), which would require the omission of the first καί. Ἅπαξ καὶ δίς occurs in Nehem. xiii, 20; 1 Macc. iii, 30; Philip. iv, 16 (Raphel. *in loc*); Herodotus ii, 121, 37; iii, 148. The opposite phrase is found in Plato, *Clitoph.*, 410 B; οὐχ ἅπαξ οὐδὲ δίς. Twice, then, did the apostle make an earnest effort to revisit Thessalonica—

καὶ ἐνέκοψεν ἡμᾶς ὁ Σατανᾶς—"and Satan hindered us." Καὶ must not be identified in meaning with δέ, as is done by Benson, Schott, Olshausen, De Wette, Koch. It simply states the result, the clauses being placed in simple contiguity, while the context exhibits that result as in contrast to the intention (Winer, § 53, 3 *b*; Philip. iv, 12).[1]

(Ver. 19.) Τίς γὰρ ἡμῶν ἐλπὶς ἢ χαρὰ ἢ στέφανος καυχήσεως; ἢ οὐχὶ καὶ ὑμεῖς ἔμπροσθεν τοῦ Κυρίου ἡμῶν Ἰησοῦ ἐν τῇ αὐτοῦ παρουσίᾳ;—"For what is our hope or joy or crown of rejoicing? or is it not also you in the presence of our Lord Jesus at his coming?"

Χριστοῦ after Ἰησοῦ, on the slender authority of F L and some of the Greek fathers, is to be rejected, the omission of the word being supported by A B D K ℵ, &c. The connection is with the previous verse, and not with verse 17; and it gives, in the form of a question, the reason (γὰρ) of his desire once and again to see them—viz., because they stood in such a relation to him and his spiritual honour and happiness. They were his "hope," not that he expected a future reward for their conversion (Estius, Fromond, Hofmann), or pardon for his earlier life, and the injury he had done to the church as Saul the persecutor; for, as Lünemann remarks, the emphasis is not on ἡμῶν, but on ἐλπίς, and the other predicates. His hope was that he and they, in spite of trials and difficulties, would be kept by divine power, so as to meet before the Master, and enjoy His acceptance and welcome. Not only ἐλπίς but χαρὰ, "joy" in them as the trophies of his toil and warfare, not only χαρὰ, but higher still, στέφανος καυχήσεως. The phrase is very

[1] A blank page in Dr. Eadie's manuscript here would probably have been filled with an exposition of the words "Satan hindered us."

expressive; it is a chaplet of triumph worn by the victor, the genitive not being that of apposition (Koch), but either of material, or, rather, of what Winer calls remote internal relation (§ 30, 2 β). The Hebrew phrase is עֲטֶרֶת תִּפְאֶרֶת, "crown of glory" (Sept., Ezek. xvi, 12; xxiii, 42; also Prov. xvi, 31, referring to the "hoary head"; Philip. iv, 1). Compare 2 Tim. iv, 8; Rev. ii, 10. As the victor boasts of his crown, the apostle might rejoice in the salvation of his converts through God's grace and by his preaching.

The epithets are natural, and are found in Greek and Latin writers—τὴν πολλὴν ἐλπίδα Νικοτέλην (*Antholog.*, vol. I, p. 225, Lips. 1794); *spes reliqua nostra* (Cicero, *Ep. Fam.*, xiv, 4); *C. Marium, spem subsidiumque patriae* (*Pro Sextio*, 17, 58); *vitae mihi pariter dulcedo et gloria* (Macrob., *Somn. Scip.*, I, 1); *Scipionem, spem omnem salutemque nostram* (Livy, *Hist.*, xxviii, 39); στέφανον εὐκλείας μέγαν (Soph., *Ajax*, 460); and the same phrase occurs in Eurip., *Supp.*, 325. Lobeck in his note refers to similar not identical phrases from other authors.

ἢ οὐχὶ καὶ ὑμεῖς—"or is it not also you?" The particle ἢ is sometimes treated in the English version as if it were a mere particle of interrogation, as in Matt. xxiv, 23; Rom. iii, 29; v, 1, 3; but it retains its real disjunctive sense as referring to a previous interrogation, not *nonne* (Erasmus, Schott), but *an non*. It introduces the second member of a double question (Klotz, *Devarius*, vol. I, 101; Winer, § 57, 1; Hand, *Tursell.* on the particle *an*, vol. I, p. 349). While some erroneously take ἢ as a mere mark of interrogation, Pelt regards ἢ οὐχὶ as meaning *nisi*. The καὶ with its ascensive force is "also," not "even," as in our version, reference being to his other converts, who were also at the same time his hope and joy—καὶ ὑμεῖς μετὰ τῶν ἄλλων, as Chrysostom explains it, and Œcumenius after him. The Vulgate and the Peshito omit καὶ; the Claromontane has *etiam*.

ἔμπροσθεν τοῦ Κυρίου ἡμῶν Ἰησοῦ ἐν τῇ αὐτοῦ παρουσίᾳ— "in the presence of our Lord Jesus at His coming." Χριστοῦ of the Received Text has little authority, and is rightly rejected. Some propose a close connection with the previous clause, as in the English version, "are not even ye in the presence of our Lord Jesus Christ." Thus Olshausen says that this expresses a doubt which is plainly put an end to in the last verse, and his meaning is, or "do not ye also (as I myself and all the rest of the faithful) appear before Christ at His second coming" (Bisping)? But such an exegesis mars the full sense of the double question. It is also partial to connect the clause immediately with the first part of the verse, "for what is our hope and joy and crown of boasting in the presence of the Lord Jesus?" For the clause belongs to both questions, and characterizes place and time. "What is our hope, joy, and crown of gloriation? or are not ye also in the presence of the Lord Jesus?" and the period is—at His coming. The two clauses are not very different in meaning: παρουσίᾳ is presence, or a being present (Æschylus, *Persae*, 167; Sophocles, *Electra*, 1232; 2 Cor. x, 10; Philip. i, 26; ii, 12). Appearance often implies advent or arrival as preceding or producing it, so that advent is a frequent meaning (1 Cor. xvi, 17; 2 Cor. vii, 6, 7; 2 Macc. xv, 21; Diodor. Sic., i, 29). The term is often, as here, employed to denote the appearance or coming of Christ, which are identical, as in Matt. xxiv; 1 Cor. xv, 23; 2 Pet. iii, 4; 1 John ii, 28, &c. Instances in Abdiel's *Essays*, p. 166.

In presence of His glorified humanity, seated on His throne, the work of redemption being finished on earth, the human species no longer, at least in present organization, living on it, but having completed its cycle of existence, specially and formally are believers accepted by Him. His coming—personal, public, and glorious—is the great hope of the church, which it ever cherishes as the epoch when it shall be full in numbers and perfect in felicity. The apostle's hope was that when he and they stood in the Master's presence, they would not be "ashamed at His coming," and he anticipated a "joy and crown of rejoicing" in their final salvation, in their rescue from temptation and suffering and death, and in their spiritual change which had ripened into glory—a change of which he by God's blessing had been the human instrument (2 Cor. i, 14; Philip. ii, 16).

(Ver 20.) Ὑμεῖς γάρ ἐστε ἡ δόξα ἡμῶν καὶ ἡ χαρά—"For ye are our glory and joy." Lünemann and many others take γὰρ, not as causal, but confirmatory, *bekräftigend—yes*, or *indeed*, ye are our glory and joy—the γὲ element of the word, according to Ellicott, having the predominance. Winer, § 53, 8; Hartung, vol. I, p. 473. But γὰρ may have its usual meaning. If the apostle virtually repeats what he had just said, the repetition must have something special, either additional or intensive, about it. "What is our hope and joy and crown of boasting? Are not ye also in the presence of the Lord Jesus? Certainly, at that future period, for ye are now in every sense our glory and joy"—ὑμεῖς ἐστέ being emphatic from position, καὶ νῦν ἐστε καὶ τότε ἔσεσθε (Theophylact). Hartung, vol. I, 473. The sense is not different whichever of these meanings of γὰρ be adopted. At the same time the temporal distinction of Flatt and Hofmann cannot be sustained—that verse 19 refers to the future, and verse 20, in contrast, to the present time. Such a distinction is not marked out by the words. The 19th verse is not expressed in the future, there being no verb written, and, though the reference is virtually to the future, the apostle views it under a present aspect, and presents it as the source of his ardent desire to revisit his converts. Chrysostom says, in reference to these epithets as applied to the Thessalonian believers, "These words are those of women inflamed with tenderness and talking to their little children. . . . The name of crown is not sufficient to express the splendour, but he has added 'of boasting.' Of what fiery warmth is this! . . . For reflect how great a thing it is that an entire church should be present planted and rooted by Paul. Who would not rejoice in such a multitude of children, and in the goodness of those children?" The book Siphra records—*Gloria est discipulo, si praecepta magistri sui observat; gloria est filiis Aaronis, quod praecepta Mosis observarunt* (Schöttgen, *Horae*, vol. I, p. 824).

The practical improvement of two very old commentators may be quoted—"Certainly the gaining of souls to God's kingdome is no small pillar to support our hope of salvation, and a pledge to us of our glory, so runnes the promise they that turne others to righteousnesse shall shine as starres, Dan. xii, 3, Prov. xi, 30" (Sclater's *Exposition of Thessalonians*, London, 1627). Bishop Jewel's reflection is—"This ought to be the case of all such which are ministers, that they should seek above all things to bring the people to such perfection of understanding, and to such godliness of life, that they may rejoice in their behalf, and so cheerfully wait for the coming of our Lord Jesus Christ" (*Exposition of Thessalonians*, 1583).

CHAPTER III

(Ver. 1.) Διὸ μηκέτι στέγοντες—" Wherefore being no longer able to bear." Διὸ, "for which reason," refers back naturally, not to the last clauses expressive of the apostle's hopeful and joyous interest in his converts (Lünemann, Hofmann), but to his intense desire to visit them and the failure of a double effort; the connection being, "because I could not come to you, Satan having hindered me, and because I was still filled with profound anxiety to hear about you, as I could not see you, I resolved to send Timothy to cheer and encourage you." The "we," as formerly limited in ii, 18, means apparently here the apostle only. The verb στέγειν is defined by Hesychius as βαστάζειν; ὑπομένειν. Its original meaning (connected with στέγη) is to cover, so as to keep out or off, as in Thucydides, iv, 37. See Poppo's note, vol. III, part iii, p. 121. The verb is used in 1 Cor. ix, 12; xiii, 7, in both cases with πάντα. It does not mean, as sometimes in the classics, *occultantes* (Wolf, Baumgarten, and Robinson), nor that he was no longer able to cover up his yearnings in silence; but the sense is, when I was no longer able to control my longing for you without doing something to gratify it (Polyb., iii, 53, 2). See Kypke *in loc.* The use of the subjective μηκέτι implies the writer's own feeling, being in such a state that I could not master my desire to see you. Winer, § 55, 5. See under ii, 15.

εὐδοκήσαμεν καταλειφθῆναι ἐν 'Αθήναις μόνοι—"we thought it good to be left behind at Athens alone." The verb belongs to the later Greek, the spelling being εὐ or ηὐ. Sturrz, p. 168. The idea of pleasing is not in the verb, though it signifies "it was our pleasure," but only that of *libera voluntas*, a resolution freely come to, not *prompta inclinatio* (Calvin), and the aorist is not to be taken as an imperfect (Grotius, Pelt), the latter of whom speaks confidently, *res ipsa docet*. Not a few refer the plural to Paul and Silas; but the limitation in ii, 18, governs this plural and the following ἐπέμψαμεν; the singular occurring again more precisely in verse 5. There is stress from its position on μόνοι, not simply, alone in Athens, *in urbe videlicet a Deo alienissimâ*, but perhaps also the feeling of solitude was deepened from his intense craving for human sympathy and fellowship. The statement is supposed to clash with Acts xvii, 14, 15. Jowett accuses the writer of the Acts of ignorance that only Silas was left behind, and Schrader supposes two visits to Athens. One theory is, that the apostle sent Timothy away prior to his own arrival in Athens—that is, as Alford expresses it, " the apostle seems to have determined during the hasty consultation previous to his departure from Beroea to be left alone at Athens, which was the destination fixed for him by his brethren, and to send Timothy back to Thessalonica to ascertain the state of their faith" (*Prolegom.*). Such is also the view of Wieseler (*Chronol. des Apost. Zeitalt.*, p. 249), and of Koppe, Hug, and Hemsen. But the natural view is that Timothy was despatched to Thessalonica from Athens. (1) For this verse plainly implies that Paul in Athens had Timothy with him, and, sending him off from Athens to Thessalonica, became himself "alone," Silas being probably absent somewhere else. The order of thought and the verbs καταλειφθῆναι, ἐπέμψαμεν, lead without doubt to such a conclusion; the two verbs indicate a mission personally enjoined by the apostle himself, and that Timothy was with him in Athens. (2) When Paul left Beroea he went away alone, but left commandment for Silas and Timothy to rejoin him, and he waited for them at Athens. Is there, then, any improbability in the supposition that Timothy obeyed the order with all speed, and that on his arrival at Athens the apostle deprived himself of his company and sent him off at once to Thessalonica? (3) The apostle, before the return of Timothy and Silas from Macedonia, had gone to Corinth, where his colleagues at length joined him, so that he writes in the beginning of the letter from the same city, "Paul and Silvanus and Timotheus." (4) The apostle could not say that it was his pleasure to be left alone at Athens, if he had been always alone during his sojourn in that city and no other had been in his company. The phrase, therefore, implies the arrival and presence of

Timothy prior to his departure to Thessalonica. There is really nothing in the narrative of the Acts, which omits this mission of Timothy altogether, to contradict this view, which is held by Schott, Koch, De Wette, Lünemann, and Ellicott.

(Ver. 2.) Καὶ ἐπέμψαμεν Τιμόθεον τὸν ἀδελφὸν ἡμῶν καὶ συνεργὸν τοῦ Θεοῦ—" and sent Timothy our brother and fellow-worker with God." There is a confusing variety of readings, showing that the copyists stumbled at some word or phrase. Though συνεργὸν τοῦ Θεοῦ, which has been conjectured by Lünemann and Alford as furnishing the occasion, is a Pauline phrase (1 Cor. iii, 9), yet perhaps the application of the phrase to one not an apostle might originate some difficulty. So B omits τοῦ Θεοῦ, and D³E K L supplant it by ἡμῶν, "our fellow-labourer," with the Syriac and Chrysostom; τοῦ Θεοῦ is placed after τὸν διάκονον, which supersedes συνεργόν in A ℵ and 67²; the Vulgate has *et ministrum Dei*, and so the Coptic; F has διάκονον καὶ συνεργὸν τοῦ Θεοῦ; the Received Text having διάκονον τοῦ Θεοῦ καὶ συνεργὸν ἡμῶν, which is vindicated by Bouman and Reiche. Amidst all this variety it is hard to come to a decided conclusion.

The text as we have given it is found in D¹17, in the Claromontane, Sangerm., and Ambrosiaster, *fratrem nostrum et adjutorem Dei*. It may be said that διάκονον is an emendation for συνεργὸν more humbly fitting to τοῦ Θεοῦ, and if this be admitted, then the reading of Lachmann, Tischendorf, and many modern editors may be safely preferred. The phrase συνεργὸν τοῦ Θεοῦ does not mean, one who wrought as a fellow with the apostle, while both belonged to God, as Flatt, Heydenreich, and Olshausen contend on 1 Cor. iii, 9; but is a fellow-worker with God, as συν distinctly belongs to the following genitive, He being the chief and primal worker himself. Bernhardy, p. 171. Compare Rom. xvi, 3, 9, 21; Philip. ii, 25; iv, 3, in all of which cases συν is connected with the associated genitive (2 Cor. i, 24; Demosth., 68, 27; 884, 2). It has been supposed by some that the apostle so eulogized Timothy to make the Thessalonians aware of the sacrifice which he made in sending such a colleague to them, and in deciding to remain in Athens alone (Theophylact, Musculus). Such a purpose is not in the context, nor can it be safely ascribed to the large-hearted apostle. As little can Chrysostom's idea be adopted, that the object of the apostle in so eulogizing his representative was to show them the honour which in this way he put upon them, lest they should be tempted to depreciate him (Hofmann). It is probable that the apostle wrote simply in the fulness of his heart, Timothy being specially dear to him, and specially useful in promoting the great work. Compare Philip. ii, 19-25. See under Col. i, 1; v, 7. Timothy was a brother beloved in many ways—the child of a pious ancestry on the female side; a convert of the apostle; an active, sympathizing, and indefatigable colleague—" working the work of the Lord, as I also do"; a fellow-worker with God himself, for the sphere was—

ἐν τῷ εὐαγγελίῳ τοῦ Χριστοῦ—"in the gospel of Christ"—God's great sphere of operation among men. Timothy preached it, and God rendered it efficacious (Rom. i, 9; 2 Cor. x, 14; Philip. iv, 3). And Timothy was sent for this purpose—

εἰς τὸ στηρίξαι ὑμᾶς καὶ παρακαλέσαι ὑπὲρ τῆς πίστεως ὑμῶν—"to establish you, and to exhort you on behalf of your faith."

The Received Text has ὑμᾶς after παρακαλέσαι, but it is rejected on greatly preponderant authority; and ὑπέρ in the last clause is to be preferred to περί, being found in A B D¹ F K ℵ. The meaning, then, is not that Paul through Timothy (a-Lapide, Grotius), but that Timothy himself should confirm them. The infinitive with εἰς τὸ, as in ii, 16, points out the special purpose of the mission, and στηρίξαι is often similarly employed (Rom. i, 11; xvi, 25; James v, 8; 1 Peter v, 10). The next infinitive, παρακαλέσαι, is plainly not to comfort, for an objective sentence dependent on it begins the next verse (Acts xiv, 22; xv, 32; 2 Thess. ii, 17), but to exhort, the exhortation being on behalf of, or in furtherance of, the faith; whereas περί would refer rather to the object or theme of the exhortation, which is distinctly put in the following verse. Winer, § 47, l. The afflictions which made this confirmation necessary are not those of the apostle only, as Œcumenius, Theophylact, Estius, Fromond, Macknight; but the whole context points to the persecution which had fallen out at Thessalonica, and in which the apostle had participated.

The next words are so closely connected with this verse that there should be no division of verses.

(Ver. 3.) τὸ μηδένα σαίνεσθαι ἐν ταῖς θλίψεσιν ταύταις—"that no one be disquieted in these afflictions." The common text has τῷ for the first word, which is not admissible (Winer, § 44, 5), and in its place F G have ἵνα. The text as given has highest uncial authority. Compare, however, 2 Cor. ii, 12; Koch *in loc.* The verb σαίνειν from σείω, used only here in the New Testament, means physically to move backwards and forwards, or hither and thither, as a dog does his tail—Ælian, *Hist. Var.*, xiii, 42; Homer, *Odyss.*, xvi, 4; Aristoph., *Eq.*, 1031. It then signifies to fawn upon to flatter (Æschylus, *Choeph.*, 191); and in this sense some take it here (Elsner, Koch, Rückert). Thus Hesychius defines σαίνει by κολακεύει. Faber Stap. has *adulationi cederet.* Beza gives *adblandiri.* Bengel says the verb is applied εἰς τοὺς ὑπούλους καὶ κολακικούς. See also Tittmann's *Synon.*, p. 189; Suidas *sub voce;* and Wetstein *in loc.* But the sense is not congruous, for such blandishment is not the result or accompaniment of persecution, which induces terror, and shakes men's constancy. Such is apparently the meaning.

The verb in later Greek signifies, to be moved in mind, to be disturbed; or, as Chrysostom explains it, θορυβεῖσθαι καὶ ταράττεσθαι· τοῦτο γάρ ἐστι σαίνεσθαι. Diogenes Laertius, viii, 41; Sophocles, *Antig.*, 1214. Hesychius gives as synonyms κινεῖσθαι, σαλεύεσθαι. The meaning of deluded or infatuated given by Hofmann has no support. The connection has been regarded in various ways.

1. Schott, Koch, and Bisping take τὸ μηδένα σαίνεσθαι as an accusative absolute, *quod attinet ad*, or, as Cocceius, *ad vos confirmandum hoc verbo.* The construction is admissible, but very rare. Bernhardy, 132; Krüger, § 50, 6, 8. Lünemann objects that Schott's appeal to Philip. iv, 10, cannot be sustained in proof, because the phrase on which the stress is laid, τὸ ὑπὲρ ἐμοῦ φρονεῖν, is the usual object accusative to the transitively employed verb ἀνεθάλετε. But another interpretation of that verse is as probable. See under Philip. iv, 10.

2. Lünemann and Alford take the clause as dependent on εἰς, in opposition to the entire sentence preceding, and as

repeating in a negative and sharper form the same thought—to stablish you and exhort you on behalf of your faith—that is, that no one of you be shaken by these afflictions. But, as Ellicott remarks, "the regimen is remote, and the course of thought is broken." Lünemann's suggestion that τουτέστι might have been written for τὸ, and Alford's, which is almost equivalent to it, are more than doubtful, and are at variance with the asserted connection—εἰς in the previous verse—for an explanatory thought is interpolated.

3. The better exegesis is that which makes τὸ μηδένα σαίνεσθαι an objective sentence, dependent on παρακαλέσαι, and explaining the theme of exhortation. Winer, § 44, 5. The meaning, then, is to stablish you and to exhort you on behalf of your faith—the exhortation being that no one be shaken. So De Wette, Reiche, Hofmann, Ellicott, and Riggenbach; A. Buttmann, p. 226. The objection, that in this case παρακαλέσαι would govern only an accusative of the thing, is not formidable. See 1 Tim. vi, 2, though Lünemann gives another explanation; Luke iii, 18, and Mark v, 22, which, however, contains an accusative of person. But, as has been stated, such infinitives have not the same immediate dependence on the verb that substantives have. On such usage see Matthiae, § 543, 2, 3, and his numerous examples. The proposal of Matthaei to insert a second εἰς before τὸ μηδένα is a desperate solution. Compare Rom. iv, 11. The sense is not materially different under any of these principal forms of exegesis. To stablish you and exhort you on behalf of your faith—that is, to the end that ye be not moved—is not very different from saying, to stablish you and exhort you on behalf of your faith—the theme of the exhortation being that ye be not shaken—

ἐν ταῖς θλίψεσιν ταύταις—"in these afflictions." Ἐν is not purely temporal (Lünemann), nor is it strictly instrumental, but it points out the condition in which they were placed; these afflictions so surrounded them that they were in them (Winer, 48, a); "these afflictions" being certainly not those special to the apostle, but common to him and to the Thessalonians. See under previous verse.

αὐτοὶ γὰρ οἴδατε ὅτι εἰς τοῦτο κείμεθα—"for yourselves know that we are appointed thereunto." Γὰρ introduces the reason for which they should not be troubled in these afflictions, and that reason, generally, is their knowledge that their subjection to them was the divine will. The verb κεῖμαι is passively used, *positi sumus* (Vulgate). Luke ii, 34; Philip. i, 17. Τοῦτο refers to θλίψεσιν, and not to the injunction, not to be shaken or perturbed. The plural verb does not refer to Paul alone (Œcumenius, Estius), but immediately to Paul and the Thessalonians, representing at the same time all believers. Those afflictions are not accidental on the one hand, and we do not court them or merit them on the other hand, but our position brings them on us, and God by his grace has set us in that position. Why then be shaken by them, for we cannot avoid them, and when with you we forewarned you of them (Matt. x, 22; John xv, 20)—

(Ver. 4.) Καὶ γὰρ, ὅτε πρὸς ὑμᾶς ἦμεν, προελέγομεν ὑμῖν ὅτι μέλλομεν θλίβεσθαι—"For verily when we were with you, we told (or, were telling) you before that we were to be afflicted."

Γὰρ assigns the reason for the αὐτοὶ γὰρ οἴδατε—καὶ laying moment upon it: for ye know because we told you before when we were with you. Winer, § 53, 8. In the phrase πρὸς ὑμᾶς, the original notion of direction disappears after verbs implying rest, and the sense is not different from παρά with the dative or the Latin *apud*. Fritzsche on Mark i, 18.

The phrase μέλλομεν θλίβεσθαι is no mere dilution of the simple future, but repeats the idea on the divine side of εἰς τοῦτο κείμεθα—that these sufferings are a portion of God's allotment which we cannot escape, as they are the characteristic and inevitable lot of believers. Μέλλομεν expresses the certainty, and implies the soonness of the sufferings.

καθὼς καὶ ἐγένετο καὶ οἴδατε—" as also it came to pass and ye know." It turned out as the apostle had foretold—the prediction had been verified, and in their history or from their experience they knew it. The words from αὐτοὶ γὰρ οἴδατε to the end of this verse are very unnecessarily marked by Griesbach and Knapp in a parenthesis.

(Ver. 5.) Διὰ τοῦτο κἀγὼ μηκέτι στέγων—"For this cause when I too could no longer forbear." "For this cause," that is, because those predicted sufferings had really broken out among them, and they had had actual experience of them. In the relative κἀγώ the καί, belonging simply to the pronoun, may refer either to Timothy, "I as well as he," or to the ὑμεῖς of the previous verse, "I as well as you," that is, "I longing to see you and you longing to see me" (Schott, Olshausen), or to those who were along with him, as in ii. 13. It is difficult to say which of these references was in the apostle's mind. The first is natural, the second is rather an anticipation of the latter part of v. 6, and the third has a historical vindication in Acts xvii. 15, that there were brethren with him for a period at Athens.

The phrase μηκέτι στέγων, "no longer forbearing," is explained under the first verse.

ἔπεμψα εἰς τὸ γνῶναι τὴν πίστιν ὑμῶν—"I sent Timothy to know your faith." Εἰς τό γνῶναι, the infinitive of purpose, specifies the design of ἔπεμψα, and the meaning plainly is not, that Timothy the sent one, but that Paul the sender, might know—the subject being the same in both verbs. The theme of information was τὴν πίστιν ὑμῶν, "your faith," what its aspects and stability were, and if it had passed through the ordeal in safety. The apostle's anxiety was—

μήπως ἐπείρασεν ὑμᾶς ὁ πειράζων καὶ εἰς κενόν γένηται ὁ κόπος ἡμῶν—"lest perchance the tempter have tempted you, and our labour might prove or turn out to be in vain." Μήπως depends naturally on γνῶναι, and not on ἔπεμψα, and introduces an indirect question, as Lünemann states. Not a few connect it with the idea of fearing (φοβούμενος), fearing lest the tempter, &c. Beza, Pelt, Turretin. The aorist indicative ἐπείρασεν specifies the tempting as having actually taken place, while the subjunctive γένηται represents the results of the temptation as conditional or doubtful, it being a possible thing that the apostle's labours should, as the result of the temptation, turn out to be fruitless. As the apprehension might be verified, or might prove groundless, the apostle's anxiety was to ascertain the actual state of things, or whether the temptation which was intended to shake them had done so. Winer, § 56, 2; Gayler, p. 323. Winer justly objects to the harsh view of Fritzsche in taking μήπως in the first clause as *an forte—an forte Satanas vos tentasset*—and in the second clause as *ne forte—ne forte labores mei irriti essent*—making it in the first clause an interrogative particle, and in the second an expression of fear or apprehension. See also Ellicott; Matthiae, § 519, 7. The verb ἐπείρασεν, as the following clause shows, does not mean "may have succeeded in tempting you," the cause for the effect (Macknight), or, *mit Erfolg versucht* (Baumgarten-Crusius). The tempter's purpose was obvious, and the apostle was only in doubt as to the result. The agent of the temptation is named in harmony with his work, as expressed by the verb ἐπείρασεν ὁ πειράζων (Matt. iv, 3; 1 Cor. vii, 5). All notion of time is excluded from the present participle used as a substantive. Winer, § 45, 7; Bernhardy, p. 316. For εἰς κενὸν γένηται, see the similar phrase under Gal. ii, 2.

(Ver. 6.) "Ἄρτι δὲ ἐλθόντος Τιμοθέου πρὸς ἡμᾶς ἀφ' ὑμῶν—"But Timothy having just now come unto us from you." The adverb of time is most naturally connected with the participle ἐλθόντος, which in itself implies time, and not with a verb so remote as παρεκλήθημεν of the following verse, which has its ground prefixed to it in διὰ τοῦτο. Lünemann's arguments for the last connection are of little weight. Not only did the return of Timothy bring comfort and that comfort prompt the writing of the epistle, but he wishes specially to connect the two things. Timothy had been sent away—his good tidings on his return cleared up perplexities, and that at once. The apostle reverts to his position in the mission of Timothy, and virtually affirms by the ἄρτι ἐλθόντος that no sooner had he come back than all doubts were cleared up, and at once his relieved and rejoicing heart gave utterance to its emotions in the epistle. The adverb ἄρτι, though originally different from νῦν, often in the later Greek represents present time. See under Gal. i, 9.

καὶ εὐαγγελισαμένου ἡμῖν τὴν πίστιν καὶ τὴν ἀγάπην ὑμῶν—"and having brought good news to us of your faith and love." The participle is used in its original meaning—ἀγαθὸν ἡγεῖτο (Chrysostom), and has its common construction, dative of person and accusative of thing (Luke i, 19; Lobeck *ad Phrynich.*, 266-8). The subjects of the good news, πίστις and ἀγάπη, are both specified by the articles. For their meaning, &c., see under Ephes. i, 15. Their faith had remained firm in spite of trial and suffering. Chrysostom explains by using βεβαίωσιν, and Theodoret τῆς εὐσεβείας τὸ βέβαιον. Their love was evincing itself—had not waxed cold because of abounding iniquity—ἡ δὲ ἀγάπη τὴν πρακτικὴν ἀρετήν. Their condition delighted him, as it proved the continued existence of unshaken faith and active love among them, and he was no less rejoiced with a third element of their character, their unfaded remembrance of himself—τρία τέθεικεν ἀξιέραστα (Theodoret). For he adds—

καὶ ὅτι ἔχετε μνείαν ἡμῶν ἀγαθὴν πάντοτε—" and that ye have good remembrance of us always." For μνεία see under i, 2; its meaning differs according as the verb by which it is followed is ποιεῖσθα, or ἔχειν. Πάντοτε belongs more naturally to the clause before it than to the participle after it (Koch and Hofmann). i, 2; 1 Cor. i, 4; xv, 58; Gal. iv, 18; Ephes. v, 20; 2 Thess. i, 3. Not only was the remembrance good, but it was continuous, the result being that they were—

ἐπιποθοῦντες ἡμᾶς ἰδεῖν καθάπερ καὶ ἡμεῖς ὑμᾶς—" longing to see us as we also (ἰδεῖν ἐπιποθοῦμεν) to see you." The simple verb ποθέω does not occur in the New Testament, and ἐπί in the compound is not intensive, greatly desiring, but retains its primary directive meaning. Ἐπιποθεῖν τι, as Fritzsche says, *idem valet quod* πόθον ἔχειν ἐπί τι (*ad Rom.*, i, 11; Sept., Ps. xli, 1). For καί see Klotz, *Devarius*, vol. II, 633; Winer, § 53, 5. They longed to see the apostle just as the apostle longed to see them. The longing was therefore mutual, for there was earnest attachment on both sides.

(Ver. 7.) Διὰ τοῦτο παρεκλήθημεν, ἀδελφοί—" On this account were we comforted, brethren." Διὰ τοῦτο compacts into one argument the three preceding statements—their unshaken faith, their fervent love, and their continuous desire to see the apostle. The verb in the perfect tense is found in A and 3, 23, 57; and such a reading may have arisen from connecting ἄρτι with it, as Koch does, though the aorist forms one of Lünemann's reasons against joining the adverb to ἐλθόντος. The aorist simple expresses the past fact that Timothy's return brought comfort, and that this comfort still existed is implied in the context—

ἐφ᾽ ὑμῖν ἐπὶ πάσῃ τῇ ἀνάγκῃ καὶ θλίψει ἡμῶν διὰ τῆς ὑμῶν πίστεως—comforted "over you in all our necessity and affliction through your faith." The first ἐπί has virtually its literal sense of "on"—you being the foundation on which the comfort rested (Winer, § 48, c). Alford, after Lünemann and Pelt, renders the preposition "with reference to you," but this is somewhat inexact. It is far wrong on the part of Koppe and Pelt to regard ἐφ' ὑμῖν as superfluous (*proprie redundat*), because of the following διὰ τῆς ὑμῶν πίστεως. For the first phrase points out the persons on whom the apostle's comfort rested (2 Cor. vii, 7), and the second points out that element of their condition by the instrumentality of which his comfort was realized; yourselves were the basis, your faith the medium of our comfort. The second ἐπὶ does not distinctly differ in meaning from the first—"over all our necessity and tribulation" —comfort was so thrown over it that it ceased to vex us and fill us with sorrow. Such is the semi-local image, the preposition, as Ellicott says, "marking that with which the comfort stands in immediate contact and connection;" you afford the comfort, and that exists over or in connection with our necessity and distress, so that these do not fill us with despondency. Some make ἐπὶ causal, others temporal. Alford suggests "in spite of" as the translation, and that is indeed the ultimate sense. To find the image it is best to adhere to the primary sense of superposition. Donaldson, *Cratylus*, § 172. Compare 2 Cor. vi, 4. The Received Text reads θλίψει καὶ ἀνάγκῃ, but only on the authority of K L and some of the Greek fathers. It is not easy to say what this affliction and necessity were, but the probability is that they were external in nature. The notion of Koch and De Wette that they were internal anxiety about the Thessalonians cannot be entertained, for in that case the report of Timothy would have removed them, but the expression implies that they continued still, though countervailing comfort was enjoyed. It is needless to distinguish the substantives nicely, as when Bouman regards the first as generic and the second as specific.

'Ανάγκη is *the unavoidable* (Wunder; Sophocles, *Trachin.*, 823) as the result of constraint or circumstances (1 Cor. vii, 37; ix, 17; Matt. xviii, 7), and the distress therefrom arising (Luke xxi, 23; 2 Cor. vi, 4; Xenoph., *Memor.*, iii, 12, 2). Θλίψις, allied to τρίβω, *tribulatio*, is *pressure* (2 Cor. ii, 4; Matt. xiii, 21). Compare Rom. ii, 9, θλίψις καὶ στενοχωρία; 2 Cor. vi, 4, θλίψις καὶ ἀνάγκῃ. It is probably wrong to restrict ἀνάγκῃ to disease, or scantiness of means, or hardness of manual labour (Schott), though these may not be excluded. The apostle may refer to his entire condition at Corinth, in the midst of peril and persecution from the Jews, "who opposed themselves and blasphemed." The words of the Lord in a vision, "no man shall set on thee to hurt thee," implies that attempts against him had been made, and these culminated at length in the insurrection against him when he was dragged before Gallio. Surrounding circumstances seemed so dark and forbidding that the apostle began to despond and was tempted to form the purpose of leaving Corinth, or at least of moderating his labours so that the enmity against him might die down. But the divine voice met him with the words quoted, and Christ's words are ever fitted to the condition of him to whom they are spoken. "Be not afraid, but speak and hold not thy peace, . . . for I have much people in this city." Compare 1 Cor. ii, 3. The comfort came—

διὰ τῆς ὑμῶν πίστεως—"through your faith," the faith of whose stability Timothy had brought so favourable a report. Grotius would very tastelessly place the phrase before ἐπὶ πάσῃ, &c., and Hofmann would join it with the following clause ὅτι νῦν ζῶμεν, with this meaning—*weil euer Glaube es ist dadurch wir jetzt leben*—a connection which Lünemann correctly calls so monstrous as to need no contradiction. Thus the apostle has in the verse ἐφ', ἐπὶ, διὰ, bringing out, as his manner is, varying but closely connected aspects of relation. See also under verse 9. The result is—

(Ver. 8.) ὅτι νῦν ζῶμεν, ἐὰν ὑμεῖς στήκητε [στήκετε] ἐν Κυρίῳ— "for now we live if ye stand fast in the Lord." The spelling of the verb in the last clause is doubtful. The received text, with D ℵ¹, and some minuscules, have στήκητε. Ellicott quotes B, but wrongly, for though Mai's reprint so spells it, Alford asserts *e codice* that it reads στήκετε, and his reason is confirmed by Tischendorf's edition *ex ipso codice*. The solecistic στήκετε is found in A B F H L ℵ³, and has therefore good authority. Scrivener's remark as to the permutation of vowels in the best MSS. is met by Alford's assertion from personal inspection that, with certain specified exceptions, it is not so in the Vatican

Codex, in any ordinary occurrences of long and short vowels. Ὅτι gives the reason of the statement which has just preceded. The language is strong. Necessity and distress had brought a species of death over the apostle, but he came out of it as soon as he heard of their firmness in the faith. Ζῶμεν is not to be explained away by the phrase *dum vivimus vivamus* (Pelt), nor is it to be exaggerated into eternal life, ζωὴν τὴν μέλλουσαν (Chrysostom). The adverb is probably not used with a purely temporal meaning—he had been as one having the sentence of death in himself, but *now* in their life he lives (Jowett, Marloratus). The particle has rather somewhat of a logical sense—referring to and implying the fulfilment of the condition introduced by ἐάν. Hartung gives as an example of the transfer of this time-particle *auf Umstande und Bedingung*—μητροκτόνος νῦν φεύξομαι, τόθ' ἁγνὸς ὤν (Euripides, *Elect.*, 979). Kühner, § 690.

The next clause is conditional ἐὰν στήκετε. If the subjunctive form be adopted, the meaning is that he did not know after all whether they would stand fast; and he states the matter hypothetically—assumes the possibility; whereas, if the indicative στήκετε be adopted, the apostle assumes as a fact that they would stand fast. Donaldson, § 502; Klotz, *Devarius*, ii, 455. See under Gal. i, 8, 9; Winer, § 41. The verb στήκειν is used in Mark xi, 25 in the literal sense of to stand; and tropically in Rom. xiv, 4; Gal. v, 1; Philip. iv, 1; and it derives its specialty of sense from the context, "stand fast." Ἐν Κυρίῳ describes the element of their stability, in union with the Lord and in fellowship with Him. The apostle had been in hard and heavy circumstances, which weighed him down to death. Opposition, unbelief, peril, disappointment, physical labour, and debility so preyed upon him that he felt as one enveloped in the shadow of death; but Timothy's news from Thessalonica so revived him, so lifted him out of the gloom, that he lived again; his soul was so joyful over the stability of his converts, that he triumphed at once over surrounding dangers and persecutions. And that conditional sentence was a warning to them for the future; the continuance of that life depended on their continuous stability.

(Ver. 9.) Τίνα γὰρ εὐχαριστίαν δυνάμεθα τῷ Θεῷ ἀνταποδοῦναι περὶ ὑμῶν ἐπὶ—"for what thanksgiving can we render God for you in return for." Some MSS.—D¹ F א¹—insert Κυρίῳ. Γὰρ, not a mere particle of transition (Pelt), confirms what has been said, and brings out one special manifestation of the power and fulness of the ζωή. Τίνα, interrogative, implies what *sufficient* thanks; or, as Theophylact quaintly paraphrases, διὸ καὶ αὐτῷ ὀφείλοντες εὐχαριστεῖν, οὐχ εὑρίσκομεν τὴν ἀξίαν εὐχαριστίαν. The apostle had given thanks for their conversion, had given thanks for the manner in which they had received the word; and now he knows not what amount of thanks to give for their stability under persecution and suffering.

The double compound ἀνταποδοῦναι is properly to give in return (ἀντί), ἀπό, as Ellicott says, hinting at the debt previously incurred. Winer's explanation is, "*ubi dando te exsolvis debito, debitum enim est oneris instar nobis impositi quo levamur cum solvimus*" (*De Verb. Praep. Comp. in N. T. Usu*, iv, p. 12). The verb is used in the sense of penal retribution (2 Thess. i, 6; Rom. xii, 19). It occurs also with a good sense (Luke xiv, 14; Rom. xi, 35; Ecclus. iii, 31. Compare Ps. cxvi, 12). It has likewise a neutral sense, τὸ ὅμοιον ἀνταποδιδόντες (Herod. i, 18; Plato, *Parmenides*, 128, c.), and is followed both by ἀγαθά and κακά in 1 Sam. xxiv, 18. This gift of life in the midst of death, and this fulness of joy were of God; and therefore to Him thanks of no common depth and fervour are due in return.

περὶ ὑμῶν is "about you" (for you), you being the objects for whom thanks are given; and the following words state the ground—

ἐπὶ πάσῃ τῇ χαρᾷ ᾗ χαίρομεν δι' ὑμᾶς ἔμπροσθεν τοῦ Θεοῦ ἡμῶν—"for all the joy which we joy on your account in the presence of our God." Ἐπί, "over," "on," gives the "ethical basis." Winer, § 48, *c*. See under verse 7. That basis is πᾶσα ἡ χαρά, "all the joy," the joy regarded in its whole extent—πάσῃ being extensive, not intensive save by inference (Pelt, Schott), *in ihrer Summe und Totalität*. Winer, § 18, 4. The attraction ᾗ for ἣν χαίρομεν, found also in Matt. ii, 10, gives the sentence a kind of periodic compactness. Winer, § 24, 1. The use of the correlative noun extends the meaning of the verb. Winer, § 32, 2; Bernhardy, p. 106;

Lobeck, *Paralipom.*, p. 501. Many examples are found in the Septuagint, New Testament, and classics. Jelf, §§ 548-9. The apostle has written περὶ ὑμῶν, "concerning you"; and to be more specific he adds δι' ὑμᾶς, the first connected with the return of thanks, and the second with χαίρομεν, on your account (John iii, 29). Compare Fritzsche *in Marc*, 205. It is his usage to distinguish varying but connected relations by varying prepositions; and he fondly dwells on the different sides of the connection of the Thessalonians with his thanksgiving and his joy. The concluding words ἔμπροσθεν τοῦ Θεοῦ ἡμῶν, used only in this epistle, are not synonymous with ἐπὶ τῶν προσευχῶν ἡμῶν, as if he meant that the emotion of joy ever brought him into the divine presence (Webster and Wilkinson); nor are they to be joined with what succeeds (Ewald, Hofmann, and the Peshito); nor is the connection with χαρᾷ (Koppe, Pelt), but with χαίρομεν, we joy in the presence of God; our gladness is pure and unselfish; it bears God's inspection, and has His approval. The reference is not to God as the author of that joy, αὐτὸς καὶ ταύτης ἡμῖν τῆς χαρᾶς αἴτιος (Œcumenius).

(Ver. 10.) νυκτὸς καὶ ἡμέρας ὑπερεκπερισσοῦ δεόμενοι εἰς τὸ ἰδεῖν ὑμῶν τὸ πρόσωπον—" night and day praying very abundantly, in order to see your face." The participle δεόμενοι is not absolute "we pray" (a-Lapide, Baumgarten-Crusius), but is closely connected with the preceding verb—what thanks can we return for the joy which you give us in our separation, praying as we do night and day to see your face? The intensity of the prayer to revisit them and perfect their faith was in proportion to the thanksgiving for the gladness which in the interval Timothy's report had produced. Schott, De Wette, Koch, and Riggenbach take δεόμενοι in apposition with χαίρομεν, which is only a subordinate thought in the verse. Luther and Von Gerlach regard the verse as an answer to the question in verse 9; but the connection is artificial, and might require a finite verb instead of the participle. The double compound ὑπερεκπερισσοῦ, "more than abundantly," expresses the fulness of the apostle's emotion. Compare 1 Thess. v, 13; Ephes. iii, 20; Sept., Dan. iii, 23. See under Ephes. iii, 20. It belongs to δεόμενοι, and not by a trajection to ἰδεῖν (Clericus). Night and day is an idiom not to be so measured as if night were specially referred to for its solitude and silence as the most fitting season for prayer (Fromond); but "night and day praying more than abundantly" is the utterance of profoundest love and longing. The purpose or object of the prayer is then given—

εἰς τὸ ἰδεῖν ὑμῶν τὸ πρόσωπον—"in order to see your face," *ut videamus* (Vulgate), the prayer being heard, that end would be obtained See under ii, 12, 16, 17. Not only to see them but in seeing them—

καὶ καταρτίσαι τὰ ὑστερήματα τῆς πίστεως ὑμῶν—"and to supply the lackings of your faith;" *et compleamus ea quae desunt* (Vulgate), *et suppleamus quae desunt* (Claromontane); τὰ ἐλλείποντα πληρῶσαι (Theodoret). The verb καταρτίζω signifies to refit or readjust literally (Matt. iv, 21; Mark i, 19 —Wetstein *in loc.*; and Polybius, i, 1, 24); then, ethically, to restore (Gal. vi, 1; Herodotus, v, 106); then to fill up, to supply, or to finish thoroughly; the meaning of the simple ἄρτιος being distinctly preserved, and κατά being intensive in force (Elsner in 1 Cor. i, 10). Philip. ii, 30; Col. i, 24.

Their faith was not perfect, it was lacking in some elements. It needed to grow in compass, to embrace yet more elements of doctrine, and have a firmer and more harmonious hold of truths already taught, such as the Second Advent. Their faith was also lacking in power; it had not led them to a universal obedience, or given them strength to surmount all heathen propensities and impurities, as is implied in the following chapter. Nor had its influence descended to every-day life in its secular aspects, enforcing honest industry and ennobling it. The visit which he so longed to make would have been improved for this purpose—to give them careful and earnest teaching and guidance on all points in which their faith needed invigoration or enlargement. Confirmation was a work which the apostle loved, it was so necessary and so beneficial. Thus he longed to visit the church in Rome, that he might impart to its members "some spiritual gift," to the end that they might be established (Rom. i, 10, 11).

In a similar spirit he writes to the church of Corinth, "I was minded to come to you before that ye might have a second benefit" (2 Cor. i, 15). Calvin's practical reflection is,

—*Hinc etiam patet quam necessaria nobis sit doctrinae assiduitas: neque enim in hoc tantum ordinati sunt doctores, ut uno die vel mense homines adducant ad fidem Christi, sed ut fidem inchoatam perficiant.*

(Ver. 11.) Αὐτὸς δὲ ὁ Θεὸς καὶ πατὴρ ἡμῶν καὶ ὁ Κύριος ἡμῶν Ἰησοῦς κατευθύναι τὴν ὁδὸν ἡμῶν πρὸς ὑμᾶς—" Now may God Himself and our Father and our Lord Jesus direct our way unto you." The Received Text has Χριστὸς after Ἰησοῦς on the authority of D³ F K L, the Vulgate, Syriac, Coptic, and Gothic versions, and several fathers; but the word is omitted in A B D² ℵ (D¹ omitting Ἰησοῦς also), and in the Claromontane Latin, the insertion being probably a conformation to the more common and familiar formula.

By δέ he passes to another aspect of the same subject, and αὐτός, emphatic in position, is not in contrast with the persons characterized as δεόμενοι (De Wette, Koch, Bisping), but it means God himself—He and none other—for He alone can fulfil such a prayer. The apostle had proposed to visit them once and again, and Satan had hindered him; but if God Himself would be pleased to direct the way to them, no hindrance would be permitted. Ἡμῶν may belong to Θεὸς καὶ πατήρ (Hofmann, Riggenbach), or simply to πατήρ. That ἡμῶν is connected with πατήρ is probable, Θεός being absolute and πατήρ relative, the relation being indicated by the pronoun, and πατήρ is often followed by a genitive (Rom. i, 7; 1 Cor. i, 3; 2 Cor. i, 2, ἀπὸ Θεοῦ πατρὸς ἡμῶν). God our Father—believers have a community of Fatherhood in Him, as they are His children, bearing His image, enjoying His guardianship, and being prepared for His house of many mansions. The words καὶ Κύριος ἡμῶν Ἰησοῦς are in direct apposition with ὁ Θεὸς καὶ πατήρ, and form with it the nominative to κατευθύναι. For the meaning and use of the names see under Ephes. i, 2. The verb κατευθύναι is the aorist optative, not the infinitive, as such usage, though found in epic and other poets, and also in prose authors, is not found in the New Testament. Winer, § 43, 5; Jelf, § 671. It means literally to make straight so that one may pass, then to guide or direct—πρὸς ὑμᾶς—the preposition indicating the direction.

It is plain that ὁ Θεὸς καὶ πατήρ and ὁ Κύριος ἡμῶν Ἰησοῦς are parallel in thought, both being related to the emphatic αὐτός, and both being nominative to the singular verb κατευθύναι.

To the mind of the apostle, therefore, God the Father and the Lord Jesus were so one that the same prayer is presented to both without distinction—there being, as the singular implies, equality of power and oneness of operation, or what Lünemann calls unity of will. But equality of power and unity of will imply a higher unity—even unity of essence; for only to one possessed of divinity can the worship of prayer be presented. It is superficial in Koch to say that the apostle here "regards Christ as the Wisdom and Power of God," for the language is directly personal in nature—the Lord Jesus is addressed as God, and the thing prayed for is to be done by Him and God as one divine and indivisible work—κατευθύναι. See under Ephes. i, 2. The Lord Jesus, though man, as the name Jesus indicates, is also Lord—at the right hand of the Father—and Governor of the universe; but this government is proof of His possession of supreme divinity, as it necessitates the possession of omnipotence and omniscience, attributes with which no creature can possibly be endowed. Who but God can roll on the mighty and mysterious wheels of a universal providence without halting or confusion?—who but He can know all hearts in their complex variety of motive and purpose, so as to be their Judge? Athanasius presses the argument derived from the singular form of the verb. After quoting the verse, he says, τὴν ἑνότητα τοῦ πατρὸς καὶ τοῦ υἱοῦ ἐφύλαξεν. οὐ γὰρ εἶπε κατευθύνοιεν ὡς παρὰ δύο διδομένης, παρὰ τούτου καὶ τούτου, διπλῆς χάριτος, ἀλλὰ κατευθύναι (*Oratio*, iii, 11, *contra Arianos*, p. 346; *Opera*, vol. II, Migne).

(Ver. 12.) Ὑμᾶς δὲ ὁ Κύριος πλεονάσαι καὶ περισσεύσαι τῇ ἀγάπῃ εἰς ἀλλήλους καὶ εἰς πάντας καθάπερ καὶ ἡμεῖς εἰς ὑμᾶς—"You may the Lord cause to enlarge and abound in love to one another and to all, even as we also to you." For Κύριος A reads Θεός; ὁ Κύριος Ἰησοῦς is found in D¹ F, and the Claromontane Latin; but there is no nominative in the Syriac, nor in the Vulgate in the Codex Amiatinus. The omission is approved by Mill, Griesbach, Eichhorn.

By δὲ he passes to another thought suggested by the previous prayer—"but you may He enlarge"; whether this prayer be heard or not as to guidance in our way to you, or whether we are privileged to revisit you or not, you may He enlarge with or without our instrumentality. May He grant this petition on your behalf. He had spoken in verse 10 of defects in their faith, and this prayer implies that their love was also in need of enlargement. The two verbs here used in a transitive sense are in the optative in continuation of the construction of the previous verse. Bretschneider wrongly takes them to be infinitives, and would supply δῴη ὑμῖν (Lex. *sub voce* πλεονάζω). Compare Sept., Num. xxvi, 54; Ps. lxx, 21; 2 Cor. iv, 15; ix, 8; Ephes. i, 8. Both verbs, similar in meaning, seem to refer to ἐν ἀγάπῃ. Œcumenius weakens the sense by giving the first a reference to number, τῷ ἀριθμῷ. Fromond similarly refers the one to *extensio*, and the other to *intensio*. Olshausen takes the one as cause and the other as effect, but the distinction is not warranted. If one is enlarged in any Christian grace, he abounds in it, enlargement and abundance being varying aspects of the same blessing. His prayer had been that defects in their faith might be filled up (verse 10), and now it is specially that their love may be augmented—first, to one another, in the same believing community, and then to all men—not to all Christians (ὁμοπίστους) of the places beyond Thessalonica (Theodoret). See under Gal. vi, 10. Men made in the image of God are to be loved as God has loved them. Our love to men, as children of a common Father, should be a likeness of His φιλανθρωπία (Titus iii, 4), man-love, having its wider circle of objects in mankind, irrespective of creed or character; while Christian love—φιλαδελφία, brother-love—has its immediate objects of attachment in the Church. Love is the fulfilment of the law. See under Gal. v, 14, and Philip. i, 9-10. In the last clause the two verbs must be supplied—καθάπερ καὶ ἡμεῖς εἰς ὑμᾶς ἐν ἀγάπῃ πλεονάζομεν καὶ περισσεύομεν—not repeating the optative which would necessitate ἡμᾶς. This filling up changes the verbs from a transitive to an intransitive sense—a change from an unusual to the more common signification. Such verbs are usually supplied from the context (Kühner, § 852), and such a supplement, although it appears clumsy, is in natural harmony with the context. Other methods are weak or artificial, as ἔχομεν, or πολλὴν ἀγάπην ἔχομεν (Pelt, Schott), *affecti sumus* (Calvin), or simply ἔσμεν (Grotius). Theophylact explains, "ye have us as the measure and example of love," μέτρον καὶ παράδειγμα. The prayer is directed to the Lord—ὁ Κύριος. The name may refer either to the Father or the Son (Alford). That it refers to the latter in this place is extremely probable. For (1) it is the common usage of the New Testament in Paul's Epistles. (2) The reader will naturally take the Κύριος of this verse to be the Κύριος of the previous verse (3) The Κύριος of this verse is also naturally the same with the Κυρίου of the following verse. (4) In the paragraph the Father is twice called ὁ Θεός καὶ πατὴρ ἡμῶν. The very distinctness of this appellation would lead one to suppose that Κύριος by itself does not refer to the Father, but to Jesus, who is twice mentioned by the same epithet in connection with Him. Basil, in his Treatise *de Spiritu Sancto*, cap. xxi, affirms that Κύριος means in this place the Holy Spirit, referring in proof to 2 Cor. iii, 17, with which it has no analogy (*Opera*, vol. II, p. 61, Migne).

The last purpose of this prayer is next given—

(Ver. 13.) εἰς τὸ στηρίξαι ὑμῶν τὰς καρδίας ἀμέμπτους ἐν ἁγιωσύνῃ ἔμπροσθεν τοῦ Θεοῦ καὶ πατρὸς ἡμῶν—"in order to confirm your hearts unblamable in holiness before God and our Father." Εἰς τό is not for the more simple καί (Kühner), but with the following infinitive indicates purpose—the purpose of the prayer that they might grow and abound in love. Love tends to confirm—for it is the bond of perfectness. When the heart is filled with this love to brethren and to mankind, it becomes established; it rises beyond the sphere of doubts and oscillations, for it is fulfilling the law, and growing in that holiness which such love sustains and develops (Matt. v, 44-48). The author of this spiritual confirmation, which has its root in enlarging love, is Κύριος to whom the prayer is addressed, not Θεός ; the subject of the verb is not ἀγάπην (Œcumenius), and certainly not ἡμᾶς the apostles (a-Lapide). Chrysostom takes notice that he says, " not you, but your hearts—for out of the heart proceed evil thoughts." The adjective ἀμέμπτους is used proleptically, " so that you may be blameless." The property expressed by the adjective does not exist in the substantive till after the action of the accompanying verb is completed. Jelf, § 439, 2; Winer, § 66, 3; 1 Cor. i, 8; Philip. iii, 21; Jude 24. The usage is not uncommon in classical writers, both in prose and poetry. Lobeck, Soph., *Ajax*, p. 230, 3rd ed., Berlin, 1866; Soph., *Œd. Col.*, 1084, Wunder's note; Matthiæ, § 446, 2, where numerous examples are given. The adverb ἀμέμπτως is found in B L. The prayer then is that He may confirm them so as to be unblamable, not vaguely, but ἐν ἁγιωσύνῃ—the more correct spelling, ἁγιοσύνῃ being found in B¹ D F (Rom. i, 4; 2 Cor. vii, 1). The noun denotes neither the process (ἁγιασμὸς) nor the quality (ἁγιότης), but the condition (Lobeck ad Phrynich, p. 350), or the sphere in which blamelessness was to evince its power as the result of the divine confirmation. It is a holy disposition or state in which the soul is freed from all disturbing and opposing elements of evil, possessing a purity which is the image of God's, and every element of which will stand His inspection and meet His approval, for it is ἔμπροσθεν τοῦ Θεοῦ καὶ πατρὸς ἡμῶν, "before God and our Father." See under i, 3; iii, 9. The phrase brings out the genuineness of the holiness and the final acceptance of him who possesses it, and in whom this prayer is fulfilled. On the relation of ἡμῶν to the two preceding nouns, see under Gal. i, 4. The phrase is not to be connected solely with the word ἁγιωσύνῃ (Koppe, Pelt), nor solely with ἀμέμπτους (De Wette, Koch), but with the entire verse.

ἐν τῇ παρουσίᾳ τοῦ Κυρίου ἡμῶν Ἰησοῦ μετὰ πάντων τῶν ἁγίων αὐτοῦ—"at the coming of our Lord Jesus with all His saints." Χριστοῦ, occurring after Ἰησοῦ in the Received Text, has in its favour F L, the Vulgate, Syriac, Coptic, and Gothic versions. But A B D K ℵ, and 20 mss. omit it, as also the Claromontane and some of the fathers; and it is therefore rightly rejected by Lachmann and Tischendorf. For the first part of the clause see under ii, 19.

The main question is, who are included under the οἱ ἅγιοι, with whom or in whose company the Lord comes? (1) Some restrict them to the saints or earlier believers, sanctified and perfected (iv, 14; 1 Cor. vi, 4). So Flatt, Olshausen, Hofmann. The word is often employed in this narrower sense. See under Ephes. i, 1. (2) Others understand by the term the holy angels.

That these are to accompany Christ is evident from many passages (Matt. xvi, 27; xxv, 31; Mark viii, 38; Luke ix, 26; 2 Thess. i, 7). So Musculus, Benson, De Wette, Olshausen, Macknight, Bisping, and Lünemann. But οἱ ἅγιοι never by itself alone in the New Testament signifies angels; and the word here cannot denote them exclusively, for it is continually or uniformly applied to human believers. (3) Some take the noun as signifying both holy men and holy angels, "with all His holy ones." In favour of this supposition there are several arguments: (*a*) For, as a fact, saints will be there (iv, 14), and angels too, as is fully told in the passage already quoted. (*b*) If the apostle had wished to exclude the angels to whom he makes special reference in the second epistle, he would have employed some unmistakeable epithet. But he uses a term that may comprehend both, according to the usage of the Hebrew and Septuagint (Deut. xxxiii, 2, 3; Ps. lxxxix, 7); קְדֹשִׁים, and οἱ ἅγιοι, without any addition, denote angels in Dan. iv, 10; vii, 13; Zech, xiv, 5. Compare Heb. xii, 22, 23. (*c*) The addition πάντων gives some weight to this opinion. (4) Angels as well as saints are called His; for the αὐτοῦ refers to Him and not to Θεοῦ (Lünemann): Matt. xiii, 41; xvi, 27; xxv, 31; 2 Thess. i, 7. So Bengel, Baumgarten-Crusius, Riggenbach, Alford, and Ellicott. True, indeed, some raise an objection from πάντων. Musculus objects that Jesus does not come with all His saints; or, in the words of Conybeare, "our Lord will not come with all His people, since some of His people will be on earth." But πάντων embraces the angels too; and iv, 14, tells us that both the dead who are raised and the living who are changed will together meet the Lord in the air. Angels, the unfallen ones so near God and so like Him, and saints redeemed and perfected, and made equal to the angels, ἰσάγγελοι, are with Him when He comes—those who owe to Him existence and glory, and those who owe to Him restoration and blessedness. Flatt proposed to join the clause ἀμέμπτους ... with μετὰ πάντων ... "that he may stablish you blameless in holiness, along with all His saints at the coming of the Lord Jesus"; as Peile paraphrases, that "you may take part in"; or as Conybeare translates, "and so may He keep your hearts steadfast and unblameable in holiness and present you before our

God and Father with all His people at His appearing." So also Musculus and Flatt, Aretius, Estius. Hofmann adopted this connection in his *Schriftbeweis*, II, 2, 1st ed.; but in the second edition and in his *H. Schr. N. T.* he has abandoned it. The connection is unnatural, and of course restricts οἱ ἅγιοι to the saints.

The word Ἀμήν, found at the end of the chapter in some codices and versions, is apparently an addition from some church lectionary, the lesson for the day ending at the place; or it may be a liturgical response.

CHAPTER IV

THE apostle commences now the practical part of the Epistle. He introduces exhortations to personal and sexual purity and to industry, in order that the believers should present a salutary and an impressive contrast to the heathen round about them.

(Ver. 1.) Λοιπὸν οὖν, ἀδελφοί, ἐρωτῶμεν ὑμᾶς καὶ παρακαλοῦμεν ἐν Κυρίῳ Ἰησοῦ—"Finally, therefore, brethren, we beseech you and exhort in the Lord Jesus." The τὸ before λοιπὸν in the Received Text has no uncial authority save B²; on the other hand, the οὖν is omitted by B¹, a few manuscripts, the Syriac and Coptic versions, with Chrysostom and Theophylact, but it is certainly to be retained. Λοιπόν, *de caetero*, Vulgate, denotes that what follows is not only additional to what has been said (*furthermore*, Ellicott), but is at the same time the concluding portion of the epistle (2 Cor. xiii, 11; Philip. iv, 8; Ephes. vi, 10; 2 Thess. iii, 1). It does not signify *überhaupt* (Baumgarten-Crusius). Chrysostom lays undue stress upon it when he paraphrases it, ἀεὶ μὲν καὶ εἰς τὸ διηνεκές; and Theodoret errs too in writing τὸ λοιπὸν ἀντὶ τοῦ ἀποχρώντως ὑμῖν τὴν ἡμετέραν παράκλησιν. See under Philip. iii, 1. The alternative explanation of Œcumenius gives the sense, though not the exact meaning—τὸ εἰς παραίνεσιν ἐλθεῖν. The οὖν introduces a conclusion based on the statement of the previous verse. As the apostle had prayed for them that they might be so confirmed as to be found spiritually perfect at

Christ's coming, on this account he sought and exhorted them to live in harmony with the divine will, or so as to please God. They should strive that their life might be in unison with his prayer. It restricts the sense unnecessarily to refer οὖν simply to the second coming (Calixtus); and it takes away from the point to give it a vaguer and remoter allusion to the report carried by Timothy to the apostle (Musculus). The first of the two verbs, ἐρωτᾶν, is used by classical writers only in the sense of asking a question. Here, however, as also in v, 12; 2 Thess. ii, 1; Philip. iv, 3, it means to entreat. The Hebrew שָׁאַל, though often rendered in the Septuagint by αἰτεῖν, as when followed by מֵאֵת or מִן applied to a person (1 Sam. viii, 10; Ps. ii, 8), is sometimes also rendered by ἐρωτάω. In the New Testament the verb has both a classical and a Hellenistic sense. Compare Matt. xvi, 13, "He asked them, saying," (ἠρώτα); John i, 19, ἵνα ἐρωτήσωσιν, on the one hand; and on the other, in addition to the texts already quoted, Matt. xv, 23; Luke xiv, 18, 19; John xii, 21. With the second sense it is followed by περί or ὑπέρ, and sometimes by the conjunctions ἵνα and ὅπως. This verb, according to Lünemann, is the entreaty of a friend; while the second, παρακαλοῦμεν, is more official in its nature—the charge enjoined by an apostle. The exhortation is ἐν Κυρίῳ Ἰησοῦ, in the Lord Jesus; not by Him (διά, per), as a formula of adjuration (Beza, Estius, Grotius, Pelt, Schott), but in Him, in fellowship with Him—He being not the source only, but also the element of our exhortation; in Him it is formed, in Him it is tendered—in Him lies its vitality and power. What the charge was is now told—

ἵνα καθὼς παρελάβετε παρ' ἡμῶν τὸ πῶς δεῖ ὑμᾶς περιπατεῖν καὶ ἀρέσκειν Θεῷ—"that as ye received from us how ye ought to walk and please God." Ἵνα is omitted in the Received Text, and is not found in A D³ K L ℵ, and in some of the Greek fathers; but it is found in B D¹ F, in both Latin versions, and in the Syriac Peshito. The repetition of ἵνα in the next clause has probably originated the omission. See Reiche on the verse. If the ἵνα be genuine, it blends the purpose of the charge with its contents. See under Ephes. i, 17; and for the verb, see under ii, 13; Gal. i, 12; the reference being to the personal teaching of the apostle during his brief sojourn among them. The verb refers simply to oral instruction, and not, as the Greek fathers, to example also. What they received is specified under one aspect by τὸ πῶς, *the how;* and thus the entire clause has given to it a substantival character. Winer, § 18, 3. Rom. iv, 13; viii, 26; Gal. v, 14; Philip. iv, 10. For περιπατεῖν, see under Ephes. ii, 2. Καὶ has a common consecutive force—how ye ought to walk, and by this walking as its medium to please God. The pleasing is the result of the walking. To walk so as to please God is to act according to His will, to live the life of His Son on the earth; and, though one may come far short of the divine ideal, yet the perfect and paramount desire so to live will enjoy the divine acceptance. The charge is not that they should begin so to walk, for he adds—

καθὼς καὶ περιπατεῖτε—"as ye also are walking." The clause, though omitted in the Received Text and also in D³ K L, the Syriac version, and the Greek fathers, is found in A B D¹ F ℵ, the Vulgate, and some other versions, and has therefore high authority, besides being a naturally interjected thought in unison with the following περισσεύητε. They had been already so walking, and in such walking they are exhorted to abound—

ἵνα περισσεύητε μᾶλλον—"in order that ye would abound still more." Καθὼς καὶ implies for its supplement a οὕτως in this clause, ἐν τῷ οὕτως περιπατεῖν (Col. ii, 6). The second or repeated ἵνα comes in naturally, after so long an intervening clause. This use of μᾶλλον characterizes the apostle's style (iv, 10; 2 Cor. vii, 13; Philip. i, 23), but it does not mean that they were to go beyond the divine commandments (Chrysostom). They had been walking so as to please God; and the charge is that they would still grow in this conformity to the precepts delivered by the apostle. It is not a bare command so to walk, but a recognition at the same time of their begun sanctification, combined with an earnest injunction to continue and make rapid progress in this holy and blessed course.

(Ver. 2.) Οἴδατε γὰρ τίνας παραγγελίας ἐδώκαμεν ὑμῖν διὰ τοῦ Κυρίου Ἰησοῦ—"For ye know what commandments we gave you by the Lord Jesus." Γάρ gives the ground of the exhortation, introducing an appeal to their present knowledge—they had not forgotten what they had received—they know it —παρελάβετε of the previous verse corresponding to ἐδώκαμεν ὑμῖν of this verse. Compare Gal. iv, 13; 1 Cor. xv, 1. The plural παραγγελίαι is not "preaching of the gospel," but means precepts (Acts v, 28; xvi, 24; 1 Tim. i, 5, 18; Polybius, vi, 27). These ethical commands were based on the gospel, and are in harmony with its spirit, true obedience being prompted by those motives which it alone supplies. The stress is on τίνας, to which the specific τοῦτο in the next clause corresponds. The preposition διά in the last clause is not to be confounded with ἐν (Pelt), but means through the Lord Jesus, as the living medium through whom the apostle was enabled to deliver them, the precepts being in origin not his own, but Christ's. Bernhardy, p. 236; Winer, § 47, 1. Before διά Grotius needlessly inserts the participle παραλαμβανομένας; and διά has not so loose a signification as Schott gives it, *auxilio seu beneficio Christi*, as if it referred to the revelations connected with the apostleship, δι' ἀποκαλύψεως Χριστοῦ. Nor is the immediate purpose of the words that which Olshausen gives, to maintain his investment as an apostle with full powers to issue moral commandments; for its object is rather to turn attention to the momentous character and obligation of the precepts so enjoined.

(Ver. 3.) Τοῦτο γάρ ἐστιν θέλημα τοῦ Θεοῦ, ὁ ἁγιασμὸς ὑμῶν —"For this is God's will—your sanctification." Γάρ introduces an illustrative reason; and τοῦτο, emphatic in position, is not the predicate (De Wette), but the subject, and refers back to τίνας, it being specially included among them; for this, about to be uttered, is the will of God—to wit, your sanctification. The omission of the article before θέλημα has been accounted for in various ways; either because what follows as a special injunction does not exhaust the whole will of God (Lünemann), or because after verbs substantive and nuncupative it is frequently omitted (Ellicott). *Nam pronomen ubi pro subiecto habendum est, substantivum autem praedicati locum obtinet, articulus omittitur* (Stallbaum, Plato, *Apolog.*, p. 57). What comes διὰ τοῦ Κυρίου is in true and ultimate source and authority the will of God. ‎Ἁγιασμὸς, in apposition to τοῦτο, preserves, according to its derivation, its active force (see under iii, 13); and ὑμῶν is the genitive of object—the sanctification of you. Estius, Koppe, Usteri, Olshausen, and Hofmann take it wrongly, with a passive meaning, as equivalent to ἁγιωσύνη, which, however, does not mean σωφροσύνη, as Œcumenius and Theophylact give it. But " the termination μος is generally found with a class of nouns which represent the action of the verb proceeding from the subject, and may be expressed by the infinitive active used as a noun" (Donaldson, *Cratylus*, § 253). On account of the τὸ μὴ before ὑπερβαίνειν of ver. 6, taken as parallel to τοῦτο, some give ἁγιασμός the more limited meaning, which that verse would suggest, of purity from sexual sin; " this is the will of God" ἀπέχεσθαι . . . εἰδέναι ἕκαστον . . . τὸ μὴ ὑπερβαίνειν. So Turretin, Pelt, Schott, Olshausen, Lünemann. But there is another and better method of explanation. (1) The explanatory infinitive ἀπεχέσθαι, without the article, defines negatively the ἁγιασμός, or, at least, a portion of it requiring immediate enforcement. (2) Then εἰδέναι, also without the article, gives a positive explanation in continuance of the negative statement. (3) But in τὸ ὑπερβαίνειν, the article brings it into a line with ὁ ἁγιασμός, and as a distinct exemplification suggested by the second clause of ver. 4.

ἀπέχεσθαι ὑμᾶς ἀπὸ τῆς πορνείας—" that ye abstain from fornication." The infinitive is explanatory of the more general ἁγιασμός. Winer, § 44, 1. Your sanctification is God's will; and His will for you under this aspect, and in your present position in Thessalonica, is that you abstain from fornication, which the heathen around you scarcely reckon a sin, and to which previous habits, beliefs, and surrounding temptations may be ever tempting you. The preposition ἀπὸ is repeated after the compound verb with which it is incorporated, as in v. 22, though it is sometimes omitted, as in 1 Tim. iv, 3. In Acts xv, 20 the preposition is inserted, and in v, 29 it is omitted, with the same construction and references. There is therefore no substantial difference of meaning, though with ἀπὸ, according to Tittmann (*De Synon.*, I, p. 225), the separation looks more *ad rem*. Πορνεία may be taken in a wide sense; and, indeed, some manuscripts and fathers read πάσης τῆς. The Syriac and some of the fathers give πάσης for the article. In every sense and aspect the sin referred to is to be abstained from, and all the more as it was reckoned among things indifferent, and was commonly practised (Terence, *Adelphi*, i, 2, 21). In Horace, *Sat.*, I, 2, 33, occurs a *sententia dia Catonis* in praise of πορνεία. Cicero says of any one who speaks as the apostle has done here, *est ille quidem valde severus;* and that the sin is not only not abhorrent *ab hujus seculi licentia, verum etiam a majorum consuetudine, atque concessis—quando enim hoc non factum est? quando reprehensum? quando non permissum?* (*Orat. pro M. Caelio*, 48, p. 285, vol. II, pars ii, *Opera*, ed. Orellius.) Consult Grotius on Acts xv, 20; Becker's *Charicles*, p. 241.

(Ver. 4.) εἰδέναι ἕκαστον ὑμῶν τὸ ἑαυτοῦ σκεῦος κτᾶσθαι ἐν ἁγιασμῷ καὶ τιμῇ—"that every one of you know how to get himself his own vessel in sanctification and honour"—another explanatory infinitival clause, without the article, and parallel to ἀπέχεσθαι (Philip. iv, 12). There has been no little debate on the meaning of σκεῦος. One may dismiss at once the more special meanings assigned to it, as *membrum virile*—the view of Er. Schmidt and others, mentioned in Wolf. The word, certainly, has such a sense in Ælian (*Hist. Animal.* xvii, 11, p. 379, vol. I, ed. Jacobs), but not in the New Testament. A great many expositors give σκεῦος the sense of body—one's own body, and as many take it in the sense of wife—one's own wife. Thus Theodoret says, τινὲς τὸ ἑαυτοῦ σκεῦος τὴν ὁμόζυγα ἡρμήνευσαν, ἐγὼ δὲ νομίζω τὸ ἑκάστου σῶμα οὕτως αὐτὸν κεκληκέναι. Theodoret had been preceded in his view by Chrysostom, and it is held by Œcumenius, Theophylact, Tertullian, Ambrosiaster, Pelagius, Calvin, Musculus, Zanchius, Hunnius, Drusius, Piscator, a-Lapide, Beza, Grotius, Hammond, Turretin, Bengel, Flatt, Schrader, Pelt, Olshausen, Baumgarten-Crusius, Macknight, and Wordsworth. Primasius explains *suum corpus castum servando sanctificet et honoret, vel certe tantum propter filios uxorem cognoscat.* But there are several objections to this view. (1) It is questioned if σκεῦος, of or by itself, can ever mean the body. It is, indeed, employed in this sense, but usually the metaphor has some distinct adjunct, or is explained in being used. Thus in 2 Cor. iv, 7, the epithet ὀστρακίνοις is added—the body being called an "earthen vessel." So in the other passages commonly quoted as τὸ σκεῦος τοῦ πνεύματος (Barnabas, Ep., vii, 4; xi, 16; xxi, p. 13, 24, 42, ed. Hefele); ἀγγεῖον is used of the body in its instrumental connection with the soul in Philo (*De Migratione Abraham*, p. 418, &c.). See Loesner. Cicero says too, "*corpus quidem quasi vas est aut aliquod animi receptaculum*" (*Tuscul. Disput.*, i, 22); *corpus, quod vas quasi constitit ejus* (Lucretius, iii, 441). But in these cases the figurative meaning is brought out by an epithet, or by the contextual phraseology. Nor can any proof be taken from the uses of the Hebrew כְּלִי, which has so many various significations, and which does not simply signify body, even in the phrase "the vessels of the young men are holy" (1. Sam. xxi, 5). The tropical uses of σκεῦος in Acts ix, 15; Rom. ix, 22, 23; 2 Tim. ii, 21, have no relation to the clause before us. It cannot be proved, then, that σκεῦος ever means by itself the body, and the instances adduced by Vorstius are not to the point (*De Hebr. N. Test.*, pp. 24, 25, 1705). (2) Nor can τὸ ἑαυτοῦ σκεῦος κτᾶσθαι mean to possess his own body, for κτᾶσθαι means to acquire, not to possess. That each one of you should acquire his own body, yields no tolerable meaning. Some of the Greek fathers, however, attempt to evade this by the paraphrase, ἡμεῖς αὐτὸ κτώμεθα ὅταν μένῃ καθαρόν, "we acquire it when it remains pure" (Chrysostom). "Sin takes possession" (κτᾶται), Theophylact says, "of the body when it is tainted by sin, but when it is purified we make it our own" (ἡμεῖς αὐτὸ κτώμεθα). But this is only repeating the verb without explaining it, and this verbal sense is rendered impossible by the negative clause μὴ ἐν πάθει, which implies another party or person. The same objection applies to the "sole admissible" explanation of Olshausen, who makes the verb signify dominion over the body—"to guide and master his body as a true instrument of the soul." Wordsworth also eludes the lexical difficulty, by rendering the verb to acquire and hold, quoting the Pharisee's boast (Luke xviii, 12), "I give tithes," πάντα ὅσα κτῶμαι, but the verb has in the quotation its proper meaning, "I get" or "acquire," *i.e.,* "of all my increase." So Matt. x, 9, where the verb is vaguely rendered "provide," but wrongly "possess" in Luke xxi, 19; "purchased," in Acts i, 18; viii, 20; in the last instances the version is coloured by the context; the word is rightly rendered "obtained" in Acts xxii, 28. (3) Nor can ἑαυτοῦ fit into that interpretation, as from its position the stress is on it. It cannot stand as the equivalent of a mere possessive pronoun; nor can it in any way denote the individuality, *die Ichheit,* by which the ψυχή is distinguished from the σκεῦος. It simply denotes his own in special possession. Neither noun, verb, nor pronoun can thus sustain the interpretation which we have been considering. Σκεῦος does not, without any adjunct or defining genitive, signify body; nor does κτάομαι denote to possess; nor does ἑαυτοῦ mark any distinction. The other interpretation gives σκεῦος the meaning of wife, a meaning which the substantive may have, while the true sense of the verb and pronoun is also preserved. Theodore of Mopsuestia has given this sense, σκεῦος τὴν ἰδίαν ἑκάστου γαμετὴν ὀνομάζει (*Opera*, p. 145, ed. Fritzsche). Augustine explains the noun by *uxor* (*Serm.* 278, *Opera,* vol. V, p. 1654, Gaume); and again, *qui suum vas possidet, id est, conjugem suam* (*Opera,* vol. X, p. 613; *Cont. Julian.,* xxxix, p. 1125, Gaume). And in favour of this view it may be noted that (*a*) The noun, as in Hebrew usage, may mean a wife. Thus the examples from Schöttgen: *In convivio illius impii regis Ahasuerus aliqui dicebant; Mulieres Medicae sunt pulchriores: alii vero; Persicae sunt pulchriores. Dixit ad eos Ahasuerus; vas meum, quo ego utor* בו משחמש שנאי כלי, *neque Medicum, neque Persicum est, sed Chaldaicum. An vultis illam videre? Illi responderunt: Volumus. Quicunque enim semen suum immittit* כשרא דלא במאא, *in vas non bonum ille semen suum deturpat* (*Horae Hebr.,* p. 827). Compare I, p. iii, 7. (2) The verb κτᾶσθαι is often used in this connection—κτᾶσθαι γυναῖκα. Thus ὁ κτώμενος γυναῖκα ἐνάρχεται κτήσεως (Ecclus. xxxvi, 29); τὴν γυναῖκα Μααλὼν κέκτημαι ἐμαυτῷ (Ruth iv, 10); ταύτην κέκτημαι, Socrates speaking of Xantippe (Xenoph., *Symp.,* ii, 10, p. 9, ed. Bornemann). (3) The pronoun ἑαυτοῦ preserves its proper significance and emphasis—his own —her who specially is his own, as his wife. (4) The context points very distinctly in this direction. There is the decided prohibition or negative aspect, to abstain from fornication, and there is now the positive and permitted aspect—the divinely appointed remedy against that sin. Comp. 1 Cor. vii, 1, 2. See Ellicott. This view has been maintained by Thomas Aquinas, Zwingli, Estius, Balduin, Wetstein, Schöttgen, Koppe, Schott, De Wette, Koch, Bisping, Ewald, Hofmann, Riggenbach, Lünemann, &c. De Wette would take the tropical σκεῦος more directly, and understands it *vom Werkzeuge zur Befriedigung des Geschlechtstriebes*, an interpretation which would include both sexes, as the woman has power over the man (1 Cor. vii, 4). Besides, in warning against πορνεία, the man is usually addressed, but the woman is implied; and so here the counsel to the husband is *mutatis mutandis* for the wife (1 Cor. vi, 15-18). This virtual comprehension of both sexes gets rid of the objection of Calvin and Olshausen to the view which we adopt, to wit, that the exhortation to purity would not apply to unmarried men or widowers, and not at all to women (1 Cor. vii, 2-9). The last phrase, ἐν ἁγιασμῷ καὶ τιμῇ, "in sanctification and honour," is connected with κτᾶσθαι as its sphere or ethical element, the active sense of the first noun being so far shaded by its connection with the abstract τιμῇ. The Thessalonian believers were to abstain from all forms of illicit sexual intercourse, and were in one way to preserve themselves from it, by each not simply getting a wife, but getting to himself his own wife according to God's ordinance in purity and honour (Heb. xiii, 4; Gen. i, 28; ii, 24). The objection to this view that it degrades woman under the appellation of σκεῦος is met by quoting the words of Peter, ὡς ἀσθενεστέρῳ σκεύει τῷ γυναικείῳ (1 Peter iii, 7), and bearing in mind that it is only in one special aspect of relation that the epithet is given.

(Ver. 5.) μὴ ἐν πάθει ἐπιθυμίας—"not in lustfulness of desire." The second noun ἐπιθυμία is the general term, and is sometimes used in a good sense in the New Testament and Septuagint, but it has often epithets and genitives attached to it which show its evil nature. See under Col. iii, 5 and Gal. v, 24. It is rather the πάθος than the ἐπιθυμία which is here condemned. The word occurs twice besides in the New Testament (Col. iii, 5; Rom. i, 26). Cicero says, "*quae Graeci πάθη vocant, nobis perturbationes appellari magis placet quam morbos*" (*Tusc.*

Disput., iv, 5). It is according to Zeno ἡ ἄλογος καὶ παρὰ φύσιν ψυχῆς κίνησις, ἢ ὁρμὴ πλεονάζουσα. Diogenes Laertius, *Zeno*, 63, p. 160, vol. II, *Opera*, ed. Huebner). Πάθος is ever wrong and sinful passion, and when ἐπιθυμία is mastered by it, when mere sensual gratification is the one pervading accompaniment, then the prohibition of the apostle is set at nought, and marriage in motive and sphere is brought down to the level of πορνεία, for it is contracted διὰ τὴν μίξιν μόνην ἁπλῶς (Theodor. Mops., p. 145, ed. Fritzsche).

καθάπερ καὶ τὰ ἔθνη τὰ μὴ εἰδότα τὸν Θεόν—" even as the Gentiles also that know not God." The particle καὶ, omitted in the Authorized Version, occurs often in such comparisons, and compares the class implied in previous words with the heathen. Klotz, *Devarius*, II, 635; Hartung, I, 126. Compare ii, 13; iii, 6-12. According to Fritzsche the article is prefixed to ἔθνη, *ubi de paganis in universum loquitur* (*ad Rom.*, ii, 14). The subjective negative μὴ is employed, as the Gentile ignorance of God is asserted from the writer's own point of view, and as the preceding clauses are "oblique and infinitival." Winer, § 55, 5. Their ignorance is not regarded as a simple fact, but as a fact which forms a portion of the argument; they sink into such vices from their ignorance. Gayler, p. 275, &c. The Gentiles know not God, and what else can be expected than that they should fall into the sin denounced, and what greater inconsistency can be predicated of believers than that they are governed by these inordinate passions which characterize the Gentiles because they are ignorant of God. See under Gal. iv, 8.

(Ver. 6.) τὸ μὴ ὑπερβαίνειν καὶ πλεονεκτεῖν ἐν τῷ πράγματι τὸν ἀδελφὸν αὐτοῦ—" that no one go beyond and overreach his brother in the matter." The previous parallel infinitive— εἰδέναι—is anarthrous, but the article gives this clause a kind of substantival force, and shows that it is not co-ordinate with εἰδέναι, but with ὁ ἁγιασμὸς of verse 3; the verse being therefore really the second parallel to that clause, and τινα, suggested by the following αὐτοῦ, and not ἑκάστον, being supplied to the infinitive. The two infinitives from the structure of the clause both govern ἀδελφόν. The first verb ὑπερβαίνειν occurs only here, and literally signifies, to pass over or beyond, such as

walls or mountains (2 Sam. xxii, 30 ; Xenoph., *Anab.*, vii, 3, 43);
then with two ethical significations, to pass by, that is, to leave
unnoticed (Herod. iii, 89 ; Isæus, p. 38, 6) ; and to go beyond,
that is, to surpass (Plato, *Timæus*, 24 D). With an intransitive sense (as in *Iliad*, ix, 497; Euripides, *Alcest.*, 1077), the verb
might mean to transgress; but with an accusative, it may signify to set one at nought by trespassing on his right. The
second verb πλεονεκτεῖν, as its composition denotes, with an
accusative of person means to take advantage of any one for
the sake of gain, or more generally, to defraud (2 Cor. vii, 2 ;
xii, 17, 18); or what Meyer on the place characterizes *als Act
der eigentlichen Habsucht* is involved in the verb. Ἀδελφός
is not a neighbour (Schott, Koch), but specifically a Christian
brother. The context shows that in ἐν τῷ πράγματι there is a
definite allusion, and the phrase cannot mean "in any matter,"
as τῷ cannot be taken for τινι. Πρᾶγμα is something involved
in the previous verses, for it cannot be changed as by Wolf and
De Wette into τοῖς πράγμασι, "matters of business" (*im
Geschäfte*). The fourth and fifth verses naturally lead to a definite interpretation of this verse as following up the previous
injunctions and presenting another example of what ὁ ἁγιασμὸς
includes. Not a few interpreters take the clause in a general
sense as a prohibition of covetousness and selfish grasping,
among whom are Zwingli, Calvin, Zanchius, Hunnius, Baldwin,
Aretius, Grotius, Koppe, Flatt, De Wette, Koch, Bouman,
Bisping, Ewald, Hofmann, Riggenbach, Lünemann, &c.
On the other hand that it is a definite warning against impurity
or breach of marriage law is held by the Greek fathers, by
Jerome, Zegerus, a-Lapide, Estius, Wetstein, Kypke, Michaelis,
Bengel, Baumgarten, Pelt, Schott, Olshausen, Ellicott, Alford,
Jowett. This is the true interpretation. (1) Because the
reason why ὑπερβαίνειν is disallowed is that God called
us—not ἐπὶ ἀκαθαρσίᾳ, which is in verse 7 put in contrast with ἁγιασμῷ. The meaning of the term in such a
connection cannot well be doubted. (2) The structure of the
paragraph points to this interpretation. First, πορνεία is forbidden, and then, secondly, its special remedy is pointed out,
with appended directions for the spirit and manner in which
a wife should be taken, and then, thirdly, and naturally, warn-

ing against any violation of marriage law is delivered, and followed up by the awful menace of divine indignation. (3) Τῷ πράγματι cannot mean business generally, ἡ πραγματεία, "in chaffering" (Wycliffe), or *in emendo et vendendo* (Piscator), but "in the matter"; and that matter is τὸ ἑαυτοῦ σκεῦος κτᾶσθαι, and the verse therefore implies impurity and adultery. The phrase refers to incestuous sin in 2 Cor. vii, 11. It is not correct in translation, though it is true in result, to explain it ἐν τῇ μίξει (Theophylact), or to say with Estius, πρᾶγμα verecunde dixit Apostolus pro concubitu. (4) It is no objection to affirm that the two verbs παραβαίνειν καὶ πλεονεκτεῖν should have their simple commercial signification, for the context demands a modified ethical sense and application. One may set at nought and defraud his brother more deeply and basely in matrimonial than in mercantile life. Πλεονεκτεῖν does not indeed in itself contain the idea of unchastity, any more than the clause in the tenth commandment (Exod. xx, 17), "Thou shalt not covet thy neighbour's wife;" yet Theodoret says, πλεονεξίαν τὴν μοιχείαν ἐκάλεσε, which only gives the desire a different object from money. Πορνεία and πλεονεξία occur together in Rom. i, 29; 1 Cor. v, 10; vi, 9, 10; Ephes. v, 3, 5; Col. iii, 5. Compare Wisdom xiv, 12, 26. The apostle's residence in Corinth at the moment may have laid upon him the necessity of the injunction. Compare 1 Cor. v, 9; vi, 9-10; 2 Cor. xii, 21. Of such impurities Burns has said—

"They harden a' within."

(5) Nor does the occurrence of the phrase περὶ πάντων τούτων, adduced by Koch, Lünemann, and De Wette, present any real objection, as if it implied that more sins than one are reprimanded, whereas in our exegesis only one is thought of. But both πορνεία and μοιχεία are included; and, as Alford observes, it is not ταῦτα πάντα which the apostle uses, and the phrase only generalizes from the sin mentioned to a wider range. (6) One might perhaps hint, too, that in cases of grasping and over-reaching, human law sternly interferes; but in the cases specified, law was in those days inoperative, and God Himself, as we are told, assumes the vindication. Chrysos-

tom thus illustrates—"He has well said τὸ μὴ ὑπερβαίνειν. For to each man God has assigned a wife, and has set bounds to nature, that there may be intercourse with one only; therefore, intercourse with another is transgression and robbery, and the taking of more than belongs to one—πλεονεξία—or rather it is more cruel than any robbery, for we grieve not so much when our wealth is carried off, as when marriage is invaded. Dost thou call him thy brother and defraudest him, and that in things which are forbidden? Here he speaks concerning adultery, but above also concerning all fornication." The earnest and plain-speaking peroration of the Golden-mouth which follows, discloses a sad state of society, and the strong terms are, alas, not inapplicable to the present day. The difficulty of the interpretation has arisen from the fact that on this subject the apostle, as Joannes Damascenus says, εὐφήμως δὲ σφόδρα καὶ ἐπικεκαλυμμένως τὴν μοιχείαν ὠνόμασε. The injunctions are enforced by the solemn thought—

διότι ἔκδικος Κύριος περὶ πάντων τούτων—" because that the Lord is the avenger concerning all these things." Ἔκδικος, used only here and in Rom. xiii, 4, has passed away from its original meaning of "without law," to signify one who maintains law, one who avenges (Wisdom xii, 12; Ecclus. xxx, 6). The verb ἐκδικέω may be followed by a simple accusative, or by τινα, to avenge one upon another—by τινὰ ἀπό τινος, or by τινι, to make retribution to him, or by περί with a noun as here, ἐκδικήσω περὶ τοῦ ἔθνους μου (1 Macc. xiii, 6). Suicer *sub voce*. The last words—" all those things"—τούτων not being masculine, as the Authorized Version supposes, but not the earlier English ones—have a wide range of reference to all the sins warned against in the previous verses. The caution against these sins has a similar basis or initiatory enforcement in Gal. v, 21; Ephes. v, 5, 6; Col. iii, 6. Lünemann adduces from Homer's *Batrachom.*, the phrase ἔχει θεὸς ἔκδικον ὄμμα.

καθὼς καὶ προείπαμεν ὑμῖν καὶ διεμαρτυράμεθα—" as also we told you before, and did solemnly testify." The spelling προειπόμεν is found in A K L and some of the fathers, the other spelling in B D F ℵ. The comparative καί is connected with καθώς as in verse 5—see under it. Πρό means before the avenging takes place, and the reference is to the apostle's words, spoken when he was among them. See under Gal. v, 21. The last compound verb witnesses to his thorough and continuous testifying on such points, so essential to Christian life and progress.

(Ver. 7). Οὐ γὰρ ἐκάλεσεν ἡμᾶς ὁ Θεὸς ἐπὶ ἀκαθαρσίᾳ, ἀλλ' ἐν ἁγιασμῷ—"for God called us not for uncleanness, but in sanctification." By γὰρ the reason is assigned for the statement just made, that the Lord is avenger of all such things. For the act ascribed to God in calling, see under Gal. i, 6, and compare ii, 12. Ἐπί denotes purpose, as in Gal. v, 13; Ephes. ii, 10 (Winer, § 48, c; Krüger, § 68, 41), and ἐν marks the spiritual element in which they were called. Nor is there any breviloquence—*um zu sein in, ut essemus*. Ἐπί, *finem*, ἐν, *indolem rei magis exprimit* (Bengel). Ἀκαθαρσία is the sexual impurity pointed out and condemned, and ἁγιασμός with its active sense is not only the opposite (iii, 13), but embraces all that growth in spiritual purity, which prepares believers for that kingdom to which God has called them.

(Ver. 8.) τοιγαροῦν ὁ ἀθετῶν οὐκ ἄνθρωπον ἀθετεῖ, ἀλλὰ τὸν Θεόν—"wherefore, then, the despiser despises not man but God." The first compound particle syllogistically introduces a strong influence, knitting together as premises what has been already stated from verse 3, and basing a solemn conclusion upon it (Heb. xii, 1; Xenoph., *Anab.*, I, 9, 18; Klotz, *Devar.*, vol. II, p. 738; Hoogeveen, p. 502). Ὁ ἀθετῶν loses the idea of time, and becomes a virtual substantive (Gal. i, 23; Winer, § 45, 7). The verb ἀθετῶ, first found in Polybius, has sometimes the strong sense of to cast aside, or violate, to annul, or make void (Mark vii, 9; and see under Gal. ii, 21), but it often denotes to despise or reject (Mark vi, 26; Luke vii, 30; x, 16—four times). There is no expressed object to the participle, and it is all the more significant without it. It is needless and enfeebling, therefore, to propose any supplement. The apostle fixes attention on the act and the actor—the despised and the despiser. Various supplements have been proposed—*istam legem* (Koppe, Schott), τὴν κλῆσιν (Pelt), ἐμὲ (Flatt), *hæc* (Vulgate and Beza). The real objective is of course the precepts already given—not repeated, particularized, or summed up, but so present to the mind of the reader that he can be at no loss about them, while the emphasis is put on the person and on the act which is shown to involve a heinous sin and an awful peril. The phrase οὐκ ἄνθρωπον ἀλλὰ τὸν Θεόν presents a direct and absolute antithesis, and is not to be softened into "not so much man as God" (Estius), or "not only man but also God" (Macknight, Flatt). Winer, § 55, 8. As ἄνθρωπος has no article, the meaning is general and may include as well the apostle himself, who has given the solemn charge (Pelagius, Beza, Schott), and the brother τὸν πλεονεκτηθέντα (Œcumenius, Pelt). Hofmann takes the reference to be, the misused woman. The article before Θεόν may not be translated, but it has a specializing power—almost as Ellicott says, *ipsum Deum*. Whatever may be the reference in ἄνθρωπος, the apostle fixes down the sin as one against God, who has forbidden sexual impurities, and who has ordained the marriage relation, so that whoever lawlessly indulges in the one, or wilfully invades the other, throws off the authority of GOD—of God—

τὸν καὶ δόντα τὸ Πνεῦμα αὐτοῦ τὸ ἅγιον εἰς ὑμᾶς—" who also gave his holy Spirit unto you." There are several various readings. A B D³, the Claromontane Latin, the Peshito, and the Gothic version, with several of the Greek Fathers, omit καί; but it is found in D¹ F G K L ℵ, the Philoxenian Syriac, the Vulgate, and others of the fathers, and may therefore be retained, though Lachmann omits it and Alford brackets it. The similar appearance of τὸν to δόντα may have led some copyist to omit it, and its insertion could not well be accounted for. Then B D F ℵ¹ read διδόντα, but δόντα is read in A K L ℵ³, most mss., very many versions, and some fathers. It is difficult to decide, only διδόντα may be a correction in order to represent the gift as a present one. The Received Text has ἡμᾶς, but on the slender authority of A, some mss., the Vulgate, &c.; but ὑμᾶς is found in B D F K L ℵ and not a few of the fathers. The change to ἡμᾶς may have been made under the impression that ἄνθρωπον meant the apostle, while this clause, taken to assert his inspiration, thus aggravates the sin of despising him. The καί introduces a new idea—God who called us in sanctification and also, that we might fully reach it, gave unto us His Holy Spirit. Bengel well says *novum hic additur momentum*. The sin is shown in its heinousness as the despisal of God, who to enable us to reach this ἁγιασμός in which he called us, has in addition conferred upon us His Holy Spirit. He then who indulges in the sins forbidden and falls into ἀκαθαρσία—as he frustrates the end of the divine call, and has nothing of its spiritual element—despises not man but God, who to elevate men above that impurity and to provide for their sanctification, gave them the Holy Spirit to do His work in securing the final perfection of His people. This divine gift is named solemnly and emphatically τὸ Πνεῦμα τὸ ἅγιον, the third person of the Ever-blessed Trinity; τὸ Πνεῦμα, the life of believers; τὸ ἅγιον, not only in essence but because His gracious function is to implant and sustain holiness—αὐτοῦ, His, proceeding from Him, carrying out His blessed purpose in those who believe. And He is a gift (δόντα) conferred on true believers, as really as the Son is a gift, for we are utterly unworthy; and a gift through Christ applying what He has provided in His incarnation and death. See under Ephes. i, 13. The concluding words εἰς ὑμᾶς are not equivalent to ὑμῖν (Koppe, Pelt), but *in vos*, the idea of direction being implied, not of *Räumlichkeit* (Lünemann). ii, 9; Gal. iv, 6. In this paragraph we have the Lord Jesus, God who calls, and the Spirit who is given—Father, Son, and Holy Ghost—a triune interest in those who have accepted salvation. Compare Luke xi, 13; John iii, 34; Acts v, 32; viii, 18; xv, 8; Rom. v, 5; 2 Cor. i, 22.

(Ver. 9.) Περὶ δὲ τῆς φιλαδελφίας οὐ χρείαν ἔχετε γράφειν ὑμῖν—"Now concerning brother-love ye have no need that I write to you." By δὲ the apostle passes to other topics somewhat in contrast to the previous statement about certain sins— to the inculcation of brotherly love and of honest industry in their secular calling. The φιλαδελφία is the love of a brother, that is, a fellow-believer or Christian brother. The last part of the compound word is the object of the love and does not characterize its name—brotherly, not because I feel that I am his brother, but because I know that he is my brother— φιλαργυρία, φιλανθρωπία, φιλανδρία.

The next clause creates some difficulties. The ordinary construction is according to Lünemann inadmissible, because this use of the active infinitive is confined to cases in which no special personal reference is attached to the verb; but here ὑμῖν belongs to γράφειν, and he affirms that either ἐμέ would be used, or the passive γράφεσθαι as in verse 1. Bouman and Reiche have no objections to ἡμᾶς or τινα (Heb. v, 11). It is true that the instances usually adduced as analogous are not strictly so, as from Soph., *Œdip. Col.*, 37, ἔχεις γὰρ χῶρον οὐχ ἁγνὸν πατεῖν, or from Thucydides, i, 38, ἦν . . . . ὁ Θεμιστοκλῆς . . . ἄξιος θαυμάσαι, or Euripid., *Med.*, 318, as in these cases there is no personal word connected like ὑμῖν with the verbs. Lünemann therefore adopts the reading ἔχομεν which is found in D¹ F ℵ⁴ (B having εἴχομεν), in the Latin and Philoxenian Syriac versions, and in Chrysostom, Theophylact, and some of the later fathers. But the common reading has good authority, A D³ K L ℵ¹, the Peshito, Theodoret, Damascenus, &c. It is probable that ἔχομεν came in on account of the grammatical difficulty in the same way as many codices have γράφεσθαι as in chap. v, 1. The construction is harsh and irregular, perhaps a colloquialism, the infinitive having virtually a passive sense—ye have no need that one should write to you, or ye have no need of one's writing to you. Winer, § 44, 8, 1; Kühner, § 640, *a*, 3; A. Buttmann, p. 223. The first clause οὐ χρείαν ἔχετε is a rhetorical touch, delicately hinting a gentle reproof, κατὰ παράλειψιν δὲ τὴν παραίνεσιν τίθησι (Theophylact). Compare 2 Cor. ix, 1; Phile. 19; chap. v. 1. The figure *prae-teritio*, assumed by some here, implies that something is omitted that might have been said in order to induce a more ready compliance—or as Chrysostom says, Νῦν δὲ τῷ εἰπεῖν, οὐ χρεία ἐστι μεῖζον ἐποίησεν ἢ εἰ εἶπεν. They did not need to be written to on brother-love, for they knew its nature and obligation (verse 10); but their practice was not quite so full as their knowledge. Compare the spirit and wording of the first verse of the chapter. There is no contrast like that assumed by Estius and Benson; they needed specially to be taught purest chastity as in the previous verses, but there was less occasion to say much about what follows—

αὐτοὶ γὰρ ὑμεῖς θεοδίδακτοί ἐστε εἰς τὸ ἀγαπᾶν ἀλλήλους—"for you yourselves are taught of God to love another." Γάρ gives the reason why there was no need for him to write to them, for they themselves are taught, and that by God — the stress lying on αὐτοὶ ὑμεῖς, coupled with δίδακτοι. They who were taught had no need of further teaching; but θεο in the compound term, which has been coined for the occasion, cannot be so subordinate as Ellicott seems to regard it. The contrast is not indeed—when God teaches, the apostle may be silent—*wo Gott lehrt, kann ich schweigen* (Olshausen); but the fact that the teaching is of God, a fact too which is expressed by a significant compound employed only here, surely gives emphasis to the entire clause, is a weighty addition to the statement—not only taught, but taught of God—though there is no formal contrast to any other teaching, παρὰ ἀνθρώπου μαθεῖν (Chrysostom). In αὐτοί does not lie the idea of *vos ipsi* or of *sponte* (Schott) which is contradicted by θεοδίδακτοι (John vi, 45 ; Isaiah liv, 13; Barnabas, *Epist.*, § 21, p. 44, *Patr. Apost., Opera*, ed. Dressel; Schöttgen, *Hor. Heb.*, p. 829). The allusion is not to the precept as uttered by Jesus in John xiii, 34 (Pelagius, Schott, Baumgarten-Crusius), nor to the divine compassion manifested towards us, and of which we should be imitators (Ambrosiaster, Pelt). The last clause with εἰς τὸ ἀγαπᾶν expresses under the purpose the contents also of the teaching (iii, 10). The compound verbal noun is not to be taken absolutely in the sense of θεόπνευστοι, and this clause regarded as describing the result. This mutual love, the tendency and purpose of the divine teaching, was an earnest actual affection, manifesting itself in such forms and spheres as the state and wants of the churches around them opened up for them. *Docti estis non modo intellectu, ut sciatis, sed etiam affectu, ut faciatis* (Estius). To be God-taught is to have divine teaching as a divine power and life. Brother-love has a special prominence, (1) for it is a testing fruit of regeneration (1 John iii, 14 ; iv, 8); (2) its visible existence is a condition of the world's conversion (John xvii, 21); (3) a token also of true discipleship (John xiii, 35); (4) while it is obedience to Christ's new commandment, and enforced by his own example (John xiii, 34 ; xv, 17 ; Eph. v, 2); and is essential to the spiritual growth of the church (Ephes. iv, 16).

(Ver. 10.) καὶ γὰρ ποιεῖτε αὐτό εἰς πάντας τοὺς ἀδελφοὺς ἐν ὅλῃ τῇ Μακεδονίᾳ—" for ye also are doing it toward all the brethren which are in Macedonia." The second τούς is omitted in A D¹ F, but retained on preponderant authority. Our version renders wrongly "and indeed," for γὰρ introduces one ground of the previous statement "ye are taught of God," and that ground is, not only were they taught it, but they were also doing it, καὶ being thus taken along with the verb. Hartung, vol. I., p. 137. De Wette takes this γὰρ as co-ordinate with the previous one, and as furnishing an additional argument that on the duty of brother-love they needed no one to write to them. But the γὰρ of this verse is best taken with the immediately preceding clause introduced by the first γὰρ. He needed not to write to them (γὰρ) for they had been taught of God. By αὐτὸ is meant τὸ ἀγαπᾶν ἀλλήλους, and εἰς marks the direction of the love toward all the fellow-believers, not only in their own city, but also in the whole province, including Philippi and Beroea, along with other places to which the gospel had been carried. It is added—

παρακαλοῦμεν δὲ ὑμᾶς, ἀδελφοί, περισσεύειν μᾶλλον—" But we exhort you, brethren, to abound still more." The apostle inculcates an increase of this love which, according to the previous verse, they already possessed, δέ implying a slight contrast between the fact and the exhortation. Their love was not perfect, but was capable of increased intensity, guided by a growing Christian intelligence and experience. The infinitive present denotes the permanence of the act. Winer, § 44, 7. What the manifestations of this brother-love were we do not know, only from the use of the verb ποιεῖτε we may infer that their love had embodied itself in some acts of substantial Christian beneficence—perhaps of hospitality, liberal relief of the poor, or kind refuge afforded to such as might be the victims of persecution. Calvin finds an argument—*a majore ad minus*; if their love spread through the whole of Macedonia, he infers that it is not to be doubted that they loved one another—*quin ipsi mutuo inter se ament*. We know that afterwards the apostle bears high testimony to their grace of liberality in the Macedonian province (2 Cor. viii, 1, 2). They are warned still further—

(Ver. 11.) καὶ φιλοτιμεῖσθαι ἡσυχάζειν—" and to make it your aim to be quiet." It is unnatural in the extreme on the part of Ewald and others to connect this infinitive with the previous περισσεύειν μᾶλλον—such a connection would be without example (see Lünemann's note on Ewald), and it is as wrong too in Lünemann to assert that there is no connection whatever. The juxtaposition of the counsels will not be thought so startling, *eingedenk der raschen Uebergänge,* if we remember the apostle's rapid transitions in the practical parts of his other epistles. But there is plainly a connection with παρακαλοῦμεν; though the themes of exhortation are not very similar, yet some inner relations must have been present to the apostle's mind. Olshausen's proposed connection is artificial and incorrect. He supposes that all the exhortations are specially connected with love—first brother-love, and then love to those beyond the church—the latter being dwelt upon in this and the following verse; but surely these injunctions to quietness, industry, and seemliness, can scarcely be summed up under the head of love (Col. iv, 5, 6).

Theodoret puts the connection in another light—"The one counsel is not," he says, "contrary to the other, for it happened that some indeed supported the needy generously; but others, on account of the munificence of these persons, neglected to work—συνέβαινε γὰρ τοὺς μὲν φιλοτίμως χορηγεῖν τοῖς δεομένοις τὴν χρείαν, τοὺς δὲ διὰ τὴν τούτων φιλοτιμίαν ἀμελεῖν τῆς ἐργασίας. That is, the brother-love was abused, and the abuse was restlessness and idleness, which, as it had a bad effect on onlookers, was rebuked by the apostle, both in itself, and on account of its deleterious results. There were of the chief women not a few who believed, and they might be imposed upon by these idlers (Acts xvii, 4). This is also the view of Estius, Benson, Flatt, Koch, De Wette, Alford, and Ellicott, and it is at least probable, when other elements are taken into account. One objection of Lünemann, that in such a case two distinct parties must be addressed by the apostle, whereas there is no trace of such division in the paragraph, is of no great moment, for often the apostle puts into general terms as if speaking to the whole church what is really applicable to one section of it. His other objection, that in this case the stress would only fall on ἐργάζεσθαι ταῖς χερσὶν ὑμῶν is denied, for the opposite of ἡσυχάζειν and πράσσειν τὰ ἴδια is as plainly condemned as idleness and is the parent of it. It is probable that mistaken notions about the immediate coming of the Saviour may have unsettled many minds and led them to live in this indolent dependence on their richer brethren, in the expectation of a new state of society, all old things having passed away. At all events the phrase "that ye may have need of nothing" or "of no man" implies that they had been dependent on some around them, and that dependence arising from their own indolence, they could surmount it by steady honest industry. Some such law of association must have suggested the connection of these precepts to the apostle's mind. Some take the first infinitive φιλοτιμεῖσθαι by itself as an independent infinitive, as in the alternative explanation of Theophylact, Calvin, and Hemming. Calvin says, that he recommends a sacred emulation, that they may strive among themselves in mutual emulation, or at least he enjoins that each one should strive to conquer himself, adding *atque hoc posterius magis amplector*. But the connection and meaning are alike unsatisfactory, especially as καὶ stands before the second verb. The verb literally means, to make it a point of honour, to be fired with ambition, to strive eagerly after or to endeavour earnestly after (Rost and Palm, *sub voce*). The word occurs in Rom. xv, 20, rendered "have I strived," that is, rather making it a point of honour not to build on any other man's foundation. In 2 Cor. v, 9, it is translated "we labour," rather too neutral a rendering. Though the idea of τιμή never wholly fades away in the verb, it can scarcely bear Koppe's translation, *honorem et laudem vestram in eo ponite ut vitam agatis tranquillam et laboriosam*. Examples may be seen in Wetstein on Rom. xv, 20, and Kypke, vol II, p. 189. Nor is Wetstein's explanation more satisfactory—*eleganter dictum: Ambite et expetite non honores et magistratus quod plerique solent*. The connected infinitive ἡσυχάζειν has its opposite in the περιεργάζεσθαι of 2 Thes. iii, 11, and in the πολυπραγμοσύνη which was a marked element of Athenian character (Plato, *Gorg.*, 526 c). The unrest or uneasiness here referred to cannot be political, as Zwingli, perhaps naturally from his own circumstances, supposes, nor can there be any allusions to seditious tumults (Koppe and Schott). Bengel's pithy clause is φιλοτιμία *politica erubescit* ἡσυχάζειν. Their unsettledness of spirits was probably produced by their erroneous belief as to the speedy advent of the Saviour. The present state seems to have been contemned and its obligations set at nought, through that feverish enthusiasm which their false expectations had excited within them. They were also in deep uneasiness about the share which departed friends and relatives would have in the blessing and glory of the second advent. They are therefore charged to study sedateness and composure.

καὶ πράσσειν τὰ ἴδια—"and to do your own business." According to Phrynichus the usage of οἱ παλαιοὶ as opposed to οἱ πολλοὶ was τὰ ἐμαυτοῦ πράττω or τὰ ἴδια ἐμαυτοῦ πράττω (Phrynichus, ed. Lobeck. p. 441). They were to mind their own affairs, engaging in that business which devolved upon them as theirs, the life that now is having its own claims as well as the life to come. Still farther and more specifically—

καὶ ἐργάζεσθαι ταῖς χερσὶν ὑμῶν καθὼς ὑμῖν παρηγγείλαμεν—"and to work with your hands as we enjoined you." The ἰδίαις of the Received Text, though it is found in A D³ K L א¹ and many mss., is probably a correction to suit the previous τὰ ἴδια, and is omitted in B D¹ F א³, and probably all the versions and the Latin fathers, the Greek fathers being divided. The infinitives are all in the present, denoting continuous action. According to Pelt, Schott, and Hofmann, the phrase means *quævis industria*, any kind of industry; but the words are to be taken in their plain literal significance, and no doubt the majority of the Thessalonian Church belonged to the working classes. They were not to cease manual labour, and by their idleness mulct the generosity of others; but they were to be as assiduous at their daily toil as they may have been before the Gospel came to the city. At his visit to Thessalonica the apostle had noticed the germs of the same evil, and warned against them, καθὼς ὑμῖν παρηγγείλαμεν, "as we commanded you." The reference is to the period of his personal labours among them. Their minds were getting unhinged by the novel and momentous truths laid open to them, of some of which they were forming a wrong conception. The clause underlies all these previous charges. The forewarning was suggested by tendencies which began to crop out during his sojourn. Minds intoxicated by new expectations, became unsettled and speculative, industry was forsaken or despised, and habits of gadding about in listless laboriousness began to show themselves. The purpose of all this instruction being—

(Ver. 12.) ἵνα περιπατῆτε εὐσχημόνως πρὸς τοὺς ἔξω—" in order that ye may walk becomingly toward them that are without." The verb is often used for the general tenor of one's life. See under verse 1. The adverb εὐσχημόνως is "honourably," or "in a becoming manner," " decently," according to the original meaning of the term (Rom. xiii, 13 ; 1 Cor. vii, 35 ; xiv, 40), the " honestly " of the English version having now changed its meaning. The opposite seems to be ἀτάκτους, verse 14, and ἀτάκτως in 2 Thes. iii, 6. The want of seemliness here referred to is plainly what is characterized in these clauses that enjoin them to study quietness and do their own business. As Theophylact says, ἐντρέπει τὰ σωματικὰ ἔργα ἀναιροῦντας καὶ μόνον τὸ πνευματικὸν ζητοῦντας, or, as Œcumenius briefly puts it, μὴ ἀσχημονῆτε ἐπαιτοῦντες. Πρός signifies direction in reference to or towards, not *coram* (Schott, Koch). Those without οἱ ἔξω are those without the Christian community—the non-Christian population around them (1 Cor. v, 12, 13 ; Col. iv, 5); and in 1 Tim. iii, 7, the phrase is οἱ ἔξωθεν. The term had been used among Rabbinical writers, הַחִיצוֹנִים (Schöttgen's *Hor. Heb.*, p. 560-599). The want of this decent behaviour towards unbelievers induced disparaging views of the gospel, created prejudice against it, and hindered its reception. Not only is our relation towards those within to be consulted, but our relation toward those without is also to be studied, lest by any inconsistency they should be repelled.

καὶ μηδενὸς χρείαν ἔχητε—"and that ye have need of no one" or of " nothing." This clause is connected with the previous charge to work with their hands, for they would thus earn the supply of their wants, and stand in need of assistance from nobody. The Authorized Version reads in its text "of nothing," but in the margin " of no man." The neuter is adopted by many. Lünemann's argument, repeated by Alford, goes for little, " to stand in need of no man is for man an impossibility," for it may as truly be said in reply, " to stand in need of nothing is equally for man an impossibility." A general saying is rightly limited by its context. The dependency of those that do not work on their fellow-men is the underlying thought, and therefore μηδενός is better taken in the masculine as by many commentators, and the Syriac reads ܐܢܫ ܡܢ, the allusion perhaps being general, not to Christians specially or to non-Christians, though if there be specialty in the reference, dependence for support on Christian brethren may be the special idea. Chrysostom says, "he had not said that ye may not be shamed by begging, but he insinuated it; if our own people are stumbled how much more those who are without, when they see a man in good health and able to support himself begging and asking help of others"; "wherefore," he adds, "they call us χριστεμπόρους—Christmongers"; or as Theodoret, "it is disgrace to live in idleness and not acquire things necessary from labour—ἀλλὰ προσαίτου βίου αἵρεσθαι καὶ τῶν ἄλλων προσμένειν φιλοτιμίαν." This dependence of one class upon another and wealthier class might soon have introduced the unnatural distinction of patron and client into the early Christian church.

(Ver. 13.) Οὐ θέλομεν δὲ ὑμᾶς ἀγνοεῖν, ἀδελφοί, περὶ τῶν κοιμωμένων—"Now we would not have you to be ignorant, brethren, concerning them that are sleeping." The singular θέλω of the Received Text has no authority, and it also reads κεκοιμημένων in the perfect, with D F K L, the majority of the minuscules, and the Greek fathers, as Chrysostom, not only on this verse, but in many quotations in various parts of his works. The present is read in A B ℵ, in some MSS., and is found occasionally in some of the Greek writers, as in the MSS. of Origen and Chrysostom. The reading of the common text has been accepted by Tischendorf in his seventh edition, though he had given it up in his second. For the present there is uncial authority high in value (there is a hiatus in C), and the word is unusual, the past tense being with one exception invariably employed, as in the following verses, 14 and 15, and in Matt. xxvii, 52; Acts vii, 60; xiii, 36; 1 Cor. vii, 39; xv, 6 and 20; Sept., Isaiah xliii, 17. The present being the rarer form there would be some temptation to alter it into the more common one, though it may be asked, why should the apostle use the unwonted tense only in this place and, under a different aspect, in 1 Cor. xi, 30? There was no such temptation, as Reiche alleges, to change the perfect into the present, in defiance of so

many examples of aorists and perfects. In the phrase οὐ
θέλομεν, &c., the apostle as usual introduces some new and
special information (Rom. i, 13; xi, 25; 1 Cor. x, 1; xii, 1;
2 Cor. i, 8). By the transitional δὲ he passes to another but
not wholly disconnected theme. Some ignorance on the subject
which he is going to discuss had apparently a share in producing that state of feeling, that indolence and restlessness which
he has condemned in the previous verses. The knowledge
which he is about to impart is given not only as consolatory,
but as a corrective element. The apostle must have taught the
doctrine of the resurrection during his abode in Thessalonica,
but some features of it may have been misapprehended,
and the special points now to be adduced may not have
been brought into prominent illustration. These points on
which he offers enlightenment are not the general state or
destiny of the departed, but specially the connection of departed
believers with the Second Advent.

He wishes them to be enlightened περὶ τῶν κοιμωμένων, "concerning those who are sleeping." The expression is a common
and natural one. See the passages quoted on the occurrence of
the participle and also John xi, 11; 2 Peter iii, 4; ὁ ποντισθεὶς
Μυρτίλος ἐκοιμάθη (Sophocles, *Electra*, 509); πεσὼν κοιμήσατο
χάλκεον ὕπνον (Homer, *Il.*, xi, 241); ἱερὸν ὕπνον κοιμᾶται θνήσκειν
μὴ λέγε τοὺς ἀγαθούς (Callimachus, *Fragm.*, x, p. 56, *Opera*, ed.
Bloomfield). The verb often represents the Hebrew שָׁכַב in the
Septuagint (1 Kings ii, 10; xi, 43; Isaiah xliii, 17; 2 Macc. xii,
45). Compare also Job iii, 13; Psalm xiii, 3; xvii, 15. The dead
here are plainly the Christian dead, not the dead generally,
as the context so distinctly shows, especially 14 and 16.
The apostle refers to their fellow-believers in Thessalonica
who had died, and concerning whom they were in great sorrow
and perplexity. But this sorrow and perplexity did not arise
from any doubts about their ultimate resurrection. That
primary article of faith the apostle must have fully proved and
expounded to them. There seems to have been no scepticism
about the fact of a resurrection as at Corinth, and no mistake
as to the nature of it as by Hymenæus and Philetus (2 Tim.
17, 18). But the point which disturbed them was the connection of dead believers with the coming kingdom. What they

seem to have feared was that those who fell asleep before that period might by their death be excluded in some way from the glories expected at the Second Advent, deemed by not a few to be so near at hand. Not their decease in itself, but their decease in the time of it, or before that epoch, troubled the survivors. The apostle therefore shows that their death is no loss, that they forego no advantage, that they rise first, and are in no way forestalled by those who shall be alive at the Saviour's second coming. The Greek fathers fall so far aside from the context that they refer the passage to the resurrection generally. Chrysostom, however, briefly points to the proper theme. "He glances at some further mystery. What then is this? We who are alive and remain shall not prevent them that are asleep." But his peroration is direct appeal to those suffering under bereavement, pressing on them the hopes and comfort of a glorious resurrection. It is wrong then to fasten any dogma on this simple and touching figure of sleep, either with De Wette, Dähne, Weizel, and others, to infer the sleep of the soul, or with Zwingli and Calvin to find in it an argument against that theory. The term is one in popular use applying to the person what is really true only of a portion of him. In this spirit allusions to the dead occur in the Old Testament as if all that formed humanity had been committed to the tomb (Ps. vi, 5; xxx, 9; lxxxviii, 10; Is. xxxviii, 18; Eccles. ix, 4, 6, 10). Sleep implies continued existence, rest, and awakening. The sleeper does not cease to be, though he sinks into a kind of unconsciousness; he is often thoughtful and active in dreams, but in this state of insensibility he enjoys repose, and then he wakens up to fresh activity. *Dormientes eos appellat Scripturæ veracissima consuetudo, ut cum dormientes audimus, evigilaturos minime desperemus* (Augustine, *Serm.* 172). The very name, "them that are asleep," as Chrysostom says, suggests consolation, εὐθέως ἀπὸ προοιμίων τὴν παράκλησιν καταβαλλόμενος. Still there is no support in the apostle's writings for the hypothesis of soul-sleep or ψυχοπαννυχία. Compare 2 Cor. v, 1, 8; Philip. i, 21-23; Matt. xxii, 23, 33.

ἵνα μὴ λυπῆσθε καθὼς καὶ οἱ λοιποὶ οἱ μὴ ἔχοντες ἐλπίδα— "that ye sorrow not even as the rest who have no hope."

A D² F L read λυπεῖσθε, not a common construction; but our text is based on the reading of B D³ E K ℵ, and has therefore at least high probability. Ἵνα prefaces the purpose of the information to be imparted. Sorrow is forbidden, plainly, absolutely. Many suppose that a certain measure or amount of sorrow only is forbidden, or that Christian sorrow should not be so immoderate as that of the hopeless heathen. So Theodoret, οὐ παντελῶς κωλύει τὴν λύπην, ἀλλὰ τὴν ἀμετρίαν ἐκβάλλει. Calvin, too, *Non autem prorsus lugere vetat, sed moderationem requirit in luctu*: also Hemming, Zanchius, Piscator, a-Lapide, Pelt, Koch, Bisping, Hofmann, Riggenbach. But the interpretation goes beyond the apostle's word, and καθώς is a particle not of measure or degree but of comparison. Christian survivors are not to sorrow. Sorrow under bereavement belongs to those who have no hope of resurrection and life. The death of a believer only translates him from sin and struggle, from disease and death, from mixed society and imperfect work, to purity, life, unwearied activity, and joyous fellowship with Christ. The apostle says virtually, believers are not to feel as unbelievers concerning the departed—the former are not to grieve, for they have no reason to grieve; the latter cannot help it, for they have no hope—καθώς καὶ οἱ λοιποί, even as also the rest, to wit λυποῦνται. For καθώς see under Ephes. i, 4. Καὶ appears in one of the members, and has its proper signification. Hartung, vol. I, p. 126; Klotz, *Devar.*, II, p. 635. "The others" are the unbelieving heathen or perhaps Jews also, round about them, and they are characterized as a class "who have not hope," or are described as such here by the apostle. For this use of the subjective μή, see Winer, § 55, 5. The sorrow which the apostle forbids is not our grief over our loss and separation caused by death, for that is instinctive and "Jesus wept," but sorrow about the state and prospects of the departed, a sorrow which was especially felt in the Thessalonian church, and produced by the fear that those who died before the second coming of Christ would be denied participation in its blessedness and triumph. Sorrow for ourselves bereaved is different from sorrow about the dark fate of those who are gone, very different from dismay and that utter desolation of heart that fell upon the heathen when friends and relations passed away, and sank, as they thought, into unbroken darkness and non-existence (Lucian *de Luctu*, vii, 211). Why this grief should not exist, the apostle proceeds to argue, for they who sleep have not ceased to be, and they will appear with Christ.

(Ver. 14.) Εἰ γὰρ πιστεύομεν ὅτι Ἰησοῦς ἀπέθανεν καὶ ἀνέστη —"For if we believe that Jesus died and arose again." By γάρ the substantiating statement is introduced, and εἰ is, as often, syllogistic or hypothetic, introducing the premiss of a conditional syllogism, and is not to be rendered "because" or "seeing that," but "if," implying at the same time the absolute certainty of the fact which is brought forward. The apostle naturally employs Ἰησοῦς, the special human name of the Saviour, so identified with men as their head and representative, that His resurrection secures as it precedes theirs. He characterizes the death of Jesus by the common verb ἀπέθανεν. Theodoret supposes without any ground that the apostle in the phrase had his eye on Doketic views, but adds more truly that "while he calls Christ's death by the proper term, he names the death of believers a sleep"—ἐν τῷ ὀνόματι ψυχαγωγῶν, "consoling them by the very name." The death and resurrection of Christ are primary objects of belief, the one event being the complement of the other, the resurrection proving that the purpose of the death had been accomplished, that the self-oblation had been accepted, that salvation had been provided in fulness and freeness, and that mortality had been conquered. The two events are often connected in the New Testament (Rom. vi). To die and to rise again specially characterize Jesus and also his people. He died and rose again. They die, and they certainly shall rise again from their connection with Him—the organic union of the members with the Head.

οὕτως καὶ ὁ Θεὸς τοὺς κοιμηθέντας διὰ τοῦ Ἰησοῦ ἄξει σὺν αὐτῷ—"even so also those who are laid to sleep by Jesus will God bring with Him." The apodosis is defective, and it might run if written fully, καὶ πιστεύομεν ὅτι οὕτως, "we believe also that those laid to sleep by Jesus will be raised," or, καὶ πιστεύειν δεῖ ὅτι. If we believe the one proposition we must believe the other which is involved in it. But (1) Οὕτως is certainly not pleonastic, as the mere sign of the apodosis (Schott, Olshausen), but maintains its full signification, "in like manner," pointing out the similarity of our condition and destiny to that of our blessed prototype, while καί strengthens the comparison or correspondence. Klotz, *Devar.*, vol. II, p. 635, 636. There is generic sameness—death and resurrection to Him, also in like manner death and resurrection to us. But there is specific difference. The result is similar, though somewhat differently arrived at. It is not simply God shall raise us as He raised Him, but more complexly, God shall bring them with Him. (2) Nor is οὕτως to be referred only to ἀνέστη, as if the meaning were *in einem solchen Zustande d. h. auferweckt, wiederbelebt*, that is, having been raised, God will bring them with Him (Flatt). For οὕτως refers to both verbs of the preceding clause and brings them into comparison with this clause. (3) It is wrong in Koch and Hofmann to give οὕτως the meaning of "under this condition," *tum vero*, or "if we believe," *nobis credentibus*, then or in that case God will bring them with Him. The cases quoted are not in point. Our faith in the resurrection is different from the fact and power of it, and the second clause under this third view would be not a consequence deduced from, but a mere confirmation of, the previous statement. Besides it is not of the resurrection of the ἡμεῖς who are believing, but of the resurrection of deceased believers, κοιμηθέντας, that the apostle is speaking. It is true that a blessed resurrection for us is connected with our faith, but the apostle is referring to a different class—to those already dead, and to our belief and hope with regard to them.

The meaning and connection of the phrase διὰ τοῦ Ἰησοῦ have been much disputed. The preposition διά cannot signify "in," as in the Authorized Version, and in an alternative explanation of Jowett; οἱ νεκροί ἐν Χριστῷ in verse 16th is a very different phrase, and so is οἱ κοιμηθέντες ἐν Χριστῷ (1 Cor. xv, 18), and οἱ ἐν Κυρίῳ ἀποθνῄσκοντες (Rev. xiv. 13). The preposition must have its true meaning when used with the genitive, "through" or "by means of"—*per* in Vulgate and Tertullian—and does not represent, as some suppose, the Hebrew בְּ.

I. Many join the phrase with ἄξει—"will through Jesus

bring them with Him"; Pelt, Schott, Olshausen, De Wette, Lünemann, Koch, Conybeare, and many others, adopt this view. But there are objections to this exegesis. (1) The order of the words is apparently against it, as in such a case one would expect διὰ τοῦ Ἰησοῦ to be placed before κοιμηθέντας for the sake of emphasis. The present unemphatic position of the words throws them back on the participle. (2) The verb ἄξει would have two accompaniments—διά and ἐν, διὰ τοῦ Ἰησοῦ and σὺν αὐτῷ—referring to Ἰησοῦ, a connection not impossible, but very improbable. (3) The sentence with this interpretation is hard and forceless, with a virtual repetition. It is, therefore, not necessary to connect the phrase with ἄξει, which has more force when taken by itself, unencumbered with any of the previous words.

II. Many connect the phrase with the participle κοιμηθέντας. Such is one opinion of Chrysostom, Theophylact, Œcumenius; and it is held by Ambrosiaster, Calvin, Hemming, Estius, Balduin, a-Lapide, Beza, Grotius, Bengel, Koppe, Jowett, Hilgenfeld, Riggenbach, Ellicott, Alford. The aorist is used from the standpoint of the resurrection—all that have gone to sleep prior to that period. Now (1) it is not necessary to give διά the sense of ἐν, as Lünemann objects; nor is it needful to take it as referring to the condition or circumstance in or out of which anything is done, as Koch, who quotes in support Rom. iv, 11; 2 Cor. ii, 4; iii, 4; 1 John v, 6. Winer, § 47 *i*. (2) It is forced and unnatural to give the strong sense that "laid to sleep by Jesus" means, put to death by Jesus—He being the cause of their death, the reference being to the martyrs. Such is the view of Salmeron, Hammond, Joseph Mede, and Thiersch. The view is untenable. The participle is too gentle a term to express a violent death. It is used indeed of the first martyr, but it could not be employed to designate the act of his murderers; besides, the context involves no reference to persecutions or to martyrdom under them, and is not in any way intended to comfort either those who are sorrowing over martyred friends, or who may expect to be put to death for their Christianity; and, lastly, the reference of the apostle is to all the sainted dead, and not merely to a section or minority of them, such as the martyrs, or to the First Resurrection of the book of the

Revelation. (3) Nor is it necessary, in the third place, to give the phrase διὰ τοῦ Ἰησοῦ any theological meaning as Chrysostom, who explains as an alternative ἢ τοῦτο λέγων ὅτι τῇ πίστει τοῦ Ἰησοῦ κοιμηθέντας, and similarly Œcumenius and Theophylact, and the scholiast in Matthæi. Subsequently Chrysostom virtually quotes the clause, giving it this connection. Ambrosiaster writes, *per Jesum*, i.e., *sub spe fidei hujus*; and Calvin, *dormire per Christum est retinere in morte conjunctionem quam habemus cum Christo*. Webster and Wilkinson say the idea conveyed undoubtedly is, that " by Him they died in peace," " those who through Jesus entered into rest." A simpler meaning is more natural.

The phrase διὰ τοῦ Ἰησοῦ is to be taken as closely connected with κοιμηθέντας, "laid to sleep by Jesus," the stress being on διὰ, which is so often used of the mediatorial instrumentality of Christ (Rom. ii, 16; v, 1; 2 Cor. i, 5; Gal. i, 1; Ephes. i, 5; Philip. i, 11; Titus iii, 6). The words will bear this interpretation, though, as Ellicott says, the examples adduced by Alford are scarcely in analogy. (Rom. i, 8; v, 1; v, 11), since in these instances an active verb is employed. Lünemann objects that the extent of the idea expressed by κοιμηθέντας here is to be taken from the relation which the apodosis in this clause bears to the previous one. The objection is not strong, for Ἰησοῦς in the first member stands in direct contrast to κοιμηθέντας διὰ τοῦ Ἰησοῦ in the second member, the noun being repeated, and the article being inserted. Jesus dead and raised is the prime subject of the first clause as an article of belief, and those laid to sleep by Jesus and awakened are the distinctive and correspondent subject of the second clause. They are called in the opening verse of the section simply κοιμώμενοι, but now the connection of that sleep with Jesus is more specially indicated, as through Him it is a sleep, and through his victory over death those in their graves are only lying in their beds, and are laid there in the sure and certain hope of a blessed awakening. The comfort and expectation implied in the clause, and the tender and beautiful conception of death which it conveys as a time of repose with the prospect of resuscitation, are all owing to Jesus, and to Him because He died and rose again. Those who are laid so to sleep—

ὁ Θεὸς ἄξει σὺν αὐτῷ—" God will bring with Him," that is, "with Jesus," not αὐτῷ, *secum*, as some would read it. The apostle does not use ἐγερεῖ, as he wishes to say more than that He will raise them, for he associates their resurrection with the Second Advent, the point on which there had been perplexity and doubt among the Thessalonian believers. The words σὺν αὐτῷ are not for ὡς αὐτὸν (Zachariae, Koppe)—" God will raise them as He raised Him" (Turnbull), but "with Him." The pregnant clause implies that they are raised already, as told in the end of verse 16, and are then brought with Him. The verb is not used of bringing from the dead, though a compound is used of Christ (Heb. xiii, 20); yet the sense is not exactly, brought to glory in heaven, as many take it, but rather, brought in Christ's train at His appearance and coming (Schrader). The reference is not so precise as Hofmann gives it—God will not bring Jesus again into the world without His brethren who sleep coming with Him. The statement is true, but the apostle, as Lünemann observes, is not teaching about Christ's coming and its mode, but only of the departed and their coming again with Christ. The signification, therefore, is not what is often given—will bring their souls from heaven that they may be reunited to their bodies; for to their souls there is no allusion, nor could their souls as such be said to be laid to sleep by Jesus. The Resurrection, as this clause asserts, is the work of God (Acts xxvi, 8; 1 Cor. vi, 14; 2 Cor. i, 9; Heb. xi, 19); but the same word is often assigned to the Mediator (John v, 21, 29; vi, 40; xi, 25; 1 Cor. xv, 22; Philip. iii, 21; in another form 2 Cor. iv, 14). The doctrine of the Resurrection occupies a prominent place in the New Testament.

(Ver. 15.) Τοῦτο γὰρ ὑμῖν λέγομεν ἐν λόγῳ Κυρίου—" For this we say unto you in the word of the Lord." Γάρ refers to the previous verse and to the statement, "them laid to sleep by Jesus God will bring with Him." Though they die before the Advent they are certainly to share in its glories, and are in no way to be anticipated by those who may happen to be alive at that momentous period, this being what so perplexed the church in Thessalonica, so that Koppe, Flatt, and Koch are in error when they refer γάρ to verse 13, and regard this verse as giving an additional reason why believers should not sorrow, taking verses 14 and 15 as parallel in the argument. But this verse is plainly an advance on the previous one, and not collateral with it. As to the destiny of the departed, there is first a negative statement, they "who are alive shall not prevent them who are asleep," and then follows a positive statement, "the dead in Christ shall rise first," &c. The previous verse affirms only that God shall bring them with Christ, and this verse and the one after it show how and in what order. Τοῦτο, emphatically placed, refers to the next statement introduced by ὅτι. What follows is of special moment, being matter of direct revelation ἐν λόγῳ Κυρίου— Κύριος being the Saviour. The phrase occurs in 1 Kings xx, 35, בִּדְבַר יְהֹוָה, rendered in the Septuagint ἐν λόγῳ Κυρίου, "in the word of the Lord" in the Authorized Version, and compare Esther i, 12; 1 Kings xiii, 2; Hosea i, 2. The preposition may bear its usual meaning, "in the sphere of" (Winer, § 48 a), that is, the following declaration is a repetition of what the Lord had revealed, and has all its truth from this correspondence. "In the word of the Lord" is, therefore, "in it" as to contents, and virtually and inferentially "by it" as to authority. None of the nouns has the article. Ἐν is not directly "by," as in the Authorized Version—that is, by divine commission, nor is it *secundum*, as Flatt and Pelt, under reference to Rom. i, 10. What the apostle is about to utter was specially revealed to him, and in that revelation his utterance had its contents and authority, the reception of it conveying the commission and the qualification to tell it. It came ἐκ θείας ἀποκαλύψεως as Theodoret says, or as Theophylact, παρὰ τοῦ Χριστοῦ μαθών. The formula of the old prophets was "thus saith the Lord," and the apostle uses κατ᾽ ἐπιταγήν (1 Cor. vii, 6), and ἐν ἀποκαλύψει (1 Cor. xiv, 6). There has been no little speculation as to the oracle referred to. (1) Many refer it to some portion of the New Testament which records Christ's eschatological sayings. Thus Pelagius, Musculus, Schott, and Pelt refer it to the twenty-fourth chapter of Matthew. Ewald unites Luke xiv, 14. Hofmann points to the special promise of Christ in Matt. xvi, 27, 28, and John vi, 44. Zwingli, as also Luthardt, selects Matt. xxv, the parable of the wise and foolish virgins, on account of the phrase εἰς ἀπάντησιν, which occurs in the first verse of that chapter, and also here in verse 17. But the apostle nowhere quotes our present gospels, and those places have not the fulness and speciality of revelation which are found in this paragraph, and they say nothing out of which one might conjecture the relations of the dead and the living to the Second Advent. (2) Others again imagine that the apostle refers to some sayings of Christ, preserved by tradition, or perhaps spoken, according to v. Zezschwitz, during the forty days between the resurrection and ascension. Calvin and Koch hold this view—the first saying generally that the utterance is taken from Christ's discourses, and the latter, that it is taken from some collection of his sayings. Theophylact compares the utterance to that (ὥσπερ κἀκεῖνο) given in Acts xx, 35. But this supposition is quite precarious, though many sayings of our Lord must have been preserved that are not found in the canonical gospels. Compare Acts xx, 35; 1 Cor. vii, 10. The opinion, if not baseless, is at least beyond all proof. No saying has been preserved to us that could, by the widest construction, form the basis of this declaration. (3) It follows, then, that we accept the clause in its simple significance, as asserting an immediate revelation from Christ to the apostle on this point. Such is the view of the majority of expositors. It is needless to inquire when, where, or how the revelation was vouchsafed to him, and it is erroneous in Jowett to affirm that Paul nowhere speaks of any special truths or doctrines as imparted to himself, for he had many direct revelations, though he does not always unfold the special subject of them—as about his special mission field (Acts xxii, 18-21); as to the position of believing Gentiles (Ephes. iii, 3); as to the Lord's Supper (1 Cor. xi, 23); and as to the reality, proofs, and results of Christ's resurrection (1 Cor. xv, 3; 2 Cor. xii, 1). See also under Gal. i, 12, and especially i, 16. On this point before us, of which no man can know anything of himself, and on which mere hypothesis would be alike audacious and vain, the apostle enjoyed an immediate revelation which he proceeds to unfold. This is, however, denied by Usteri, and the revelation is described as subjectivity, this especially being said to rest *auf dem allgemeinen Glauben und der Fortbildung der Tradition verbunden mit einer lebendigen combinatorischen Imagination* (p. 341). The revelation is—

ὅτι ἡμεῖς οἱ ζῶντες οἱ περιλειπόμενοι εἰς τὴν παρουσίαν τοῦ Κυρίου—"that we the living, the remaining over unto the coming of the Lord." The participle περιλειπόμενοι occurs only here and in verse 17 in the New Testament—the inclusive preposition signifying "around" and then "over," the idea being that of overplus—and means "remaining over" or "behind." It is an epithet applied to the water left over after a sacrifice, τὸ περιλειπόμενον ὕδωρ (2 Macc. i, 31). Orthryades is called τὸν περιλειφθέντα, the only surviving one of the three hundred Spartans. Herodot., i, 82; Herodian, II, 1, 16; Plato, *De Legibus*, III, 677 E, p. 295, *Opera*, vol. X, ed. Stallbaum. These words naturally suggest the idea that the apostle by his use of ἡμεῖς expected to be among them—among those who should not die before the Second Advent. Many modern commentators adopt this view; while as many, regarding such a notion as derogatory to the apostle and his inspiration, strive by various expedients to get rid of it. That an inspired man should be guilty of so gross a blunder as to believe and affirm that he should live on to the Second Advent would be extraordinary, and yet more extraordinary when he is professedly speaking from a special divine revelation. But many of the arguments against the view we have stated as the apparent one are utterly void. (1) Œcumenius, after Methodius, adopts the opinion that the two participles refer to the souls of the departed as being immortal, ζῶντας τὰς ψυχὰς, κοιμηθέντα δὲ τὰ σώματα λέγει—the statement being that those souls shall not precede their bodies into the presence of the Lord, but shall resume them ere they ascend to meet the Lord. But the class indicated by the two participles is plainly opposed to the other class who are laid to sleep before "that day." The term ζῶντας moreover describes living men and not their mere souls. (2) By some the participial clause is taken hypothetically, "provided that we live, provided that we survive." Thus Turretin *si modo ex eorum numero simus*; Cornelius, a-Lapide, *nos qui vivimus, inquit, i.e., quicunque vivent, sive ex nobis sive e posteris nostris, quorum personam hic induo et subeo*. But in that case, as Lünemann states, the two articles must be omitted, and the statement of the apostle is direct and unconditional in its words. (3) Nor can these present participles admit of a future signification, after some supposed Hebrew usage (Flatt, Pelt), for they are both present and ideally describe some men as a class alive and surviving at the Second Coming, in opposition to another class who have fallen asleep, the apostle putting himself among the former number—ἡμεῖς. (4) Nor can ἡμεῖς οἱ ζῶντες mean them who live and remain behind (J. P. Lange), that is, we, so far as we in the meantime represent those who shall then be alive. This sense is forced and ungrammatical. (5) In the opinion of Calvin the apostle in using ἡμεῖς makes himself one of the number who will live until the last day, and in doing so meant to impress on the Thessalonian church the duty of waiting for the Advent, and to hold all believers in suspense about it, adding what appears to convey a charge of simulation against the apostle, "granting that he knew by a special revelation that Christ would come at a somewhat later time, it was nevertheless necessary that this doctrine should be delivered to the church in common," which really means that the apostle did not consciously speak truth when he put himself among the ἡμεῖς. The earlier and indeed the commoner view has been that the apostle uses ἡμεῖς by a figure of speech, that he speaks *communicative*, adopts what is called *enallage personæ, ἀνακοίνωσις*. The sense then is, those of us Christians who at the Advent shall be in life. This is the view of Chrysostom and his followers, with Erasmus, Zanchius, Hunnius, Balduin, Bengel, Flatt, &c. Thus Chrysostom writes, τὸ δὲ ἡμεῖς, οὐ περὶ ἑαυτοῦ φησιν· οὐ γὰρ δὴ ἔμελλεν αὐτὸς μέχρι τῆς ἀναστάσεως μένειν, ἀλλὰ τοὺς πιστοὺς λέγει. A modification of this view may be held. When the apostle says, we the living and remaining behind, he means himself and includes those addressed by him. Did he then affirm that he and they without exception would survive till the second coming, or that he and they so surviving would without exception be caught up to meet the Lord in the air, every one of them being a genuine believer? Certainly not. It seems best therefore to suppose that as Paul distinguishes the two classes, the living and the dead, he naturally puts himself among those to whom at the moment he belonged, and who as the living and surviving are contrasted with those who had fallen asleep or died. For there will be a like distinction when the Saviour comes; and to describe the one class the apostle employs the present time and says, "we who are alive and remain." If the Advent were to take place just now, the classification would be literally correct. To the mind of the apostle the second coming was ever present, and under this aspect he puts himself and his contemporaries in the one category without actually intending to affirm that they should not taste of death till the Redeemer should appear. The clause is thus a vivid way of characterizing all the living as represented by himself and the Thessalonians to whom he writes, while the deceased Thessalonian believers represent all who have died before His appearance and coming. Alford says, "Doubtless he expected himself to be alive together with the majority of those to whom he was writing at the Lord's coming." Must not the declaration on which this inference is based be a portion of the λόγος Κυρίου, "this we say by the word of the Lord, that we living and remaining over"? Dean Alford, however, quite neutralizes his argument when he says, "at the same time, it must be borne in mind that this inclusion of himself and his hearers among the ζῶντες and περιλειπόμενοι does not in any way enter into the fact revealed and here announced, which is respecting that class of persons only as they are and must be, *one portion* of the faithful, at the Lord's coming, not respecting the question who shall or who shall not be among them in that day." This is in other words the conclusion we have come to, and the exegesis does not compel us on the Dean's own showing to hold the strict belief that Paul expected himself and his contemporaries to survive the Second Coming. The apostle's use of "I" and "we" for argument's sake may be seen in Rom. iii, 7; 1 Cor. iv, 6; xiv, 14. There is no distinct or independent proof that the apostle really expected to live till the Second Advent; nay, he says (1 Cor. vi, 14), "God hath both raised up the Lord, and will also raise up us by His own power;" and again (2 Cor. iv, 13), "knowing that he which raised up the Lord Jesus shall raise up us also by Jesus, and shall present us with you." The declaration (1 Cor. xv, 51), "We shall not all sleep, but we shall all be changed," can be satisfactorily explained without supposing that the apostle expresses his belief that he would not die, and the paragraph adduced by Alford (2 Cor. v, 1-10), if this belief be supposed to underlie it, contradicts itself; for how could the man who believed that he was not to die and who longed to be clothed upon without mortal change, declare in almost the same breath that he was willing rather to be absent from the body and to be present with the Lord. These Corinthian epistles were written not more than four or five years after those sent to Thessalonica. Towards the end of his life indeed the apostle says very decidedly, "to die is gain," and that he "had a desire to depart and to be with Christ"—not a word of any hope that Christ was coming in his lifetime, and that therefore he should not die; or should be still among living men when the Master returned. This longing for the day of the Lord might work itself into a belief that it was near, and this was the common impression, for its period had not been revealed, and it was ardently hoped for. But the apostle in the midst of such fervent expectations, warns this church a few months after writing the clause before us, that the belief "that the day of Christ is at hand" is a serious delusion, for prior to it there must be the development of the mystery of iniquity. He might regard the Advent as possible in his lifetime, but never apparently as certain. He never distinctly teaches that it would either be or not be before his death. He was not so presumptuous as to fix a date for an event known to the Father only, and not revealed to angels or even to the Son Himself. If he taught its nearness, he assigned it to no year; if he taught its certainty as a fact, he also dwelt on the uncertainty of its time. In a word he never expresses surprise that the day had not come so soon as he had anticipated, never utters a word of disappointment that it seemed more than ever at a great and indefinite distance. For παρουσία see ii, 19; and the phrase εἰς τὴν παρουσίαν belongs, by the arrangement of the sentence, to περιλειπόμενοι, and not to the following verb φθάσωμεν.

οὐ μὴ φθάσωμεν τοὺς κοιμηθέντας—" shall in no wise anticipate them that are laid to sleep"—"prevent" in the old English sense, and according to its Latin derivation, meaning "go before." You may go before one to help or to hinder him; the latter being so common an impulse in our poor fallen nature, the word has now sunk into the second sense exclusively. The verb φθάνειν—sometimes followed by εἰς τι, the object, sometimes by ἐπί τινα, the person, and sometimes by the participle of another verb—here governs the simple accusative. Jelf, § 694. For οὐ μή, as a strengthened negative, see Winer, § 56, 3, where he remarks that Hermann's rule, given under Œdip. Col., 853, as to the difference of those negatives with the future and the aorist, must not be pressed in the interpretation of the New Testament, as the MSS. vary so much in so many passages, and the subjunctive is the predominant usage. The two negatives occur often similarly in the Septuagint. Gayler, p. 441. Strengthened negatives, like compound verbs, characterize the later Greek. The idiom is supposed by many to be elliptical, and thus to be resolved, " there is no fear that," or as Alford, " there is no reason to fear that." See also Ellendt, *Lex. Soph.*, II, p. 409, *sub voce* οὐ. The meaning is, that they who are found alive when the Saviour comes shall have no priority in any sense over those who have died—shall not, because they survive and need not to die, start sooner into the Master's presence, or come into participation of His glory and honour earlier than those who have gone down to the bed of rest. The living shall in no privilege or blessing forestall the dead, and the dead lose nothing by their earlier decease. The Thessalonian believers need not sorrow over the deceased as if they had in any degree fallen short of the prize, or were in any way to come behind the others who shall be alive, and remaining over at the Second Advent. So far from being anticipated by this class, the dead anticipate them— " the dead in Christ shall rise first," or before the living are changed (1 Cor. xv). It is a strange thought that some shall outlive all history, and see the end of all kingdoms, of all scientific development, and of all human affairs; shall see the world at its last moment, and humanity in its final phase, as it ceases as a species to exist upon earth.

(Ver. 16.) ὅτι αὐτὸς ὁ Κύριος . . . καταβήσεται ἀπ' οὐρανοῦ —" because the Lord himself . . . shall descend from heaven." Ὅτι might be taken as parallel to the previous ὅτι, and as introducing another portion of the λόγος Κυρίου, and as dependent on λέγομεν (Koch, Hofmann). But it develops the order and the proof more distinctly to take it as the ancient versions do, *quoniam* in the Vulgate, *quia* in the Claromontane Latin. The Syriac has ܡܛܠ, and some of the Greek fathers interpret by γάρ—καὶ γὰρ αὐτὸς (Theophylact), αὐτὸς γὰρ πρῶτος (Theodoret).

The phrase αὐτὸς ὁ Κύριος is not "He the Lord," as De Wette and Hofmann, which is, as Alford says, to the last degree flat and meaningless. Nor is the reference expressly to His holy person, to His glorified body, for the purpose of excluding any meaning of mere operation or influence, as Olshausen and Bisping, after Estius and Fromond. This interpretation does not bring out the whole truth. The sense is also fuller than Alford gives it, "the words being," he says, "used for solemnity's sake, and to show that it will not be a mere gathering unto Him, but He himself shall descend." For the meaning is that Himself and none other, Himself in person and glory will descend—not Himself as the principal person, and as in contrast to believers (Lünemann)—not Himself as the first of all the host of heaven to come down—but Himself in proper person. The work is delegated to no substitute, but Himself, the same Jesus who ascended into heaven, will return from it, καταβήσεται ἀπ' οὐρανοῦ. He went up in person, and in person He descends (Mark xvi, 19; Acts i, 10, 11; ii, 33; Ephes. i, 20; iv, 8, 10). Ἐκ is usually employed in the connection, save here and in Luke ix, 54. Compare Sept., Dan. iv, 10. He shall descend—

ἐν κελεύσματι—"with a signal shout," the Latin versions having *in jussu*. The noun κέλευσμα, which occurs only here in the New Testament, is the word of command, or any sounded signal. It is used of the shout of a huntsman to his dogs (Xenoph., *Ven.*, vi, 20); of the shout of a chariot-driver to his steeds, ἄπληκτος, κελεύματι μόνον ... ἡνιοχεῖται (Phædrus, p. 253 D); of the cry of the captain to the rowers, by which they kept stroke, ἔπαισαν ἅλμην ... ἐκ κελεύσματος (Æschylus, *Persae*, 403); ἐκ κελεύσματος (Euripides, *Iphig. in Taur.*, 1405; Silius Italicus, vi, 360; Ovid, *Metam.*, iii, 10); of the word of military command, ἀφ' ἑνὸς κελεύσματος ... ὥρμησαν (Thucydides, ii, 92). It is also used of the shout of a man with a stentorian voice, φωνέων μέγιστον, who hailed another across the Ister, and that other heard τῷ πρώτῳ κελεύσματι, and brought up all the ships (Herod., iv, 14); of the flight of the locusts (Prov. xxx, 27); and Philo, in a phrase not unlike that before us, uses it of divine command—God can easily gather together all men from the ends of the earth into one place, ἑνὶ κελεύσματι (*De Praem.*, § 19). On the spelling κέλευμα, κεκέλευμαι, and the similar variety in other words, Lobeck has a long note (*Ajax*, 704, p. 268, 3rd ed.). See also a long note of Bloomfield's (*Persae*, 403). The prevailing sense then is a battle-shout, or a signal sounded to a fleet or army. It is wrong in Hunnius and Bisping to identify the κέλευσμα with the trump of God, as if the meaning were *horribilis fragor inclarescentium tonitruum*. The three prepositions ἐν—ἐν —ἐν, point to three distinct circumstances accompanying the Descent. The preposition has its usual sense—something in which an event takes place—a concomitant circumstance; and it may therefore be rendered "with." The idea may be that in the κέλευσμα, or surrounded by it, the Descent takes place. That κέλευσμα is a mighty shout of warning and command, but who can tell what it is as it heralds and accompanies the Second Advent? It is not the shout of the army, as is sometimes supposed, but the shout of the general to his army; therefore it cannot mean, as Macknight says, "*the loud acclamation which the whole angelic hosts will utter to express their joy at the Advent of Christ to raise the dead and judge the world.*" But it may be the thunder-shout which ushers in the Great Day, perhaps sounded by the archangel through the trump of God, and may be addressed to the ἅγιοι who are to accompany Him, and as if to summon them to the royal progress. See under iii, 13; 2 Thess. i, 7. Theodoret and Œcumenius refer the κέλευσμα to Christ, "He will bid the archangel sound," and so after them Grotius and Olshausen. But the clauses with ἐν refer to concomitants of Christ's Descent, and therefore not naturally to Himself, and the κέλευσμα may be explained by the following clauses—

ἐν φωνῇ ἀρχαγγέλου—"with the voice of an archangel." Ἀρχάγγελος occurs in the New Testament only here and in Jude 9. Like similar terms as ἀρχιτρίκλινος, ἀρχιτελώνης, ἀρχιποίμην, ἀρχιερεύς, ἀρχισυνάγωγος, ἀρχιτέκτων, it means not chief angel, but chief of the angels—a head or leader, as is implied in the phrase "Michael and his angels." The word occurs only in the singular, and with the definite article, in Jude 9. According to the apostle there are various ranks of angels (see under Ephes. i, 21); Jesus when he comes is surrounded by troops of them (Matt. xxv, 31), and an archangel may be leader of the στρατιᾶς οὐρανίου (Luke ii, 13). Who this archangel is it is vain to inquire. Michael is the only one mentioned in the New Testament, but in Dan. x, 13, he is called אַחַד הַשָּׂרִים הָרִאשֹׁנִים, "one of the chief princes," as if apparently there were others of similar rank; though some signal eminence still attaches to him, as he is styled הַשַּׂר הַגָּדוֹל (Dan. xii, 1). They are sometimes said to be seven, "the seven lamps" burning before the throne; and sometimes ten; and in the Jewish writings four are especially named, corresponding to the "thrones, dominions, principalities, and powers," in Ephes. i, 21. The names also of these serving angels have thus been given: Michael and his company stand on the right hand of the throne, and Gabriel similarly on the left, Uriel in front, and Raphael behind, the Shechinah being in the centre (Tobit xv, 15; Book of Enoch). With these speculations we have no special concern. One archangel is here singled out—one of those most glorious beings, the eldest of the creation, godlike in splendour and attributes. To say that he is Michael may have probability, but no sure foundation (Hunnius, Estius, Ewald, Bisping). Nor can the term mean the Lord Jesus himself (Ambrosiaster, Olshausen), for such a notion would destroy the symmetry of the verse, and give to the Saviour first a distinctive, and then a unique and unfamiliar title; for Olshausen admits that nowhere else is Christ called archangel. Olshausen refers the κέλευσμα to Him, and holds that to mention a creature next in order would be startling, but the κέλευσμα is not necessarily to be referred to Christ (Bishop Horsley), "it belongs rather to the archangel." Honertius and Alphenius, in Wolf's *Curae*, think that the Holy Ghost is meant by the archangel. It is hard to say how such a notion could originate, though the idea sprang apparently from an attempt to find the Trinity in the verse—the Father in the last word, the Son being the Lord, Himself, and the Holy Spirit under the name of the archangel. Φωνή is ascribed to the archangel—a voice no doubt like himself, "powerful and full of majesty," the form, perhaps, which the κέλευσμα assumes. This mighty voice heralds and accompanies the descending Lord, reaching through the universe, and summoning all its ranks into His presence, and to adoration—startling those who are alive and remain, and piercing even "the dull cold ear of death" (Theodoret, Schott).

καὶ ἐν σάλπιγγι Θεοῦ—" and with the trumpet of God." The genitive Θεοῦ is not the so-called Hebrew superlative (Nordheimer). Winer, § 36, 3 *b*. The phrase, therefore, does not mean a large or a far-sounding trumpet, excelling vastly the trumpet of men (a-Lapide, Benson). Bengel has "*tuba Dei adeoque magna,*" and Storr, "*tuba longe lateque sonans.*" Nor is the meaning a trumpet blown at God's command, as Balduin, Pelt, Schott, Olshausen. These things may be true, but they are inferential only; the genitive is simply that of possession—the trumpet which is God's, and being His may possess the qualities which those expositors assign to it. The trumpet is His, as being employed in His heavenly service. The many allusions to the trumpet in the Hebrew poetry, as a signal and warning blast, afford no illustration. Compare, however, Isaiah xxvii, 13; Zech. ix, 14; Rev. viii, 2. But the trumpet used at the Jewish festivals comes somewhat nearer, since by divine command it blew various signals of assembly under the theocratic government, and might be an earthly image of what is super-celestial, "a pattern of things in the heaven." Compare Numbers x, 2; xxxi, 6; 1 Chron. xvi. 42; Ps. lxxxi, 3; Joel, ii, 1. But the trumpet is often associated with Old Testament Theophanies. In Psalm xlvii, 5, the trumpet is associated with a divine ascension—the reverse in idea of this place. The descent on Sinai was accompanied by such peals—thunder, lightnings, a thick cloud on the mount, and the voice of the trumpet exceeding loud—nay, the voice of the trumpet sounded long, and waxed louder and louder (Exod. xix, 16, 19; Heb. xii, 19). As Milton has it—

> "The Son gave signal high
> To the bright minister that watch'd ; he blew
> His trumpet, heard in Oreb since perhaps
> When God descended ; and perhaps once more
> To sound at general doom."

The distinct announcement is made in the New Testament—" He shall send his angels with a great sound of a trumpet, and they shall gather his elect from the four winds, from one end of heaven to the other" (Matt. xxiv, 31)—a passage which has a close connection with the verse before us, for the trumpet-blast is associated with the second Advent—" The son of man coming in the clouds of heaven with power and great glory." More distinctly still the apostle says, " We shall not all sleep, but we shall all be changed—in a moment, in the twinkling of an eye, at the last trump, for the trumpet shall sound." What the trumpet-peal accomplishes we know not. It gathers apparently the elect together—it may raise the dead, and give universal warning that the Lord is come.

> *Tuba mirum spargens sonum*
> *Per sepulcra regionum,*
> *Coget omnes ante thronum.*

The voice of the archangel may be uttered by the trumpet. Chrysostom gives a choice of three suppositions as to the theme of utterance, "it is either as in the parable, 'The Bridegroom cometh,' or, ' Let the dead arise,' or, ' Make all ready, for the Judge is at hand.'" The phrase, " the last trump " (1 Cor. xv, 52), is supposed by the same author to imply previous trumpets, at the last of which the Judge descends, while others identify it with the seventh trumpet of the Apocalypse ; but these notions, the second especially, are exceedingly precarious—the phrase, " the last trump," being apparently a popular one, and meaning the trumpet in connection with the End. The power of God can at once raise the dead, but undoubtedly, for the best of reasons, He has chosen to employ the instrumentality dimly disclosed in this verse. It would on the one hand be presumptuous to speak dogmatically upon it, or to refine upon it, and spiritualize it as a mere image—as is done to some extent by Olshausen. On the other hand, in some of the Jewish books, the trumpet and its seven blasts are dwelt upon with puerile exaggeration, as may be seen in Eisenmenger *Entd. Jud.*, vol. II, pp. 929, 930. " The trumpet is a thousand ells long, according to the ells of God ; at each peal a certain result follows ; at the first peal the world is awaked, and at the others, the various parts of the human body are collected and reorganised," &c., &c.

What the passage may show is, that as the trumpet blast was supposed in Jewish theology to herald or accompany God to legislation or judgment—as it did in the awful manifestation at Mount Sinai—so the doctrine of the apostle, though a new disclosure on this point, was in unison with the traditionary Jewish faith.

καὶ οἱ νεκροὶ ἐν Χριστῷ ἀναστήσονται πρῶτον—" and the dead in Christ shall rise first." Some manuscripts and fathers read πρῶτοι, the Latin versions having *primi*, an evident emendation, prompted by the idea of a first resurrection. The text has superabundant authority, the connecting καὶ is consecutive " and so," introducing the result of the Advent or Descent from heaven as just described—though it would be precarious to connect the clause solely with ἐν σάλπιγγι Θεοῦ.

Ἐν Χριστῷ is by Krause, Pelt, Schott, and Peile, wrongly connected with the verb, " shall rise in Christ." Winer adopted this connection in his earlier, but abandoned it in his later editions (§ 20, 2 *a*, ed. 6th), his objection being that the distinction is superfluous, there being no allusion to non-believers. Schott and Pelt render "*mortui primum resurgent per Christum,*" *i.e.* διὰ Χριστοῦ, deriving in this way the idea of a first and then that of a general resurrection. Schott adds, "*pro mortuis omnibus in vitam revocandis, parte pro toto posita, cultores Christi resuscitandi commemorari poterant,*" quoting in proof 1 Cor. xv, 23. But the idea of a second resurrection is nowhere found in the context. The dead are opposed to the living—the resurrection of the Christian dead is in contrast to the change and rapture of Christian survivors, and to the first, therefore, the distinctive ἐν Χριστῷ is naturally added. The question is not by what means the dead shall rise, but what is the relation which they shall bear to the

Ver. 16.] FIRST EPISTLE TO THE THESSALONIANS 167

Redeemer at his advent. He has said that the dead shall not take precedence of the living, and this order which had been asserted negatively in the previous verse, is asserted positively in this clause. The Vulgate has *et mortui, qui in Christo sunt, resurgent primi*, and the Syriac has ܡܝܼܬܸܐ ܕܲܒܡܫܝܼܚܵܐ ܢܩܘܼܡܘܼܢ ܠܘܼܩܕܲܡ. The connection of ἐν Χριστῷ with the verb would therefore leave the character of the νεκροί undefined, and by putting the stress on ἐν Χριστῷ would introduce confusion into the sentence, as if it were meant that the dead, all the dead, would rise through Christ, an idea quite foreign to the context, and the apostle's immediate object. Ἐν Χριστῷ has the common meaning—in union with Christ; that union is not dissolved by death; they were in Christ—the source of their spiritual life when in the body, in Him when they died, and they are in Him still; yea, so in Him that His resurrection secures theirs. He cannot rise without raising all included in Him, and livingly and organically united to Him as the members to the Head.

Πρῶτον has its distinct and momentous position in the clause, for it solves the perplexity which was felt in the Thessalonian church. Not only shall the dead share in the glories of the Advent, but they shall share first; its first result is their resurrection. They lose no privilege by dying before the Advent, they even win this priority over those who shall then be alive. Πρῶτον corresponds to ἔπειτα, the dead rise first, and then the living are with them caught up. Πρῶτον has no reference to the resurrection of unbelievers; it is simply first, or before the rapture of the living and surviving saints. The apostle thus refers to the two great results of the Advent—first, the resurrection of the dead saints; and, secondly, the assumption of the living saints. To identify the resurrection asserted in this verse with the "first resurrection" of Rev. xx, 6, is quite unwarranted. The view is held by the Greek expositors with Pelagius, Ambrosiaster, Estius, Turretin, and Olshausen. For, 1st, if the πρώτη ἀνάστασις, the prophetic picture in the Apocalypse, be a literal resurrection, it is confined to the martyrs; 2nd, the first resurrection is that of "souls"—said to live, not to be reclothed—and it is in contrast to the "second death," which is explained to be "the lake of fire." Are the martyrs only to escape the second death? Is not that death, the death of a soul severed for aye from God, the source of life? Of a general resurrection there is here no mention, as there is no allusion to the resurrection of unbelievers; their destiny is here undisclosed and is left under awful shadow. Three reasons are adduced in Œcumenius for the omission, but only one of them is of any weight, viz., that any allusion to the fate of unbelievers was foreign to his immediate purpose of enlightening and consoling the Thessalonian church. Macknight is verbose and tenacious in expounding his theory that the wicked shall be raised with their present bodies, and that as, after the righteous ascend, the earth is to be burned, they will, in all probability, remain on it to be consumed in the general conflagration. But this passage is totally silent as to such a fate, and it cannot be found in it even by implication. Nor does any other Scripture give any countenance to the conjecture. On the other hand Karsten (*die letzten Dinge*) supposes, with as little proof, that the wicked are raised in order to be disembodied.

The apostle does not say where the souls of the dead are. The thief went to Paradise, not to Heaven. Hades represents generally the world of spirits, both good and bad, and Hades ceases to exist at the last day. They themselves—that is, their bodies—shall be raised, personality being attributed to them though one portion is wrapt in unconsciousness.

(Ver. 17.) Ἔπειτα ἡμεῖς οἱ ζῶντες οἱ περιλειπόμενοι ἅμα σὺν αὐτοῖς ἁρπαγησόμεθα ἐν νεφέλαις εἰς ἀπάντησιν τοῦ Κυρίου εἰς ἀέρα—" Then we who are alive and remain over shall be caught up at the same time along with them in clouds to meet the Lord in the air." Some MSS. as D¹ F read εἰς ὑπάντησιν τῷ Χριστῷ, and the Latin versions similarly have *obviam Christo*, and so Tertullian and Jerome. The adverb ἔπειτα (ἐπ' εἶτα) "then," not only introduces the second result of the Lord's descent, that the living shall be caught up, but also implies that the last event is closely connected with the former. Erfurdt on *Antig.*, 607, remarks *ubi quum praecedat τὰ πρῶτα, necessario ea temporis pars intelligi debet, quae τὰ πρῶτα proxime sequitur—i. e.*, ὁ ἐνεστώς (vol. I, p. 139, 3rd ed.). It is almost equivalent to καὶ τότε. Heindorf, Plato *de Republica*, p. 336 C. The two events are consecutive, the one follows close upon the other. For ἡμεῖς οἱ ζῶντες, &c., see under verse 15. Ἅμα may mean *simul*, at the same time, or all in one company. But as σὺν αὐτοῖς follows, the temporal meaning of ἅμα is to be preferred, and it also implies that the one event, though behind the other in time, is in close proximity to it. Klotz, *Devarius*, vol. II, p. 95. Σὺν αὐτοῖς comprehends those who have been raised — we who are alive and remain shall be caught up at the same time with them who are raised, and shall form one company. The resurrection precedes, and though the dead are prior in resurrection, the living are not posterior to them in this rapture, but both simultaneously are lifted up in one band to meet the Lord. In ἁρπαγησόμεθα is the idea of sudden and irresistible seizure by a power beyond us. For the form of the verb, see Buttmann, §144. Ἐν νεφέλαις is connected with the verb, and seems to characterize either manner or instrument "in the clouds," enveloped by them and borne up by them. Lünemann and De Wette render "on the clouds," *auf Wolken—mitten auf ihnen thronend*. The phrase does not mean "into the clouds," as if ἐν were εἰς (Beza and Hammond), nor does it, as if it were νέφος, signify in clusters or a great multitude (Koppe, Rosenmüller, Macknight). Clouds are often associated with the divine presence—"He maketh the clouds his chariot" (Psalm civ, 3); "the clouds are the dust of his feet" (Nahum i, 3); Jesus went away in a "cloud"; "a cloud received Him out of their sight" (Acts i, 9); and in the clouds he returns, ἐπὶ τῶν νεφελῶν (Matt. xxiv, 30; xxvi, 64); ἐν νεφέλαις (Mark xiii, 26); μετὰ τῶν νεφελῶν (Rev. i, 7). The rapture of the living in some way corresponds in majesty to Him and His coming, or, as Theodoret says, ἔδειξε τὸ μέγεθος τῆς τιμῆς. The purpose of the seizure is—

εἰς ἀπάντησιν τοῦ Κυρίου—"to meet the Lord." The phrase comes from the Septuagint, where it usually represents the Hebrew לִקְרַאת, as often in Judges and in the historical books, also in Jer. xli, 6; li, 31; and is followed by a genitive and occasionally by a dative. Polybius, v, 26, 5; Winer, § 31, 3. The word belongs to the later Greek. Matt. xxv, 1, 6; Acts xxviii, 15. The Lord is descending to the earth, they are caught up on His progress to meet Him, and thus God "brings them with Him" (verse 14). Theophylact, after Chrysostom, likens the meeting to a king's entrance into a city—all its aristocracy coming out to meet him. The meeting is one of welcome and praise. He is coming in fulfilment of His promise and to crown His work.

The last words, εἰς ἀέρα, are connected with the verb ἁρπαγησόμεθα, *in aëra*, and cannot mean through the air (Flatt), nor, as is the opinion of the same author, can ἀήρ denote heaven. The air is not to be regarded as the heaven of believers, as virtually Pelt, Usteri, and others. The New Testament affords no basis for this dream, nor does this place say more than that the dead who are raised and the living along with them meet the Redeemer, not in heaven as he leaves it, nor on earth if He come down to it, but between heaven and earth in the air, which, in our imagination, is the pathway up to glory (Augustine, *De Civit. Dei*, xx, 20, 2). It is not said, on the one hand, that they will descend with him to earth, nor, on the other hand, that He will return with them to heaven. What shall follow after His saints meet Him the apostle does not declare; he affirms nothing of the judgment or the admission to final blessedness. He pauses at the point when he had shown how groundless was the perplexity of the Thessalonian believers concerning the position and destiny of the dead at the second Advent. But he adds in a word as the grand conclusion—

καὶ οὕτως πάντοτε σὺν Κυρίῳ ἐσόμεθα—" and so we shall ever be with the Lord." "And thus," not, under these circumstances, but as the consequence of being caught away to meet Him into the air. We meet and never more part from him. Thucydides, i, 14. The subject of the verb is the sainted dead and the sainted living—who simultaneously are snatched up to meet the Lord. Σὺν (not μετά) implies close fellowship, and πάντοτε expresses its endless duration without limit of time—not simply to "the end," when the mediatorial government shall pass into that of God in simplicity and immediateness. The fellowship of the saved with the Saviour is this unending spring of blessedness. It is plainly implied in these words that those who survive till the second Advent do not die. Some have doubted this, because death is so often asserted to be the sure and common destiny of mankind. Disturbed by a various reading of 1 Cor. xv, 51, some took ζῶντες in a spiritual sense, "those who are spiritually alive." Jerome gives Origen's view thus: *nos qui vivimus quorum corpus mortuum est propter peccatum; spiritus autem vivit propter justitiam*. Jerome reports another opinion: *vivi appellantur, qui numquam peccato mortui sunt, qui autem peccaverunt, et in eo quod peccaverunt, mortui sunt, . . . mortui appellantur, quia peccaverunt; in Christo autem mortui, quia plena ad Deum mente conversi sunt* (*Epist.* 119, vol. I, p. 811, ed. Vallarsii). That these living survivors should in some way die, has been held by many. Augustine says: *nec illi per immortalitem vivificabuntur, nisi, quamlibet paululum, tamen ante moriantur; ac per hoc et a resurrectione non erunt alieni, quam dormitio praecedit, quamvis brevissima, non tamen nulla* (*De Civitate Dei*, xx, 20, vol. VII, p. 963, *Opera*, Gaume, Paris, 1838). A similar view was held by Ambrosiaster, Aquinas, and Anselm, the death taking place according to Augustine, Anselm, and a-Lapide *in aëre et raptu;* according to others *in terra, qui locus est morientium*. See a-Lapide *in loc*. Ambrosiaster says: *in ipso enim raptu mors proveniet et quasi per soporem, ut egressa anima in momento reddatur* (*Opera Omnia*, vol. II, p. 450). The same hypothesis occurs in the exegesis given by Œcumenius, which states that the living are spirits and the dead are bodies. But the apostle in 1 Cor. gives us a glimpse of the truth—" we shall not all die, but we shall all be changed." A sudden and mysterious change passes over the living—the change of their animal body into a spiritual body; this is supposed to have taken place at the point where the apostle says, "We who are alive and remain shall be caught up." The exposition of a-Lapide ends by showing from the rapture of the saints, quick and dead, how the valley of Jehoshaphat, the scene of judgment, will be able to hold all—*omnes homines qui umquam fuerunt, sunt, aut erunt*.

(Ver. 18.) ὥστε παρακαλεῖτε ἀλλήλους ἐν τοῖς λόγοις τούτοις—" wherefore comfort one another with these words." Ὥστε, consequently, or, so then, *itaque*—the verse being an inferential exhortation. Winer, § 41, 5. The verb corresponds to the purpose of the paragraph indicated in verse 13, ἵνα μὴ λυπῆσθε—in order that ye should not sorrow; and such being the blessed hope as now revealed, the injunction is, comfort one another—not each one laying up the hope in his own heart for his own individual comfort, but pressing it on others in all its blessed adaptation and fulness. By the use of ἐν the παράκλησις is conceived of as residing in "these words." It is not a Hebraism, as Grotius supposed, for it is often found in classical writers, the dative, as Wunder says, being used for the Latin ablative of instrument, signifying that the power of doing something is contained in that thing to whose name the preposition is prefixed, as is conversely the case with ἐκ and ἀπό (Sophocles, *Philoct.*, 60). Ἐν here thus indicates the instrumental adjunct. Donaldson, § 476 *a*; Matthiae, § 396, 2, 2. See Raphel. *in loc.* There is stress on τούτοις, as in 1 Tim. 4, 6 —"these words," from verses 15, 16, 17. Λόγοι is words, "not things here or anywhere" (Alford), nor arguments (Pelt), nor *argumentis et rationibus* (Aretius), nor λόγοι τῆς πίστεως (Olshausen). These words, spoken by immediate divine revelation and authority, contain the elements of genuine and lasting consolation. The dead are not lost, and they forego no privilege by dying before the Advent; the living obtain no advantage over them, for these words tell that the dead rise first, and that the living being suddenly changed, both are simultaneously snatched up to meet the descending Lord, to whose merit and mediation all those hopes and glories are owing, and with Him shall they be for ever. The inference given by Theodoret is foreign to the context—ταῦτα τοίνυν εἰδότες φέρετε γενναίως τοῦ παρόντος αἰῶνος τὰ σκυθρωπα, though the hope here unfolded will not only bear up Christians under bereavement, but under every form and kind of evil which may fall upon them.

CHAPTER V

THE question of the disciples was a natural one, "Tell us when shall these things be, and what shall be the sign of Thy coming." Such curiosity must have been evinced in Thessalonica, excited by the apostle's preaching on the duty of waiting for His Son from heaven. And he seems to have given them the Lord's words, "of that day and hour knoweth no man." This statement had been distinctly made, so that they knew it perfectly. At least the suddenness of the Advent had been impressed on them. The Lord had said "in such an hour as ye think not the Son of Man cometh," using also a figure here briefly repeated, "know this, that if the goodman of the house had known in what watch the thief would come, he would have watched" (Matt. xxiv, 43). There is no need therefore to conjecture with Olshausen that the Thessalonians had sent a special question as to the period of the Advent to Paul, and prayed for his solution of the mystery. In such a case the language of the first verse would have borne some trace of being a response. The apostle has told them what had been revealed to him by immediate revelation, and he has exhorted them to apply to their own comfort such words of wonder, hope, and assurance. And now he passes by $\delta\acute{\epsilon}$ to a different but collateral subject.

(Ver. 1.) Περὶ δὲ τῶν χρόνων καὶ τῶν καιρῶν, ἀδελφοὶ—" But of the times and the seasons, brethren." The nouns are thus distinguished by Ammonius, the first as defining ποσότης, quantity, and the second ποιότης, quality; or, the first means simple or indefinite duration, while the second carries with it limitation and character, and thus comes to denote epoch, season, or opportunity —involving the notion of transitoriness. Tittmann, *De Synon.*, I, p. 39; Trench, II, p. 27. Καιρός is probably allied to κείρω as *tempus* to τέμνω, a special period cut out of time, for time comprehends all seasons, or as Bengel says, χρόνων partes καιροί. Hence the phrase χρόνου καιρὸν (Sophocles, *Electra*, 1292). Χρόνος may stand generally for καιρός, but not the reverse (Luke i, 20; Acts iii, 20, 21; Gal. iv, 10). The Latin tongue, as Augustine acknowledged, has no special term to represent καιρός, as *opportunitas* has in it the idea of fittingness or favourableness, whereas καιρός may bear the opposite meaning. The Vulgate renders here *de temporibus autem et momentis* as in Acts i, 7; *über Zeit und Stunde* (Lünemann). The same Greek terms are used in Acts i, 7; Wisdom, vii, 18; viii, 8; and in the singular in Eccles. iii, 1; ἡμέρα and ὥρα, general and special, occur in Matt. xxiv, 36; Mark xiii, 32. The plural is employed here in reference to the number of times and seasons, not to their absolute length, though it does imply some extent of duration. The object is the Second Advent, the period of which may comprise a variety of times and seasons preparing for it, characterizing, and fixing it.

οὐ χρείαν ἔχετε ὑμῖν γράφεσθαι—" ye have no need that it or anything be written to you." See under iv, 9. This version is more in accordance with the Greek idiom than the common ones, " that I write unto you," or " to be written unto," as it preserves the force of the dative and the infinitive passive. The ground of the statement has been variously given. (1) The Greek fathers suppose that the apostle regarded information on the point as superfluous and unprofitable, ὡς περιττὸν, καὶ ὡς ἀσύμφορον (Chrysostom). (2) Others imagine the reason to be, that no one can know these things. Fromond, Koch, Pelt, Estius, Baumgarten-Crusius. (3) Bengel assigns a moral reason—*qui vigilant, his non opus est dici, quando futura sit hora, nam semper parati sunt.* (4) The true and simple reason probably is that the apostle had already instructed them during his sojourn among them, and as he had taught them orally, he did not need to write now to them. For he affirms in the following verse that they know with perfect accuracy, not indeed the times and seasons, but they knew this —that the Second Advent would take men by surprise. They had been taught not its period, that being undisclosed, but its suddenness.

(Ver 2.) αὐτοὶ γὰρ ἀκριβῶς οἴδατε—" for ye yourselves know perfectly." This verse assigns the reason (γὰρ) why they had no need to be written to on the times and seasons—they themselves had correct information; the emphatic αὐτοὶ in contrast with the writer himself as in iv, 9. The adverb ἀκριβῶς occurs only once more in Paul's epistles, and is rendered "circumspectly"

(Ephes. v, 15). It is rendered "diligently" in Matt. ii, 8, and in Acts xviii, 25, "perfect," (Luke i, 3), "having had perfect understanding"; the comparative adjective is used in Acts xviii, 26; xxiii, 15, 20, and the superlative in Acts xxvi, 5. Their knowledge of what he is going to state was not dim, uncertain, or fluctuating, but precise, clear, and accurate.

ὅτι ἡμέρα Κυρίου ὡς κλέπτης ἐν νυκτί, οὕτως ἔρχεται— "that the day of the Lord as a thief cometh in the night, so it cometh." The article which the Received Text places before ἡμέρα is omitted in B D F ℵ, but is found in A K L and many mss. and fathers. It may have been omitted, as ἡ stands so close to ἡμέρα succeeding it, but its insertion may have been owing to grammatical precision. It is not needed, for the sense is not affected by the omission, "the day of the Lord" being a definite and unique expression. Compare Philip. i, 6, 10; ii, 16; 2 Peter iii, 10. Winer, § 19, 1, 2 b. The phrase in the usage of the Old Testament, יוֹם יְהוָה, is used in the prophets to denote the appearance of Jehovah's direct and glorious self-manifestation in his awful rectitude and power (Is. ii, 12; Ezek. xiii, 5; Joel i, 15; ii, 11; iii, 14; Zeph. i, 14; Mal. iv, 5). Here the Lord is Jesus Christ, who returns on this day, specially His as fixed by Him—His, as showing His glory and crowning His mediatorial work, as declared in the previous paragraph. On Κύριος, see Ephes. i, 2. The day of the Lord is the period of the Second Coming, as may be seen by comparing Luke xvii, 30; 1 Cor. i, 8; v, 5; 2 Cor. i, 14; Philip. i, 6, 10; ii, 16; 2 Thess. ii, 2. (1) The phrase, as it is suggested by the 14th, 15th, 16th verses of the previous chapter, cannot refer to the destruction of Jerusalem as Schöttgen, Hammond, Harduin. See Whitby's reply to Hammond *in loc.* (2) Nor, for the same reason, can it refer to each man's death, or to this and to the end of all things (Zwingli, Bloomfield, and Riggenbach). Chrysostom writes οὐχ ἡ κοινὴ μόνον ἀλλὰ καὶ ἡ ἑκάστου ἰδία, "for the one resembles the other." That may be the self-application for each one, since death to him is the day of the Lord, but it is not the true meaning and reference of the clause under review—

ὡς κλέπτης ἐν νυκτί . . . ἔρχεται—"as a thief in the night cometh." The day cometh not simply in the night, but in the night as a thief. Winer, § 20, 4 *note*.

It is not simply nocturnal, but sudden and unexpected. The figure is common in Scripture (Matt. xxiv, 43; Luke xii, 39; 2 Peter iii, 10; Rev. iii, 3; xvi, 15). The allusion is first found in Job xxiv, 14; Jer. xlix, 9. The house is unguarded, deep sleep has fallen on its unprepared inmates, and in such a night the thief comes and makes sudden and effectual entrance to "kill and to steal and to destroy." It is added emphatically οὕτως ἔρχεται, so it cometh, the manner of the Advent being brought into formal prominence, ὡς being resumed in οὕτως, not as Bengel puts it, *uti dicetur versu sequente*. The present is not for the future (Koppe, Flatt, Pelt), nor does it express the suddenness of the event (Bengel, Koch), but its absolute certainty. Bernhardy, p. 371; Winer, § 40, 2. Though the Advent be future, the present gives it an abiding characteristic. There is no need of saying with Riggenbach, *das Bild des Diebes scheint unedel zu sein*; or with Schott, *si quid parum decori huic comparationi inesse videatur perpendamus necesse est, minime personam Christi redituri cum fure adventante, sed rem ipsam cum furis adventu conferri*. Such a distinction serves no purpose. The figure in its suggestiveness is easily understood. He comes as the thief comes without warning, in such an hour as men think not, and when they are not looking for him. Theodoret says, τὸ αἰφνίδιον τῆς δεσποτικῆς παρουσίας ἀπείκασε κλέπτῃ. The suddenness of the event is therefore the idea specially suggested by the image, so far as dead saints and the surviving ones are concerned. The terribleness of the event which Schott, Hofmann, and Alford find in the figure is brought out only in the following verse, and as regards unprepared unbelievers, as has been remarked. There is no doubt that this verse and others having a similar figure originated in the early church the opinion that the Lord would come in the night, and especially on Easter Eve, as He came when the first passover was held in Egypt, and solemn vigils were kept in expectation of the event. Lünemann. Bingham, vol. VII, p. 236. The language employed by the apostle has a strong resemblance to that of our Lord in Matt. xxiv, 43; xxv, 6; and he ascribes to his readers a perfect knowledge of the statement. Most probably the information was acquired through the apostle's own personal teaching when he was with them. There is no proof of Ewald's supposition that he had left with them a written document, *Urkunde*, a so-called gospel referred to in the previous words λόγος Κυρίου (iv, 15). Nor is there any foundation for Wordsworth's hypothesis that they might have had a written gospel, " either Matthew or Luke, probably the latter." The apostle had in his preaching at Thessalonica dwelt on the suddenness of the Second Advent; the ignorance of its period imposing constant preparedness and watchfulness. And they knew this correctly. What they knew was that they did not know the time, but only the solemn suddenness, of the Lord's coming (Luke xii, 39).

(Ver. 3.) ὅταν λέγωσιν Εἰρήνη καὶ ἀσφάλεια—" when they may be saying peace and safety." The Received Text inserts γὰρ after ὅταν with K L, many mss., the Vulgate (*enim*); δέ in place of γὰρ is found in B D ℵ³, in the Philoxenian Syriac, and in Eusebius, Chrysostom, and Theodoret; ὅταν stands alone, A F ℵ, in four mss., the Claromontane Latin, the Peshito, the Gothic, and in many of the Latin fathers. There was ever a strong temptation to supply connecting particles, so that very probably δέ is to be rejected as well as γάρ. The two particles are often exchanged in codices, as Rom. iv, 15; xi, 13; xv, 8; Gal. i, 11; iv, 25; v, 17. The description is all the more vivid from its apparent abruptness and the want of any copula. In cases parallel to this, the Authorized Version often uses the present, as in Matt. vi, 2, 5, 6, 16; x, 19, 23; though here it employs the future. The persons implied are not merely, as Hammond supposes, the Jews who persecuted those who received the faith with all bitterness, and all "temporizing Christians who complied and joined along with them—Jews and Gnostics, who were the cockle among the wheat in every Christian plantation." Chrysostom also partly holds the same view, "those who warred upon them," οἱ πολεμοῦντες αὐτούς. The reference, as the context shows, is to unbelieving men who are wholly unprepared for the sudden crisis—

Εἰρήνη καὶ ἀσφάλεια—" peace and safety," that is, are on all sides, perhaps a reminiscence of Ezek. xiii, 10, 16, "saying peace and there was no peace." The first term may be inner quiet and the second outer tranquillity, nothing within or without disturbing or menacing their ominous repose, which is so fallacious and so soon to be sternly and suddenly broken and destroyed. The unheralded storm dashes on them in a moment, as if from a clear and unclouded sky, or, in the apostle's figure—

τότε αἰφνίδιος αὐτοῖς ἐφίσταται ὄλεθρος—"then suddenly on them does come destruction." The adjective αἰφνίδιος, "unforeseen," from its position emphatic—a species of predicate of manner—is more, as Ellicott says, than a mere epithet, and may be rendered by an adverbial phrase, *repentinus eis superveniet interitus* (Vulgate), the Syriac having ܡܥܠܝܐ ܢܣܘܒ Kühner, § 685; Winer, § 54, 2; Ellendt's note, Arrian, vol. I, p. 174; Thucydides, vi, 49; viii, 28. The same happens often in Latin—as *subitus irrupit* (Tacitus, *Hist.*, iii, 47); Kritz, Sallust, note on the phrase *aspera fœdaque evenerant*, i, p. 125, compared with do., ii, p. 174. The present verb ἐφίσταται is to come upon by surprise (Luke xxi, 34; Acts iv, 1; xvii, 5); τὸ αἰφνίδιον καὶ ἀπροσδόκητον (Thucydides, II, 61). It has here the simple dative, ἐπί being used in the passage just quoted from Luke xxi, 34. Ὄλεθρος (ὄλλυμι) means death in the Homeric poems, and then destruction in a general sense (1 Cor. v, 5), ruin inflicted as a divine penalty or as the result of sinful courses (2 Thess. i, 9; 1 Tim. vi, 9; Sept., Pro. xxi, 7; Obadiah 13). This state of false peace is suddenly broken, and they are destroyed in their dream of security.

ὥσπερ ἡ ὠδὶν τῇ ἐν γαστρὶ ἐχούσῃ· καὶ οὐ μὴ ἐκφύγωσιν—"as travail upon her with child, and they shall in no wise escape." The form ὠδίν instead of ὠδίς, like ἀκτίν, belongs to the later Greek. Winer, § 9, 2, note 1; Buttmann, § 41, 3. The phrase ἐν γαστρὶ ἐχούσῃ is the usual formula denoting pregnancy (Matt. i, 18, 23; xxiv, 19; Mark xiii, 17; Luke xxi, 23; Rev. xii, 2). The phrase in *Iliad*, vi, 58 is γαστέρι φέρειν, and ἐν γαστρὶ φέρειν occurs in Plato, *De Legg.* vii, 792 E. This comparison is found often in the Old Testament (Ps. xlviii, 6; Is. xiii, 8; xxi, 3; Jer. vi, 24; Hosea xiii, 13; Micah iv, 9, 10). The point of comparison is the suddenness and uncertainty of the birth-pang. The throe of agony comes in a moment upon the woman, no matter where she is or in what she is engaged. Other points of analogy have been sought for, but they unnecessarily strain the figure. (1) Rieger and Calvin suggest that, as the woman carries in herself the cause of her anguish, so these unbelieving men bear their sin, the source of their suffering, within them. (2) Pelt mars the unity of the figure by laying undue stress on the inevitableness of the travail. (3) Chrysostom combines in his illustration the severity as well as the suddenness of the spasm. Theodoret's words are "she knows that she is pregnant, but does not know the time of her travail, so we know that the Lord of all will come, but we have not indeed learned the time of His Advent." Œcumenius adds, "that indeed she has signs of birth, but she knows not its hour or day." (4) De Wette, approved by Koch and Lünemann, in the same spirit, thus puts it—"that the figure assumes the day to be near, as such a woman, though she does not know the day and hour, has yet knowledge of the period." The idea so far contradicts the context which represents the unbelieving world as wholly taken by surprise; and, besides, it is not the pregnancy nor the birth, but the proverbially sudden pang which seizes such a woman, that the apostle puts into prominence. (5) Olshausen brings out another idea foreign to the figure in its present use, that a higher life is to be produced in humanity by the will of God, through the ordinance of these pangs; and Bisping thus enlarges, "the end of all things is the time of the birth-woe, which is followed by the new birth of humanity *im grossen Gange*, and of all nature (Rom. viii, 22)." But it is not the result or product of the birth which is here presented, it is the sudden rush of destruction upon those who are lulled in a false and carnal security. Or it is the unexpectedness of the Advent to all who are not prepared for it and looking for it; that is the apostle's statement in itself, and as pointed by the double figure. The Lord himself delivered and illustrated the same awful truth—as it was in the days of Noah, when the flood, swift and undreamed of, came on a busy and self-indulging world; as it was in the days of Lot when Sodom was absorbed in social merriment and prosperity, and when in a moment it rained fire and brimstone from heaven upon it, so shall also the coming of the Son of Man be. Compare Is. xxx, 13; Matt. xxiv, 36, 39; Luke xvii, 26-30.

καὶ οὐ μὴ ἐκφύγωσιν—" and they shall in no wise escape."

There is no accusative expressed, and it narrows the sense to supply one, so that the verb is to be taken in its fullest significance (Heb. ii, 3; xii, 25; Ecclus. xvi, 13). A direct accusative is, however, sometimes added (Rom. ii, 3; 2 Macc. vii, 35; vi, 26). Whatever is threatened, whatever they merit, they shall not escape, but shall meet with the opposite of peace and safety. For the double negative οὐ μή, see under iv, 15. Compare Ps. lxxiii, 18, 19.

(Ver. 4.) Ὑμεῖς δὲ, ἀδελφοί, οὐκ ἐστὲ ἐν σκότει—"But ye, brethren, are not in darkness." Their character is placed in contrast, δέ, with that of those whose doom is told in the previous verse. Ἐστέ is not imperative, but indicative. (1) The imperative would have required μή (Schmalfeld, p. 143). (2) Besides, Christians are in profession and character, not in darkness. (3) As Koch remarks, the imperative ἐστέ does not occur in the New Testament. The clause is simply an assertion, and ἐν σκότει appears to have been suggested by the previous ἐν νυκτί. The σκότος is not simply ignorance (Theodoret and others), but spiritual darkness or depravity—darkness of soul as well as of intellect—without the saving enlightenment of the truth—the state of unthinking and unbelieving men, who though on the verge of ruin are in self-delusion, saying "peace and safety" (Rom. xiii, 12). See under Ephes. v, 6. The apostle uses the abstract ἐν σκότει—in it as their enveloping element. (Greek fathers). See under Col. i, 13.

ἵνα ἡ ἡμέρα ὑμᾶς ὡς κλέπτης καταλάβῃ—" that the day should overtake you as a thief." The order ἡ ἡμέρα ὑμᾶς is supported by B K L ℵ, nearly all mss., and by the Greek fathers Epiphanius, Chrysostom, Theodoret, Damascenus; while the order ὑμᾶς ἡ ἡμέρα is found in A D F, both Latin versions, and many Latin fathers, and is adopted by Lachmann, Tischendorf in his first edition, and Ellicott. The authority is not very decided either way, and it may be said on the one hand that ὑμᾶς was emphasized purposely by putting it first, or, on the other hand, that it was put after ἡμέρα according to the simpler order which is preferred by Tischendorf in his 2nd and 7th editions, and by Alford. The reading κλέπτας, received by Lachmann, and found in A B and the Coptic version, is favoured by Grotius, De Wette, and

Ewald, but cannot be sustained, for though it be the more difficult reading, it wants the authority of manuscripts, versions, and fathers. Ἵνα is not to be rendered ecbatically as ὥστε (Pelt, Schott, Olshausen, Baumgarten-Crusius, Bisping, Jowett), but with its usual telic signification so far modified that result is combined with purpose (Winer, § 53, 6), or purpose is viewed as embodied in result. Lünemann states the connection thus, "the penalty which falls on the unbelieving and God-estranged, may that not fall upon you." Hofmann regards it differently—"the being in darkness would be indispensable in order to such a surprise." The sense then is, ye are not in darkness, for this blessed purpose, that the day may not overtake you as a thief. The purpose of your enlightenment is that the day may not surprise you, as it must and will those who are still in darkness. The verb καταλάβῃ has from κατά an intensified meaning, that of eager or sudden seizure, and not necessarily that *des feindlichen Ergreifens* (Koch). A similar sense modified by the context is found in Mark ix, 18; John viii, 3, 4; xii, 35; Philip. iii, 12. The phrase ἡ ἡμέρα has been taken by many as synonymous with ἡ ἡμέρα Κυρίου. Hence F adds ἐκείνη, the two Latin versions have *illa*, and the Syriac reads ܠܝܘܡܐ ܗܘ. But the reference is wrong, as the following verses show in the phrases, "children of the day," "not of darkness," "let us who are of the day." The noun ἡμέρα is now used as in contrast with σκότος, and is the period of light, that light which, breaking in upon the soul, so benignly fills it that it is no longer ἐν σκότει, and which shineth more and more unto the perfect day—the day of the Lord. The day—the period of light, the day-spring from on high—should not surprise them like a thief stealing suddenly upon them, for they were not in darkness, they were already children of light, familiar with it, and prepared for the fuller light of "that day." If the reading κλέπτας be adopted, the meaning would be—The day bursting upon the thief surprises him in his nocturnal prowling, or seizes him unawares when not suspecting the dawn to be at hand; but ye are not in that predicament, ye are not like thieves "who ply their work in the night" (De Wette) The inference or lesson is given by Ambrose, *nobis enim non scire proderat; ut dum certa futuri judicii momenta nescimus, semper tanquam in excubiis constituti, et in quadam virtutis specula collocati peccandi consuetudinem declinemus; ne nos inter vitia dies Domini deprehendat; non enim prodest scire, sed metuere quod futurum est* (*De Fide*, v, 14, Paris, 1845).

(Ver. 5.) πάντες γὰρ ὑμεῖς υἱοὶ φωτός ἐστε καὶ υἱοὶ ἡμέρας—"for all ye are sons of the light and of the day." There is overwhelming evidence in uncials, versions, and fathers for the insertion of γὰρ, which the Received Text omits. Ye are not in darkness, " for ye are all sons of light." The Hebraic form גֵּן הָאוֹר, υἱοὶ φωτός, denotes genetic relationship, light in the aspect of a parent to his children. Winer, § 34, 3 *b* 2. The usage with the genitive of an abstract noun is common in Hebrew—the light is their origin and life. Many examples may be seen in Glassii *Philologia Sacra*, vol. I, p. 95, ed. Dathe. All the six sections of examples are not so distinguishable in meaning or reference as Glassius makes them. Compare Luke xvi, 8; John xii, 36; Matt. viii, 12; xiii, 38; Acts iv, 36; Ephes. vi, 8. See under Ephes. ii, 2, 3. There are phrases remotely similar in classic Greek, but none of them has the genitive of an abstract noun; and even with regard to them Bloomfield remarks, *notandum, hoc genus loquendi apud sophistas et scriptores neotericos maxime in gratia fuisse* (*Persae*, 408; Goettling, Hesiod, *Theog.*, 240, p. 26). The relation expressed being derivative, the sense is not that of the Greek expositors, οἱ τὰ φωτὸς πράττοντες, or οἱ τὰ δίκαια καὶ πεφωτισμένα πράττοντες (Œcumenius), though such is the result. The "light" and "the day" are so far synonymous, as the day is the period of the light, which puts an end to the darkness. Divine enlightenment fills the believer—the light is his life, the birth and growth of his spiritual existence.

οὐκ ἐσμὲν νυκτὸς οὐδὲ σκότους—" we are not of the night nor of darkness." Ἐστέ, found in a few codices, is a conformation to the previous clauses. It is wrong in Estius, Pelt, and Schott to supply υἱοί; the genitive by itself rather denotes the sphere to which one belongs. Acts ix, 2; xxiii, 6; 1 Cor. vi, 19; Heb. x, 39; Winer, § 30, 5; Ast *Lex. Platon.*, *sub voce* εἰμί; Bernhardy, p. 165. We believers in general belong not to the night nor to darkness; night being the period of darkness, it is not our sphere of origin or action. The night has passed away; the darkness is gone; and we are light in the Lord. The apostle passes from the meaning of ἡμέρα, as the point of time when the Lord comes again, to its more common meaning of daytime as the period of light in contrast with night-time and darkness, these being taken at the same time as symbols of spiritual states. Being now sons of the day, we live in its light, which is only brightened by the day of the Lord when it comes, for it brings fuller and endless radiance. In Rom. xiii, 11, 12, 13, the apostle makes a similar transition from the use of day, as meaning the Advent, to its natural or spiritual signification. The startling reverse of the picture is given in Amos v, 18, 19, 20.

(Ver. 6.) "Ἄρα οὖν μὴ καθεύδωμεν ὡς καὶ οἱ λοιποί—" So then let us not sleep even as the rest." After ὡς, καὶ is wanting in A B ℵ¹ and in the Vulgate (Codex Amiatinus); but it is found in D F K L ℵ³, in the Vulgate, Peshito, and several of the fathers. It is found in similar clauses, 1 Cor. ix, 5 ; Ephes. ii, 3 ; 1 Thess. v, 13. The authorities for the omission are about as valid as those for the insertion.

Ἄρα is inferential, such being the case, and οὖν is collective and argumentative; then, therefore, as things are, let us in consequence of our being so. Klotz, *Devarius*, ii, pp. 181-717; Donaldson, *Cratylus*, § 192. As we are sons of the day, and are not sons of the night, let us, I and you, not sleep—sleep and night go together, but sleep and day are incompatible. Sleep is the image of spiritual lethargy and indifference, without earnestness or activity. "The others" are the unbelieving world around them, that cared for none of these things, wrapped in a profound slumber, never awakened to the reality of the soul's condition and prospects, and the spiritual consciousness so wholly sunk into torpor and death as to be unsusceptible of saving impressions. See under Ephes. v, 14. Compare Matt. xiii, 13, 14, 15.

ἀλλὰ γρηγορῶμεν καὶ νήφωμεν—" but let us watch and be sober." The clause is the direct positive contrast to the previous negative one. The verb γρηγορέω, used as a present, is from the perfect of the verb ἐγείρω, ἐγρήγορα. Buttmann, vol. II, pp. 114, 115; Phrynichus, ed. Lobeck, p. 118. For the use of the subjunctive, see Winer, 41, 4. Wakefulness is enjoined by the apostle, on himself, and all his fellow-believers. The verb νήφωμεν may be from νη+εφ=eb, Sanscrit *ap*, water, *der nocht nicht getrunken hat*, connected with *ebrius* and πίνω. (Benfey, *Wurzellex.*, vol. II, p. 75). Thomas Magister says νήφει τις ὅταν μέθης ἐκτὸς ᾖ . . . γρηγορεῖ ὅταν ἐκτὸς ὕπνου ᾖ. Let us who are not in the world's great dormitory not only be wakeful and ever on the alert, but also wary in our vigilance, serene and circumspect in thought and act, neither dreaming on the one hand, nor suddenly thrown off our guard on the other hand, unbeguiled by "dreams and fantasies," ὀνειράτων καὶ φαντασίας (Chrysostom); as the same father remarks, "for even by day if one watches, but is not sober, he will fall into numberless dangers"—ὥστε γρηγορήσεως ἐπίτασις ἡ νῆψις ἐστίν. Mark xiii, 35, 36, 37. This is probably not strictly correct, for the two verbs are taken as being nearly synonymous, as Huther on 1 Peter v, 8; but the second is rather the result of the first, and cannot exist without it. There may be a watchfulness devoid of that self-discipline which is implied in sobriety. Then follows the confirmatory illustration—

(Ver. 7.) οἱ γὰρ καθεύδοντες νυκτὸς καθεύδουσιν, καὶ οἱ μεθυσκόμενοι νυκτὸς μεθύουσιν—"for they that sleep sleep in the night, and they that be drunken are drunken in the night." The last half of the verse is rendered in the Claromontane Latin *et qui inebriantur nocte ebrii sunt*. So Bengel says, μεθύσκομαι *notat actum;* μεθύω *statum vel habitum*. Macknight makes the same distinction, "the first verb signifies the act of getting drunk, and the second the state." Similarly, Erasmus, Beza, and Piscator. But the distinction does not seem to be tenable, at least it serves no purpose to make it here. Compare John ii, 10; Ephes. v, 18; Rev. xvii, 2. Both verbs represent the same Hebrew word in the Septuagint, שָׁכַר—the first, however, in its Piel form שִׁכֵּר. The second Greek term is often used figuratively with αἷμα in the Septuagint, and also in the New Testament, as Rev. xvii, 6. As the verb is repeated in the first half of the verse, the variation need not be insisted on in the second half. The Vulgate has *et qui ebrii sunt, nocte ebrii sunt*—the stress of the sentence lying on the repeated νυκτός. By many the verse has been taken in a figurative or spiritual sense. Thus Chrysostom, "the drunkenness of which he here speaks is not that from wine only, but that also which comes from all sins. For wealth and the lust of possession is a drunkenness of the soul, and so is carnal lust (σωμάτων ἔρως), and every sin you can name is a drunkenness of the soul." Then he says, "Sin is a sleep, because in the first place the vicious man is inactive with regard to virtue, and again because he sees everything as a vision, he views nothing in its true light, but is full of dreams—ὁ πλοῦτος ὄναρ, ἡ δόξα, πάντα τὰ τοιαῦτα." The illustration is repeated by Œcumenius and Theophylact, and is virtually adopted by Baumgarten-Crusius, Koch, Hofmann, &c. Baumgarten-Crusius thus gives it, "Defect in spiritual life and immorality, belong to the lightless condition, therefore not to you"; or as Hofmann, "with those who sleep and get drunk it is night." Pelagius explains, *qui dormierunt obliti sunt sui; curae quoque inebriant mentem.* Augustine is still more decided, *noctem dicens iniquitatem, in qua illi obdormiunt cupiendo ista terrena,* &c., (*Enarrat. in Ps.* 131, vol. IV, p. 2102, *Opera*, Gaume). But it is better to take the words in their natural sense, the meaning being that in ordinary experience night is the common time for sleep and for drunkenness. The repetition of the verbs, as subject and predicate, shows, as Lünemann remarks, that νυκτός is only a designation of time. The verse is thus a familiar illustration of the use and abuse of night. *Admonet indecorum atque turpe esse dormire medio die aut inebriari* (Calvin). Peter's disclaimer was, "these men are not drunk, seeing it is but the third hour of the day" (Acts ii, 15); and in his second epistle he brands some persons as guilty of an uncommon and aggravated sin, "that shall perish in their own corruption," viz., "that count it pleasure to riot in the daytime" (ii, 13). Sleep and drunkenness belong to the night season, it is the natural time for the one, and it is for many reasons taken advantage of for the other. Believers, on the other hand, are to be wakeful and sober, are not to be like the rest, οἱ λοιποί, who are of the night in every sense, it being their element and sphere. What is true of sleepers and drunkards literally is true in a higher and more awful sense of those who want spiritual illumination. See under Gal. v, 20.

(Ver. 8.) ἡμεῖς δὲ ἡμέρας ὄντες νήφωμεν—" but let us as being of the day be sober." By the emphatic ἡμεῖς he identifies himself with his readers, and by δέ he passes to contrasted conduct. The participle has a quasi-causal, or what Schmalfeld calls a temporal-causal force (p. 207), "inasmuch as we are of the day," an argument to be sober and to arm ourselves. See under verses 5 and 6. The Peshito inserts ܒܢܝ, "sons," and some expositors, as Estius, Whitby, Schott, &c., needlessly do the same, and mar the idiom. See under verse 5. It would seem that ἡ ἡμέρα and ἡμέρα are kept distinct in the paragraph, the first being the definite day of the Lord, and the second the present period of illumination and activity. This sobriety, in which the mental powers are preserved in strict discipline, is necessary, and yet it is not enough to be never off our guard, there must also be the assumption of armour—ἀλλὰ δεῖ καὶ καθοπλίζεσθαι (Chrysostom).

ἐνδυσάμενοι θώρακα πίστεως καὶ ἀγάπης καὶ περικεφαλαίαν ἐλπίδα σωτηρίας—" having put on the breast-plate of faith and love, and for an helmet the hope of salvation." Not merely *induti* (Vulgate). The past participle describes the action as just preceding the state inculcated by the verb, or contemporaneous with it. Winer, § 45, 2. He has said in verse 6, "let us watch and be sober"; and now, assuming that believers are watchful, he repeats, " let us be sober." Sobriety is self-restraint, self-discipline, indispensable to our getting the benefit of the armour which we are to assume. An armed man not watchful, an armed man undisciplined, will soon be seized and vanquished. The figure of a Christian soldier is common with the apostle (2 Cor. x, 4; Ephes. vi, 11; 1 Tim. vi, 11; Sept., Is. lix, 17). Perhaps the idea of watching suggested that of being armed for defence, the underlying thought being that we must not be so subdued, and so kept in spiritual captivity, that the day of the Lord should surprise us. Resistance against evils, which are apt to overpower and fetter us so as to throw us into unpreparedness for the Advent of the Master, is the soul of the figure—the being armed not for aggression but for safety.

The three genitives, πίστεως, ἀγάπης, σωτηρίας, are without the article, as being well known and unique terms, and by correlation they cause the governing substantives, θώρακα, περικεφαλαίαν, also to want the article, and that in cases " where the governing noun might seem to require the definite form." Winer, § 19, 1; Middleton, *Greek Article*, p. 48, ed. Rose. For the use of the verb ἐνδύειν, compare Herod., vii, 218; Xenoph. *Cyrop.*, vi, 4, 2; Wisdom, v, 17; Ephes. vi, 11; Rom. xiii, 12.

In the phrase θώρακα πίστεως καὶ ἀγάπης, the genitives are those of apposition. Winer, § 59, 8. Faith and love are the defence of the person. The breast-plate or coat of mail covers the heart, the helmet or military cap defends the head. Πίστις is a θώραξ, for it is a faith which realizes one's position, its dangers and its means of safety; which grasps the truth, and is filled with its living power; steady in its dependence on the Master, and in its conscious union with Him; heroic from His example, and self-sustained by His presence. Ἀγάπη, which with πίστις forms the καρδιοφύλαξ, is a love which lives in self-consecration; which does all duty, and bears all trial from paramount affection to Him; being knitted to Him, and, through Him, to all that bears His image. These in their combination form an armour of mail tempered so that no weapon can pierce it; a harness through whose joints no arrow can find an unsuspected entrance (1 John v, 4, 5).

"And for an helmet the hope of salvation." The genitive σωτηρίας may be taken as that of object, not the basis on which hope rests, but the object which it embraces, or what it desires and expects. See under i, 3. Σωτηρία, used in the abstract, has its most comprehensive meaning, of deliverance from sin and death, from all the penal and polluting effects of the fall— a deliverance incipiently and partially enjoyed now, and to be fully and finally possessed at the Second Advent. The hope of such salvation covers the head in the day of battle, preserves from despondency, nerves to face danger, and braces up under fatigue and difficulty by fixing the gaze on the glorious issue which is no uncertainty, as is told in the following verse. " It is not possible that one fortified by such armour as this should ever fall" (Chrysostom), or as Theodoret pithily puts it, γενέσθω δὲ ἡμῖν κράνος ἀρραγὲς ἡ τῆς ἐπηγγελμένης σωτηρίας ἐλπίς.

What keeps believers sober, vigilant, armed, and thus prepared, is the possession of the three primary graces, faith, love, and hope, arranged as in i, 3. See under it. When these are in lively exercise, the soul is ever wary and watchful, ever prepared for the Master's coming, nay, longing for it—faith believing it, love embracing it, hope ardently anticipating it—and then the day will not overtake us unawares or as a thief.

Between this and the somewhat corresponding passage in Ephes. vi, 13, &c., there are some points of difference. First, in the Epistle to the Ephesians, there is a fuller description of the defensive armour—the girdle, the sandal, and the shield, omitted here, are there mentioned. Secondly, there is also mention in that epistle of an aggressive weapon—the sword. And, thirdly, there is some variation in the explanatory terms—there it is the breast-plate of righteousness, but here the breast-plate of faith and love, the distinction between them being that of process and result; there it is the helmet of salvation, but here the hope of salvation; and the shield, not enumerated here, is there called the shield of faith. Heart and head being such vital organs are selected as needing special and fitting defence, the shield as well as the breast-plate being said to be faith; the idea of self-defence is common to both. "Salvation" is also exchanged for the "hope of salvation," the difference being that between salvation, partial now but consciously enjoyed, and the prospect of a perfect salvation in heaven, so that the various figures are not to be pressed too closely, as in Chandler's paraphrase or Gurnall's *Christian Armour*. For the meaning of the military terms see under Ephes. vi, 14, 17.

(Ver. 9.) ὅτι οὐκ ἔθετο ἡμᾶς ὁ Θεὸς εἰς ὀργήν—"because God did not appoint us to wrath." Alford calls this verse epexegetical of ἐλπίδα σωτηρίας, but it rather assigns the ground of that expression—the basis of the "hope"—given first in a negative and then in a positive form. It is not a new motive for watchfulness (Musculus), nor yet generally a motive to assume the armour mentioned, as the Greek fathers, Œcumenius and Theophylact. Nor is ὅτι to be rendered "that" as if it introduced the contents or object of the hope (Hofmann). Rom. viii. 20, 21, is not in analogy, for there ἐπ' ἐλπίδι has no object genitive attached to it as here. In this use of the verb τιθέναι, that with an accusative of person followed by εἰς pointing out the object, τινὰ εἰς τι, there is a species of Hebraism,—at least the Hebrew verbs שׂים, נתן or שׁית are used similarly with לְ. Thus in Sept., Ps. lxvi, 9; Is. xlii, 15; Jer. ix, 11; xiii, 16; Ezek. xiv, 8; John xv, 16; Acts xiii, 47 (τέθεικά σε εἰς φῶς); 1 Tim. i, 12 (θέμενος εἰς διακονίαν); 1 Peter ii, 8 (εἰς ὃ καὶ ἐτέθησαν). See under iii, 3. God did not appoint us to wrath, to be the victims of it, or to suffer under it, though we had sinned against him and were by nature children of wrath. The ἡμᾶς are those who believe, and therefore escape the awful penalty. The indefinite aorist refers to a past period, though not perhaps to the eternal decree, but to its embodiment in time or its temporal manifestation. See under i, 10. We are destined not to punishment, to "death" or "destruction" (2 Cor. vii, 10; Philip. i, 19), nor to mere escape but to positive blessing. In sending the gospel and giving us His Spirit, God did not set us out for wrath. Ὀργή is divine wrath against sin, the converse of ἔλεος. The one implies the other, love to the sinner, ὀργή to his sin.

ἀλλ' εἰς περιποίησιν σωτηρίας διὰ τοῦ Κυρίου ἡμῶν Ἰησοῦ Χριστοῦ—" but to the obtaining of salvation through our Lord Jesus Christ." For the various meanings which περιποίησις and its verb may bear or which have been assigned to them, see at length under Ephes. i, 14. The verb denotes to acquire for oneself (Gen. xxxvi, 6; Prov. vii, 4; Is. xliii, 21; Acts xx, 28; also in the classics, Thucyd., iii. 102; Xenoph., *Cyrop.*, iv, 410; Herod., i, 110; vii, 52). In the Definitions ascribed to Plato, the words occur, σωτηρία, περιποίησις ἀβλαβής. The meaning of *conservatio* is sometimes attached to the word, as in 2 Chron. xiv, 13, where it represents the Hebrew מִחְיָה; in Heb. x, 39, "to the saving of the soul"; but it is needless here to give this meaning and make the following genitive that of apposition. Acquisition therefore is the probable meaning of the noun, as in 2 Thess. ii, 14, "Whereunto he called you by our gospel εἰς περιποίησιν δόξης"; Heb. x, 39. Hesychius defines it by πλεονασμός, κτῆσις. In Ephes. i, 14; 1 Peter ii, 9, the word represents the Hebrew סְגֻלָּה, and the noun is collective in sense (Exod. xix, 5; Deut. vii, 6; xiv, 2; Matt. iii, 17). The Latin versions rightly and simply have *in acquisitionem salutis*. See under previous verse. God's appointment was that we should obtain salvation, deliverance from the ὀργή, with final acceptance and perfection. The Greek fathers do not give any definite assistance as to the precise shade of meaning. Generally, Chrysostom and Œcumenius give the result, "that he might save us." Theodoret has ἵνα σωτηρίας ἀξιώσῃ καὶ οἰκείους ἀποφήνῃ, and Theophylact merely exchanges the noun for the verb and adds καὶ σώσῃ— God did appoint us to obtain salvation, and this being so, that salvation comes not as an immediate gift, but—

διὰ τοῦ Κυρίου ἡμῶν Ἰησοῦ Χριστοῦ—"through our Lord Jesus Christ. The clause is not to be connected with ἔθετο (Estius), but with the words immediately before it, to obtain salvation. Nor does it refer to the securing of salvation (Hofmann), for the participation of it is the present thought. Nor does it mean, through his doctrine (Grotius), nor through faith in Him (Lünemann), but through Himself—through His mediation, and, as the next verse shows, especially through His atoning death. This is the uniform doctrine of Scripture. Salvation having God for its source, has Christ for its medium. Only through Christ is God known and accessible to us, and only through Him are spiritual blessings conferred upon us by God. See under Ephes. i, 7, and for the meaning of those proper names see under Ephes. i, 2, and under Gal. ii, 16. "Through our Lord Jesus Christ"—

(Ver. 10.) τοῦ ἀποθανόντος ὑπὲρ ἡμῶν—"who died for us." ὑπὲρ has preponderant authority, περί being found in B א¹, 17, a similar difference of reading occurring in other places. The clause points out the process by which salvation is obtained, through His death—not His teaching or example, but His death. Not that the clause is properly causal, as the participle in that case would have wanted the article. Donaldson, § 492. It simply describes the death of Christ in immediate connection with our obtainment of salvation, and as showing its preciousness and certainty.

ἵνα εἴτε γρηγορῶμεν εἴτε καθεύδωμεν ἅμα σὺν αὐτῷ ζήσωμεν— " in order that whether we wake or sleep, we should together live with Him." Ἵνα points out the great purpose of His atoning death. The compound εἴτε follows generally the construction of the simple εἰ, and it may be connected with a subjunctive. Nor may such a connection be called unclassical, though it is not the ordinary usage, at least among Attic prose writers, *paucis admodum locis*. Klotz, *Devarius*, ii, 501. The usage is admitted by Thomas Magister, οὐ μετὰ ὑποτακτικοῦ δὲ, πλὴν ἐπὶ τῶν αὐθυποτάκτων οἷον εἰ λάβωμαι (p. 267). In Plato occurs the phrase εἴτε τις ἄρρην εἴτε τις θῆλυς ᾖ (*De Legibus*, xii, 9 D, p. 958). See the first note of Stallbaum on the point, vol. X, p. 399; that of Wex, *Antig.*, vol. II, p. 187; and that of Poppo (Thucydides, i, 139); Hermann *De Particula* ἄν. Though the optative in such a case be commonly employed, the subjunctive in the secondary clause may, as Winer suggests, be the result of conformity to the subjunctive in the principal clause (§ 41, 2 c, note 2). The purpose of Christ's death is our life, and that life is independent of the states implied in γρηγορῶμεν and καθεύδωμεν; we may be in the one condition, or we may be in the other, it matters not, we shall together live with him, for on the certainty and reality of this life waking or sleeping has no influence.

But what is the meaning of the alternative clauses, "whether we may sleep, whether we may wake"? (1) The opinion of Musculus, Aretius, Whitby, and Fell, which is, whether He comes during the day when we are awake, or during the night when we are asleep, cannot be entertained. This explanation is wholly meaningless and unsatisfactory, and is also out of harmony with the solemn statement, and it does not relieve us from the difficulty of a change of meaning in the verbs. (2) Nor can the verbs be taken in an ethical sense, as in the previous paragraph, verses 6-8. For the declaration is that they who being in darkness are asleep, shall be overtaken by the day of the Lord as a thief in the night. To be asleep in this spiritual sense is to be in death, and such a state is wholly incompatible with the possession or prospect of the life described in ἵνα ζήσωμεν. (3) The opinion proposed but not adopted by Alford is sufficiently refuted by himself. His statement is, "To preserve the unity of metaphor we may interpret in this sense, that our God died for us, that whether we watch, are of the number of the watchful, that is, already Christians; or sleep, are of the number of the sleeping, that is, unconverted—we should live." Thus it would be, "who died that all men might be saved," "who came not to call the righteous only, but sinners to repentance." There is to this interpretation the great objection that it confounds the οἱ λοιποὶ with the ἡμᾶς, who are definitely spoken of as set by God, not to wrath, but εἰς περιποίησιν σωτηρίας. And the expression would be a rough and somewhat misleading statement of the general purpose of Christ's death; but its special purpose toward himself and his fellow-believers is the aspect of it present to the apostle's own mind. (4) The words are to be taken in their figurative sense, the first as descriptive of physical life, and the second of physical death. The meaning of the first verb is changed from its ethical sense, and the second is equivalent to κοιμᾶσθαι in chap. iv. Compare Matt. ix, 24; Sept., Ps. lxxxviii, 6; Dan. xii, 2. Chrysostom says, ἀλλ' ἕτερον ἐκεῖ τὸν ὕπνον φησὶ καὶ ἕτερον ἐνταῦθα. The first verb will thus correspond with "we who are alive and remain," and the second with those "who are fallen asleep." The verb γρηγορεῖν, however, is nowhere found in the sense of to live, and it gets such a meaning here only from its immediate contrast with καθεύδειν, and the employment and meaning of both are shaped by the following ζήσωμεν. Besides, the two verbs do not simply signify living and dying in themselves, but the first expresses life in its spiritual attitude of watchfulness and preparedness for the Lord's coming, and the second describes that condition or form which death has assumed through the mediation and atonement of the Lord Jesus (iv, 14). Compare Matt. xxiv, 42; xxv, 13; Rev. iii, 2, 3; Titus ii, 13.

There is, as has been said by De Wette, a want of perspicuity in this necessary change of sense, but the signification is apparent. Von Gerlach's observation, that the sleep of death is itself a portion of the curse of the sleep of sin, however true, does not explain the change of meaning in the two verbs, and would introduce a confusing reference. The final cause of Christ's death is wholly uninfluenced by these two states, living or dying; they who survive have no advantage over those who sleep, they who sleep are waked up to a higher life.

ἅμα σὺν αὐτῷ ζήσωμεν—"we should together live with Him." The connection of ἅμα has been variously given. (1) Hofmann and Riggenbach take the whole clause as one thought, "together with Him," that is, in closest union with Him. Such is probably the purport of the Authorized Version, and the other earlier English ones. But it does not need ἅμα to express this idea. (2) Bengel takes ἅμα in a sort of temporal sense—*simul, ut fit adventus. Totum institutum est*, περὶ τῶν χρόνων—but this idea neither suits the train of thought nor the connection. (3) The adverb ἅμα is suggested by the two states described in the previous clause. They who die before the Advent are severed from them who survive till that period, but both parties in spite of this separation shall be in company as a band of contemporaries living with Christ (iv, 17). "Ἅμα is together, that is, "in one society" (Rom. iii, 12). It refers immediately to the connection of believers with one another, and not to their union with Christ, which is expressed by σὺν αὐτῷ. That we should live is the great purpose of His death, and the life is plainly an existence above and beyond the life that ends in sleep. The waking and sleeping have immediate reference to the Second Coming, and the life purposed (ἵνα) for us is in connection with the same period. The entire paragraph points to this grand destiny, it underlies all the teaching from verse 13 of the previous chapter; the dead rise and the living are changed when the Lord descends, and both together shall be for ever with the Lord. So that the notion of Möller and Hofmann, that the living with Christ is that which is enjoyed now—the living being united to Him, and the dead being asleep in Him —though true in itself, falls short of the full meaning of the declaration before us. The starting-point was the relation of the dead and the living to Christ's Second Coming, ignorance or misconception of that relation having filled the Thessalonian church with sorrow over departed friends and kindred, and the paragraph now closes with an annunciation of the comforting truth that the dead and the living, though severed in the meantime, are so comprised in the final purpose of our Lord's atoning death that both of them at His return are united, live as one company, and in fellowship with Him. As the result of His death for them they live, life in every form and in every sphere of their nature being secured for them by the surrender of His life for them; they shall together live for ever with Him

—in His presence, and in communion with Him. Of that life, so blessed and unending, His presence is the primal element and the "chiefest joy" (Rom. xiv, 8, 9; 2 Cor. v, 9). Ζήσωμεν is a more definite and expressive term than the ἐσόμεθα of iv, 17; John xiv, 19; Col. iii, 3, 4.

(Ver. 11.) Διὸ παρακαλεῖτε ἀλλήλους—"wherefore comfort one another." This verse is the inference from the foregoing section—διό. οὖν = *quod quum ita sit*, διὸ = *quamobrem, ut etiam hoc aptius duas res conjungat*. Klotz, *Devarius*, II, p. 173. See under Gal. iv, 31. The Claromontane Latin has *exhortamini*, the margin of the English version has "exhort," and this rendering is allowed by Turretin, Pelt, De Wette, Peile, Koch, Conybeare, Hofmann, &c. It is a favourite word of the apostle, and its precise meaning in any place can only be gathered from the context. As the exhortation in this place has comfort for its theme, the verb is better taken, as in iv, 18, as meaning "comfort," and the entire preceding context necessitates or at least suggests such a meaning. Even the edification commanded in the following clause requires this meaning of comfort, as Pelt supposes, *ut ejus sit effectus*. Baumgarten, Rosenmüller, and Schott would combine both meanings. Theodoret explains by ψυχαγωγεῖτε. The hortatory part begins in verse 6, passing, as Lünemann remarks, into the consolatory, and the 10th and 11th verses are parallel to iv, 17, 18. The discussion of these momentous themes was brought on by the perplexity and sorrow of the Thessalonian church: they were not to grieve over departed fellow-believers, and the grounds of comfort are then distinctly set before them. The first portion of the paragraph ends with "wherefore comfort one another;" while the second portion, prolonging the illustration on some points in a more ethical form, leads to the same result, followed up by a similar practical inference, "wherefore comfort one another." There is need of comfort under bereavement, but all true comfort lies in these utterances of the apostle, and they were to ply one another with them. In a word, this wonderful paragraph starts with the monition "that ye sorrow not," and, after opening up the grounds of consolation in the death, resurrection, and final return of Jesus—securing the union of His people with Him as Saviour, representative, and pledge, and their communion with one another—it ends with the charge, *"comfort one another."* This is the only place where the authorized version renders ἀλλήλους, "yourselves together," Luke xxiii, 12, and xxiv, 14, being somewhat similar; the usual translation is "one another," or "among themselves" or "yourselves," &c.

καὶ οἰκοδομεῖτε εἷς τὸν ἕνα, καθὼς καὶ ποιεῖτε—"and edify one another, even as also ye are doing." The figure in the verb is common with the apostle. See under Ephes. ii, 20, where the figure of ναὸς Θεοῦ is developed at length. Compare 1 Cor. iii, 9, 16; viii, 1; x, 23; 2 Cor. vi, 16. The phrase εἷς τὸν ἕνα, "the one the other," is not without parallel in later classical writers, as Lucian, Dionysius Halicar., Plutarch, Arrian, and also in Theocritus, *Idyll.* xxii, 65. Examples may be found in Kypke, vol. II, p. 339. Compare Plato, *De Leg.*, εἷς πρὸς ἕνα (I, p. 626 c), and see the remarks of Winer, § 26, 2 *b*. The phrase is in meaning equivalent to ἀλλήλους—οἱ καθ' ἕνα (Ephes. v, 33). But this natural sense is too simple for many. The words will not bear the meaning assigned by Faber, *ad unum usque,* to a man—no one omitted, ἕως ἑνός; nor that given by Whitby, "edify yourselves into one body," εἰς ἕν; and still less that proposed by Rückert—so as to show, the one the other, that it is Christ as the foundation on whom the building should be reared, ἐπὶ τῷ ἑνί; such an idiom would be without example (*Römerb.*, vol. II, p. 249). All these proposals conjecture εἰς for εἷς.

And they did not need to begin obedience to this injunction as to mutual comforting; they were doing it; it had already been their practice, and the counsel virtually implies praise for previous work, and encouragement to proceed with yet profounder mutual sympathy. For καθὼς see under Ephes. i, 4; καθὼς καὶ as in 1 Cor. xiii, 12; xiv, 34. Klotz, *Devarius,* II, 635; Winer, § 53, 8. In several earlier verses of the epistle, as in iv, 1, 10, the apostle has a similar allusion to the Thessalonian church as having commenced to do what he is enjoining upon them. The church had set itself in earnest to do the Master's will, and the apostle urges not only a continuous, but a still fuller compliance. Calvin's remark is *sed ne videatur eorum negligentiam perstringere simul dicit eos sponte facere quod præcipit. Verum quae nostra est ad bonum segnities, qui optime omnium sunt animati, stimulis tamen semper indigent.*

The apostle has been enjoining the duty of mutual comforting and edification, and he turns now to one special form in which his counsel could be obeyed. The connection proposed by Chrysostom is peculiar, "rulers stir up opposition, so do physicians, and parents, and so does the presbyter; he who is rebuked is sure to become an enemy." But this connection is far-fetched and is probably a reflection from the commentator's own times and experience. For he suffered for his fidelity and died a virtual martyr. This other proposed connection has apparently a similar origin, to wit, the desire of the laity on the smallest encouragement to become teachers. "And lest they should imagine that he had raised them to the rank of teachers by bidding them edify one another, he has subjoined this—all but saying, I give leave even to you to edify one another, for it is impossible for a teacher to say everything." Similarly Œcumenius and Theophylact. Such a connection presupposes a state of things which, in any extreme form at least, could scarcely have existed at that early period in the Thessalonian community. There is no clear trace of any such difference as Olshausen supposes, between the church and its rulers; and verse 27 does not distinctly imply it. Hofmann's remark is also beyond the context—"forget not in your activity what you owe to the office-bearers." All we can say is that if there were any untoward tendencies to neglect the duties now to be enjoined, the injunction would be read with a special point and significance. The apostle, naturally and without any polemical motive, turns from mutual edification to those whose special function it was to instruct the church.

(Ver. 12.) Ἐρωτῶμεν δὲ ὑμᾶς, ἀδελφοί—"Now we beseech you, brethren." Δὲ marks the transition to another theme. On the verb, see under iv, 1. This brief preface shows the special earnestness with which he utters the counsel now to be given. On obedience to it depended, in no small measure, the peace and the spiritual prosperity of the church.

εἰδέναι τοὺς κωπιῶντας ἐν ὑμῖν καὶ προϊσταμένους ὑμῶν ἐν Κυρίῳ καὶ νουθετοῦντας ὑμᾶς—"to know them that are labouring among you, and are presiding over you in the Lord, and are admonishing you." As the absence of the article in the two last participles shows, the same class of persons is described in the three clauses, and they are characterized by their functions, or, as the use of the participle shows, by their actual exercise of those functions. More generally, they are described as "labouring among you." In the verb κοπιάω (κόπος, κόπτω) lies the notion of severe toil, exhausting labour. It is applied again and again to ministerial industry (Rom. xvi, 12; 1 Cor. xv, 10; Gal. iv, 11; 1 Tim v, 17). The Christian ministry rightly discharged is no sinecure, it is the highest and hardest of human enterprises; the reward is proportionate. It is sometimes followed by εἰς defining its object, as in Philip. ii, 16; Col. i, 29; or its final purpose, 1 Tim. iv, 10; Rom. xvi, 12. Ἐν is sometimes used to mark its sphere or its spirit, but here it seems to have a local reference, *inter vos* (Vulgate); not as Pelt (*in vobis*), in your hearts; nor as Hofmann, "on you," as its objects, *ut ipsi veri fierent Christiani*. The clause being somewhat vague in reference is defined by the following one—

καὶ προϊσταμένους ὑμῶν ἐν Κυρίῳ—"and are presiding over you" (1 Tim. v, 17). These presidents are the class designated generally as they who are labouring among you. The labours here recognized are not those of hearty zeal and fatiguing toil on the part of any in the church who might spontaneously undertake them, but are specially those of the presbyters. Two functions are assigned to them, labour and presidence; they wrought among them, and they were over them; laboured in virtue of being presidents; their presidency was therefore no idle or neutral oversight, no mere position of preferment and honour. The church could not exist in order and usefulness without some species of government, law being essential to liberty, superintendence and control being indispensable to harmony and development. The phrase ἐν Κυρίῳ, not *juvante Domino* (Schott), marks the sphere of presidency—in Him, in union with Him, in harmony with His authority and purposes, not "lording it over God's heritage," but in an administration "distinct from, and not subordinate to, civil government." The explanation given by Chrysostom, and more distinctly put by Theodoret, is wholly wrong—τὸ δὲ προϊσταμένους ὑμῶν ἐν Κυρίῳ ἀντὶ ὑπερευχομένους ὑμῶν, &c. Examples from Josephus of the participle governing the genitive may be found in Krebs, p. 346. Justin Martyr describes the work of the president in his day.

καὶ νουθετοῦντας ὑμᾶς—" and admonish you." The verb signifies to put in mind, to correct by word—a word of encouragement, or a word of remonstrance (νουθετικοὶ λόγοι, Xenoph., *Mem.*, i, 2, 21), though it does also signify correction by deed (ῥάβδου νουθέτησις, Plato, *De Leg.*, 700 c). See under Ephes. vi, 4; Trench, *Synon.*, § 32. This admonition is another element or sphere of the labour referred to in the first clause. It implies teaching, but means particularly, practical counsel, suggestion, and warning; earnest, pastoral instruction; unwearied, tender, and watchful guidance in the midst of trial, struggle, and temptation (Ephes. iv, 11). In this way the apostle describes the presbyters of the Thessalonian church as labouring, their labour being superintendence and admonition, not two distinct offices held by different individuals, but combined apparently in one—"warning every man, and teaching every man in all wisdom, in order to present every man perfect in Christ Jesus" (Col. i, 28). And these they are charged first to know, εἰδέναι. The verb seems to mean, to know emphatically, like ידע, almost equivalent to recognize (Fürst, *Heb. Lex.*, *sub voce*); other senses have been assigned which usage will not warrant. They were to know their office-bearers, that is, not simply how it was with them, or what they had in them, but in themselves, in their position and duties—in effect, so to understand their value, as to esteem them highly in love. Compare 1 Cor. xvi, 18, where ἐπιγινώσκω is used (ἐπιγινώσκετε οὖν τοὺς τοιούτους); and for somewhat similar Hebrew usage compare Ps. cxliv, 3; Prov. xxvii, 23; Nahum. i, 7.

(Ver. 13.) καὶ ἡγεῖσθαι αὐτοὺς ὑπερεκπερισσῶς ἐν ἀγάπῃ διὰ τὸ ἔργον αὐτῶν—"and to esteem them very highly in love for their work's sake." As De Wette, Lünemann, and Ellicott have remarked, the sense of the clause depends on the connection of ἐν ἀγάπῃ. If it be kept in what seems its natural position, the meaning will be, "regard them very highly, and that in love," love being the element in which this superabundant esteem is to embody itself. So Theodoret, Estius, Grotius, De Wette, Koch. Or ἐν ἀγάπῃ may be joined more closely to the verb, as the Vulgate, *habeatis illos abundantius in charitate*, "esteem them in love very highly." So several Greek fathers, Beza, Pelt, Schott, Olshausen, Hofmann, Riggenbach. Neither connection is free from difficulty, for, in the first mode, the neutral verb which means to reckon or hold must signify emphatically to regard with esteem, and would require, therefore, some supplement as περὶ πλείονος, Theodoret changing it in explanation into πλείονος αὐτοὺς ἀξιοῦτε τιμῆς; and, in the second mode, a supplement is also indispensable, which Œcumenius inserts thus, ἡγεῖσθαι αὐτοὺς ἀξίους τοῦ ἀγαπᾶσθαι; Chrysostom simply saying, μὴ ἁπλῶς ἀγαπᾶτε ἀλλ' ὑπερεκπερισσοῦ ὡσανεὶ παῖδες πατέρας. There is, however, no strict example of such a construction. Some quote τί τοῦτο ἡγήσω ἐν κρίσει (Job xxxv, 2), and the phrase ἐν τοιαύτῃ ὀργῇ εἶχεν occurs (Thucydides, ii, 18), but neither of these instances is analogous. The sense, however, seems to be what the second mode indicates.

The reading of the Received Text, ὑπὲρ ἐκπερισσοῦ, has good authority, as it is found in A D³ K L ℵ; the ending ως has in its favour B D¹ F; the ως might have been changed into οῦ as being the more common form. The compound adverb, which is quite in the apostle's style, is to be taken with ἐν ἀγάπῃ. See under iii, 10. Œcumenius remarks πολλὴ δὲ ἡ ἐπίτασις τοῦ ὑ π ὲ ρ καὶ τοῦ ἐ κ. The presidents were to be held in love very abundantly "for their work's sake"; that work was so momentous in itself—the care of souls—and it was to be performed so thoroughly, that it could be characterized as toilsome labour (Heb. xiii, 17). They who felt the spiritual benefit of such work, such presidence, and such practical counsels, belonged to a church so blessed in its pastorate that they were surely under no common obligation to cherish deep regard and love for the presbyters, to whom such affectional esteem must have been very welcome as a recognition of their ardour and self-denial, and a proof that their efforts had not been in vain. Indifference and indolence on the part of church rulers preclude, therefore, all claim to this affection. To claim or extort it in virtue of the office is to miss or forfeit it—it must be won by the earnest discharge of duty.

εἰρηνεύετε ἐν ἑαυτοῖς—" be at peace among yourselves." The English version and the Syriac Peshito, with codex א¹, supply an unauthorized "and." This verb, with the exception of Mark ix, 50, is found only in the Pauline writings. Though there is no connecting particle, the clause is not so wholly disconnected from the previous part of the verse as Lünemann supposes. Next to knowing and loving those who were over them in the Lord was the duty of preserving internal peace, and the injunction prepares the way for the more detailed and special inculcations of the following verses. The reflexive ἑαυτοῖς is used for the reciprocal ἀλλήλοις (Col. iii, 13; Ephes. iv, 32; 1 Peter iv, 8). The permutation, as Kühner remarks, has no other cause *quam ut varietur oratio*. *Gr. Gr.*, vol. II, § 628; Winer, § 22, 5. Xen. *Mem.*, ii, 6, 20, φθονοῦντες ἑαυτοῖς μισοῦσιν ἀλλήλους. A different reading, ἐν αὐτοῖς, is found in D¹ F א and some minuscules, in the Syriac, Vulgate, and some of the Greek fathers; but ἑαυτοῖς is warranted by A B D³ K L, *in ipsis* being employed in the Claromontane Latin. The other reading is not therefore to be adopted, though Theophylact says γράφεται καὶ ἐν αὐτοῖς. It was probably felt that the very short injunction appeared awkwardly between the larger entreaties immediately before and after it in verses 11, 13, and 14. Nor could even that reading bear the interpretation of the Syriac ܗܘܰܘ ܒܫܠܡܐ, or of the Vulgate, *pacem habete cum eis*, that is, " be at peace with the presidents." So also Theophylact and Luther, Calvin, Zuingli, Balduin, a-Lapide, Fromond, and others, guided by the Latin version. Chrysostom, like the Peshito, apparently connects the clauses, " for their work's sake be at peace with them." Theodoret puts it, καὶ μὴ ἀντιλέγειν τοῖς παρ' αὐτῶν λεγομένοις. But to sustain such a meaning μετ' αὐτῶν would be requisite (Rom. xii, 18); and the injunction of peace in regard to the presbyters would not be suitable, for submission would be enjoined, as in Heb. xiii, 17. Zuingli proposes another rendering, "in or through them ye have peace"; but even allowing the reading αὐτοῖς, this version would require a different order of the words. Peace was a blessing essential to growth and usefulness; the want of it destroyed edification; jealousies, alienations, turmoil lead to ultimate extinction (1 Cor. vii, 15; xiv, 33; Gal. v, 15; Ephes. iv, 31; 2 Thess. iii, 16; 2 Tim. ii, 22; James iii, 14, 16).

(Ver. 14.) παρακαλοῦμεν δὲ ὑμᾶς, ἀδελφοί—"Now we exhort you, brethren;" δὲ being transitional. This address is to the brethren, believers in general. The apostle has alluded to those who held office and wrought and counselled; but his mind is not wholly occupied by them, or their official prerogative. The church itself must act as well as its officers; the presbyters do not so represent the church, or are not so identified with it, as to preclude congregational industry and co-operation. Duty lies on them which they cannot devolve on their rulers. From the time of Chrysostom, however, who says without any argument πρὸς τοὺς ἄρχοντας διαλέγεται, this charge has been taken as addressed to the office-bearers. The Greek fathers have been followed in this interpretation by Estius and Fromond in the Catholic church, and by Benson, Bloomfield, Macknight, Conybeare, and Peile. But the words are addressed to the ἀδελφοί, parallel to the ἀδελφοί in verse 12, or generally to the members of the church. Conybeare lays a wrong emphasis on ὑμᾶς, "but you, brethren (that is, rulers) I exhort." The order of the words will not bear that exegesis, and the repetition of νουθετεῖτε, and the charge in verse 27, will not sustain it. The allusion to the rulers comes to an end when a new clause intervenes—be at peace among yourselves, you, the people—and the address in this verse has the same continuous congregational reference. Nor is the verse to be regarded as taking up what had been said in verse 11, which is the fitting inferential conclusion (διὸ) to the previous section. The first injunction is—

νουθετεῖτε τοὺς ἀτάκτους—"admonish the unruly." For the verb see verse 12 and under Ephes. vi, 4. Ἄτακτος is found only here in the New Testament, but the adverb and verb occur in the second epistle—the adverb (2 Thess. iii, 6, 11), and the verb (2 Thess. iii, 7). It means out of rank; a soldier in rank is τεταγμένος; ἄτακτοι are οὐ ταχθέντες, *inordinati* (Xenoph., *Mem.*, III, 1, 7; Plato, *De Leg.*, vii, 806 c). See Sturz, *Lex. Xenoph.*, sub voce, vol. I, p. 455.

The term naturally came to denote men lawless in life or disorderly (Plutarch, *De Puer. Educ.*, 7). See Ast's *Lex. Platon.*, *sub voce*, vol. I, p. 298. The translation of the Peshito is too vague, and so is the explanation of Chrysostom and his followers, who class under the epithet all who do contrary to the will of God—as the drunken, the riotous, the covetous, καὶ πάντες οἱ ἁμαρτάνοντες. But it is plain that the apostle does not include all sinners under the epithet, which is intended to specify a certain class. From the use of the word in the second epistle, "the disorderly" appear to be those whose minds and habits had become unhinged from their misapprehension of the nearness of the Lord's coming; those who were neglecting the duties of common life, and had ceased to maintain themselves by such honest labour as characterized the apostle himself when he sojourned among them. See under iv, 11, 12; 2 Thess. iii, 6, 12.

παραμυθεῖσθε τοὺς ὀλιγοψύχους — "comfort the feeble-minded." For the verb see under ii, 11. The compound adjective occurs only here in the New Testament, though it is found in the Septuagint, Is. liv, 6; lvii, 15; Prov. xviii, 14; in Artemidorus, iii, 5, διὰ τὸ ὀλιγόψυχον. The verb occurs also in Isocrates (p. 392 *b*). Who the feeble-minded are has been disputed. One can scarcely apply the epithet to those who from a sense of sin despaired of divine mercy, or, with Theodoret and Theophylact, to those who had not courage to endure trial or persecution, the latter, after Chrysostom, comparing them to the seed that fell on the rocky ground. The reference, considering the strain of the previous context, is to the class who were inclined to "sorrow as those who had no hope," who had not grasped the great truth of the safety of the dead as propounded by the apostle—so Theodoret in one of his explanations—and they are distinguished from the weak generally in the following clause. Hofmann's objection that theirs was a case of error and not of faint-heartedness, *nicht Kleinmuth sondern Irrthum*, is of no weight, as Riggenbach remarks, for the error led to feeble-mindedness. They, then, who were faint-hearted and could not realize the hope of immortality and resurrection at the Master's return, so as to be filled with the sure and certain prospect, were to be comforted—not to be chidden as dull, or rebuked as sceptical, but to be encouraged.

ἀντέχεσθε τῶν ἀσθενῶν—" support the weak "—*sustinete infirmos* (Claromontane). The verb is used only in the middle in the New Testament (Luke x, 9; Acts iv, 9; v, 15; 1 Cor. xi, 30; Sept., Prov. iv, 6; Is. lvi, 2, 4, 6). From signifying "to hold against" literally, or "stand firm against," it came to signify "to hold on by" or "to keep close to," and thus "to care for, to assist." Thus the Greek fathers generally understand it (1 Cor. xi, 30). The weak are not the physically infirm, but the weak in faith or in other Christian graces, τοὺς ἀσθενοῦντας περὶ τὴν πίστιν (Theophylact). Rom. xiv, 1; xv, 1; 1 Cor. viii, 7, 11, 12. Pelagius explains by *sustinete nuper credentes, qui nondum sunt confirmati*. Those whose faith had not risen to that ascendency which governs and inspires the whole nature, or whose knowledge had not acquired clearness and symmetry, who had not come to the riches of the full assurance of understanding, or a perfect and unshaken confidence and hope, were to be helped and not frowned upon; were not to be neglected, but cherished with assiduous and kind painstaking—

μακροθυμεῖτε πρὸς πάντας—" be long-suffering towards all." The verb is opposed to ὀξυθυμεῖν, and denotes that mild and patient temper which does not easily take offence, which is not excited to immediate anger by hasty words or deeds, which does not fly into a rage when one's zeal is thwarted or his motives disparaged, but bears and forbears in the midst of provocation. And this spirit was to be exercised πρὸς πάντας. The reference is limited to the three classes specified in the verse—the unruly, the faint-hearted, and the weak—by Chrysostom and Theophylact, Koppe, De Wette, Hofmann, and Jowett. But it is better to take it as unrestricted—all men and not all fellow-believers. Long-suffering towards all with whom one is brought into contact in the church and out of it is enjoined. See under Ephes. iv, 2.

(Ver. 15.))ὁρᾶτε μή τις κακὸν ἀντὶ κακοῦ τινὶ ἀποδῷ—"see that no one render evil for evil to any one." The optative form ἀποδοῖ is found in some codices; ἀποδοίη is read in D[1], but there is no ground for accepting it. Βλέπειν μή is commoner in the New

Testament than the formula commencing this verse, which is found, however, in Matt. xviii, 10 ; Mark i, 44, and also among classical writers. Gayler, p. 316, 17; Phrynichus, ed. Lobeck, p. 345. Ἀποδῷ is explained at length by Winer, *De Verborum cum Praepositionibus Compositorum in N. T. Usu*, part IV, which treats of verbs compounded with ἀπό. The original reference is to what one possesses, κακόν, and out of which he gives, in return for what he got, κακοῦ. The exhortation is general, and with an individualizing application to the church and to every member of it without exception. The cautionary form of the charge shows that it was needed, that they were living in the midst of inducements to cherish retaliation. De Wette argues that because the apostle does not write τις ὑμῶν, he implies that revenge could not be imputed to believers, and enjoins that the better among them were to labour to prevent its outbreak in others. But the apostle is writing to the church, ὑμῶν being implied, and what power could they have to restrain vengeful words and acts in the case of others around them ? The recency of their conversion made it possible, if not probable, that, on the part of many, the habits of heathen times had not been wholly surmounted. Compare Matt. v, 30, &c.; Rom. xii, 17 ; 1 Pet. iii, 9. All retaliation is forbidden, and the prohibition is peculiar to Christianity (Koch). See under Ephes. iv, 26, 27. It is needless to say with Schrader that the prohibition refers to the heathen from whom believers had so much to endure, though they are also included. The negative is followed by the positive inculcation—

ἀλλὰ πάντοτε τὸ ἀγαθὸν διώκετε—" but always follow after what is good." The precise meaning of ἀγαθόν has been disputed. Lünemann and Riggenbach take it to mean morally good, *sittlich Gute* ; Koppe, Flatt, Schott, and Olshausen regard it as the beneficial or the useful; Hofmann and Möller, "what is good for one" ; Beza, Piscator, Pelt, and Baumgarten-Crusius view it as special beneficence. As it is opposed to κακὸν, evil embodied in word or act, it will naturally mean the opposite, or good embodied in word or act, and this comprises all the other opinions, for it is what is morally good according to the divine law, and must from its nature tend to his good who receives it. See under Gal. vi, 10; Ephes. iv, 28. And this good was not to be studied accidentally or periodically, they were not to be surprised into it, nor yet driven away from it by provocation—πάντοτε διώκετε, pursue it always, neither intermittently nor languidly—they were to set their soul upon it. This verb is often followed by an abstract noun (Rom. ix, 30, 31; xii, 13; xiv, 19; 1 Cor. xiv, 1; Heb. xii, 14; Sept., Ps. xxxiii, 15; Prov. xxi, 21). It is similarly used in Plato, and sometimes with the contrast οὔτε διώκειν οὔτε φεύγειν (*Gorg.*, 507 B). The next clause is read in the Received Text—

καὶ εἰς ἀλλήλους καὶ εἰς πάντας. Καὶ, however, is doubtful. In its favour are B K L ℵ⁴, very many mss. the Philoxenian Syriac, the Amiatine codex of the Vulgate, and the Greek fathers. Tischendorf inserts it in his second and seventh editions. But it is not found in A D F ℵ¹, many mss., nor in the Peshito, the Claromontane Latin, the Coptic and Gothic versions. The evidence is thus rather against it, and it may have been inserted for the sake of fulness, or for the balancing of the two parts of the clause. On the other hand it might be left out as unnecessary. The continuous pursuit of good was to have for its objects not only the members of the church, or a select circle of fellow-believers, but all men around them— even, as Theophylact says, καὶ εἰς ἀπίστους. Their Christian beneficence was to be continuous in its exercise and universal in its range. See under Gal. vi, 10. Compare Matt. v, 44; Rom. xii, 17, 19.

(Ver. 16.) Πάντοτε χαίρετε—"Rejoice always." This clause is not detached from the previous exhortations, though they have relatively others in view, and this is absolute or personal. It means far more than salutation, *lebt immer wohl* (Bolten), or *semper bene valete* (Koppe). Joy springs from the possession of present good. It is the natural result of escape, of conscious safety, of deliverance from so great evil and peril—and by such a process as His self-gift—into a condition so blessed as to give the hope of living for ever with Him, implying assimilation to His image, and an intense delight in His presence, and in fellowship with Him. This joy is virtually connected with faith (Philip. i, 25), it "is in the Lord" as its sphere (i, 6), and "in the Holy Ghost," by whose special influence it is created and diffused; joy unspeakable and full of glory (1 Pet. i, 8). And they were to rejoice "always," their joy was not to be spasmodic and intermittent, but continuous as the source of it is unchanging, and even in days of trial and suffering though it may be clouded, it is not to be extinguished, as it should be independent of external incumbrances, and as "all things work together for good to them that love God" (Rom. v, 2, 5; James i, 2). See under Philip. i, 4; iv, 4. The close connection, proposed by Chrysostom, between this verse and those preceding it is, "when we possess such a soul that we avenge ourselves on no one, whence, tell me, will the sting of grief be able to enter into us?" But this is too precise, though it may be true, that had we a spirit so elevated, so disinterested, and so Christ-like, we should rejoice evermore. The exhortation appears to be general, and is proposed to those who from their history, position, and experience, might have many causes of sorrow, or might find it difficult to cherish perpetual gladness.

(Ver. 17.) ἀδιαλείπτως προσεύχεσθε—"pray without ceasing" (Ephes. vi, 18; Col. iv, 2; i, 3; ii, 13). This injunction is not to be obeyed as to its external form, for on bended knees one cannot always be. The apostle himself travelled and preached as well as prayed; but the journey and the sermon had their birth, strength, and success in prayer. Did one only bear in mind that God is benefactor, ever giving, and ever to be inquired of to give more, that we are always receiving and therefore ought to be always asking, the precept would not seem so strange as it does to some; for what attitude is more becoming, in our condition of close and constant dependence on God, than to be ever looking up and expecting an answer—the supply of our wants to-day only edging our appetite and intensifying all our yearnings for still larger supplies for the morrow. It is not right therefore to say that this command can be fulfilled only in idea—it is a real and a blessed privilege to pray always; there is no place where one may not pray; no time when one may not pray; no blessing which one may not solicit; no human being for whom intercession may not be offered; no step should be taken without asking divine counsel, and no enterprise engaged in without invocation of the divine blessing. Theodoret refers to the time of taking a meal and making a journey as special periods for prayer. This injunction, "pray without ceasing," the apostle did not think it necessary to explain any more than the declaration "praying night and day that we might see your face" (iii, 10); nor did he seek to show the congruity of both with the other and apparently contradictory expression, "labouring night and day, because we would not be chargeable unto any of you" (ii, 9). Prayerfulness therefore should always characterize us, that spirit of devotion which ever realizes the nearness of God and our relation to Him, the heart filled with unspoken adoration, and with those profound and struggling aspirations which the apostle calls unutterable groanings. Prayer in its fulness comprises all this complex variety of emotions. So great are our wants and so weak is our faith, that the old words are still true, "hitherto ye have asked nothing." The precept is not fulfilled by observing set hours of prayer, nor does obedience to it necessitate monastic seclusion (Augustine, iv, 427). Chrysostom's connection is, that prayer is the way or means of enabling one to rejoice evermore, or as Theophylact adds, ὁ γὰρ ἐθισθεὶς ὁμιλεῖν τῷ Θεῷ will always possess ground of joy.

(Ver. 18.) ἐν παντὶ εὐχαριστεῖτε—"in every thing give thanks." See under i, 2. The precept is universal in sphere, as the two before it are continuous in time (Philip. iv, 6). The phrase ἐν παντὶ cannot mean at every time but in "every thing." See 2 Cor. ix, 8, where πάντοτε is associated with it. See under Ephes. v, 20; Col. iii, 22, 23. As there is no exception, adverse things are not excluded. In the dungeon at Philippi Paul and Silas sang praises unto God, and it is good to be afflicted. There is nothing on this side of eternal punishment that ought not to fill us with thankfulness. Thanks especially for mercies—for privileged existence; for continued means of grace; for the growth of divine life in the soul; for what blesses us now; for what is promised to bless us through eternity, as well as for all that disciplines us for it— for all this should humble and hearty thanks be given.

τοῦτο γὰρ θέλημα Θεοῦ ἐν Χριστῷ Ἰησοῦ εἰς ὑμᾶς—"for this is God's will in Christ Jesus toward you." The minor variation of reading need not be noticed, ἐστιν being found in D¹ E¹ F G. The singular τοῦτο seems to refer to the previous clause only, and not also to the other clauses before it. Grotius and Schott take in the clauses commanding prayer and thanksgiving, and the precept enjoining joy is also comprised in the reference by a-Lapide, Möller in De Wette, Jowett, and, with hesitation, Alford. The apostle can scarcely have regarded all these precepts as being so much in unity, that he might characterize them by τοῦτο. This θέλημα is not the *decretum divinum*, special or unique, as Schott supposes, though it may imply it, —such a reference would have required the use of the article— but it is God's will in its nearer form given or expressed for us. The absence of the article may, as Ellicott suggests (iv, 3), point out that thanksgiving is only one of many portions of the divine will. The phrase ἐν Χριστῷ Ἰησοῦ represents the sphere in which this divine will exhibits itself. Theophylact and Œcumenius in their explanations exchange ἐν for διὰ, as if it denoted means or medium, διὰ τῆς τοῦ Ἰησοῦ Χριστοῦ συνεργίας. Εἰς ὑμᾶς is "towards you," and not, as the Vulgate, *in vobis*.

(Ver. 19.) Τὸ Πνεῦμα μὴ σβέννυτε—"Quench not the Spirit." The verb often occurs, and means literally "to put out a fire or a light" (Matt. xii, 20; xxv, 8; Ephes. vi, 16; Heb. xi, 34; Sept., Is. xlii, 3; Lev. vi, 12; Job xxi, 17). Its tropical sense is evident, τὴν ἀγάπην (Song of Solomon viii, 7); τὴν χάραν (Joseph., *B. Jud.*, vi, 1, 4); θυμόν (Ælian., *Hist. Var.*, vi. 1; Plato, *De Leg.*, 888 A); τὸ ἔμφυτον πνεῦμα (Galen, *De Theriac.*, i, 17); ἀποσβῆναι τὸ πνεῦμα (Plut., *De Defect. Orac.*, p. 419 B). The word is also applied to the wind, and there are similar phrases in the Latin classics. Wetstein *in loc*. The πνεῦμα is viewed as a flame, "He shall baptize you with the Holy Ghost and with fire" (Matt. iii, 11). Compare Acts ii, 3; xviii, 25; and in 2 Tim. i, 6, ἀναζωπυρεῖν is the opposite of σβέννυτε. Τὸ Πνεῦμα is the Spirit of God, and this meaning is not to be diluted in any way. This Divine Being dwells in the hearts of believers; their bodies are His shrine. He is the Enlightener, Purifier, Intercessor, Comforter, Sealer, the Earnest, the First Fruits. The figure in the verb is striking, and did the verse form part of a series of ordinary practical counsels, it might mean that the Spirit within us as Quickener and Sanctifier was not to be thwarted by unthankfulness (Calvin), or, as the Greek fathers, by an unholy life, by sprinkling water upon it or not supplying oil (Chrysostom). The joy, the prayer, and the thanksgiving enjoined in the previous verses are the fruit of the Spirit, and He Himself, the Divine Producer and Sustainer, is now referred to in person. The verse would thus be nearly parallel to Ephes. iv, 30. But the following context suggests a more special signification. The apostle seems to refer to the Spirit in His extraordinary manifestations, so frequent in the church at that early period, and one of them he specifies in the following verse. Some of these are described in 1 Cor. xii—" word of wisdom," "word of knowledge," "faith," "gifts of healing," " working of miracles," " prophecy," " discernment of spirits," " divers kinds of tongues," " interpretation of tongues," " diversities of gifts, but the same spirit," " these all wrought by one and the selfsame spirit," " dividing to every man severally as he will." Those gifts of the Spirit appearing in the church were not to be rudely repelled, for they were "given to profit withal." We do not know the state of the Thessalonian church, so that it is perhaps too much to say with Olshausen, on the one hand, that the apostle had no presentiment that the Thessalonians were in danger of becoming a prey to fanaticism, though this was the case later, as is seen in the second epistle, and too much to deny on the other hand, with Hofmann, that there was any disinclination to spiritual utterances. The counsel is general, but may imply that there was a tendency to repress such spiritual utterances, from a rigid love of order and dread of irregular and infectious enthusiasm, for all these gifts were liable to abuse. From the abuse they were not to argue against the use, or forbid the genuine because of the spurious manifestation.

(Ver. 20.) Προφητείας μὴ ἐξουθενεῖτε—" despise not prophesyings." The verb, literally " to set at nought," is found in various parts of the New Testament; the other form, ἐξουδενοῦν, being found in Mark ix, 12, οὐθεν being also a later form of οὐδεν (Lobeck, *Phrynichus*, p. 182). For an account of the rank

and office of the προφήτης in the New Testament, see under
Ephes. ii, 20, and iv, 11. The prophet was next in honour and
position to the apostles; he was a teacher directly inspired by
the Holy Ghost, uttering, suddenly and consciously, and with
strange power, revelations which had not of necessity in them
any disclosure of the future. The prophet's impulse was under
his own control, and his teaching was to "edification, exhortation,
and comfort." His special function was toward them which
believe—it was not to win converts, but to promote spiritual
progress, though not specially or exclusively, for there belonged
to him the awful power of laying bare men's hearts and character
by flashing a sudden light upon them; and a plain man (ἰδιώτης),
or an unbelieving man (ἄπιστος), who felt his nature so read
would be so struck that, "falling down on his face, he will
worship God, and report that God is in you of a truth" (1 Cor.
xii, 14). Prophecy, therefore, in the primitive church, served a
vital and momentous purpose. Compare Acts xi, 27; xiii, 1;
xv, 32; xix, 6; Rom. xii, 6. Teaching, as distinct from prophesying, was more human and equable in its character " as the
reflective development of thought," was not so original, and
might not produce those instantaneous and alarming results.
These prophesyings they were not to despise, but were ever to
welcome them as divine manifestations. The apostle gives
direction to the prophets themselves in 1 Cor. xiv, 26-33. A
proneness to set prophesyings and all such uncommon *charis-
mata* at nought might originate in the church, because either
impostors might make pretensions to the gift and lead the
simple astray by their false lights, or because fanatics might
become their own dupes, and give out for supernatural utterances
their own wretched delusions. But there is no ground for
supposing that in Thessalonica prophecy was depreciated in
comparison with the more dazzling gift of tongues, as was the
case at Corinth (1 Cor. xiv, 1, 5). We find Paul disobeying
prophecy, and the earnest dissuasives based upon it (Acts xxi,
4, 14).

(Ver. 21.) πάντα δὲ δοκιμάζετε—" but prove all things."
The particle δὲ is omitted in the Textus Receptus, and is not
found in A ℵ[1] and many mss., nor in the Peshito or Coptic
versions, nor in many quotations in the fathers. But it is

found in B D F K L ℵ³, in both Latin versions, in the Philoxenian Syriac, in the Gothic version, and in several patristic citations. The genuineness is thus amply supported. Some of the fathers might omit it *pro libertate citandi*, and it might fall out from being next to δο in the following word, or be left out from a desire to make the verse a terse and disconnected maxim. The reading δοκιμάζοντες has no real authority, nor has καὶ in connection with the next clause. The verb means, to put to the test, to try whether a thing should be accepted, "the proved becoming the approved." See 1 Cor. iii, 13. The injunction, begun by δὲ after a negative clause, stands in antithesis to the previous command, and πάντα is thus restricted by the context. The clause by itself is an excellent maxim of general significance and application, but the sense is fairly limited to the subject in hand. "Do not put down the prophesyings, but subject them to the proof—τὰς ὄντως προφητείας—this being said lest they should think that he had opened the βῆμα to all" (Chrysostom). What the test to be applied is we are not here informed. In 1 Cor. xiv, 29, 30, 31, one rule is given, prescribing the order and succession of the utterances to prevent confusion. There was also a gift in the early church —the discernment of spirits, διακρίσεις πνευμάτων (1 Cor. xii, 10; xiv, 29). Ellicott, after Neander, would apply this injunction specially to the class so gifted, but the text does not directly warrant such a limitation. The church so admonished would, however, fulfil the command in and through a χάρισμα, if any of her members possessed it; if not, they must apply their own spiritual discernment, which in those days of spiritual enlightenment and fulness might be endowed with sufficient keenness of insight for the purpose. Compare the injunction in 1 John iv, 1, δοκιμάζετε τὰ πνεύματα—a general injunction, accompanied by a simple and decisive test, the confession of Christ come in the flesh being proof of possessing the Spirit of God, while the denial of this primary truth characterized Antichrist.

τὸ καλὸν κατέχετε—"hold fast the good." For the adjective, which is not here in result different from ἀγαθόν in v, 15, see under Gal. vi, 9. Donaldson's *Cratylus*, § 334. For the verb, compare Luke viii, 15; 1 Cor. xi, 2; xv, 2; Heb. iii, 6. Though there be no connecting particle, the clause seems to be naturally joined to the one before it. The meaning will then be, "hold fast that element or species of prophesying to which the epithet καλόν is applicable." It is not a general or disconnected maxim, though the clause is asyndetic, as if it meant, keep the good you at present possess (Hofmann). On the other hand, Flatt takes it as referring as much to the following clause as to the preceding one. While it does refer especially to the clause, "prove all things," and is its natural consequent, the testing being satisfactory, it may be regarded as transitional to the more general injunction coming after it, καλόν suggesting its antithesis πονηροῦ; and κατέχετε, "hold by," being opposed to ἀπέχεσθε, "hold away."

(Ver. 22.) ἀπὸ παντὸς εἴδους πονηροῦ ἀπέχεσθε—"abstain from every kind of evil" (Rom. xii, 9). Εἶδος is originally what presents itself to the eye—figure, or form—often used in Homer of a human appearance; also in Luke iii, 22, σωματικῷ εἴδει; Luke ix, 29, τὸ εἶδος τοῦ προσώπου; John v, 37, οὔτε εἶδος αὐτοῦ ἑωράκατε; 2 Cor. v, 7, "we walk by faith," οὐ διὰ εἴδους, "not by appearance," the objects of faith being unseen; Xenoph., *Cyrop.*, i, 2, 1, εἶδος μὲν κάλλιστος. In these cases appearance is equivalent to form, and does not mean mere semblance without reality. The Authorized Version reads, "all appearance of evil," that is, avoid even what bears the aspect of evil, though it may not be really evil, *externa species quae mali suspicionem concitare possit* (Wolf). This notion is found in some of the older English versions—in Wycliffe, in the Rheims, and in Cranmer; Tyndale having, "all suspicious things," and the Vulgate, *ab omni mala specie*. It is also adopted by Luther, Calvin, Piscator, Grotius, Michaelis, Wordsworth, and Webster and Wilkinson. But, as has been said, the antithesis is not between what is really good and what is evil only in appearance—*schein*—a meaning also which εἶδος cannot bear. But the noun may signify sort, kind, or species—species under the genus—and the *specie* of the Vulgate is by many so understood: thus, εἶδος καὶ γένος (Plato, *Epin.*, 990 E). This is the view of the majority of modern interpreters. See Wetstein *in loc.* The Greek fathers seem to have entertained the same view, as Chrysostom explains the clause after quoting it, μὴ τούτου ἢ ἐκείνου ἀλλ' ἀπὸ παντός. This exegesis assumes that πονηροῦ is a substantive; but Bengel, Pelt, Schott, and Lasch take it as an adjective, *von jeder Bösen Art; ab omni specie mala* (Vulgate), and the Syriac has ܡܢ ܟܠ ܨܒܘ ܒܝܫܐ. Bengel, Middleton, Tittmann, and Schott contend that if πονηροῦ were a substantive, it would have the article prefixed to it. But, first, the article would be necessary if πονηροῦ referred to some distinct element of the πάντα in the previous verse; and, secondly, the article is not necessary to abstract adjectives when the totality of what is specified is not intended, but only a part (Kühner, § 486); κακὰ καὶ αἰσχρὰ ἔπραξεν: τρίτον ... εἶδος ἀγαθοῦ (Plato, *Rep.*, II, 357 c). Heb. v, 14. Chrysostom, in one of his Homilies, has οὐδέν ἐστιν κακίας εἶδος ὅπερ ἀτόλμητον. Then, thirdly, if πονηροῦ were an adjective, the antithesis to τὸ καλόν would be greatly weakened; and, lastly, an adjective would scarcely agree with εἶδος as signifying kind or species. From every kind or form of evil were they to abstain in thought and deed; from whatever would prompt them to retaliate, chill their joy, hinder their prayers, interrupt or limit their thanksgivings, or lead them to frown on spiritual utterances; from everything "in doctrine or in conduct" (Theodoret) which might bring them spiritual injury in their individual or ecclesiastical capacity.

The commentators have remarked that some of the fathers use a peculiar quotation which has been thought to throw some light on these clauses. The phrase is γίνεσθε δόκιμοι τραπεζῖται, "become ye approved money-changers." The clause is connected immediately with this verse, and quoted as if it formed a portion of this epistle by Clement of Alexandria, Basil the Great, Ambrose, and Athanasius; the citation of the Alexandrian Cyril and that of the apostolical constitutions are somewhat different, and do not directly connect themselves with the verses before us. Various sources have been assigned to it by those who have employed it. Clement of Alexandria assigns it generally to Scripture, ἡ γραφή; Cyril of Alexandria ascribes it to Paul, and after quoting it adds verses 21 and 22 of this chapter. Similarly, and without quoting these verses so fully, Origen, Jerome, and Epiphanius ascribe it to Christ. Usher thought that it was taken from the Apocryphal Gospel according to the Hebrews. The probability is that it is one of Christ's unwritten utterances, many of which must have been preserved and handed down in the early church. Compare 1 Cor. vii, 10; Acts xx, 35. But the connection of this $ῥῆμα$ $ἄγραφον$ with the verses under discussion, though somewhat striking in the patristic writings, is in reality very slender. It is but the echo of $δόκιμοι$ in $δοκιμάζετε$, with some slight resemblance of thought which might be imaged in the work of a *nummularius*. Hänsel, however, imagining that the apostle had the utterance before his mind, has wrought out the idea to its full extent, in the belief that it throws a new light upon verses 21 and 22. His paraphrase is, "The good money keep; with every sort of bad money have nothing to do; act as experienced money-changers; all the money presented to you as good, test." The illustration is artificial and far-fetched, though it is adopted by Baumgarten-Crusius, and allowed by Neander. But if such were the usage, the wording must have been different, as Lünemann. Besides, $εἶδος$ cannot of itself mean money—$εἶδος$ $νομίσματος$—nor would the verb $ἀπέχεσθε$ be at all applicable, for the turn of thought would be, not keep away from it, but put it away from you. The quotations from the fathers referred to in this paragraph may be found in Suicer's *Thesaurus*, *sub voce* $τραπεζίτης$; and a list of the supposed unwritten utterances of Christ may be seen in Fabricius, *Codex Apocr. Novi Testamenti*, pp. 321-335, with a long note on the one in question.

(Ver. 23.) Αὐτὸς δὲ ὁ Θεὸς τῆς εἰρήνης ἁγιάσαι ὑμᾶς ὁλοτελεῖς—" Now may the God of peace Himself sanctify you wholly." Δέ is transitional to another theme—not in full contrast to what has been stated, but rather complementary. They are enjoined to abstain from vengeful acts, and to cherish beneficent feelings; to act towards those among them as their condition and character suggested and required; to be continuous in spiritual gladness, in prayer and thanksgiving; not to repress spiritual manifestations, but to apply a spiritual discernment to them; to appropriate what was good in them, and to abstain from every species of evil. These are so many detached elements of sanctification, which are pressed upon them, and which only through divine grace they could possess or exhibit, and through frailty often only in an imperfect degree. His heart's desire for them is now summed up in this concluding and comprehensive prayer. It can scarcely be said to be in contrast with them and the efforts which they might be able to make, as De Wette, Ellicott, Alford, Lünemann—for though in form, indeed, prayer is in contrast with precept, yet this is rather a prayer to God to strengthen them for all those duties which had been set before them, by developing their perfect sanctification. They are bidden to do those duties, and God himself is implored to sanctify them. Δέ implies that the subject, though connected, is different from what precedes; they are enjoined to do, but He is implored to give. Αὐτὸς is emphatic—Himself and none other; and indeed none other than He can be so appealed to, or can answer such an appeal. Winer, § 24, 5. The genitive εἰρήνης points to Him as its continuous giver or producer, and thus characterizes Him, *die dominirenden Eigenschaften* (Scheuerlein, p. 115). Peace is that inner tranquillity resulting from divine acceptance and growing assimilation to the divine image, which is inwrought by God, and sustained by His Spirit. See under Ephes. i, 2; Col. iii, 15; and especially under Philip. iv, 7. It is out of the question to refer the noun to the distant cognate verb in the 13th verse. Ἁγιάσαι, not used by the classics, occurs often in the Septuagint and New Testament, and means to make ἅγιος; hence believers are called οἱ ἡγιασμένοι (Acts xx, 32; xxvi, 18; 1 Cor. i, 2; Jude 1). See under Ephes. i, 1.

The adjective ὁλοτελεῖς occurs only here in the New Testament, though it is sometimes found in later Greek writers; and the adverb occurs in the version of Aquila (Deut. xiii, 17). It signifies, complete in reference to amount, that in which nothing is wanting essential to aim or end. Thus the Vulgate, *per omnia*, or as Œcumenius explains it, τουτέστι ὅλους δι' ὅλων. The emphatic order of the words is thus preserved, and the pronoun and adjective kept in natural concord. Others, however, take ὁλοτελεῖς in an ethical sense, and as the accusative of result—sanctify you so that you become entire or perfect. So the Claromontane Latin, *ad perfectionem;* Jerome gives us the alternative, *per omnia vel in omnibus sive plenos et perfectos;* and this last view is adopted by Ambrosiaster, Erasmus, Estius, Koppe, Pelt. But the other interpretation is preferable, as being the simpler, and as it keeps distinct the meaning of the two compound adjectives—

καὶ ὁλόκληρον ὑμῶν τὸ πνεῦμα καὶ ἡ ψυχὴ καὶ τὸ σῶμα ἀμέμπτως . . . τηρηθείη—"and entire may your spirit and soul and body be preserved blameless." By καὶ he passes on to the particulars, annexing to the more general prayer the specific petition. Winer, § 53, 3. The adjective ὁλόκληρος is, whole in all its parts, explained in James i, 4, as ἐν μηδενὶ λειπόμενοι, "wanting in nothing," and this is the only other place of the New Testament in which the word occurs. The cognate noun, ὁλοκληρίαν—"his perfect soundness"—is applied in Acts iii, 16, to the state of the lame man after being healed, and the adjective describes the unchipped or unbroken stones of which an altar might be built, in Deut. xxvii, 6. In Ezek. xv, 5, it represents the Hebrew מְלָאכָה, and similarly in 1 Macc. iv, 47, λίθους ὁλοκλήρους κατὰ τὸν νόμον; applied also to a full week in Lev. xxiii, 15; and in Deut. xvi, 6, in the Alexandrian Recension. Is. i, 6; Wisdom xv, 3. Josephus employs it to denote the physical symmetry of the priests (*Antiq.*, iii, 2, 2); and Philo uses it both of priests and victims (*De Vict.*, 2; *De Off.*, 1). Plato, *Leg.*, vi, 759 c; Stallbaum's Note, vol. X, § 2, p. 140; *Phaedrus*, p. 250 c; Ast., *Lex. Platon.*, *sub voce;* Trench, *Synon.*, § 22; Wetstein, *in loc.* The adjective standing here as a secondary predicate belongs to all the substantives, πνεῦμα, ψυχὴ, σῶμα, though agreeing in gender with the nearest one, to which the Authorized Version wrongly confines it. Winer, § 59, 5. It describes a sanctification in which no element of God's purpose is unrealized, or of a believer's perfection is absent or defective, and that in every part of our nature. The verb τηρέω is used of divine guardianship (John xvii, 11, 12, 15; Rev. iii, 10; Jude 21). The preservation of spirit, soul, and body, is characterized as ἀμέμπτως, the adverb qualifying the verb. Compare ii, 10; iii, 13. The preservation is embodied in this holiness which shall incur no censure, as being perfect in nature (ὁλοτελεῖς), and complete in extent (ὁλόκληρον); and the period is—

ἐν τῇ παρουσίᾳ τοῦ Κυρίου ἡμῶν Ἰησοῦ Χριστοῦ, "in the coming of our Lord Jesus Christ,"—not "unto," as in the Authorized Version. This prayer for the preservation of our whole nature will be found answered at the Second Advent (1 John ii, 28). See iii, 13. The clause is closely connected with ἀμέμπτως. And the apostle rested his confidence on God's unchanging truthfulness, for he at once adds—

(Ver. 24.) Πιστὸς ὁ καλῶν ὑμᾶς ὃς καὶ ποιήσει—"Faithful is he that calleth you who also will perform or do it." Πιστὸς is emphatic in position, and the participle designates God as the Caller, the idea of time being dropped. Winer, § 45, 7. It is not to be taken for the aorist, and the reference is to God, as in the Pauline theology. See under Gal. i, 6; v, 8. The faithfulness of God is unchallenged, carrying out every purpose which He has formed, and fulfilling every promise which He has made (1 Cor. i, 9; x, 13; 2 Cor. i, 18; 2 Thess. iii, 3; 2 Tim. ii, 13; Heb. x, 23; Is. xlix, 7). Calling is God's initial work, leading to justification and final glorification (Rom. viii, 30). Whatever pledge that calling implies—and it implies perfection—He will fulfil; as He calls so also (καὶ) will He perform. There needs no formal accusative to ποιήσει, as is supplied in some codices; neither πάντα ταῦτα (Olshausen), nor *was ich wünsche* (De Wette), nor yet exactly ἐφ' ᾧ ἐκάλεσεν, though that be the result. The verb is used alone in relative sentences (Thucydides, v, 70, and Poppo's note). Koch refers to Schoemann, *ad Isaeum*, p. 372. He will do what is involved in the call, and comprehended in the prayer; not merely, τὸ ἀμέμπτως ὑμᾶς τηρηθῆναι (Lünemann), but also what is included in the previous part of the prayer, ἁγιάσαι ὑμᾶς ὁλοτελεῖς. Baumgarten-Crusius takes occasion to remark, *Der Klang solcher Stellen ist prädestinativisch;* and then proceeds to reply to his own observations, that he may remove from his readers such an impression. Three injunctions follow. First—

(Ver. 25.) Ἀδελφοί, προσεύχεσθε περὶ ἡμῶν—"Brethren, pray for us." The same request is made in other epistles (Rom. xv, 30; Ephes. vi, 19; Col. iv, 3; 2 Thess. iii, 1; Heb. xiii, 18. Compare 2 Cor. i, 11). The verb is sometimes followed by ὑπέρ, and for the distinction, if any, between the two prepositions, see under Ephes. vi, 19. For their use in another connection, see under Gal. i, 4. The Greek commentators call attention to the request as a proof of the apostle's humility. That Timothy and Silvanus are included is quite likely as they are comprised in the opening salutation. Prayer for them on the part of the church would prove its living interest in them, and a sympathy with their labours and trials, and would doubtless comprehend earnest petition for divine blessing on them in person, and in all the arduous evangelical toil in which they were engaged. A second injunction is—

(Ver. 26.) Ἀσπάσασθε τοὺς ἀδελφοὺς πάντας ἐν φιλήματι ἁγίῳ—" Salute all the brethren with a holy kiss." Had the injunction been "Salute one another," as in some other places, it might have been regarded as addressed to the church. But it is given to one class, and they are charged to salute all the brethren—the class on whom the obligation devolved being probably those who were over them in the Lord. The presbyters were to salute all the brethren, probably in the apostle's name—"being absent he greets them through others"—ὡς ὅταν λέγωμεν φίλησον αὐτὸν ἀντ' ἐμοῦ (Chrysostom). The verse plainly implies that those who received the epistle were to salute all the others. Hofmann, approved by Riggenbach, wrongly holds, on the other hand, that as verse 25 is addressed to all the Thessalonians, this verse also has the same application, the meaning being—"Deliver my salutation in connection with the holy kiss to all the brethren; and this the Thessalonians did collectively, when on hearing these words they kissed one another." But the simple terms will not warrant such a deduction.

The greeting was to assume a special form—ἐν φιλήματι, ἐν being instrument; the kiss conveyed the salutation. It is called holy, ἁγίῳ, as being the token and symbol of Christian affection, and not the form of mere civility or worldly courtesy. The same epithet is employed in Rom. xvi, 16; 1 Cor. xvi, 20; 2 Cor. xiii, 12, where also ἀλλήλους is employed. In 1 Peter v, 14, the phrase is ἐν φιλήματι ἀγάπης. The apostle sometimes reverses the position of the noun and adjective, as in some of these passages—the difference being, according to Fritzsche, as between *osculum Christianum*, and *Christianum osculum* (*Ad. Rom.*, vol. III, 310). Theodoret from the epithet ἅγιον infers that the kiss was not to be a δολερὸν φίλημα like that of Judas. As may be seen from many passages in the Old Testament, not only near relations of both sexes kissed one another, as parents and children and members of the same household, but also persons unrelated, in token of friendship or under the guise of it. Among the Greeks and Romans the custom prevailed; and, among Persians and Arabs, the mode of kissing part of the person and dress was indicative of rank. The Christian kiss here enjoined was continued in the early church—both in the East and West. It was apparently observed at first without distinction of sex, as the verse before us would seem to imply. The Apostolical Constitutions say—"Then," that is, at the end of the service, "let the men give the men, and the women the women, the Lord's kiss, but let no one do it in deceit, as Judas betrayed the Lord with a kiss" (*Lib.* ii, 57). Again, at the end of a form of prayer for the faithful, "let the deacons say to all, Salute ye one another with a holy kiss" (*Lib.* viii, 11). In the Eastern churches the men and women sat on opposite sides of the building. Justin the martyr records, that after the administration of baptism and the prayers accompanying it, "we salute one another with a holy kiss" (*Apol.*, i, 65). Thus Tertullian argues that a Christian woman should not marry a heathen, as he would be unwilling to allow her to go to the prisons to embrace the martyr in his chains, or at other times to give the kiss of peace to a brother. The kiss was also given to persons newly baptized, as is mentioned both by Cyprian and Augustine (Cyprian, *Ep.* 59; Bingham, iv, 49). Tertullian says, *Jejunantes habita oratione cum fratribus subtrahunt osculum pacis, quod est signaculum orationis* (*De Oratione,* xviii, vol. I, p. 569, *Opera,* ed. Œhler). The kiss was given before the distribution of the elements at the Eucharist, and it was also given to the bishop and to the presbyter on their consecration (Bingham, *Antiquities,* ii, 11, § 10; ii, 19, § 17; iv, 6, § 15). It was called εἰρήνη, *pax,* and *osculum pacis*—hence the phrase *dare pacem,* τὴν εἰρήνην δίδοσθαι; and Clement of Alexandria gives it the epithet μυστικόν, as in contrast to the shamelessness of those who do nothing but make the churches resound with kissing, not having love within. "We dispense the affections of the soul by a chaste and closed mouth"

(*Pædag.*, iii, 11, vol. I, p. 329). Athenagoras warns against the abuse of the custom—" the Logos has said, If any one kiss a second time because it has given him pleasure, he sins" (*Legat.*, 32). See a chapter on the subject in Augusti, *Handbuch der Christ. Archaeol.*, vol. II, p. 718. The custom is still found in the Coptic church, and in the Greek Church at Easter, though in the early church it was omitted on Good Friday in reference to the kiss of Judas. It fell into disuse in the Latin church about the thirteenth century, and a relic or picture called *osculatorium* was handed round the congregation that each one might kiss it. Du Cange, *sub voce Osculum*. Palmer's *Origines Liturg.*, II, p. 102.

(Ver. 27.) Ἐνορκίζω ὑμᾶς τὸν Κύριον, ἀναγνωσθῆναι τὴν ἐπιστολὴν πᾶσι τοῖς ἀδελφοῖς—" I adjure you by the Lord that this epistle be read to all the brethren." D³ F K L ℵ have the simple verb ὁρκίζω—the compound being found in A B D¹ E, 17. The Received Text inserts ἁγίοις before ἀδελφοῖς, with A K L ℵ³, many versions, and some fathers. But the epithet is omitted in B D F ℵ¹, and the Claromontane Latin. The evidence from the MSS. is strongly against the word, though the versions are in its favour. Lachmann refuses it, but Tischendorf has admitted it in his seventh edition; Ellicott and Riggenbach bracket it, but Lünemann and Alford reject it. The word is at all events suspicious. The verb with its two accusatives—that of the persons adjured, and that of Him by whom adjuration is made—involves an argument for the Lord's divinity (Mark v, 7; Acts xix, 13). Grotius, Pelt, and Olshausen needlessly understand νή before Κύριον. On the verb as condemned by the Atticists, see Phrynichus, ed. Lobeck, p. 360.

The verb ἀναγινώσκω in the active is often followed by the thing or author read, and occasionally by ὅτι; in the passive it has here the dative after it—not of those by whom, but of those to whom the epistle was to be read (Luke iv, 16; Acts xv, 11; 2 Cor. iii, 15; Col. iv, 16). The infinitive aorist in sentences of command may not refer to a single act (Alford), but it may imply that the thing is to be done instantly, for the use is more general in such sentences, though the present would have implied that the action was in course of performance, and the future that it would take place at some indefinite period to come. According to Stallbaum the action is represented as unconditioned by time (*Euthyd.*, p. 140), or it may command the simple performance of the action (Lobeck, *Phrynichus*, p. 751 ; Schmalfeld, p. 346). "All the brethren" implies a public assembly of the brotherhood in Thessalonica, not in the whole of Macedonia (Bengel, Flatt), in the same way as the Old Testament was read in the synagogue. The command, then, is simply that the epistle be openly read to the assembled church, but not for the purpose of recognizing it as a genuine letter of the apostle (Michaelis). The letters forged in his name belong to a later period. (There was often a *recitatio* of a newly composed work prior to its publication. Tacitus, *Dialog. De Oratore*, 9, p. 358, vol. IV, *Opera*, ed. Ruperti.) But why this strong adjuration to do a work so natural and so necessary as to read to the church an epistle sent to them by their founder ? The adjuration is not meant to secure that the epistle should not be undervalued as the substitute for the apostle's own personal presence, so earnestly longed for (Hofmann). Nor is it any proof of a later origin, or of a time when an epistle was reckoned a sacred composition, treated with a special solemnity, and frequently read. The aorist does not imply such a frequency, and there is nothing abnormal in the request that a letter designed for a Christian community should be read by all of them, πᾶσιν having the stress upon it. Jowett's two surmises are alike groundless—either that the apostle doubted the good faith of the rulers, or was not completely master of his own words. The one has no sure basis, and the other is derogatory to the writer, and unsubstantiated by any critical analysis of his style, or by any true estimate of his modes of expression—words being with him the faithful vehicle of thought and emotion. Nor can we say with Theodoret, that there was a likelihood (εἰκός) that those who got the epistle might keep it back from some members of the church, there being no hint that the presbyters were so alienated from the church that they might be tempted to such a course (Olshausen). Still the language is strong, and is not found anywhere else. All that we are warranted to say is that the apostle felt that the contents of the letter were so important, so suited to the spiritual wants of the people, that he was very anxious that every member of the church should hear it read, and therefore puts them under solemn oath to secure this result. For the letter touched on their first reception of the gospel and its blessed fruits; on the trials which they had encountered, and his own earnest desire and frustrated efforts to revisit them; on his disinterestedness when he laboured among them, and the joy which he had in their progress; on the fulness of comfort set apart for those distracted by sorrow and anxiety about the relation of the dead to the Second Advent—that solace edged with a word of warning to those whose minds had become unsettled, and who, by their indolence, were bringing discredit on the new religion. The entire epistle—so simple, and somewhat historical—was the immediate and natural disclosure of his heart toward them. Perhaps in the prospect of writing letters to other churches, he enjoined the reading of this first one written by him. They might not know how they were to deal with it, or when, how far, or to whom, to make known its contents. He, therefore, solves all such difficulties, and at once adjures them to read it publicly to the assembled church. *Quod Paulus cum adjuratione jubet, id Roma sub anathemate prohibet* (Bengel). The inferential structure raised on this verse by Wordsworth is conjecture without great plausibility, so far, at least, as the Thessalonian church is concerned, however it might be in subsequent centuries.

(Ver. 28.) Ἡ χάρις τοῦ Κυρίου ἡμῶν Ἰησοῦ Χριστοῦ μεθ' ὑμῶν—"The grace of our Lord Jesus Christ be with you." For these names see under Ephes. i, 2. The grace of the Lord Jesus Christ, in its fulness, he implored upon them—of Him who in love took upon Him their nature and became Jesus—of Him the Anointed One, the Christ, who is now at the right hand of the Father, as Lord of all. That grace adapts itself to every want, to every variety and element of spiritual condition. See under Ephes. i, 2.

In the epistles are found varying forms of the concluding salutation. Those most resembling the one before us are Rom. xvi, 24—"the grace of our Lord Jesus Christ be with you all;" 2 Thess. iii, 18—"the grace of our Lord Jesus Christ be with you all;" 1 Cor. xvi, 23—"The grace of the Lord Jesus be with

you." There are shorter forms—Col. iv, 18 ; 2 Tim. iv, 22—
"Grace be with you;" Titus iii, 13—"Grace be with you all;"
1 Tim. vi, 21—"Grace be with thee;" and there are also longer
ones—Gal. vi, 18—"The grace of our Lord Jesus Christ be with
your spirit, brethren;" Philip. iv, 23, and Phile. 25—"The
grace of our Lord Jesus Christ be with your spirit;" and the
full benediction is (2 Cor. xiii, 14)—"The grace of the Lord
Jesus Christ, and the love of God, and the communion of the
Holy Ghost be with you all;" and in Ephes. vi, 24, it is—
"Grace be with all those that love our Lord Jesus Christ in
sincerity."

The 'Aμήν of the Received Text, though supported by
A D²³ K L ℵ, and some fathers, is scarcely to be accepted—it
is not found in B D¹ F, and the Latin versions. Lachmann
and Tischendorf omit it, as it may have been an ecclesiastical
addition or response.

The subscription, with its many variations, has no authority,
being added by some copyist of an unknown date.

COMMENTARY

ON

SECOND THESSALONIANS

SECOND THESSALONIANS

CHAPTER I

(Ver. 1.) Παῦλος καὶ Σιλουανὸς καὶ Τιμόθεος τῇ ἐκκλησίᾳ Θεσσαλονικέων ἐν Θεῷ πατρὶ ἡμῶν καὶ Κυρίῳ Ἰησοῦ Χριστῷ— "Paul and Silvanus and Timotheus to the Church of the Thessalonians in God our Father and the Lord Jesus Christ." The address is the same as in the First Epistle, with the addition of ἡμῶν after πατρί. See under i, 1, for some of its peculiarities. There are some minor variations and corrections in the reading which need not be recounted.

(Ver. 2.) χάρις ὑμῖν καὶ εἰρήνη ἀπὸ Θεοῦ πατρὸς ἡμῶν καὶ Κυρίου Ἰησοῦ Χριστοῦ—" grace to you and peace from God our Father and the Lord Jesus Christ." The ἡμῶν after πατρός is doubtful, though it has in its favour A F K L ℵ, the Vulgate, both the Syriac versions, and the Coptic version, with Chrysostom, Theodoret, &c. It is omitted in B D, in the Claromontane Latin, and in Theophylact. The external authority is great, and probably prevails over the conjecture that ἡμῶν may have been inserted for the sake of conformity to the opening salutations in many other epistles (Rom. i, 7; 1 Cor. i, 3; 2 Cor. i, 2; Ephes. i, 2; Philip. i, 2; Col. i, 2; Phile. 3). There is little probability that the pronoun was omitted in this verse on account of its occurrence in the first verse. Tischendorf omits it, Lachmann brackets it, Griesbach prefixes his mark of *omissio minus probabilis*. Πατρὸς is used absolutely in Gal. i, 3, and in the pastoral epistles, 1 Tim.

i, 2; 2 Tim. i, 2; Titus i, 4; but in the two first citations there is a various reading, not, however, of preponderant value. For the sense of the terms see under Ephes. i, 2; Gal. i, 1, 3.

The apostle, as is his wont, now thanks God for them—for their spiritual progress, and for their patience under persecution and afflictions, those afflictions being tokens of God's righteous judgment, which will reward them and punish their enemies; and the period of retribution is the personal revelation of the Lord Jesus from heaven in glory at the final day.

(Ver. 3.) Εὐχαριστεῖν ὀφείλομεν τῷ Θεῷ πάντοτε περὶ ὑμῶν, ἀδελφοί—"We are bound to give thanks to God always for you, brethren." See under 1 Thess. i, 3; Ellicott on Col. i, 12. Not only does he give thanks, but he feels a profound and irrepressible obligation to give thanks. Not that he was ever reluctant or forgetful to bless God; not that his thanksgiving needed a special impulse to express itself; but that in this case there sprang up, from all the circumstances, a sense of duty so profound that the thanksgiving is not simply a becoming form at the opening of the epistle, but a devout act which, from the healthy condition of the Thessalonian Church and his intense paternal interest in it, had become to him a holy necessity. And he adds—

καθὼς ἄξιόν ἐστιν, ὅτι ὑπεραυξάνει ἡ πίστις ὑμῶν, καὶ πλεονάζει ἡ ἀγάπη ἑνὸς ἑκάστου πάντων ὑμῶν εἰς ἀλλήλους— "as it is meet, because your faith groweth exceedingly, and the love of every one of you all to each other aboundeth." By not a few the clause καθὼς ἄξιόν ἐστιν is taken as a parenthetical insertion—*uti par est* (Beza)—and ὅτι is joined to ὀφείλομεν, "we are bound to give thanks (as is meet and right)—bound to give thanks, that your faith," &c. Others, who hold the same connection, regarding such a sense as flat and pointless, infuse other thoughts, as in one of Theophylact's explanations, ἵνα μηδὲ ἐπὶ τῇ εὐχαριστίᾳ αὐτῇ ἐπαιρώμεθα, ὡς ξένον τι συνεισαγαγόντες; he adds, in one place, that ἡ ἄξια εὐχαριστία is to be shown by words and by deeds. Œcumenius writes, ἢ τὸ μεγάλως ἐξακουστέον, as if the clause meant the greatness of the thanksgiving, great thanks for great mercies. So Bengel too, *ob rei magnitudinem*. Schott explains the phrase as showing *modum eximium, quo animus gratus declarari debeat.* Hofmann says, "with the acknowledgment of personal obligation he joins a recognition of the circumstances of the case." So Erasmus, Fromond, Pelt, and others—De Wette being in doubt.

But (1) if ὅτι be joined to ὀφείλομεν, the intervening clause, καθὼς ἄξιόν ἐστιν, is superfluous. (2) The insertion of ἀδελφοί breaks the connection, and, making the clause independent, severs ὀφείλομεν from ὅτι, &c. (3) As Lünemann remarks against Schott's exegesis, καθὼς does not signify measure or degree, as is implied in *modum eximium*. (4) The clause καθὼς ἄξιόν ἐστιν does not gather the stress upon it, but only carries forward the thought to the distinct and enumerated grounds of thankfulness, and therefore the clause connected with the first words of the verse is specially linked to what follows. We are bound to give thanks as is most due, because your faith groweth exceedingly—the brief assertion of the meetness of the thanksgiving leading so naturally to the production of the reasons for it. Nor is there in the clause any pleonasm (Schott), or that tautology which Jowett imagines—"tautology which with the apostle is often emphasis, ἄξιον expressing a higher degree of the same notion than ὀφείλομεν." Such an exegesis, however, does not create tautology—"it is not merely an obligation, but a noble and worthy thing," is his own paraphrase. The two thoughts are quite distinct—duty in itself and in the character of the deed comprised in it. Nor is the connection so poor and unnatural as Jowett asserts, for in ὀφείλομεν the duty is represented in its subjective aspect, as obligation felt by the apostle and his colleagues, our "bounden duty," and καθὼς ἄξιόν ἐστιν introduces its objective basis—the spiritual experience and progress of the Thessalonian Church. The clause, therefore, is followed by ὅτι—*quoniam* in both Latin versions—because your faith groweth exceedingly. Winer, § 53, 8.

Though verbs compounded with ὑπέρ are favourites with the apostle, the verb ὑπεραυξάνει occurs only here. Fritzsche, *Rom.*, vol. I., p. 351, who, besides Rom. v, 20—the verse commented on —refers to Rom. vii, 37; 2 Cor. vii, 4; xi, 5; Philip. ii, 9; 1 Tim. i, 14. The simple verb is used transitively in other places, but intransitively, as here, in Acts vi, 7. Their faith was growing exceedingly; expanding out of its original germ, as a tree from its seed; increasing in the intensity of its confidence, and of its regulating and ennobling power; and opening up so as to embrace a wider cycle of truths. It would not have been a living faith if it had not grown. And as it had increased so much (ὑπέρ)—not merely beyond expectation (Riggenbach), but beyond measure—the apostle felt bound to give thanks to God. Olshausen finds in the verb an indulgent reference to too great an eagerness of belief or credulousness by which they afterwards brought reproof upon themselves. So also Baumgarten-Crusius. But surely the apostle could not make such a faith the ground of thanks to God, nor can ὑπέρ have in it what is really a satirical allusion.

Not only their faith in its growth, but their love also in its enlargement, formed the ground of the apostle's thanksgiving. That love is specified in no vague terms, but is individualized—not simply your love of the church as a mass, but the love of each one of you all toward one another—the whole body of believers in Thessalonica. It is a freak of Hofmann to take πάντων ὑμῶν as in apposition with ἑνὸς ἑκάστου. The love, ἡ ἀγάπη εἰς ἀλλήλους, is brother-love—not man-love, or love of all (Pelt), but the love of fellow-Christians—there being no reference to those without the church, as in 1 Thess. iii, 12, or to any supposed antipathy to the heathen unbelievers (Schrader). While ὑπεραυξάνει characterizes their faith in its growth, πλεονάζει characterizes their love in its extension, or, not only in its increasing fervour, but specially in the enlargement of its sphere; every one loving, every one conscious of being beloved—universal reciprocal affection—"equal," as Chrysostom says, "on the part of all." Chrysostom notices the distinction in the use of the two verbs, but the figure employed by him fails to explain it. See under 1 Thess. iii, 12; Ephes. i, 15. There might be, as Olshausen remarks, some differences in the church, as the third chapter indicates; but they were so merged in universal attachment that the eulogy of the apostle was warranted. Faith, hope, love, and patience already characterized them, as is said in 1 Thess. i, 3; iii, 6; iv, 9; the apostle had prayed for an increasing abundance of love among them, and in this clause he thanks God virtually that his prayer had been heard.

For the signal spiritual progress of the Thessalonian Church the apostle felt bound not only to thank God, the source of all good, but he always had peculiar pleasure in Thessalonica, and he gave it an honourable and prominent place in his addresses and ministry among the other churches—

(Ver. 4.) ὥστε ἡμᾶς αὐτοὺς ἐν ὑμῖν ἐγκαυχᾶσθαι ἐν ταῖς ἐκκλησίαις τοῦ Θεοῦ—"so that we ourselves glory in you in the churches of God," "make a boast of you" (Coverdale). There are some various readings—B ℵ, and a few minuscules read αὐτοὺς ἡμᾶς, and this order is preferred by Alford. These are two old and high authorities. C is here deficient. The Received Text has καυχᾶσθαι after D K L, and many of the fathers, F having καυχήσασθαι; but A B ℵ have ἐγκαυχᾶσθαι, the more unusual form, which is therefore to be preferred. It is found in the Sept., Ps. li, 3; Ps. cvi, 47. The first pronouns are emphatic—we ourselves, not we of our own accord (Hofmann), but we as well as others, who know you, and honour, appreciate, and praise you for your spiritual prosperity; we ourselves who prayed and laboured for you, and have a tender and abiding interest in you, as being the instruments by which God has brought you into this happy condition. The insertion of καὶ is not needed for this meaning—1 Thess. iv, 9, where, however, it is αὐτοὶ ὑμεῖς with a slight change of emphasis. But (1) it is to be questioned if the clause can sustain the contrast in Ellicott's paraphrase—" ourselves, as well as others, who might call attention to your Christian progress more naturally and appropriately than those who felt it, humanly speaking, due to their own exertions, but who, in the present case, could not forbear." Such an expression of feeling is in no way opposed to what the apostle says in 1 Cor. i, 31; iii, 21. The apostle felt himself so wholly an instrument in the Master's hand that he never scrupled to mention his services—ever ascribing humbly and gratefully to Him the strength to do them, and any success which might attend them (1 Thess. i, 8, 9; ii, 19, 20). (2) The contrast is not that presented by Jowett—" so that it is not only you who boast of yourselves, but we ourselves who boast of you." Similarly Chrysostom—" if we give thanks and glory to God for you among men, much more ought you to do so for your own good deeds." "We ourselves" is not in opposition to you—"your self-gloriation" is in no sense hinted at—but is in opposition to others who also glory in you. Surely this reference of the apostle to the exultant feelings of himself and his colleagues is so natural in the circumstances that the language has no "semblance of a false emphasis, or of awkwardness of expression." (3) Nor is the contrast that indicated by Schott and Pelt, *de se potissimum Apostolo intelligi vult*, ἡμᾶς αὐτοὺς being equivalent to ἐμαυτόν—for verse 3 refers to himself and his companions. Such a contrast would be abrupt and unnatural, and it is disproved by the close logical connection of the verses. The boasting is ἐν ὑμῖν, "in you," you being its object and sphere. Winer, 48; Bernhardy, p. 210. Comp. Exod. xiv, 4; Isaiah xlix, 3. The churches of God in which this boasting had taken place must be those which the apostle visited and addressed—those in Corinth and its neighbourhood the Achaian capital being his headquarters. The inference of Chrysostom that patience is shown by much time, and not in two or three days, must not be unduly pressed as settling in any way the date of the epistle. Still further—

ὑπὲρ τῆς ὑπομονῆς ὑμῶν καὶ πίστεως ἐν πᾶσιν τοῖς διωγμοῖς ὑμῶν καὶ ταῖς θλίψεσιν αἷς ἀνέχεσθε—" for your patience and faith in all your persecutions and the afflictions which ye endure." Ὑπέρ points out the elements of spiritual character, over or on account of which he boasted. Bengel's connection of the preposition with εὐχαριστεῖν is too remote and unnatural. The Hendiadys supposed by Pelt and others is not to be thought of, ὑπομονῆς τῆς πίστεως—πίστις ὑπομένουσα, or τῆς ὑπομονῆς ἐν πίστει. The noun ὑπομονή, "bearing up under," means quiet and steadfast endurance—not the bearing of evil in apathy or stoical unresistance, but in a spirit of serene firmness, and of earnest expectation that God would vouchsafe final deliverance. Πίστις has its common signification, confidence in God and Christ, as in the previous verse; and there is no necessity for Lünemann to give it the sense of "*Treue*," or for Bengel to explain it as *fidelem constantiam confessionis*. Similarly

Olshausen. Though the omission of the article before πίστεως places it and ὑπομονή under one conception, the signification of "fidelity" is not warranted. Their patience and their faith are closely allied. That their faith had been growing is his general statement, and he thanks God for it; and here he again mentions the same faith in a more special aspect and connection. Suffering for Christ they still believed on Him—persecution did not uproot their faith or even bring it into suspense. They were enduring, and in spite of this endurance believing, when the apostle gloried in them (Rev. xiii, 10). Their endurance tested their faith, and showed its stability, and their faith was the inner element of that patience which was one of its fruits. In the next phrase, as the repetition of the article before θλίψεσιν shows, πᾶσιν belongs to διωγμοῖς ὑμῶν, and θλίψεσιν is specialized by αἷς ἀνέχεσθε which takes up again the ὑμῶν. The term διωγμός appears to be the more special and θλῖψις the more general—the first being that injury done to the person, property, or character of believers by the powerful and unscrupulous opponents of the gospel; and the other, those evils that came upon them on account of their faith, many of them connected with persecution—hardship, poverty, disease, loss of friendship, rupture of family ties, the pressure of other trials—all on account of their Christian professsion, maintained so boldly and patiently in a city so hostile and powerful as Thessalonica. And these are still endured by them—

αἷς ἀνέχεσθε—"which ye are enduring" at the moment or at the time when the epistle was written. There had been earlier persecutions, as during the apostle's own brief sojourn; and these are alluded to in 1 Thess. i, 6; ii, 14, by the aorist, as having passed away. But they appear to have been renewed, and the church was suffering from some fresh outbreak when the apostle was writing this epistle. Fritzsche maintains that αἷς ἀνέχεσθε is a regular poetical construction, as the verb may govern the dative, as in Euripides, *Androm.*, 981. He assigns to it a passive meaning *sustinendo premi*. But while the verb in the classics governs the accusative of person, in the New Testament it uniformly governs the genitive both of person and thing—the former as in Matt. xvii, 17; Mark ix, 19; Luke ix, 41; Acts xviii, 14; 2 Cor. xi, 1, 19; Ephes. iv, 2; Col. iii,

13 ; 2 Tim. iv, 3, and the latter in Heb. xiii, 22 ; in other passages it is used indefinitely, so that very probably αἷς is here an attraction, not for ἅς, as Schott, Olshausen, De Wette, and Hofmann, but for ὧν—the case regularly governed by the verb. A. Buttmann, p. 140.

Timothy had been sent to them for the purpose of comforting them concerning their faith, that no man should be moved by those afflictions, and the clauses before us assert the success of that mission. The apostle's heart poured itself out in thanksgiving to God, and he had gloried in the Thessalonian church and held it up as a model to other Christian communities. But there were ethical lessons in those afflictions, and these the apostle proceeds to unfold and apply.

(Ver. 5.) ἔνδειγμα τῆς δικαίας κρίσεως τοῦ Θεοῦ—" which is a token of the righteous judgment of God." In a similar connection (Philip. i, 28) ἥτις ἐστίν is expressed, and similarly ὅ τι ἐστίν may be supplied here. Compare Rom. viii, 3. The clause is not to be resolved into εἰς ἔνδειγμα, as is read in Cod. 73, and explained by Theophylact, supported by Koppe, Flatt, and Olshausen, the Vulgate having also *in exemplum*. The noun occurs only here, but the other verbal, ἔνδειξις, is found in Rom. iii, 25 ; Philip. i, 28. The apposition is nominatival. Winer, § 59, 9. The reference or connection has been variously taken ; what is declared to be the ἔνδειγμα ? (1) Some take it to be the Thessalonians themselves—the ὑμεῖς involved in ἀνέχεσθε (Erasmus, Camerarius, Estius). Such a connection is simple indeed, but it would have required the participle ὄντες to be expressed ; nor does it yield a sense at all in harmony with the context. Estius finds in it an argument for *adhuc luenda poena temporalis*. (2) Some take the reference to be to πᾶσιν διωγμοῖς, &c., as Calvin, Bullinger, Aretius, Pelt, Schrader, Ewald, Bisping. But the afflictions themselves, apart from their nature and source, and apart from the character and spirit of those who endure them, cannot be the ἔνδειγμα. (3) The connection is better taken with the entire clause, not themselves simply, or their afflictions, but themselves so conditioned—" your patience and faith in all your persecutions, and the sufferings which you are enduring." The patience and faith manifested by you in severe suffering—

not the suffering, but the noble spirit in which it had been borne, forms the ἔνδειγμα. The phrase ἡ δικαία κρίσις τοῦ Θεοῦ presents in itself an undoubted and universal truth— God judges, and He "judges righteous judgment." But in its present connection the phrase presents difficulty. There are two extremes of opinion. Olshausen, on the one hand, followed by Riggenbach, restricts the judgment to the present time, while Ellicott, on the other hand, confines it to the future judgment. The use of the articles proves nothing on either point. That it is not wholly present judgment the entire coming context shows—on from the following verse where the revelation of Christ from heaven with angels and in fire is brought into view, and, by the very terms, into immediate relation with the verse before us—"the righteous judgment of God," "seeing it is a righteous thing with God to recompense tribulation," on the one hand, and "rest with us," on the other. Nor is the reference wholly to the future tribunal, for the just judgment begins now, not simply by the effect of such suffering in purifying and perfecting them—the judgment is for condemnation to enemies and unbelievers—but because the patient sufferings of believers demonstrate that there is now righteous judgment on the part of God; the grace that so sustains them is from Him; He as Judge accepts and approves them by the bestowal of such gifts of patience and faith; and this experience is a further token or presage that a period of fuller manifestation is coming when the persecutors shall receive condign retribution, and their victims shall be brought into perfect and eternal repose. Their condition, and that of their persecutors, both here and hereafter, were in contrast; but there is a mutual reversal in the world to come—the future compensating the present (Luke xvi. 25). Suffering here, especially the suffering of the good at the hand of wicked oppressors, implies under God's righteous government a future state of balancing and compensation, of reward and penalty, equitably administered. Compare De Wette, Lünemann, Hofmann.

εἰς τὸ καταξιωθῆναι ὑμᾶς τῆς βασιλείας τοῦ Θεοῦ—"that ye may be counted worthy of the kingdom of God." The connection of this clause has also been variously taken. (1) Some would connect it with αἷς ἀνέχεσθε, as Estius, Bengel, Hofmann,

Bisping. "The suffering makes them worthy of the kingdom" —τὸ pati facit dignos regno (Bengel); Estius advancing farther and saying, against the heretics, that eternal life is not so to be ascribed to the grace of God—*ut non etiam dignitati et meritis hominum a gratia Dei profectis retribuatur.* But though this connection may not necessarily include the Popish doctrine of merit, while it would bring out the purpose of the suffering, yet as Lünemann remarks, it reduces to a parenthesis the momentous clause, "which is a token of the righteous judgment of God"—a clause from which spring the thoughts which, taken up in verse 6, lead to the startling disclosures of the following verses. (2) Nor does it belong to the whole sentence, ἔνδειγμα τῆς δικαίας κρίσεως τοῦ Θεοῦ, "a token of the righteous judgment of God, which has this end in view, that ye may be accounted," &c. (Schott). For the token itself is not directly connected with the end or result, but belongs especially to the κρίσις, while εἰς τό introduces the purpose. (3) The connection is directly with τῆς δικαίας κρίσεως—the aim or result of the righteous judgment (Lünemann, Ellicott, Ewald, Alford). Winer, § 44, 6. Result is expressed in 2 Cor. viii, 6, and De Wette queries if it may not mean the substance or contents of the judicial decision. Surely it is refinement to debate in such a case whether εἰς τό refer to result or purpose, as the result is simply the embodied purpose, and the purpose by appointed and fitting means works out the result. The purpose or result of the κρίσις was that such sufferers in patient heroism for Christ should be accounted worthy of his kingdom. For the infinitive compare Luke xx, 35; xxi, 36; Acts v, 41. Joseph., *Antiq.* xv, 38. It is by the righteous judgment of God that they are counted worthy, or declared to be meet for the divine inheritance (Lillie). The righteous sentence of God, efficient even now in the creation and sustenance of faith and patience in the midst of suffering, shall at the appointed time relieve and accept the sufferers, and translate them into God's eternal kingdom. For the kingdom, see under 1 Thess. ii, 12.

ὑπὲρ ἧς καὶ πάσχετε—"on behalf of which ye are suffering." The preposition ὑπέρ means "on behalf of," as in Acts v, 41; ix, 16; Rom. i, 5; xv, 8; 2 Cor. xii, 10; xiii, 8. Winer, § 47, 6.

The καὶ points out the connection, as in Rom. viii, 17—Alford making it equivalent to "ye accordingly"—Ellicott saying, "it has a species of consecutive force, and supplied a renewed hint of the connection between the suffering and the being counted worthy." Suffering gave them no claim on the kingdom, but it separates the two classes, and by God's grace inworks or develops those elements of character which enable and induce believers to suffer for the kingdom, and prepare them for the ultimate enjoyment of it.

> "The path of suffering, and that path alone,
> Leads to the land where sorrow is unknown."

John xvi, 33; Acts xiv, 22; Rom. viii, 17.

(Ver. 6.) εἴπερ δίκαιον παρὰ Θεῷ ἀνταποδοῦναι τοῖς θλίβουσιν ὑμᾶς θλῖψιν—"if so be that it is a righteous thing with God to render back to those who afflict you affliction." In εἴπερ there is no doubt implied—the argument is stated hypothetically for the sake of confirmation. Compare Rom. viii, 9, 17. Εἴπερ *significat proprie, si omnino,* quod nostro sermone dicas— *wenn überhaupt;* ubi vim ac rationem condicionis magis vis efferre—*wenn anders.* Klotz, *Devarius,* vol. II, p. 528. Hartung. I, p. 343. Hermann's note under Gal. iii, 4. Thus Chrysostom interprets τὸ Εἴπερ ἐνταῦθα ἀντὶ τοῦ, ἐπεὶ, κεῖται, ὅπερ ἐπὶ τῶν σφόδρα ὁμολογουμένων καὶ ἡμεῖς τίθεμεν καὶ ἀναντιρρήτων ... τίθησι τὸ εἴπερ τοῦτο, ὡς ἐπὶ τῶν ὡμολογημένων. So Theodoret—οὐκ ἐπὶ ἀμφιβολίας ... ἀλλ' ἐπὶ βεβαιώσεως—according to a familiar idiom. In the phrase παρὰ Θεῷ, there is a quasi-local reference to the divine tribunal and judgment (Rom. ii, 13; 1 Cor. iii, 19; Gal. iii, 11; 1 Peter ii, 3; Herod. iii, 160). Winer, § 48, *d*; Rost and Palm, *sub voce* παρά. The term δίκαιον takes up the δικαία κρίσις of the previous verse—the characteristic element of justice in the divine judgment being the foundation of the argument, which is presented under a human aspect and analogy, "if such a course with men much more so with God" (Chrysostom). In order to substantiate his statement the apostle appeals virtually to our innate sense of justice, which by analogy declares that it is a right thing with God, and the hearer cannot but respond, ἀλλὰ μὴν δίκαιον. For the verb see under 1 Thess. iii, 9. What is just or righteous is the divine retaliation, "affliction to those who afflict you," like sin like penalty, "with what measure ye mete" (Ps. xviii, 47; lvii, 6; Rom. ii, 5). See under Col. iii, 24, 25. By this *jus talionis*, the penalty in kind is not only entailed by the sin, but also fashioned by it as a reproduction of itself. Totally wrong is the remark of Pelt, that the phrase makes mention *non de essentiali Dei justitia, sed de gratia potius;* and that of Hunnius—*justitia Dei, quemadmodum illa in Christo est misericordia erga nos affectu tincta atque temperata.* But there is another aspect—divine rectitude is not one-sided—

(Ver. 7.) καὶ ὑμῖν τοῖς θλιβομένοις ἄνεσιν μεθ' ἡμῶν—" and to you who are afflicted rest with us." The participle is passive, not middle, as in Bengel's explanation, *qui pressuram toleratis.* The noun ἄνεσις is used in the classics in contrast to ἐπίτασις—tightening and slackening τῶν χορδῶν (Plato, *Rep.*, I, p. 349 E); τῆς πολιτείας (Plutarch, *Lycurg.*, 29; *Vitae*, vol. I, p. 94, ed. Bekker). It signifies also relief, as from labour (Joseph., *Antiq.*, iii, 10, 6); from immediate execution (2 Chron. xxiii, 15); from close confinement (Acts xxiv, 23); from moral obligation, and in contrast to θλῖψις (2 Cor. viii, 13); and then generally it denotes rest—Hesychius defining it by ἀνάπαυσις. In 2 Cor. ii, 13; vii, 5, it is in contrast again with θλῖψις. It is rest from all that persecution which they were suffering from the fury of unbelieving Jews and heathens—rest μεθ' ἡμῶν—with us, Paul, Silvanus, and Timothy, for we have suffered from persecution, and hope for rest (1 Thess. ii, 2). Turretin and De Wette err in giving the phrase a wider reference to all believers, for all of them are not exposed to such sufferings. Bengel similarly errs in rendering *nobiscum, i.e., cum sanctis Israëlitis,* and after him Macknight, and virtually Ewald. This ἄνεσις is the immediate aspect of heaven to the suffering, rest to the weary and worn-out, release from all the disquiet, pain, and sorrow of the earth, stillness after turmoil, the quiet haven after the tempest. This view of heaven was specially natural and welcome to them, who were suffering for its sake, for it was a complete reversal of their present condition (Luke xvi, 25; Acts iii, 19; Heb. iv, 3, 11; Rev. xiv, 13). Ἄνεσιν is governed by the double ἀνταποδοῦναι, for which see under 1 Thess. iii, 9. The period of introduction to the "rest" is—

ἐν τῇ ἀποκαλύψει τοῦ Κυρίου Ἰησοῦ ἀπ' οὐρανοῦ—"in or at the revelation of the Lord Jesus Christ from heaven." The clause specifies the time when the judicial retribution implied in ἀνταποδοῦναι is to take place, the period of the Second Advent. Παρουσία is the word commonly employed (see under 1 Thess. ii, 19; iii, 13), but ἀποκάλυψις is a more vivid term, pointing to the visible, personal, and gracious manifestation of the Lord Jesus Christ (1 Cor. i, 7). Compare Luke xvii, 30; Rev. ii, 5. Ἐπιφάνεια is also employed, as in ii, 8; 1 Tim. vi, 14; 2 Tim. iv, 1, 8; Titus ii, 13. This term seems to imply previous or present concealment (the heavens have received Him), in contrast with His immediate and magnificent appearance "in His own glory," and "in the glory of His Father, and of the holy angels". (Matt. xvi, 27; xxv, 31; Luke ix, 26). The words ἀπ' οὐρανοῦ indicate the locality whence he comes. He is now in heaven, at the right hand of God, pleading, reigning, and preparing a place for His people; and the economy of redemption being completed, in itself and in the number of its recipients, He descends to raise the dead, and usher all His own perfected ones in the fulness of their humanity into everlasting blessedness. See under 1 Thess. iv, 16, 17. That personal revelation is now characterized as being—

μετ' ἀγγέλων δυνάμεως αὐτοῦ—"with the angels of his power." The preposition means "in company with," the angels being His attendants or retinue. The genitive δυνάμεως is that of possession; the power is not theirs but His. They are the servants of his power, manifesting and fulfilling it. Winer, § 34, 3 b. The Advent is accompanied by the voice of the archangel when the dead are raised, and angels are referred to in a similar connection, as gathering together the elect, and as "gathering out of this kingdom all things that offend, and them which do iniquity" (Matt. xiii, 41; xxiv, 31). "All the holy angels" are with Him when "He shall come in glory, and shall sit on the throne of His glory" (Matt. xxv, 31). The work performed by Him at the Second Advent is momentous and mighty—resurrection and final victory over death; judgment, and the ultimate separation of believers and the wicked; and the angels of His might, as its heralds and ministers, are specially connected with Him and His glorious appearance. (1) While the margin of the Authorized Version presents the right translation, the version itself, "His mighty angels" is in no way to be justified, though it may be an inference. The mistranslation is an old one. Theophylact explains, δυνάμεως γὰρ ἄγγελοι, τούτεστι δυνατοί, and the alternative explanation of Œcumenius is similar. It has been followed by Piscator, Benson, Flatt, Tyndale, and in the Genevan version. But αὐτοῦ is to be construed with δυνάμεως, not with ἀγγέλων, the sense being "not the angels of might," as if the genitive might have an adjectival meaning, but the angels of His might, He being the central figure. (2) Another and as erroneous translation has been given in the Syriac, ܒܚܝܠܐ ܕܡܠܐܟܘܗܝ, with the power of His angels, that is, with the host of them; and the view has been followed by Drusius, Michaelis, Koppe, and Hofmann who for this purpose attaches αὐτοῦ to the following διδόντος—δύναμις being taken as representing the Hebrew צבא. But, first, δύναμις has never this meaning in the New Testament, and Hofmann's reference to Luke x, 19; xxi, 26; Matt. xxiv, 29, will not sustain him; second, the order of the words with this sense would require to be μετὰ δυνάμεως ἀγγέλων αὐτοῦ. The next clause is read in the *Textus Receptus*—

(Ver. 8.) ἐν πυρὶ φλογός, after A K L ℵ, with nearly all mss., Theophylact, Ambrosiaster, Chrysostom, Theodoret, and Damascenus. It is also preferred by Reiche, Tischendorf, and Alford. The other reading, ἐν φλογὶ πυρός, is found in B D F, and both Latin versions, the Peshito and Gothic versions, and in Œcumenius, Tertullian, and others of the fathers, and is adopted by Lachmann and Ellicott. No assistance can be got from the similar clauses in Exod. iii, 2, or Acts vii, 30, for in each there is also a difference of reading. Both readings are well sustained by diplomatic authority, though the last has the appearance, in spite of its apparently higher evidence, of being a correction as to sense, flame of fire being more natural than fire of flame. The Hebrew in Exod. iii, 2, reads בְּלַבַּת־אֵשׁ, in a flame of fire; followed by A of the Seventy, ἐν φλογὶ πυρός; which B of the same version reads ἐν πυρὶ φλογός. Compare in the Septuagint Ps. xxix, 7; Is. xxix, 6; Joel ii, 5; Dan. vii, 9: also Sirach xlv, 19; Heb. i, 7; Rev. xix, 12. The former is apparently the more usual form. The clause specifies another element or accompaniment of the ἀποκάλυψις. He is revealed in, or enveloped in, a fire of flame—no dulled or veiled glow, but a radiance, bright, pure, and flashing; a fire burning with intensest brilliance. That was a familiar symbol of the divine presence and glory—the cloud that guided Israel being as the veil by day of the inner brightness, which shone out in the night as fire. Compare Gen. xv, 17; Exod. iii, 2; xiii, 21, 22; xix, 18; Ps. xcvii, 3, 4; Is. xxx, 30; and the other passages already quoted. What characterizes the Theophanies of the Old Testament characterizes the Advent of the Son in our nature—similar majesty of manifestation betokening the Godhead of the Redeemer, Jehovah-Jesus (1 Cor. iii, 13).

It serves no good object to attempt any minute detail of the meaning and purpose of the phenomenon, either as Zachariae and Koppe, to refer it to thunder and lightning, or to say that the fire is meant to consume the world of unbelievers, as Zuingli, Aretius, a-Lapide, Fromond, for the context does not assert any such purpose, though the punctuation of the English version would seem to imply it. Some connect this clause with the following one, διδόντος ἐκδίκησιν, "in flaming fire awarding vengeance." So Estius, a-Lapide, Macknight, Hofmann, Hilgenfeld, regard the previous words as instrumentally connected with the judgment to which, according to Hilgenfeld, the flaming fire belongs. Hofmann's exegesis is strained and unnatural; he connects αὐτοῦ with διδόντος, referring the pronoun to God, and begins the sentence with ἐν τῇ ἀποκαλύψει. But, as Lünemann remarks, in that case αὐτοῦ would require to be left out, and the genitive διδόντος changed into διδόντι, with the article prefixed. Theodoret regards the fire as τῆς τιμωρίας τὸ εἶδος, and similarly Theophylact in the first of his explanations. Jowett needlessly combines both references, expressing at once the manner of Christ's appearance, and the instrument by which he executes vengeance on His enemies. It is best to keep the clause ἐν πυρὶ φλογός by itself, and as parallel to it, μετ' ἀγγέλων δυνάμεως αὐτοῦ, and to regard the words as descriptive of the awfulness and sublimity of the ἀποκάλυψις, the glory in harmony with the work; while διδόντος, connected with Ἰησοῦ, tells the purpose of the Advent by asserting the fact—

διδόντος ἐκδίκησιν τοῖς μὴ εἰδόσιν Θεὸν καὶ τοῖς μὴ ὑπακούουσιν τῷ εὐαγγελίῳ τοῦ Κυρίου ἡμῶν Ἰησοῦ—" awarding vengeance to those who know not God and to those who obey not the gospel of our Lord Jesus." The Received Text has Χριστοῦ after Ἰησοῦ, with A F ℵ, the Latin, Peshito, and Gothic versions, and some of the fathers, but it is omitted in B D K L, 25 mss., in the Philoxenian Syriac, in the Coptic, and many of the fathers, and is probably to be rejected as a conformation to common usage. The first and awful phrase, διδόντος ἐκδίκησιν, occurs only here in the New Testament, but in Ezek. xxv, 14, we have the words καὶ δώσω ἐκδίκησιν μου ἐπὶ τὴν Ἰδουμαίαν, and ἀποδοῦναι is employed with the substantive in Num. xxxi, 3, representing the Hebrew נְקְמַת־יְהוָֹה. This vengeance is and must be just, as it is His sentence, who is the righteous Judge, and who has also been the loving Saviour; the Lamb of God, by whose gentleness the apostle adjures the Corinthian church. As man and mediator, Jesus is Judge; all judgment is committed to the Son; He awards merited penalty "to them that know not God"; and by the subjective μὴ the apostle records this as his own opinion of them. Winer, § 55, 5. Whatever their own flattering impressions on the point, he asserts their ignorance—an ignorance that might have been enlightened in Thessalonica. The clause characterizes the heathen. See under 1 Thess. i, 9, and iv, 5; Gal. iv, 8; Ephes. ii, 12. Compare Jer. x, 25; Rom. i, 28. Ignorance of God prevents all confidence in Him, and all intelligent service to Him. The contrast is stated in John xvii, 3, 25. The class referred to did not know God, and in their wilful ignorance persecuted His servants.

The second clause, by the repetition of τοῖς, indicates another distinct class. Winer, § 19, 5. Matt. xxvii, 3; Luke xxii, 4. Schott, De Wette, Riggenbach, Turretin, Pelt, and Hofmann suppose it to include all who reject the Gospel, whether as Jews or not. In the second clause the words Κυρίου ἡμῶν Ἰησοῦ are solemnly written, as in distinction from

Θεόν of the previous clause. Schrader understands the first clause of heathen, and the second clause of Christians, or as Aretius puts it, *pestes in sinu ecclesiae latitantes*—plainly against the context. In Hofmann's view the first clause describes heathen, and the second Jews and heathen, but the two clauses are distinctive delineations. The basis of safety is to obey the Gospel of our Lord Jesus—so to listen, understand, and believe, that the heart is induced and enabled to obey, accepting its invitation, believing its doctrines, trusting its promises, and obeying its precepts. That Gospel is no vague thing, it has a living personal source—our Lord Jesus, who as Jesus brought the good news of divine mercy to the world, and as Lord is sending his Spirit to give His truth a deep and vital lodgment in men's hearts. This clause will thus characterize the Jews. They had knowledge of God, but would not accept the Gospel, spurned it from them, and in their fanatical rejection of it persecuted Christ's servants who proclaimed it (Rom. x, 3, 16, 21). See under 1 Thess. ii, 14, 15, 16. Both classes, though differing in spiritual condition, united in afflicting the Thessalonian believers, and the prophetic words are verified to them, τοῖς θλίβουσιν ὑμᾶς θλίψιν. Ignorance of God and disobedience to the Gospel urged them to molest and harass the Thessalonian believers, a course of conduct which not only insures the penalty, but moulds its nature, as a retribution in kind.

(Ver. 9.) οἵτινες δίκην τίσουσιν, ὄλεθρον αἰώνιον ἀπὸ προσώπου τοῦ Κυρίου καὶ ἀπὸ τῆς δόξης τῆς ἰσχύος αὐτοῦ—" who shall suffer punishment, everlasting destruction away from the presence of the Lord, and away from the glory of His power." The qualitative and generic pronoun οἵτινες characterizes the persons referred to as being of a class just specified. This relative may sometimes bear a causal sense, *saepissime rationi reddendae inservit*, according to Hermann (*Praef. ad Soph. Œdip., Tyr.*, p. xiii). Such a sense, advocated by Lünemann and Alford, is not formally needed here. The two parties referred to are men who as a class have been already characterized. The phrase δίκην τίσουσιν, "shall pay the penalty," occurs only in this place. Compare Jude 7. But its meaning is clear, as it is often employed in classical writers, the verb being sometimes followed by the accusative of that for which penalty is borne, or atonement is made—φόνον (*Iliad*, xxi, 134), ὕβριν (*Odyss.*, xxiv, 350); and often as here it is followed by δίκην—τίσουσά γ' ἀξίαν δίκην (Soph., *Electra*, 298). A long list of instances is given by Wetstein from the tragedians, and from Plato, Thucydides, Lucian, Ælian, Arrian, Plutarch. The noun is also used with διδόναι, when the meaning is, punishment awarded or legal penalty. The sinners referred to not only feel the inner ruin wrought by ignorance and disobedience—for all sin punishes as it degrades, and hardens, and widens the distance from God—but a positive penalty is laid on them, δίκη. And that δίκη is declared to be ὄλεθρον αἰώνιον, "everlasting destruction." The reading ὀλέθριον has but very slender support. Ὄλεθρος (ὄλλυμι) means death in the Homeric poems, and then destruction in a general sense; ruin as the result of a sinful course, or inflicted as a divine penalty. For the word see under 1 Thess. v, 3. The words are awful; and the next clause deepens the awe—

ἀπὸ προσώπου τοῦ Κυρίου—"from the face of the Lord." (1) The simplest and most natural meaning of ἀπό is local, in separation from the face of the Lord, the source of joy (Rom. ix, 3; 2 Cor. xi, 3; Gal. v, 4). So Schott, Lünemann, Bisping, Riggenbach. His face or countenance throws its benign radiance over his saints, who in their nearness worship Him, and are ever in fellowship with Him. His personal presence is the life and joy of heaven, and to see His face is supreme blessedness, so that to be severed from it is gloom and death, and in that sad severance (ἀπό) is the penalty to be endured (Ps. xi, 7; xvi, 11; xvii, 15; Matt. v, 8; xviii, 10; Heb. xii, 14; Rev. xxii, 4). Compare Septuagint, κρύπτεσθε . . . ἀπὸ προσώπου τοῦ φόβου Κυρίου καὶ ἀπὸ τῆς δόξης τῆς ἰσχύος αὐτοῦ (Is. ii, 10), the clauses being repeated in verses 19 and 21 of the same chapter. The language of the verse before us has apparently its origin in this portion of Isaiah. See also Jer. iv, 26. (2) But the earliest interpretation of ἀπό takes it in a temporal sense, the eternal destruction takes place "at" or "after" the manifestation of His presence. So the Greek fathers; Œcumenius explaining it by ἄμα; Chrysostom more fully, ἀρκεῖ παραγενέσθαι μόνον . . . καὶ πάντες ἐν κολάσει, repeated virtually by Theophylact. This interpretation is adopted by Erasmus, Vatablus, Fromond, Webster and Wilkinson. But, first, ἀπὸ is specially connected with ὄλεθρον, and seems to explain its awful nature in a local sense; secondly, the term πρόσωπον has this species of local meaning attached to it, and thus differs from παρουσία or ἀποκάλυψις; thirdly, the phrases adduced, in which ἀπό has a temporal meaning, describe an act, event, or period, which forms an epoch (Rom. i, 20; Philip. i, 5). (3) A third interpretation takes ἀπό as causal, an idea virtually involved in the interpretation of the Greek fathers. His presence will be the means of their punishment. His mere look brings the penalty. So Bengel, Pelt, De Wette, Ewald, Baumgarten-Crusius, and Hofmann who compares Jer. iv, 29, where, however, this meaning is not necessary. But this signification, to sustain itself, virtually inserts some epithet before πρόσωπον, *zornigen* or *finsteren*, angry or dark; and as ἀπό in this sense is used to denote a personal source, such a meaning would be more plausible if only ἀπὸ τοῦ Κυρίου had been written, and for this the phrase, as we have it, is merely a *circumscriptio* according to Pelt. Winer, § 47. Besides, it would with this sense be a mere repetition of the previous statement, "awarding vengeance." De Wette lays stress on the following ἰσχύος, as if it threw back into this clause the idea of power put forth, and so far suggested or corroborated the causal signification of ἀπό. But ἰσχύος belongs to δόξης as its source, and that δόξα is repeated in the verb of the next verse, ἐνδοξασθῆναι—

καὶ ἀπὸ τῆς δόξης τῆς ἰσχύος αὐτοῦ, "and from the glory of His power." The preposition has the same local sense, the glory being that glory which springs from His power, and which may be conceived of as a visible splendour, gathered up like the old Shechinah into one spot. The phrase is therefore not to be diluted either into ἰσχὺς ἔνδοξος or δόξα ἰσχυρά, "mighty glory" (Jowett). The glory is so connected with His might that, as it is originated by it, it characterizes and envelops it—all its outgoings are ever encircled with glory. That power manifests its glory in the perfection and happiness of His saints, who have been rescued and blessed by Him, and lifted at length beyond death to supreme and immortal felicity. This glory so won by His power is reflected upon Him from His glorified ones, as the next verse intimates, and from such living splendour surrounding Christ's and Christ are the unbelieving for ever exiled.

(Ver. 10.) ὅταν ἔλθῃ ἐνδοξασθῆναι ἐν τοῖς ἁγίοις αὐτοῦ—"when He shall have come to be glorified in His saints." The clause defines the period when the judgment or penalty of the previous verse is to be inflicted. Ὅταν is used with the aorist subjunctive in reference to the future occurrence of an event or action objectively possible, when there is no certainty as to the period of such occurrence. Winer, § 42, 5; more fully, Schmalfeld, § 121. The coming though future in itself is conceived of as having taken place prior to these contrasted results. The infinitive ἐνδοξασθῆναι is that of purpose, and the compound verb is used only, in the New Testament, in this verse and in verse 12; but it is found in the Septuagint, Exod. xiv, 4; Is. xlv, 25; xlix, 3. The ἅγιοι are plainly human saints, not angels, as Schrader and Macknight; and angels are already mentioned. See under 1 Thess. iii, 13, where a more comprehensive meaning may be assigned to the term. Ἐν is not to be taken for διά, as Chrysostom and his followers, and after them Pelt, Bengel, and Schott; nor does it signify among (Michaelis), but, with its usual force, it points out the element in which this glorification takes place. He is glorified in them—in their persons, in the saving power which pardoned and changed them, in their spiritual maturity, in all the prior steps and processes by which it has been reached, in His own image indelibly enstamped upon them, in their perfect and unchanging blessedness, in their full and final glorification—in all these elements of their history and destiny Christ's glory is reflected, He himself is glorified (Ephes. i, 6, 12). His love and His atoning death, His spirit and His intercession, have wrought out His own hallowed purpose in them, and in them as the fruit of His mediation He is glorified. Not only to be glorified, but—

καὶ θαυμασθῆναι ἐν πᾶσιν τοῖς πιστεύσασιν—"and to be admired in all them that believed." The Received Text has the present πιστεύουσιν, but on no uncial authority, and indeed no authority worth mentioning. The aorist refers back to the earthly period when they possessed faith in Jesus Christ, a period past when looked at from "that day." The adjective πᾶσιν, not prefixed to ἁγίοις, enhances the value of faith—in every one without exception who has faith in Christ—the element wanting in those who suffer the righteous penalty. Bengel, from the use of the same term, and without any ground, distinguished the ἁγίοις from the πιστεύσασιν, as if πᾶσιν gave the latter epithet a wider signification than the former, "saints being those of the circumcision, believers they of the Gentiles." The Lord Jesus is to be not only praised, but wondered at—wonder being excited by what is great and unwonted, or when the result far transcends the instrumentality, or turns out beyond expectation, or, when actually realized and beheld, surpasses every conception. The results of faith are so marvellous—a gift so great as forgiveness, a change so thorough and benign as from death to life, the continuous sustenance of that life amidst many defects and struggles, preparation for glory, and welcome entrance into it—these results so rich, lasting, and godlike, wrought out for believers by Jesus, surely so single Him out and exalt Him that He is to be wondered at. When believers appear on that day so pure, lovely, and Christlike; when their present glory is contrasted with their first condition on earth—so guilty, so frail, so defiled, and so helpless; when they call to mind by what a work they have been saved—His cross and passion; and by what a simple instrumentality—a child's trust in the Son of God; then He who has done such great things for them will command their admiration and homage. It creates wonder at Him that He purposed to save us at all in our low and lost estate; greater wonder still that His purpose involved His becoming the Infant of Days, the Man of Sorrows, and the victim of sacrificial agony; and greatest wonder of all that believers in Him are not only raised to their original status, but elevated to a loftier honour, bearing the image of the Second Adam, and admitted into the heavenly inheritance. It is a mere surmise of Theophylact, that this admiration is to happen in the presence of τοὺς οἰκτρούς. The ground is now given—

ὅτι ἐπιστεύθη τὸ μαρτύριον ἡμῶν ἐφ' ὑμᾶς—"because our testimony unto you was believed." The verb ἐπιστεύθη with the stress upon it takes up the participle πιστεύσασιν, and places the Thessalonian believers among the number. Christ is to be admired in them that believe, and you believed our testimony, and therefore possess this joyous anticipation. That testimony was directed to them, ἐφ' ὑμᾶς, and the absence of the article gives to the clause unity of conception, connecting ἐφ' ὑμᾶς immediately with μαρτύριον. Winer, § 30, 2; § 49, l. "Our testimony" is the testimony borne by us, ἡμῶν being the genitive of efficient or proximate origin, and that testimony in itself was the divine message of the Gospel, which they are said in the First Epistle to have "received in much affliction with joy of the Holy Ghost." The apostle and his colleagues brought and delivered the testimony. The Thessalonians heard and believed, remained firm in the midst of trials and persecutions, and are commended by the apostle for their patience and faith; their spiritual growth and their afflictions being a token of the righteous judgment of God, when the solemn scenes now described shall take place; and they take place—

ἐν τῇ ἡμέρᾳ ἐκείνῃ—"in that day," the previous clause being parenthetical. This clause is thus to be joined to θαυμασθῆναι, defining the period, and put last to gather up the whole from ὅταν ἔλθῃ into a solemnity of emphasis. "That day" must have been the theme of his earlier lessons to them, and the manner of this allusion shows their familiarity with it. Calvin's note is that the day is so named to check impatience—*ne ultra modum festinent.* Some, however, propose for the clause a different connection. Bengel takes the connection back to ἔλθῃ, and Webster and Wilkinson to δίκην τίσουσιν. The Syriac Peshito version reads ܕܐܬܗܝܡܢ ܣܗܕܘܬܢ ܕܥܠܝܟܘܢ ܒܝܘܡܐ ܗܘ, "for our testimony concerning you will be believed in that day." So Damascenus, Estius, a-Lapide, Grotius, Storr, Flatt, Baumgarten-Crusius. They join ἐν τῇ ἡμέρᾳ ἐκείνῃ either with μαρτύριον or ἐπιστεύθη. This construction either necessitates ἐφ' ὑμᾶς to be translated "about you"; or the aorist ἐπιστεύθη to be translated as a future or a future perfect (Grotius and Rosenmüller) with a new meaning, "will be made good or substantiated"; or ἐν τῇ ἡμέρᾳ, "about that day," as Luther, "our testimony to you about that day ye believed" (a-Lapide);

a vobis respicientibus ad illum diem creditum fuerit (Estius); or, as others, "our testimony about you will then be substantiated," or "our testimony to you shall be believed even by the wicked in that day." Grotius, "*Quod de salute vestra prædiximus, id illo tempore eventu firmatum erit, ut fidem negare nemo amplius possit.*" Storr, *Opusc.*, vol. II, p. 106. Somewhat similarly Ewald, *Dass beglaubigt war unser Zeugniss an euch*, &c.

(Ver. 11.) Εἰς ὃ καὶ προσευχόμεθα πάντοτε περὶ ὑμῶν—"In reference to which we also pray always concerning you." The phrase εἰς ὃ is not to be rendered "wherefore," as in the Authorized Version, as if it were δι' ὅ; *quapropter* being the rendering also of Grotius, Pelt, Baumgarten-Crusius; *itaque* being given by Koppe. Nor is it equivalent to ὑπὲρ ὅ (De Wette). But the clause has the original meaning of direction—to or towards which, viz., the realization of the glorification of Christ in saints and believers. Winer, § 49 *a*. Lünemann's objection to the rendering "with a view to which," that it would make the consummation predicted dependent on the apostle's prayers, is not formidable. For the Thessalonians are regarded as believers, and therefore as belonging to that happy company; and certainly the divine purpose never renders unnecessary the prayers and aspirations of faith. Nay, by them, and in perfect consistency with divine immutability and human responsibility, it realizes itself. The same objection might be taken against the following ἵνα, referring to or introducing the subject or purpose of the prayer. Καὶ, "we also," that is, according to Ellicott, "not only longing and hoping, we avail ourselves also of the definite accents of prayer." The result being so glorious, with a view to it as portrayed by him, the apostle also prayed for preparatory grace to all the members of the Thessalonian Church. Alford suggests that to support Lünemann's view, that the prayer was added to the fact of the ἐνδοξασθῆναι, the words should have stood καὶ ἡμεῖς προσευχόμεθα. For περί after this verb, see under Ephes. vi, 18. The prayer was continuous, πάντοτε, as there was need of continuous grace. And its object was—

ἵνα ὑμᾶς ἀξιώσῃ τῆς κλήσεως ὁ Θεὸς ἡμῶν—"that our God may count you worthy of your calling," ὑμᾶς having the stress upon it. The εἰς ὅ at the beginning of the verse is so far different from ἵνα that the former refers back to what had just been written—the glorification of Christ in His saints; and the latter points forward to blessings needed by the Thessalonians in the prospect of it, and to qualify them for it. In ἵνα the purpose and theme of the prayer are blended, as sometimes. See under Ephes. i, 17. The verb ἀξιοῦν means to count or reckon worthy, followed here by the accusative of person and genitive of object, though sometimes by the accusative and the infinitive (Luke vii, 7); in the passive by the simple genitive (1 Tim. v, 17; Heb. iii. 3 x, 29; Sept., Gen. xxxi, 28); and by the infinitive (Xen., *Mem.*, i, 4, 10). Compare Joseph., iii, 8, 10. Luther, Grotius, Flatt, Bengel, Olshausen, and Ewald give the verb the meaning of "to make worthy"—a meaning which, as the passages cited show, does not belong to it. See Liddell and Scott, *sub voce*. There is some difficulty about κλήσεως. If κλῆσις be the initial divine act alone, then as it was past, how could the apostle pray that God would count them worthy of it? This difficulty has induced Olshausen to attach to the verb the unsupported sense of "to make worthy." Lünemann takes κλῆσις in a passive sense—the blessing to which one is called—the heavenly blessedness of the children of God. Ellicott and Alford view it as descriptive of the Christian life which springs from effectual calling. See under Ephes. iv, 1; Philip. iii, 14. Hofmann gives it somewhat differently—"that He may count you worthy of a calling which brings to completion what began with our testimony and your faith therein." Allied to this is another view proposed by Riggenbach, that, as is illustrated by the parable of the supper, this call may be the last, decisive, energetic call—the δεῦτε (Matt. xxv, 34). But Scripture usage does not warrant this supposition. There is, however, little reason to give κλῆσις other than its usual meaning. See under Gal. i, 6; v, 13; Philip. iii, 14. Compare Rom. viii, 30; ix, 11, 24; xi, 29; 1 Cor. i, 9, 24; 1 Tim. vi, 12. The call was divine—it had summoned them from death unto life; and the apostle's prayer is, that God in that day would deem them worthy of it—would judge that their entire life had been in harmony with it (1 Thess. v, 24). Compare the use of the adjective (Matt. iii, 8; Luke iii, 8; Acts xxvi, 20) and of the adverb (1 Thess. ii, 12). To secure such a result, or that this ἀξιοῦν may be realized, it is added—

καὶ πληρώσῃ πᾶσαν εὐδοκίαν ἀγαθωσύνης καὶ ἔργον πίστεως ἐν δυνάμει—" and may fulfil every good pleasure of goodness and the work of faith in power."

I. The Authorized Version renders "the good pleasure of His goodness," along with Œcumenius, Zuingli, Calvin, Estius, Justiniani, Beza, Bengel, Pelt, Bisping, &c. But to this exegesis —which by itself might be true, as the noun εὐδοκία is used in reference to God in Ephes. i, 5, 9; Philip. ii, 13—there are various objections in the verse itself. (1) Such a sense would necessitate πᾶσαν τὴν εὐδοκίαν. (2) The following phrase ἔργον πίστεως, also without any pronoun, must refer to those on whose behalf the prayer is offered, so that by parity of thought the first clause must have a similar reference, and εὐδοκίαν ἀγαθωσύνης belong to the Thessalonians also. (3) The noun ἀγαθωσύνη is never used of God by the apostle. It occurs in three other places—" ye also are full of goodness" (Rom. xv, 14); in the catalogue of the fruits of the Spirit (Gal. v, 22); and similarly in Ephes. v, 9—" the fruit of the Spirit is in all goodness." See 2 Chron. xxiv, 16.

II. Some are disposed to combine a divine and human reference. Grotius has, *omnem bonitatem sibi gratam;* Olshausen, "God fills you with all the goodness which is well pleasing to Him"; Theophylact, καὶ οὕτως ἦτε ὡς βούλεται ὁ Θεὸς μηδενὸς ὑμῖν λείποντος. But εὐδοκία is closely connected in relation with ἀγαθωσύνης, and cannot have that Godward signification. Jowett says, without any good foundation, that the apostle uses mixed modes of thought, and has not distinguished between the Word of God as the cause, and as the effect. Strangely does Thomas Aquinas understand it, *de sola humanæ voluntatis mutatione,* the decree of God, on the other hand, being immutable. The clause is rendered by Fritzsche, *ut expleat omnem dulcedinem honestatis (Ad. Rom., x, 1).* Tyndale translates, "every delectation of goodness." The meaning may be, all or every delight in goodness—comprising every purpose or impulse toward it, and complacency in it (Rom. x, 1; Philip. i, 15). For the spelling of ἀγαθωσύνη with o instead of ω, see Buttmann, § 119, 10 c, and Thomas Magister,

p. 391, ed. Ritschl). Ἀγαθωσύνη is not, well-doing or beneficence (Schott, Chandler), but moral goodness. See under Gal. v, 22. Ἀγαθωσύνης does not seem to be in apposition—a good pleasure consisting in goodness—but is rather the genitive of object, that on which their good pleasure specially turned, so that it delighted to expend itself on it. And not this or that, but "every" (πᾶσαν) good pleasure having this earnest propension and aim.

καὶ ἔργον πίστεως ἐν δυνάμει—" and the work of faith with power." The words ἔργον πίστεως are not in apposition. See 1 Thess. i, 3. The concluding phrase ἐν δυνάμει belongs to πληρώσῃ, indicating the element in which it shall realize itself, or the manner in which it is prayed that it may be brought about. The clause has thus really an adverbial force (Col. i, 29).

(Ver. 12.) ὅπως ἐνδοξασθῇ τὸ ὄνομα τοῦ Κυρίου ἡμῶν Ἰησοῦ ἐν ὑμῖν καὶ ὑμεῖς ἐν αὐτῷ—" in order that the name of our Lord Jesus may be glorified in you, and ye in Him" or "it." The Χριστοῦ of the Received Text rests on the rather slender authority of A F, the Vulgate, both Syriac versions, and Chrysostom, but it is wanting in B D K L ℵ, the Claromontane Latin, the majority of mss., Œcumenius, and Damascenus. Ὅπως indicates the final purpose, and does not differ materially from ἵνα in meaning, though it does in construction (Klotz, *Devarius*, II, p. 629). Ὄνομα is certainly not a periphrasis for Κύριος (Turretin, Koppe). The "name" is not Himself, but Himself as made known to men in those elements of character, relation, and glory which ὄνομα contains and implies—the name which he has made for Himself. See under Phil. ii, 10. That name wins for itself a new lustre in the salvation of the Thessalonian believers, ἐν ὑμῖν—as He is glorified in all His saints in that day (verse 10). And the glorification is reciprocal—καὶ ὑμεῖς ἐν αὐτῷ. The pronoun may refer to ὄνομα (Lünemann and Hofmann), but though in that case the reciprocity would be more formally balanced, the meaning is not so expressive, as our glorification in His name is not so significant as glorification in His person. The familiar but expressive phrase ἐν αὐτῷ is that union with Him, which so identifies His people with Himself that they are glorified in Him, are "partakers of His glory." His, the glory of Saviour; theirs, the glory of being saved in Him, and of being with Him for ever (1 Thess. iv, 17).

κατὰ τὴν χάριν τοῦ Θεοῦ ἡμῶν καὶ Κυρίου Ἰησοῦ Χριστοῦ—" according to the grace of our God and the Lord Jesus Christ." Κατὰ passes, as Winer remarks, § 49, "from the idea of norm into that of result," or the signification "in consequence of" naturally springs out of "according to," or is blended with it. For χάρις, see under Ephes. ii, 8. Though there is no τοῦ before Κυρίου, it would be wrong to identify it immediately with Θεοῦ, as is done by Hofmann, Riggenbach, and others, for Κύριος had become as a proper name, and therefore may want the article when it is joined to a preposition, or is used in the genitive, or precedes Ἰησοῦς Χριστός (Winer, § 19, 1). See especially Middleton's remarks on the non-applicability of Granville Sharpe's rule to this clause, p. 379, &c. See also under Ephes. v, 5. But it is plainly implied that this grace has a unity of origin, both in God and Christ; it is a possession common to both, and equally characterizing both. The final aim indicated by ὅπως recognizes both equally as answering the prayer which includes such a purpose κατὰ τὴν χάριν. Such oneness of attribute and gift implies the divinity of the Saviour, and His oneness of essence with the Father. Nor is such theology at all un-Pauline, though Hilgenfeld adduces it as a proof of the spuriousness of the epistle. It is found in the common benedictions at the beginning of many of the epistles. See under Gal. i, 1, 3.

CHAPTER II

THE apostle now passes to one special purpose of the epistle—to check and correct those erroneous and premature anticipations of the Second Coming which had become prevalent in Thessalonica, and were doing damage, and producing an unsettledness of mind which led to various irregularities. The apostle therefore tenders to them reassuring prophetic instruction—

(Ver. 1.) Ἐρωτῶμεν δὲ ὑμᾶς, ἀδελφοὶ, ὑπὲρ τῆς παρουσίας τοῦ Κυρίου ἡμῶν Ἰησοῦ Χριστοῦ καὶ ἡμῶν ἐπισυναγωγῆς ἐπ' αὐτόν—" Now we beseech you, brethren, in regard to the coming of our Lord Jesus Christ, and our gathering together unto Him." By δέ the apostle passes to his main point—the slight contrast being a transition from his request for them to his request of them. For the verb see under 1 Thess. iv, 1. The epithet ἀδελφοί—the expression of his attachment—is meant to gain their affectionate attention, while with the verb it implies the momentous nature of the following charge.

The Authorized Version takes ὑπέρ as a formula of adjuration, "We beseech you by the coming of our Lord Jesus," and so the Vulgate (*per adventum*), Pelagius, Erasmus, Calvin, Beza, Fromond; by the solemnity or certainty of it, by the interest you have in it, or the fervent expectation which you cherish about it. The preposition, like πρός, may be so used, as in Homer—

λίσσεθ' ὑπὲρ τοκέων γουνούμενος ἄνδρα ἕκαστον.
(*Il.*, xv, 660, 665; xxii, 338.)

καί μιν ὑπὲρ πατρὸς καὶ μητέρος ἠϋκόμοιο,
λίσσεο καὶ τέκεος (*Il.*, xxiv, 466).

λίσσομ' ὑπὲρ θυέων καὶ δαίμονος (*Odyss.*, xv, 261).

But this construction never occurs in the New Testament, and it would be strange, as Lünemann remarks, that the apostle should adjure them by the very thing which he was about to open up to them. The preposition ὑπέρ is to be taken as not very different from περί. Lünemann gives it the sense of " in behalf of," " in the interest of"—so virtually Wordsworth, Ellicott, and Jowett—the Second Coming being misunderstood, he was about to do it justice. But this is regarded by some as rather a refinement, though ὑπέρ does imply interest in the person or thing referred to (Acts v, 41; Rom. ix, 27; 2 Cor. viii, 23; xii, 5, 8; Philip. i, 7; iv, 10). Chrysostom explains it by περί—in reference to that event in which we have so profound an interest, and which on account of this very interest you so sadly misunderstood, we entreat you. For παρουσία see under 1 Thess. iii, 13. It is the second personal and glorious Coming of our Lord at the end of the present dispensation, and for its double purpose, see under 6—10 of previous chapter. The apostle during his visit had told them of the Advent, and the twin features of their converted state were, turning from idols and waiting for His Son from heaven. The double compound ἐπισυναγωγή occurs only here, and in Heb. x, 25, with a very different reference. Lünemann suggests that ἐπί must mean "up to," but though that is really the case (1 Thess. iv, 17), the preposition does not express it, ἐπί merely "marking the point to be reached "—εἰς ἀπάντησιν τοῦ Κυρίου. See Mark v, 21. The ἡμῶν is objective, the gathering together of us—us at present in life—not us, the living and the dead raised up as contemporaries, but us spoken of in the previous epistle as living and surviving till the Second Coming. The living are at that epoch to be caught up, and the result is, their "gathering together unto Him." The τῆς is not repeated before ἐπισυναγωγῆς; the two events are joined in unity, the one bringing with it the other as a synchronous result. No notice is taken here of the resurrection—though when Christ comes down, the dead in Him rise—for the appeal is to the present generation of believers who regarded the Advent as on them, and their gathering together without suffering death as about to take place. Their own death is not implied, and the death of friends, which had grieved them, precedes this wondrous assemblage. The aim or purpose of his request is next stated, and it contains also the theme.

(Ver. 2.) εἰς τὸ μὴ ταχέως σαλευθῆναι ὑμᾶς ἀπὸ τοῦ νοὸς μηδὲ θροεῖσθαι—"that ye be not quickly shaken from your mind, nor yet be troubled." For εἰς τό see 1 Thess. ii, 12; iii, 10. The verb σαλευθῆναι, from σάλος, agitation, tossing of the sea (Luke xxi, 25; Sept., Jonah i, 15), and of an earthquake (Is. xxiv, 20), denotes besides its physical sense (Matt. xi, 7; Acts iv, 31), to be mentally agitated or disturbed (Acts ii, 25; xvii, 13; Heb. xii, 26, 27, &c). The adverb ταχέως has been variously taken—so soon after my exhortations to you either orally or in the First Epistle (Piscator and Olshausen), or so soon after my departure, or even perhaps so soon after they heard any doctrine of the kind (De Wette, Lünemann). But the adverb may refer to manner rather than time, " soon and with small reason " (Alford). It implies certainly a mental disturbance, quickly, easily, and unthinkingly brought about, and, on this solemn subject, they are specially warned against it. The phrase ἀπὸ τοῦ νοὸς is rendered adverbially by the Authorized Version, " in mind," and as the Syriac ܡܶܢ ܪܶܥܝܳܢܟܽܘܢ ; better in Wycliffe, " from your witte," and in Tyndale, " from your mind," the Rhemish version having " from your sense," " *a vestro sensu*" (Vulgate): But νοῦς is not *sensus verborum Pauli* (Wolf), nor your earlier and more correct view, *sententia* (a-Lapide, Grotius), *deserentes id quod tenetis* (Fromond). Rom. vii, 23, 25; xiv, 5. Νοῦς is to be taken in its general sense, as mind or reason, your sober or right mind —" from your common sense " (1 Cor. xiv, 14; Philip. iv, 7). The construction is pregnant, shaken so as to be driven out of your mind, *ita concuti animo, ut dimovearis seu abducaris ἀπὸ* (Schott). Rom. vi, 7; vii, 2; ix, 3; 2 Tim. ii, 26. Winer, § 66, 2. The language implies that something like a panic had taken place, or that they were in imminent danger of falling into one. In the clause, μηδὲ θροεῖσθαι is climactic, " nor yet be troubled or terrified "; the verb is more significant than that of the previous clause, as terror rises above disturbance, and is occasioned by it. The disjunctive μηδέ has high authority over μήτε, a reading suggested by its triple occurrence in the next clauses. It has a slight ascensive force. See under 1 Thess. ii, 3.

μήτε διὰ πνεύματος μήτε διὰ λόγου μήτε δι᾽ ἐπιστολῆς ὡς δι᾽ ἡμῶν—" neither by spirit, nor by word, nor by letter, as by us." The clause is divided into three co-ordinate and connected negations (Matt, v, 34, 35; Luke ix, 3; Acts xxiii, 8, 12, 21; 1 Tim. i, 7; James v, 12). Winer, § 55, 6; Wex, *Antig.*, ii, 156, &c.; Klotz, *Devarius*, II, p. 715; Hermann, *Opuscula.*, vol. III, p. 151, &c. Μήτε διὰ πνεύματος, " neither by spirit," some oracle or saying embodying or professing, but falsely, to embody spiritual wisdom and foresight on the doctrine, or rather the period of the Second Advent. Theophylact explains it by διὰ προφητείας. The phrase cannot mean *signa quasi per Spiritum facta*, nor the prophecies of the Old Testament falsely understood (Krause), " nor delusive spiritual apparitions " (Schrader). Some take πνεῦμα as the abstract for the concrete πνευματικός (Chrysostom, Koppe, Storr). Compare 1 John iv, 1. This meaning would yield quite a good sense—the man who framed the false oracle under assumed spiritual influence, for some human agency is implied; but it is out of harmony with the words that follow, λόγου and ἐπιστολῆς, which cannot be taken as abstract, but are definite terms. There had been some one in the Church at Thessalonica that, under assumed spiritual influence, uttered the false and alarming doctrine.

μήτε διὰ λόγου, "nor by word." Λόγος has been understood in different ways. (1) Some take it in the sense of calculation, as if the reference were to some wrong computation based on the prophecies and "times" of Daniel, and bringing out the result that the day of the Lord was immediately imminent (Michaelis, Tychsen). Such a meaning is groundless and artificial to the last degree, and λόγος by itself could not convey such a sense. (2) Some regard it as a word of Christ, some falsified saying of His on the last day, resting on the prophecies of Matt. xxiv, Mark xiii, and Luke xxi (Baumgarten-Crusius, Noesselt). But such a reference would have required from the apostle some more definite expression. (3) Macknight would give it the sense of verbal message, as if sent from the apostle to the Thessalonians; and Grotius similarly renders it *rumores de nobis*, to this effect, that we are now speaking otherwise than we had done formerly. Both conjectures need no refutation. (4) Others put λόγου in contrast with πνεύματος, and regard it as a teaching (διδαχή), which did not deliver itself in prophetic rapture, but perhaps rather took its proofs from Scripture. Chrysostom explains by πιθανολογία, Theophylact by διδασκαλίας ζώσῃ φωνῇ γινομένης, and the view generally is held by Zuingli, Calvin, Ewald, Hofmann, and Riggenbach. But the natural contrast is not between λόγος and πνεῦμα, but between λόγος and the following ἐπιστολή, what is spoken being contrasted with what is written. The same contrast is repeated in verse 15. Λόγος is therefore an oral utterance ascribed to the apostle, and here falsely ascribed to him, as ὡς δι' ἡμῶν implies. For διὰ λόγου is not to be taken as an independent statement, or as connected simply with δι' ἐπιστολῆς, but the meaning is that both utterances and letters of a fictitious character were ascribed to the apostle.

The last phrase, μήτε δι' ἐπιστολῆς, has been strangely supposed by not a few to refer to the first epistle and to some misinterpretation of it—so Jerome, Kern, Hilgenfeld, Hammond, Krause, Paley, Reuss, Bleek, and Webster and Wilkinson —his former letter, but comprehended under the general signification "any communication by letter"; hence the omission of the article. But a reference to his former epistle would have necessitated the article or some phrase equally definite, and the epistle would not as here have been disowned. Compare 1 Cor. v, 9-11; 2 Cor. vii, 8. The last words, ὡς δι' ἡμῶν, have been connected in various ways. Some join them to all the preceding words, as Erasmus, Reiche, Noesselt, Jowett, Webster and Wilkinson. Not to repeat that λόγος and ἐπιστολή are connected closely in verse 15, and are taken so here, it may be replied that ὡς δι' ἡμῶν cannot apply to πνεῦμα, as it could not be feigned for him in his absence; the πνεῦμα must have been in the midst of themselves—the immediate witnesses of its manifestations. It could in no way be said to be by our agency, δι' ἡμῶν, as are the "word" and "letter" supposed to have the apostle for their medium. The particle ὡς, *as* = as so represented—implies the fictitious nature of the assumption. Ellicott, Fritzsche, Winer, Vulgate (*tamquam per nos*); Syriac, ܐܝܟ ܕܡܢ ܠܘܬܢ.

This warning apparently implies that forgery was early at work, and that during the few months elapsing from the date of the first epistle a fictitious utterance and a letter had been circulated in the apostle's name, teaching what the apostle intimates in the last clause of the verse. Nothing farther do we know of them. Jowett says that the apostle refers only to the possibility of such a speech or epistle being used against him, but the language describes an actual occurrence. The 15th verse of this chapter places the genuine word and letter in contrast with the spurious, and the 17th verse of the third chapter describes a guard against a forged epistle, by showing the token of a true one—" the salutation of me, Paul, with mine own hand, which is the token in every epistle. So I write." It is needless to wonder why any men at that early time could be so audacious as to attach to any forgery, written or oral, the apostle's name and authority, for we know nothing of the motive and almost nothing of the contents save in the one point. Nor can we now say why the apostle treated the matter so leniently, by averring that the deception was innocent in motive, or that the letter was anonymous. The apostle could not prevent sayings being put in his name—he could only deny or disclaim them; but he took precautions against the repetition of such literary forgery.

ὡς ὅτι ἐνέστηκεν ἡ ἡμέρα τοῦ Κυρίου—"as that the day of the Lord is come." For Κυρίου the Received Text has Χριστοῦ, with D³ K, most mss., and the Gothic; but Κυρίου is read in A B D¹ F L ℵ, both Latin and both Syriac versions, with the Greek and Latin fathers. The ὡς introduces the statement not as actual, but as so represented, its falsehood being implied. The "day of the Lord" is the day of the Second Advent—His, as He appears as Judge, His last and loftiest function—His, as on it He crowns His work, and His church becomes complete in happiness and in numbers—His, as then He is glorified in His saints and wondered at in all them who believe. On that day He rises into a pre-eminence hitherto unwitnessed.

The true meaning of the verb ἐνέστηκεν is not "is at hand," but "is come," or "is present." The rendering of the English version, "at hand," has been adopted by many—Calvin, Jowett, &c. Thus Hammond, "were instantly a-coming;" Benson, "just at hand, and will happen shortly;" Bloomfield, Conybeare, Webster, and Wilkinson, "near or close at hand;" Wordsworth, "instantaneously imminent." (1) Now the verb is used in six other places of the New Testament, and in all of them it bears the sense of "present." Rom. viii, 38, οὔτε ἐνεστῶτα οὔτε μέλλοντα, "neither things present nor things to come;" 1 Cor. iii, 22, εἴτε ἐνεστῶτα εἴτε μέλλοντα, "whether things present or things to come;" 1 Cor. vii, 26, διὰ τὴν ἐνεστῶσαν ἀνάγκην, "on account of the present distress;" Gal. i, 4, ἐκ τοῦ αἰῶνος τοῦ ἐνεστῶτος πονηροῦ, "out of this present world, an evil one;" 2 Tim. iii, 1, ἐνστήσονται καιροὶ χαλεποί, "grievous times shall be present," i.e., the grievous times are not to follow the last days, but to be included in them; Heb. ix, 9, παραβολὴ εἰς τὸν καιρὸν τὸν ἐνεστηκότα, "a figure for the time now present," spoken of the Jewish economy. In all these cases, except 2 Tim. iii, 1, for which there is some apology, the Authorized Version renders by "present"; and there was no reason, therefore, to deviate from the true sense in the verse before us. The translation "is come," "has arrived," is fully justified by the uniform meaning of the verb in the New Testament, and is the rendering also, save in two cases, in the Authorized Version. (2) To show that our translators were swayed by other than philological reasons, it may be remarked that the rendering "is at hand" occurs in twenty other places in the New Testament, and in none of these, of course, does that rendering represent the Greek verb before us. It rightly stands for ἤγγισε nine times, ten times for ἐγγύς, and once for ἐφέστηκεν (2 Tim. iv, 6), where Luther renders *ist vorhanden*. (3) The Septuagint usage is similar to that of the New Testament. In Dan. vii, 5, εἰς μέρος ἓν ἐστάθη, the simple verb has a different meaning, where it represents the הקמת, *stare facta, constituta est*. But we have in the Apocrypha, 1 Esdras v, 46, ἐνστάντος δὲ τοῦ ἑβδόμου μηνός, "the seventh month being come," not "being at hand," as in the Authorized Version; ix, 6, τρέμοντες διὰ τὸν ἐνεστῶτα χειμῶνα, "trembling on account of the present foul weather;" 1 Macc. xii, 44, πολέμου μὴ ἐνεστηκότος ἡμῖν, "there being at present no war between us;" 2 Macc. iii, 17, τὸ κατὰ καρδίαν ἐνεστὸς ἄλγος, "the sorrow at present in his heart," or, as in the Authorized Version, "what sorrow he had now in his heart; vi, 9, τὴν ἐνεστῶσαν ταλαιπωρίαν, "the present misery;" xii, 3, ὡς μηδεμιᾶς ἐνεστώσης πρὸς αὐτοὺς δυσμενείας, "as if there had been no ill-will at present between them;" 3 Macc. i, 16, τῇ ἐνεστώσῃ ἀνάγκῃ. The same meaning is found in the Hellenistic writers. Joseph., *Antiq.*, xvi, 6, 2, οὐ μόνον ἐν τῷ ἐνεστῶτι καιρῷ, "not only in the present time," but also in the past time; Philo, *De Plantat. Noe*, ὅς εἰς τὸν παρεληλυθότα καὶ ἐνεστῶτα καὶ μέλλοντα, "it is of the nature of time to be divided into the past and the present and the future" (*Opera*, vol. III, p. 136, ed. Pfeiffer). (4) Nor does the classical usage differ. Xenoph., *Hellen.*, ii, 1, 6, περὶ τῶν ἐνεστηκότων πραγμάτων, "concerning the present state of affairs;" Polybius, i, 60, τὸν ἐνεστῶτα καιρόν; do., 75, εἰς τὸν ἐνεστῶτα πόλεμον; xviii, 38, κατὰ τὸν ἐνεστῶτα βασιλέα, "against the present king." Examples from Æschines and Demosthenes, as applied to καιρός, πόλεμος, are given by Rost and Palm. There may be some cases where it may bear the sense of, impending, as good as come, ideally present; but the prevailing temporal meaning is what we have given. Nay, Hesychius defines ἐνεστῶτα by πάροντα. Χρόνος ἐνεστηκώς is the grammatical name of the present tense, and μετοχὴ ἐνεστῶσα is the present participle. Sextus Empiricus divides time into τὸν παρῳχημένον καὶ τὸν ἐνεστῶτα καὶ τὸν μέλλοντα. Theodore defines the term by παρών. Not simply "at hand," but "is present" or "has begun," is the correct translation, even taking the classical usage which Webster and Wilkinson assume, though they wrongly render it "imminent." (5) How could the doctrine that the day of the Lord is at hand be treated by the apostle as an error? That the day of the Lord is at hand is the uniform teaching of the New Testament (Matt. xxiv; Rom. xiii, 12; Philip. iv, 5; Heb. x, 25, 37; James v, 8; 1 Peter iv, 7; 1 John ii, 18; Rev. xxii, 20). Could the apostle disclaim the teaching of such a doctrine as that "the day of the Lord is at hand," or warn the Church against it as an error and a species of deception? The rendering "at hand" cannot therefore here be the correct translation of ἐνέστηκεν. (6) Were the doctrine against which the apostle warns, and which he so solemnly disowns, only that the day of the Lord was at hand, how could such a doctrine throw the Church into panic and confusion—how could they be driven from their sense and alarmed, as he calls it? For they were familiar with it; they were waiting for His Son from heaven, and His Coming is again and again referred to in the first epistle. The imminence of the Advent was no new theme to them, and they could not be so startled by it. Nay, such was their spiritual condition and temperament, that such a doctrine, if disclosed for the first time to them, would have filled their spirits with unutterable gladness. They were waiting for His Son from heaven; they were meanwhile characterized by works of faith, labours of love, and patience of hope; the word had wrought effectually in them; their faith had grown exceedingly, and their mutual love abounded; they were children of the light; they were the apostle's joy, hope, and crown of rejoicing in the presence of our Lord Jesus Christ at His coming. His prayer for them was, that "God would establish their hearts unblameable before Him at the coming of our Lord Jesus Christ with all His saints," and that "their whole spirit, soul, and body might be preserved blameless unto the coming of our Lord Jesus Christ." He "comes to be glorified in His saints," and He comes suddenly, "as a thief in the night;" and how, in such a spiritual state, could they be filled with consternation at the thought that the period was near when all their own anticipations and all these prayers for them should be fully realized. As the nearness of the Advent was no new doctrine, it could not have so alarmed them; and as their character was such as to lead them to love His appearance and to lift up their heads as their redemption drew nigh, it could not have so excited and confounded them, nor could the apostle have branded such a doctrine as false, or have ascribed it to some spurious spiritual manifestation or to some utterance or some letter forged and circulated in his name. Thus, both philologically and doctrinally, the rendering "is at hand" cannot be sustained.

Lastly, the translation we give seems to be the oldest one. The Syriac has ܕܡܪܢ ܐܬܐ ܠܗ ܝܘܡܐ ܕܗܐ "Lo the day of our Lord is come." At all events the same Syriac term, which is but the Syriac form of the Chaldee אתא, stands for ἦλθον in Acts viii. 36; for ἐπέστησαν, Acts x. 17, "were arrived and standing at the gate;" for κατήντησεν, Acts xviii. 19, "he came to Ephesus, &c." The meaning in these places is "is come" or "arrived." Compare Daniel vii. 13, 22. Chrysostom identifies the error here condemned with that of those who said that the resurrection is already past, adding that believers, henceforth hoping for nothing great and splendid, might faint under their sufferings. Theodore of Mopsuestia understands this to be the error condemned ὡς ἂν ἐγγύθεν παρόντος ἐκείνου τοῦ καιροῦ (*Catena in Thessal.*, p. 386, ed. Cramer). Œcumenius puts it thus—"the apostle does not say when the resurrection shall be, ὅτι δὲ οὐ νῦν ἐφέστηκεν ἀποδείκνυσι"; and more distinctly in his preface, ὡς ἤδη τῆς παρουσίας ἐνστάσης—ἤδη παρεῖναι αὐτήν; and in the same preface, Theodoret is quoted as asserting that some seducers ἔλεγον παρεῖναι λοιπὸν τὴν παρουσίαν τοῦ Κυρίου;

Pelagius, *ne quis vos seducat ullo modo, dicentes: hic Christus, ecce illic;* and Ambrosiaster has *de adventu quasi imminentis Domini.* But it may be asked—how could these early believers persuade themselves that the day of the Lord was come—how could they hold that the Lord had descended—that the trumpet had been heard—that the dead had been raised and the living caught up? It will scarcely do to conjecture, with Lillie, that they might imagine that "the day had come in some different way from that in which they had been taught to look for it, or else, that this great crisis had actually transpired, and in that precise shape, while they were not aware of it." They must in such a case have thought that they had forfeited their share in the glory of the kingdom. We cannot imagine the possibility of such delusion, and the hallucinations which Lillie brings in proof are not at all to the point. The first instance adduced by him is that of a party in the church of Corinth who said that "there is no resurrection." But this denial is a very different error from saying that it had already taken place without their participation in the result, or their witnessing its glories and mysteries. The other instance, that of those who said that the resurrection is past, was based on a false spiritualistic philosophy, which identified resurrection with the revivification of the soul; surely a very different error from the imagination that the resurrection of the dead in the physical sense had already taken place. It was scarcely possible that the error had proceeded so far as to impugn the reality and universality of the resurrection. The apostle had said that "the day of the Lord cometh as a thief in the night," suddenly and without warning, but could they persuade themselves that the sudden destruction then threatened had fallen on their enemies, and that none of them had escaped? The phrase employed, $\dot{\eta}\mu\epsilon\rho a \ \tau o\hat{v} \ \mathrm{K}\nu\rho\iota o\nu$ may not be identical with the actual $\pi a \rho o \nu \sigma \iota a \ \tau o\hat{v} \ \mathrm{K}\nu\rho\iota o\nu$, but may denote its period and comprehend the events which are its antecedents and concomitants. Not the $\pi a \rho o \nu \sigma \iota a$ itself, but its period had come. The day of the Lord, the epoch of the Second Advent had now dawned upon them, and the persecutions now falling on them were tokens of its presence. They regarded the day of grace as apparently at an end, so that in fancy they were in the period of judgment, which was to witness the dissolution of society and the introduction of a new state of things. This error was taught as if on the apostle's authority—his teaching or letter—and it may have been the more readily adopted from his own words, which seemed to imply that he himself was to be alive at the Advent; or the error may have been given out not as a retractation, but as a farther expansion of his oral teaching and his doctrine as given in the first epistle.

(Ver. 3.) Μή τις ὑμᾶς ἐξαπατήσῃ κατὰ μηδένα τρόπον—"Let no one deceive you in any way." The anxiety of the apostle on the point leads him to a virtual repetition of the warning. The doctrine that the day of the Lord had set in was a deception; whatever might be the motives of those who taught it, it was a perilous error and they were to guard against being its dupes. The ἐκ in the compound verb has an intensive force, the verb meaning "to deceive out and out." The phrase κατὰ μηδένα τρόπον does not allude merely to the three ways specified in the preceding verse, as if it meant by any of these means (Œcumenius, Theophylact, Bengel, Baumgarten-Crusius), but is absolute and inclusive, "in no way," by no method of deception whatever its form or character.

ὅτι ἐὰν μὴ ἔλθῃ ἡ ἀποστασία πρῶτον—"because the day will not set in unless there come the apostacy first." The ellipse is easily supplied—ὅτι οὐκ ἐνέστηκεν ἡ ἡμέρα τοῦ Κυρίου (Lünemann), or, as Ellicott, ἡ ἡμέρα οὐκ ἐνστήσεται, or, as Theophylact, οὐ γενήσεται ἡ παρουσία τοῦ Κυρίου. The clause involving the use of a finite verb is omitted; the mind of the writer is fixed specially on the event which must intervene, the mental negation implied in the two previous verses, namely, "the day of the Lord has not taken place," involving the consequent unexpressed negation, "nor will it take place unless." Winer, § 64, 7; Hermann, *Vigerus*, II. p. 694. On ἀν with the subjunctive, see Donaldson, § 583 β. There are two proposed constructions which are hard and unnatural. Storr and Flatt propose to get rid of the ellipse by giving ἐὰν μή a sense analogous to the Hebrew אִם לֹא, *ganz gewiss, certissime* (Numbers xiv, 28; Ezek. xvii, 19; Heb. iv. 3, 5); but in those places the phrase has the form of an oath. Knatchbull's connection is as unsatisfactory, for he places a comma after ὅτι, joins it to ἐξαπατήσῃ, and supplies ἐνέστηκεν, "let no man deceive you that the day of the Lord is come, if it shall not come before the apostacy, *ne quis seducat vos ullo modo quod instet dies Domini si non venerit prius apostasia.*

Ἀποστασία is a more recent form for the older ἀπόστασις. Lobeck, *Phrynichus*, p. 528. The word is found in Acts xxi, 21—a charge against Paul that he taught defection from Moses; in Sept., 2 Chron. xxix, 19—the idolatrous defection of Ahaz; in Jer. ii, 19, with a similar sense—παιδεύσει σε ἡ ἀποστασία σου; and in 1 Macc. ii, 15, in reference to enforced idolatry—οἱ καταναγκάζοντες τὴν ἀποστασίαν. The verb is used in 1 Tim. iv, 1, followed by τῆς πίστεως, and in Heb. iii, 12, with ἀπὸ Θεοῦ. This usage shows that by the term spiritual defection is meant, and such a meaning is in harmony with the context, for its connection is with the Man of Sin and the Mystery of Iniquity. It is therefore wrong for this double reason—

I. To refer it to any political dissatisfaction or revolt either (1) to that of the Jews from the Romans—*singularis et notabilis illa rebellio* (Schöttgen, vol. I, p. 840; and so Clericus, Noesselt, Rosenmüller, and partly Usteri, *Paulin. Lehrbegr.*, p. 349); or (2) to the mutiny against, and the assassination of Galba, Otho, and Vitellius, prior to the consolidation of the empire by the gens Flavia (Wetstein), or (3) to any mingled religious and political defection (Aretius, Vorstius, Kern); or (4) to the breaking up of the Roman Empire, as a-Lapide. "*Quis, nisi Romanus status, cujus abscessio in decem reges dispersa Antichristum superducet?*" (Tertullian *De Resurr. Carnis*, vi, p. 499, vol. II, *Opera*, ed. Oehler); *discessio . . . ut omnes gentes quae Romano imperio subjacent, recedant* (Jerome, *ad Algasiam*, p. 887, vol. I, *Opera*, ed. Vallarsi).

II. Equally wrong is the notion of Hammond that the word describes "a notable discernible apostatizing of Christians to that abominable impiety of the Gnostics," quoting 1 Tim. iv, 1. But no Gnostic aberration expresses the full meaning of the term, nor does it harmonize with the contents of the prophecy. Hammond, however, understands by the Advent, the infliction of divine judgment on the Jews.

III. Nor can ἀποστασία be taken as the abstract for the concrete, meaning Antichrist himself, as Chrysostom, and the Greek fathers, with Augustine. Thus Theophylact, ἀποστασία τουτέστι ὁ Ἀντίχριστος; Augustine, *diemque judicii non esse venturum, nisi ille prior venerit, quem refugam vocat* (*De Civitate Dei*, lib. vol. VII, p. 958, *Opera*, Gaume, Paris). But such a personification confuses the order of the prophecy; the apostacy precedes, and prepares for the revelation of the Man of Sin. "The falling away," therefore, is not the result of the appearance of the Man of Sin, but the antecedent; not as Pelt, *secessionem cujus ille erit auctor et signifer*. Thus ἀποστασία, so signalized by the article ἡ, is something distinct, something so far familiar to them, and on which they had enjoyed previous instruction. See verse 5. It is a spiritual falling away, the opposite of that growth in Christian excellence which the apostle commends in them—faith fled, love dead, hope collapsed, and the truth forsaken; all spiritual graces and energies fallen out of recognition and existence; God ignored, Christ forgotten, and the Spirit grieved and gone. Such a defection is so sad and fatal that it opens the way for the daring and defiant revelation of the Man of Sin. He seizes the opportunity when all is asleep and fearless because faithless, to found his kingdom, diffuse his falsehood, and fortify his impious pretensions. This man would not be suffered to show himself, would not be permitted to gather strength and hardihood in a healthful and vigilant condition of the church (Luke xxi, 8). The elements of that apostacy seem to be gathered up at length, and to culminate in a single personality, as its last appalling embodiment. The καὶ of the following clause has something of a consecutive force—marking its clause as the result of the previous one.

καὶ ἀποκαλυφθῇ ὁ ἄνθρωπος τῆς ἁμαρτίας, ὁ υἱὸς τῆς ἀπωλείας—"and there be revealed the Man of Sin, the Son of Perdition." For ἁμαρτίας, ἀνομίας is read in B ℵ and several of the fathers, but the text has good authority. The phrase has resemblance to איש און (Isaiah lv, 7). The genitive τῆς ἁμαρτίας is that of predominating quality, *die dominirenden Eigenschaften* (Scheuerlein, § 16, 3). He is the Man of Sin, whose inner element and outer characteristic is sin and nothing but sin; who has his being, plans, and activity in sin and in nothing else; who, as the living embodiment of it, is known and recognized as the man of sin. The following verse shows that he fully verifies his awful and significant name—a name in terrific antagonism to the Holy and Loving One, and His holy and benignant government, the purpose of which is to put down sin and deliver sinners. The ἀποκαλυφθῇ suggests a contrast with the same word in i, 7, "the Lord Jesus shall be revealed from heaven"—a sudden and distinct personal manifestation is implied (Turretin, Pelt). There are to be secret preparations, causes in hidden operation, prior to the final embodiment and outburst. The man of sin is also—

ὁ υἱὸς τῆς ἀπωλείας—"the Son of Perdition." A similar phrase τέκνα ἀπωλείας occurs in Isaiah lvii, 4. The man of sin stands to perdition as child to parent (John xvii, 12; Ephes. ii, 2). Sonship indicates in Hebrew idiom a variety of relations, even among inanimate things. The son of perdition is he on whom perdition falls as his due and his heritage, who is so indissolubly related to it, and so bound up with it, that he cannot escape it. Being the Man of Sin, he must be in God's righteous government the Son of Perdition. Such sin entails and measures out its own retribution.

Ἀπώλεια is the perdition which he himself is to suffer, not that which he brings on others (Pelt), nor are the two ideas in combination, as Theodoret, Œcumenius, Bengel, Heydenreich, and Schott suppose. Thus Œcumenius, διὰ τὸ ἀπολλύειν πολλοὺς καὶ αὐτὸν ἀπόλλυεσθαι. The one intransitive meaning is most in harmony with the idiom. The person so described is a man —ἄνθρωπος—a single man, and not a series or succession of men, not the personification of evil influences, or the head of any human organization. This man, made of sin, and the representative impersonation of it, is the counter-Christ, "he who opposes;" both are individual men, both come to view, or are "revealed" in immediate personal manifestation, both are signalized in character, the one by righteousness, the other by sin. The one has life and glory as his destiny, but the other ruin and perdition. At the same time the idea of a Satanic incarnation is not to be admitted, as Pelagius curtly puts it, *diabolus scilicet.* "Is it then Satan?" asks Chrysostom. "By no means, but some man that admits his full inworking in him, πᾶσαν δεχόμενος (τοῦ Σατανᾶ) τὴν ἐνέργειαν," and more fully in Theodoret. It is an inspiration, rather than an incarnation, as verse 9 also implies.

(Ver. 4.) ὁ ἀντικείμενος καὶ ὑπεραιρόμενος ἐπὶ πάντα λεγόμενον Θεὸν ἢ σέβασμα—" he who opposes and exalts himself above every one called God, or an object of worship." These participles, connected with ἀποκαλυφθῇ, carry forward the description begun by the nouns of the previous clauses and add several dark features to it. Ὁ ἀντικείμενος, the opposing one, or one who opposes = the opposer. His characterizing work or function, or that which gives him distinctive notoriety is, that he opposes; there is no object mentioned, and Christ is to be understood, as may be inferred from verse 8, for the Lord is at His coming to consume and destroy him. The opposing is not directed against mankind (Michaelis, Baumgarten), there being no idea of this kind in the context, nor generally against God and Christ (De Wette, Riggenbach), but specially and pointedly against Christ, *corde, lingua, stilo, factis, per se, per suos* (Bengel). This gives him a character not unlike that of ὁ ἀντίδικος, διάβολος, הַשָּׂטָן (1 Peter v, 8; Rev. xii, 10). Compare Job i, 6; Zech. iii, 1. Filled with the devil's spirit, he is noted as the devil's workman, withstanding, counteracting all that Christ is planning and doing—his heart so set upon it that his uniform attitude toward it is that of a daring and defiant antagonist. Satan entered into the heart of Judas, the son of perdition, and he takes possession of the Man of Sin, inspiring him with power, intensifying his malignity, feeding his pride and profanity till he is tempted to self-deification, which is now described. As the verb ἀντίκειμαι is always followed by a dative in the New Testament, and as no object is here expressed, the participle may be regarded as absolute, as being virtually a substantive, and there is no need therefore of a zeugmatic construction, as is supposed by Benson, Koppe, Flatt, Pelt, Hofmann, and Riggenbach—the clause beginning with ἐπὶ belonging only to ὑπεραιρόμενος. The omission of the article before the second participle does not unite both participles under one construction, but only shows that both refer to the same person. Winer, § 19, 4.

καὶ ὑπεραιρόμενος ἐπὶ πάντα λεγόμενον Θεὸν—" and exalting himself above every one called God. The compound verb occurs only in 2 Cor. xii, 7, ὑπέρ being a favourite preposition with the apostle. The modifying participle λεγόμενον does not mean every so-called God (Peile), as that would exclude the one true God, " nor every one that entitled himself a God" (Wakefield), but it is used to prevent the conclusion that the God and gods are placed in the same category; "every God" would be a profane and erroneous expression, impossible for a Christian believer, who acknowledges one God only. One is rightly called God, others are falsely so-called, λεγόμενοι Θεοί (1 Cor. viii, 5). Compare Ephes. ii, 11. The phrase then means the true God and every other one bearing the name—the false gods of heathenism. The preposition ἐπί, *supra* in the Vulgate, means "upon," "over," or "above" "motion with a view to superposition" (Donaldson, *Gr. Gr.*, § 483 c), motion followed by rest on or over. It is used sometimes with a hostile reference (Matt. x, 21 ; 2 Cor. x, 2); such a reference being here reflected from the previous participle (Winer, § 49 *l*). The clause bears a strong resemblance to Daniel xi, 36—" and the king shall do according to his will, and he shall exalt himself and magnify himself above every god, and shall speak marvellous things against the God of gods." This description portrays a heathen and polytheistic king, and the phrases ἐπὶ πάντα θεόν . . ἐπὶ πάντας θεούς in verse 37 are quite analogous. The Man of Sin exalts himself above and against every one called God. He puts himself into a position higher than that of any God, refuses to worship anything divine, as if he himself possessed a higher divinity.

ἢ σέβασμα—" or an object of adoration," *aut quod colitur,* Syriac " worshipful." Σέβασμα occurs in Acts xvii, 23, " objects of divine reverence," and with the same meaning in Wisdom xiv, 20 ; xv, 17; Bel and the Dragon, 27. Περὶ τὰ θεῖα σεβάσματα. Dionys. Halicar., *Antiq.*, I, 30, v, 1. It cannot here at all refer to the Roman Emperor called Σεβαστός, and denote the majesty and power of Cæsar which the Man of Sin subjects to himself and defames. Whatever bears a divine name or claims divine worship, he will put beneath himself in a spirit of overbearing and self-glorifying hostility, and of blasphemous insolence, as if to himself alone divine homage were due. He that lifts himself above everything divine in person or homage puts himself in its room as divine. The inference is that this 'Ἀντίθεος thrusts God out of His place, usurps it, and arrogantly and impiously claims the worship due to Him. The apostle adds in proof—

ὥστε αὐτὸν εἰς τὸν ναὸν τοῦ Θεοῦ καθίσαι, ἀποδεικνύντα ἑαυτὸν ὅτι ἔστιν Θεός—"so that he sitteth down in the temple of God, showing himself that he is God." The Received Text has ὡς Θεόν, with D³F K L, the Syriac, Chrysostom, and Theodoret; but the words are omitted in A B D¹ ℵ, both Latin versions and the Coptic, with very many of the Greek and Latin fathers. They are to be rejected therefore, and they are a species of gloss. The result is introduced by ὥστε. In this unparalleled and audacious wickedness, the antagonist and exalter of Himself above every one divine in title enters into the shrine of God and there sits down a self-made God. The connection has been taken by Conybeare thus, so as to seat himself in the temple, (αὐτόν for αὑτόν) and as if καθίσαι were transitive (Grotius, Koppe, Pelt); but καθίσαι is usually intransitive in the New Testament, so that αὐτόν is the subject, and has the stress upon it. Καθίσαι . . . εἰς is a pregnant construction—goes into and sits down (Matt. ii, 23; xiii, 2). Arrian, Ellendt, note, vol. I, p. 247; Schaefer, do.; Demosth., vol. I, p. 194; Winer, § 50, 4. The aorist describes the act—he sits down, and it is implied that the sitting lasts after the act. By ναός (ναίω) is meant the temple proper, as distinct from ἱερόν, the cluster of sacred buildings around it (Herodotus, i, 181-183); and the distinction is observed in Josephus, Philo, the Septuagint, and New Testament. Trench, *Synon.*, I, § 3. Into the temple proper does this proud opposer thrust himself—as if he were its divine inhabitant with his throne in the Holy of Holies. But what is this ναός? (1) The term may be used figuratively for the Church (1 Cor. iii, 17; 1 Cor. vi, 19; Ephes. ii, 21, 22). So the Greek fathers, Theodoret, Œcumenius, and Theophylact, after Chrysostom who says—" for he will not introduce idolatry, but will be a kind of opponent to God, and he will abolish all the gods and will order them to worship him instead of God, and he will be seated in the temple of God—οὐ τὸν ἐν Ἱεροσολύμοις μόνον ἀλλὰ καὶ εἰς τὰς πανταχοῦ ἐκκλησίας." Theodoret says that by the temple is to be understood the churches in which he will snatch the primacy—προεδρείαν. Similarly Theophylact— "not specially in the temple at Jerusalem, ἀλλὰ εἰς τὰς ἐκκλησίας ἁπλῶς, καὶ πάντα ναὸν θεῖον," and to the same effect Œcumenius. The same view is held by many commentators, among whom are Musculus, Hunnius, Estius, Aretius, Benson, Wolf, Heydenreich, Pelt, Olshausen, Bisping, Hilgenfeld. The opinion is so far sanctioned by the usage of Scripture. But the places quoted in support of it are not wholly analogous; the spiritual temple is in them said to be built up of individual believers as living stones; they are affirmed to be a temple, and the appeal is to them in this character. The phrase is an immediate and impressive symbol of their purity and consecration and of their being the dwelling-place of God, "an habitation of God through the Spirit." In those ethical passages, describing spiritual privilege, blessing, and destiny, the meaning lies on the surface, and is so clear that it cannot be for a moment mistaken, for the metaphor carries its own explanation, and believers are asserted to form the temple. See Howe's *Living Temple;* see also Essay on the Man of Sin.

But the case is somewhat different in a picture like this where, without any explanation, the profane and daring usurper, as the acme of his antagonism, is said to take his seat in the temple of God. (1) There is no allusion in the context to believers as being God's temple, but in the text quoted believers are directly asserted to constitute it. (2) The sitting in the temple does not harmonize so fully with the notion of an ideal or spiritual structure. The citations adduced by Alford are scarcely in point, as 1 Cor. vi, 4, where, ἐν τῇ ἐκκλησίᾳ occurring, the meaning is evident, and the clause signifies, set them as judges for a definite purpose; Matt. xxiii, 2, where sitting in Moses' chair is without ambiguity; and the image is as evident in Rev. xx, 4. The places where Jesus is said to sit on the right hand of God are not in analogy; his royal seat is the symbol of highest exaltation and of universal dominion. (3) If the temple of God be the church, what is meant by the Man of Sin entering and seating himself in it, what is the position which he thus occupies, what is his locality? for he is no ideal usurper, no personified evil influence, but a man with human conditions. (4) Could those for whom the epistle was written easily understand by the phrase the Church of Christ; or would not their first and most natural conclusion be that the Man of Sin was to intrude into some actual edifice, set apart to God as His shrine, like that at Jerusalem, and appropriate it. (5) The next clause, "Showing that He is God," leads to the same conclusion—he that sits in God's temple takes God's place and prerogative, for the temple is His dwelling—a conclusion which could not have the same force and evident connection with the premises, if the temple were the church so symbolized, for the usurpation would in that be more directed against Christ, the Head of the Church, or the Holy Spirit who fills it. (6) Were the Church to permit such intrusion, and such impious self-assumed exaltation on the part of the Man of Sin above all divine persons and worship, it would cease to merit the appellation of the temple of God, and also on account of the previous apostacy which made such self-deification possible. (7) The entire prophecy is distinct and personal, of prosaic and plain directness in its description of a man possessing a certain character, bringing on himself a certain destiny, and as he is at length to be consumed by the Lord at His Second Advent; may it not therefore be said that it would be out of harmony with this literal style of prediction, if in the midst of it should occur an unfamiliar image as the name of a place which is the scene of a usurpation without parallel? (8) This is also the earliest interpretation. Irenæus says expressly, "Besides he has also pointed out, which in many ways I have shown, that the temple in Jerusalem was made by the direction of the true God. For the apostle himself, speaking in his own person, distinctly calls it the temple of God . . . in which temple the adversary shall sit, trying to show himself off as Christ, "*tentans semetipsum Christum ostendere . . . transferet regnum in eam, et in templo Dei sedet, seducens eos qui adorant eum, quasi ipse sit Christus* (*Contra Haeres.*, v, 25, 2, 4, pp. 784, 786), *et sedebit in templo Hierosolymis* (do., v, p. 803, vol. I, *Opera*, ed. Stieren). Cyril of Jerusalem, who had a natural interest in the matter of prior possession, asks, ποῖον ἆρα ναόν the ruined temple of the

Jews? μὴ γένοιτο· γὰρ τοῦτον ἐν ᾧ ἐσμέν, adding that the temple is that built by Solomon, which Antichrist shall rebuild, ὁ τοῦ Σολομῶνος ναὸν κατασκευασθέντα μέλλων οἰκοδομεῖν (*Catech.*, xv, 7, p. 212, ed. Miller). Jerome refers to the same opinion, though he does not adopt it, *et in templo Dei, vel Hierosolymis, ut quidam putant* (*ad Algas.*, Lit. 121, p. 888, vol. I, *Opera*, ed. Vallarsi). Gregory of Nazianzus held a like opinion, φασὶν ὅτι ὁ ναὸς ὁ ἐν Ἱεροσολύμοις οἰκοδομηθήσεται ὕστερον, ὡς τοῦ Ἀντιχρίστου πιστευθησομένου ὑπὸ Ἰουδαίων Χριστοῦ (vol. I, *Orat.*, 47, p. 724 D, *Opera*, ed. Paris, 1630). All these arguments are not very strong, but may somewhat incline the balance in favour of this opinion, though certainly the difficulty of interpretation is increased, if the old temple of Jerusalem be regarded as the scene. Yet such is the view of Grotius, Clericus, Schöttgen, Whitby, Kern, De Wette, Lünemann, Wieseler, Döllinger. See Essay.

ἀποδεικνύντα ἑαυτὸν ὅτι ἐστὶν Θεός—"showing himself off that he is God." The compound verb means, according to Winer, *spectandum aliquid proponere*, and its participle is more than, trying to show himself, πειρώμενον ἀποδεικνύναι (Chrysostom); he is actually doing so, though he cannot succeed. He is showing himself that he is God, as he sits in the temple; this his claim to be regarded as God is a present, characteristic, continuous self-exhibition as God. Θεός is not *a* god, or a possessor of divinity, one among many, but God. The expressed ἐστίν emphasizes the assertion. How this self-deification is done, or how this wretched assumption and exhibition of divinity is held up, we know not. The impious pretence is not kept up by false miracles, as many contend, such as the Greek fathers, Heydenreich, Schott, Olshausen, De Wette, Riggenbach, for these lying wonders are not introduced till verse 7, and they belong more to his mission as a seducer than to this culmination of blasphemy—usurping God's place and prerogatives, and giving out that he is God. This is the crowning act of impiety—not putting his statue in the temple, but sitting in state in it himself; not multiplying false gods, or setting up many idols, but himself claiming godhead, either as a rival, or to the exclusion of the one true God. For a creature, for a man, to venture upon this divine treason, and, from pride and insolent ambition and antipathy, to take God's seat and claim His honour, is surely the most awful consummation of wickedness and blasphemy that can be imagined, and he who rises to the height of such flagrant, "damnable" enormity, is truly named the Man of Sin, the Son of Perdition. One can scarcely imagine the possibility of such God-defying and God-personating rebellion, and we must surely wonder why it is tolerated at all, not why vengeance is flashed upon it in God's time at the Second Advent.

(Ver. 5.) Οὐ μνημονεύετε ὅτι ἔτι ὢν πρὸς ὑμᾶς ταῦτα ἔλεγον ὑμῖν—"Remember ye not that when I was yet with you I was telling you these things?" For πρὸς ὑμᾶς see under 1 Thess. iii, 4. Ταῦτα refers to the contents of the two previous verses —the things just touched on by him, and more fully communicated during his very brief residence at Thessalonica. The imperfect implies more than a solitary communication—"I used to tell you." Winer, § xl, 3 b. He had been in the habit of giving them such lessons and disclosures, no doubt for some good purpose. His eschatology was no idle or purposeless speculation; it ever had influence on present duty, patience, and hope. The commencing interrogation, "Do ye not remember?" has in it *tacita objurgatio*. If they had only remembered his definite and repeated lessons, they could not have been so perplexed and seduced as to imagine that the day of the Lord had set in; for they would have sustained themselves by the thought that defection must precede it, and the terrible development of the Man of Sin.

(Ver. 6.) Καὶ νῦν τὸ κατέχον οἴδατε, εἰς τὸ ἀποκαλυφῆναι αὐτοῦ ἐν τῷ ἑαυτοῦ καιρῷ—"And now what hinders ye know, in order that he may be revealed in his own time." They knew what this restraining power or influence was—knew it from his previous personal teaching, and therefore he does not here repeat the information. We have not the same knowledge, and so must be contented to conjecture his meaning. Because they knew it so well, we know it so imperfectly. The particle νῦν has been variously taken. (1) It has been taken as a particle of time, qualifying κατέχον—what now hinders. So Heydenreich, Schrader, Olshausen, Baumgarten-Crusius, Bisping, Wieseler. But in that case the order would require to be τὸ νῦν κατέχον, the emphatic adverb having its natural position between the article and the participle. The places adduced to exemplify such a hyperbaton as these expositors assume are not parallel instances, as verse 7; Rom. xii, 3; 1 Cor. vii, 17. The use of ἄρτι and of ἤδη with ὁ κατέχων, in verse 7, does not favour this view. For as ἔτι refers to his sojourn, and qualifies ὤν, ἄρτι after ὁ κατέχων, as Lünemann says, has not the stress upon it, but the participle has, and therefore ἄρτι is not connected with νῦν as the repetition of its meaning; while ἤδη, again, is in contrast with the phrase "in his own time." Some connect it with οἴδατε, and as in contrast to ἔτι—while he was yet with them he told them of those things already mentioned, and now after his writing they knew, or when they recalled his instructions they knew (Riggenbach). They knew either what hindered—the previous, or intermediate and necessary happening of the apostacy (Bengel, Storr, and Flatt); or, under another aspect suggested by Kern and Hilgenfeld, "ye now know what preventeth the coming of Christ—namely, the prior manifestation of this self-deifying Man of Sin." But as these topics imply additional knowledge, the words would be νῦν δὲ καὶ οἴδατε.

(2) The particle νῦν may be taken with its logical signification as an advance to a new thought. See under 1 Thess. iii, 8. Compare Acts vii, 34; x, 5; xii, 11; 1 Cor. xiv, 6. "And now, those things being so," or passing away from the question and implied rebuke of the previous verse to another point— "ye now know what withholds;" so De Wette, Lünemann, Ewald, Alford, Ellicott; not "and thus" (Koppe), nor *igitur* (Flatt, Pelt). Schott takes νῦν in the sense of *etiam nunc, compertum habetis, non illo tantum tempore, quo vos de his omnibus coram edocui, cognovistis, quid adhuc illum cohibeat.* But the idea expressed by κατέχον is a new idea, and not contained in the ταῦτα, and the words as Lünemann argues, would require to be τὸ οὖν κατέχον οἴδατε καὶ νῦν, "ye knew it then; ye know it also now." The participle denotes what restrains or hinders or τὸ κωλύον (Chrysostom). Luke iv, 42; Rom. i, 18; Sept., Gen. xxiv, 56; Xenoph., *Mem.* ii, 6, 9.

There are two important questions. What is the restraining power, and from what does it restrain? The former will be considered in the appended Essay, and various answers have been given to the latter. (1) The meaning cannot be what hinders me from speaking more fully to you on Antichrist—to wit, the fear of incurring the wrath of Nero: such is the absurd view of Heinsius, which is contradicted by verses 7 and 8. (2) Nor is it the Second Advent which is so hindered (Noack), for αὐτόν does not refer to Christ, as κατέχων in verse 7 distinctly shows; and therefore the true reference is to ἄνθρωπος τῆς ἁμαρτίας, the main theme of the present section, the ἀποκαλυφθῆναι of this verse being identical with the ἀποκαλυφθῇ of verse 3 and the ἀποκαλυφθήσεται of verse 8, and κατέχον is in contrast with "revealed in his time"; the restraining power holds him back from being revealed—from any premature manifestation. The following εἰς τό introduces not the result (Flatt), but the design of this restraining power, in order that he may be revealed ἐν τῷ ἑαυτοῦ καιρῷ, " in his own time "—not before it, but in it (Matt. xx, 18; Luke i, 20; 1 Tim. vi, 15). A set time is appointed by God for the manifestation of the Man of Sin— a time neither to be antedated nor postponed, and the restraining power which prevents his immediate appearance is also in God's hand. It is a mistranslation of εἰς τό to make it *donec* or *usque dum*, for it is not equivalent to ἕως in the next verse. The revelation of the Man of Sin is so prearranged that it was not impending, and does not come by chance or at any self-selected epoch. Christ came in the fulness of the time, and his great, dark, and last counter-worker and caricature comes also in his own time.

(Ver. 7.) Τὸ γὰρ μυστήριον ἤδη ἐνεργεῖται τῆς ἀνομίας—" For the mystery already is working of lawlessness." Γάρ introduces confirmative explanation, as μυστήριον is opposed to ἀποκαλυφθῆναι, what is hidden to what is manifest. Ἤδη is in contrast with εἰς τὸ ἀποκαλυφθῆναι, present as contrasted with future, and ἐνεργεῖται is in antithesis with τὸ κατέχον, working and yet retarded from open outbreak. For μυστήριον see under Ephes. i, 9; v, 32. It is not something incomprehensible, but here something veiled and hidden, and apparently as yet unknown to the church, yet working its way toward the awful consummation. Ἐνεργεῖται, middle, has an active sense as usually in the New Testament; not "is being wrought," or *efficax redditur*, but "worketh" (Estius, Calovius, Noesselt, Storr, Schott). See under Gal. ii, 8. Ἀνομία—rendered "iniquity," Matt. xiii, 41; "unrighteousness," 2 Cor. vi, 14; "transgression of the law," 1 John iii, 4—is lawlessness, the reference being to the law of God (1 John iii, 4, ἡ ἁμαρτία ἐστὶν ἡ ἀνομία). This ἀνομία is utter and wanton disrespect for divine law; not only the wilful non-recognition of it, but perhaps the virtual superseding of it by some godless self-constituted and usurping authority. Trench, *Synon.*, ii, § 16. In—

τὸ μυστήριον τῆς ἀνομίας, the genitive does not seem to be that of opposition (Lünemann, De Wette, Alford); nor is the meaning *von derselben und für dieselbe gemacht*; nor is it the hidden plans of wickedness (Kern, Baumgarten-Crusius); nor does it signify the agent or source, τῆς ἀνομίας πάγην (Theodoret). The genitive is that of the characterizing principle, *die dominirenden Eigenschaften* (Scheuerlein, p. 115), or that of contents. This mystery is characterized specially by ἀνομία as its leading and distinctive principle, or it is so filled with it as to take its character from it. Nor does the phrase mean, evil working under pretext of good (Flatt). But the moment lies on μυστήριον from its position, and by its emphatic separation from its genitive by the adverb and verb. Nor can the reference of the phrase be to a person, as Simon Magus (Grotius), as if the mystery was in apposition with the Lawless one. Thus Chrysostom, "He speaks here of Nero as if he were the type of Antichrist, for he too wished to be thought a God." The opinion of Olshausen is similar. Christ, according to him, is called the mystery of godliness in 1 Tim. iii, 16, and that too because in Him God Himself appeared in the flesh; so His counterpart is here called the mystery of lawlessness, because in him the devil was manifest in the flesh, ὁ διάβολος ἐφανερώθη ἐν σαρκί. But the Man of Sin is, according to verse 9, not an incarnation of the devil (of which Scripture knows nothing), but an inspiration of the devil—not *diabolus, sed diaboli praecipuum organum*, and the mystery is not a person, but a process. Nor can the meaning proposed by Krebs, then by Hofmann and Heydenreich, be sustained, "a confounding and inconceivable extreme of wickedness"—Joseph., *De Bello Jud.*, i, 24, 1, being quoted in proof. But this signification is not in harmony with the context, which places the mystery in virtual antithesis with the revelation. Τὸ Μυστήριον τῆς ἀνομίας is allied to the ἀποστασία, not as identical with it, but as connected with it, both being preparatory to the public manifestation of this self-made God. The mystery of lawlessness was working at the moment, but its nature was undetected and its huge development unguessed at. That wickedness existed already in germ, but the germs were of continuous and unsuspected activity and growth; there were principles of incipient lawlessness at work, which would gather into them kindred elements, and combine and ripen at length into that terrible personal manifestation—the Man of Sin.

This mystery was to work up to a certain point, until the power that bore back the Man of Sin should be removed.

μόνον ὁ κατέχων ἄρτι ἕως ἐκ μέσου γένηται—"only till he who now restraineth be taken out of the way." Many have thought that this verse required in some way to be supplemented. (1) Some supply ἔστι—only there is one who restraineth (Knatchbull, Benson, and Baumgarten); but a word of such importance and as something more than a mere copula, could scarcely be omitted, and there is no necessity for the supplement, which mars the compact brevity of the clause. (2) Numerous expositors supply a verb to the participle, *tantum ut qui tenet nunc teneat, donec de medio fiat* (Vulgate), "only he who letteth will let until he be taken out of the way." Instead of *teneat* some supply *tenebit* or *obstabit*, some κατέχει, some καθέξει, and others κατεχέτω. Various are the objects which the verb so supplied is imagined to govern—*qui tenet nunc fidem catholicam teneat eam firmiter* (De Lyra), and similarly Zegerus and Estius, while Vatablus gives it as *solus hodie Christi adventum detinens, et remorans, donec per ipsius Christi adventum tollatur;* τὴν ἀρχήν—*qui imperium tenet*—is the filling up of Bos, and ἀνομίαν of Schott. But the masculine cannot have a different meaning from the neuter participle in the previous verse, and the withholding plainly refers to the manifestation of the Man of Sin. Others transpose ἕως and put it before ὁ κατέχων ἄρτι, till only he who still withholds it, shall be taken out of the way (Rosenmüller, Heydenreich, Schott); but such a version does not correspond with ἤδη. Olshausen and Pelt regard the clause as a fusion of several propositions into one, but such a supposition is quite unwarranted. Μόνον is not to be taken with the first clause, either with μυστήριον, as Jowett—"the hidden mystery is already at work, but only as a hidden mystery"; or with ἐνεργεῖται, as Wordsworth—"worketh inwardly only, to be hereafter revealed outwardly." But μόνον belonging to ἕως states the temporal limitation of ἐνεργεῖται, and commences a protasis, the apodosis being in the following verse, καὶ τότε, &c. The moment is on ὁ κατέχων, placed therefore before ἕως as in Gal. ii, 10, μόνον τῶν πτωχῶν ἵνα μνημονεύωμεν, and ἄρτι is closely connected with it—not actually at the present time, but present time in the conception of the writer. The mystery works already and will work in preparation for the Lawless one, till the restraining power which bars back his open revelation of himself be removed. The century or year implied in ἕως is not given. The last words ἐκ μέσου γένηται, are not necessarily to be understood of a violent removal (Olshausen, Baumgarten-Crusius); the fact is given without any assertion of the manner (1 Cor. v, 2; Col. ii, 14). The opposite phrase ἐν μέσῳ εἶναι means to be in the way, to be a hindrance, so that ἐκ μέσου γίγνεσθαι means to be taken out of the way, to cease to be a hindrance. Plutarch, *Timol.*, p. 238; Herodot., viii, 22; Xenoph., *Cyrop.*, v, 2, 26; Sept., Is. lvii, 2. The nominative to γένηται is ὁ κατέχων without doubt, and therefore Zuingli, after Augustine, is wrong in referring it to the Man of Sin—his interpretation being, "only he who holds any element of truth now should hold it fast till Antichrist is taken away." Similarly Calvin, who says that the apostle makes both statements in reference to one person, Antichrist being thus the person to be taken out of the way, adding *et participium* "*obtinens*" *resolvi debet in futurum tempus.* This exegesis requires a different meaning to be given to the masculine participle from the neuter one, and connects this verse with verse 5. The neuter κατέχον of the previous verse is exchanged for the masculine κατέχων, the restraining power being now regarded as in an embodied form or individuality.

(Ver. 8.) Καὶ τότε ἀποκαλυφθήσεται ὁ ἄνομος—"And then shall be revealed the Lawless one," ἀνομία like κατέχον being now viewed as a living personality. The emphasis is on the phrase καὶ τότε, "and then," when the power or person withholding shall have been removed out of the way, taking up the point of time indicated by μόνον ἕως and echoing ἐν τῷ καιρῷ. Ἀποκαλυφθήσεται looks back to τὸ μυστήριον ἐνεργεῖται—no longer a veiled working, but an open undisguised personal manifestation—repeating the ἀποκαλυφθῆναι of verse 6, and the ἀποκαλυφθῇ of verse 3, and ὁ ἄνομος takes up τῆς ἀνομίας, viewed now as a living personality. There is no doubt that ὁ ἄνομος is the same with αὐτός in verse 6, and with the ὁ ἄνθρωπος τῆν ἁμαρτίας of verse 3. The opposite opinion of Grotius is utterly baseless. The terms ἀνομία, ἄνομος point out so far what the form of wickedness is which the Man of Sin will assume—lawlessness, as described in verse 4—not heathenism, nor polytheism, but the audacious and profligate setting aside of all rule, the casting off of all divine supremacy, and the establishment of an autonomy, his arrogant and godless self-will being the only law. What has been so long working as a mystery and growing in lawless energy, and which in the interval has been kept back by a stronger hand from open manifestation, shall at length assume a personal shape, and appear as a "man" verifying his title as the Lawless one; not an outlaw or one beyond law, but one above law, subject to no rule save his own as the highest power—God disowned and His legislation superseded, not by atheism, or by dull negative anarchy, but by wild and virulent antitheism, enthroned in blasphemous and God-defying outrage. As Christ glorified all divine law in His obedience unto death and was the righteous one, the servant of Jehovah, so this counterpart—not a pseudo-Christ, but truly an Antichrist—flings all divine law off and away, and stands out as the Lawless one and as a God-personating usurper. The apostle adds in haste and to comfort the believers—

ὃν ὁ Κύριος Ἰησοῦς ἀνελεῖ τῷ πνεύματι τοῦ στόματος αὐτοῦ καὶ καταργήσει τῇ ἐπιφανείᾳ τῆς παρουσίας αὐτοῦ— "whom the Lord Jesus shall consume with the breath of His mouth, and shall destroy with the appearance of His coming." The Received Text omits Ἰησοῦς with B D³ K L, many mss., and some of the fathers, but ὁ Κύριος Ἰησοῦς has the authority of A D¹ F L² א, both Latin and both Syriac versions, the Coptic, and very many of the fathers, both Greek and Latin. For ἀνελεῖ the Received Text has ἀναλώσει, with D³ K L, and some of the fathers; ἀνελεῖ is found in A B and some of the fathers. This form has authority from the fact that a somewhat similar reading ἀνάλοι occurs in א¹, and ἀνέλοι in D¹ F א³. The reading of D¹ is, however, doubtful, and ἀνελεῖ may be a conformation to Isaiah xi, 4. These twin clauses have the ring of the old Hebrew prophetic parallellism, and are, perhaps, an echo of Isaiah xi, 4; καὶ πατάξει γῆν τῷ λόγῳ τοῦ στόματος αὐτοῦ; καὶ ἐν πνεύματι διὰ χειλέων ἀνελεῖ ἀσεβῆ. The apostle has not finished his account of the Lawless one, but he hastens, ere he adds some dark features to the picture, to assure his readers of his final and certain destruction. If he verify his name as "The Man of Sin," he shall also verify his name as "The Son of Perdition." If ἀνελεῖ be adopted, the verb ἀναιρέω signifies often to put away, or to put out of the way—spoken of death, or a public execution, &c.,—in many places both of the gospels and Acts. Compare also Heb. x, 9; Polyb., xxxii, 1, 3; Xenoph., *Cyrop.*, i, 1, 1. See on a similar form Phrynichus, ed. Lobeck, p. 183. If ἀναλώσει be adopted, it means in the classics "to use up," as money, in a bad sense, and the verb ἀναλίσκω is also used of persons in the New Testament (Luke ix, 54; Gal. v, 15), representing in the Sept. the Hebrew אכל, "to eat up," "to devour" (Jer. l, 7), and it describes the result of fire four times in Ezekiel and twice in Joel. It also stands for כלה in Gen. xli, 30, and Is. xxxii, 10. Πνεῦμα is used with its original signification of breath (Is. xi, 4; Rev. xi, 11, &c.) Compare Gen. vi, 17; vii, 22. The figure is a very expressive one. His mere breath as he comes the second time will consume his terrible antagonist. Compare Ps. xxxiii, 6; Wisdom xi, 20, 21. It is needless to take off from the impressive force and simple majesty of the figure by any rude and prosaic analysis. But (1) Theodoret and Theodore of Mopsuestia refer the term to a cry or word uttered; the first has φθέγξεται μόνον, and the second μόνον ἐπιβοήσας, followed by the quaint explanation that we employ breath in articulate speech (*Opera*, ed. Fritzsche, p. 148). (2) Vatablus and a-Lapide take it as meaning the condemnatory sentence of a judge, *jussu suo, verbo suo, sua sententia*—a tame explanation. Similarly Calvin explains πνεῦμα by *verbum*, and Pelagius more vaguely, *cœlesti imperio, vel solo*. (3) Athanasius understands by πνεῦμα the divine or Holy Spirit (*Epist. ad Serap.*, 1, 6, p. 547, *Opera*, vol. II, Migne); and the same view is given in the alternative explanation of Theophylact. But the phrase carries on the face of it its plain and natural sense, and implies the ease and perhaps the suddenness of the annihilation of the Lawless one. The verb καταργεῖν, often used by the apostle, is "to put down," " to do away with," " to destroy " (Rom. vi, 6; 1 Cor. vi, 13; xv, 24; 2 Cor. iii, 7). The meaning is not to make inoperative, as Calovius, Olshausen, and Riggenbach, referring to Rev. xix, 15-19, which describes the fate of the beast and the false prophet. Παρουσία is here, as everywhere in this connection, the Second Personal Advent, and the places are so numerous that they need not be quoted. See under 1 Thess. ii, 19.

᾿Επιφάνεια is simply appearance, and it is usually in the Authorized Version rendered "appearing," as 1 Tim. vi, 14; 2 Tim. i, 10; iv, 1, 8; Titus ii, 13; but here the Authorized Version, after the Genevan and the Bishops', gives "brightness," Tyndale, however, having "appearance," and the Latinized Rheims, "manifestation of His Advent," the Vulgate, *illustratione*, but the Claromontane, *aspectu*. The idea of brightness or glory does not belong to the term — τῆς δόξης is added in Titus ii, 13; an immense number of expositors, however, unwarrantably attach such an idea to the word in this place. The appearance must be glorious, but the apostle does not say so, and the expression is all the more significant that he does not say so. The term is applied to the First Coming (2 Tim. i, 10), " made manifest by the appearing of our Saviour Jesus Christ, who hath abolished death;" and it is, as applied to the Second Advent, followed by some title of the Saviour (1 Tim. vi, 14), "until the appearing of our Lord Jesus Christ" (Titus ii, 13); once it is connected with βασιλείαν (2 Tim. iv, 1), "who shall judge the quick and the dead at His appearing and His Kingdom'"; once it stands by itself (2 Tim. vi, 8); ἐπιφανής is applied to ἡμέραν Κυρίου (Acts ii, 20). The noun is used in the classics of the appearance of a deity to aid a worshipper (Diodor. Sic., i, 17 ; Athenæus, xii, 542). Compare 2 Macc. iii, 24; the so-called second epistle of Clement 12; Suicer, Thes., *sub voce;* and Wetstein, *in loc.* Olshausen's distinction serves no good purpose—that the first is the subjective, and the second the objective aspect; the meaning is that His coming has only to make itself visible, when the result described by καταργεῖν shall take place. The first gleam of His presence shall destroy His antagonist. "Let God arise," sang the Psalmist in a similar spirit, "and let His enemies be scattered." The bringing to nought of the Man of Sin, therefore, does not happen till the Second Advent. The phrase on that account does not mean the entrance of Christ's word into the heart (Zuingli). Chrysostom says, "it is enough for Him to be present, and all these things are destroyed. He will put a stop to the deceit by only appearing." The two clauses are not different things, though the one may precede the other, but the words mean that the coming shows itself as a visible reality. The first clause also is clearly connected with this one as its preceding feature. The breath is not His word and spirit operating *in hominum animis* (Hunnius) invisibly in time, nor is wind or storm as heralding Him to be thought of, but it is the breath issuing from His mouth, as He is coming nearer and nearer to destroy this blasphemous assumer of divine prerogative.

(Ver. 9.) οὗ ἐστὶν ἡ παρουσία κατ' ἐνέργειαν τοῦ Σατανᾶ— "whose coming is after the working of Satan." The relative takes up ὁ ἄνομος, after his awful, irresistible, and sudden doom is told by anticipation. By the use of παρουσία the apostle brings the Man of Sin into immediate connection and contrast with the personal Jesus, though at different points of time. Παρουσία belongs to each—to Christ at His last coming; to Antichrist at an earlier period of his human manifestation, but at an epoch future to the composition of the epistle. Ἐστὶν, the ethical present, asserts the certainty of the coming event (Lünemann), "either as unchangeably determined, or about to take place by some unalterable arrangement." Winer, § 40, 2. For παρουσία, see under last verse, and 1 Thess. ii, 19. Or ἐστὶν may be used doctrinally, describing, as Alford says, "*the essential attribute*" (1 Cor. xv, 35). Κατά is best taken with its usual signification, "according to," not "in consequence of," *in Folge* (De Wette). It serves no good purpose to take κατ' ἐνέργειαν τοῦ Σατανᾶ as an independent clause, ὁ ἄνομος appearing as a working or energy of Satan. It is better to connect the clause with ἐστὶν—ἐν. The one view is, that the coming is after the energy of Satan, and the second that it is a coming in false wonders, κατ' ἐνέργειαν τοῦ Σατανᾶ, pointing to the source of the power so put forth. The Syriac, indeed, has ܘܟܠܗ ܡܐܬܝܬܗ ܗܘܐ ܒܡܥܒܕܢܘܬܗ ܕܣܛܢܐ. The entire coming of the Man of Sin is full of Satan's power, and is displaying itself in these false miracles. Just as in Christ the fulness of the Godhead dwelt bodily, so without there being an incarnation, without there being a personal union, Satan's fulness dwells in the Man of Sin, dowering him with superhuman craft and might, and finding a fitting agent and organ in him. This παρουσία of the lawless one is a Satanic counterpart, or infernal mimicry of Christ's παρουσία, as the following context also shows. Being according to the inworking of Satan, its sphere is—

ἐν πάσῃ δυνάμει καὶ σημείοις καὶ τέρασιν ψεύδους—"in all powers and signs and prodigies of lying." Πάσῃ singular, used with the first noun, yet agrees with all three of them, and with its extensive signification denotes "all kinds of" (Winer, § 59, 5 *b*; Matt. iv, 23; Eph. i, 21), and ἐν denotes the sphere (Winer, § 48, 3). The genitive ψεύδους is probably that of the characterizing qualities. But Lünemann and De Wette take it as the genitive of purpose—*der Genitivus des Gesichtspunktes*—"wonders whose aim is lying." Winer, § 30, 2 *b*. And so Chrysostom explains alternatively εἰς ψεῦδος ἄγουσι. But the characterization of these miracles would seem to be a more immediate necessity than a statement of their purpose; and if they were false themselves, they could not but lead to falsehood, and they must have had their origin in it. In fact, Alford brings together the three possible meanings of source, character, and result—all have falsehood for their basis, essence, and aim; and so also Riggenbach, Theodoret, Calovius, Turretin, Olshausen take the word in a somewhat similar way. Theodoret's illustration is, they show gold which is not gold, χρυσὸν οὐκ ἀληθῶς ὄντα χρυσὸν. Chrysostom, Œcumenius and Theophylact mention both interpretations of the genitive—character and result—but do not decide. Hofmann finds the epithet specially verified in the antagonism of these miracles to the truth. The nouns δυνάμεις, σημεῖα, τέρατα, are words of similar meaning, and the three are found in a somewhat different order in Acts ii, 22, and in Heb. ii, 4—"God also bearing them witness both with signs and wonders, and with divers miracles." These phenomena are works of power, signs or tokens of divine interposition, and also prodigies or rare and startling manifestations. Σημεῖον is the highest term applied to a true miracle, and it often occurs in the gospel of John. The words are allied in signification, and the phrase may set them over against the true miracles of the Son of God, "a man approved of God among you by miracles, and wonders, and signs." Compare Matt. xxiv, 24; Rev. xiii, 14. There is no proof whatever that these are miracles in the proper sense of the term; real miracles misleading into the belief that they are done by divine power (Augustine). Riggenbach calls them "monstrosities without any saving object, but not, therefore, mere juggleries." But can any one but God work a miracle? See Farmer on the one side and Trench on the other. No doubt the wonders referred to are to be startling and portentous, the last exhibition of Satan's craft and power through the Lawless one, the last concentration of all hellish energy and cunning; and men may be led to regard them as proofs and indications of divine power on the part of him who sits in the temple of God, dispossessing God of His seat; showing himself in this way among others, that he is God. Falsehood is Satan's essence and element, and it is embodied in this, his last and chosen human organ, the Man of Sin, not only the usurper of God's prerogative, but also the malignant arch-deceiver.

(Ver. 10.) καὶ ἐν πάσῃ ἀπάτῃ ἀδικίας—"and in all deceit of unrighteousness." The Received Text has τῆς before ἀδικίας, with D K L ℵ³, and some of the fathers, but the omission has the higher authority of A B F ℵ¹, &c. The conjunction introduces a fuller statement, which gathers up into itself the previous particulars. Winer, § 53, 3. What was said of ψεύδους may be said of this genitive. The deceit is characterized by unrighteousness, or it leads to it (Estius, Aretius, Grotius, De Wette); its utterly iniquitous nature may be specially dwelt on. The Lawless one is wholly iniquitous and deceitful; he lives in guile, and that guile is ever hostile to righteousness. He does his work by seduction and lying, both in the false wonders and also in every possible form of wicked imposture. There is thus a terrible accumulation of epithets throughout the paragraph—a man of sin, a counter-God, mystery of iniquity, lawless one, working of Satan, false miracles, and every sort of iniquitous deceit. No wonder that perdition and thorough destruction are associated with them. But this deceit of unrighteousness does not prevail over every class; it has efficacy only—

τοῖς ἀπολλυμένοις—"for those that are perishing." The Received Text has ἐν before τοῖς with D³ K L ℵ³, but the preposition is wanting in A B D¹ F ℵ¹, in the Latin and Coptic versions, and in several of the Greek and Latin fathers. The phrase is therefore in what is called *dativus incommodi*. The Authorized Version, by its punctuation, connects the words exclusively with the previous clause, "deceivableness of unrighteousness in them that perish," and so Heydenreich, Flatt, Hofmann, Baumgarten-Crusius. The reference is better taken to the whole previous verse, the entire false and Satanic diplomacy there characterized. But the connection cannot be that indicated by Schott, *fraudibus impiis, quae patrantur inter homines miseros*, nor that given by Benson, "by their fraudulent practices the Man of Sin and his adherents will greatly prevail. But among whom? Among men, but men of corrupt minds." The τοῖς ἀπολλυμένοις are those who are perishing, and the reason of their perishing state follows. Turretin gives the meaning as *qui exitio digni sunt adeoque certissime sunt perituri*; Grotius, *apud eos, qui evangelio credere noluerunt, ac propterea perituri sunt*. The present tense characterizes their future perdition as already decided (Lünemann), as those who are perishing at the time in contemplation (Ellicott). 1 Cor. i, 18; 2 Cor. ii, 15; iv, 3. Theodoret describes them as those who, though the Lawless one had not come, had deprived themselves of salvation. The sentence that consigns them to perdition is God's sentence, as we are told in i, 6, 9; but they bring their sentence on themselves, as the apostle goes on very distinctly to affirm—

ἀνθ' ὧν τὴν ἀγάπην τῆς ἀληθείας οὐκ ἐδέξαντο εἰς τὸ σωθῆναι αὐτούς—" because they did not receive the love of the truth that they might be saved." The significant phrase, ἀνθ' ὧν is "in return," "in requital for" (Luke i, 20; xix, 44; Acts xii, 23; Sept., Lev. xxiv, 20; 1 Kings xi, 11; Joel iii, 5; Xenoph., *Anab.*, i, 3, 4; v, 5, 14; Winer, § 47 *a*; Raphelius and Wetstein *in Luc.*, i, 20). In the phrase ἀγάπην τῆς ἀληθείας, the genitive is naturally that of object—the love that has the truth for its object. The meaning, therefore, is not *charitatem veram* (Anselm), nor does the love of the truth here mean Christ, as the Greek fathers supposed, He being the love of the truth because He truly and really loved us. The truth is especially Christian truth, in which all truth culminates; the truth by the love and reception of which men are saved. But to receive the love of the truth is more than to receive the truth (Kern, Jowett). To want the love of the truth is to be wholly indifferent to its claims, and to be wholly unsusceptible of its beauty, power, and adaptation. The truth might be received in some faint and fragmentary form—held so lightly, and understood so superficially, that no true love for it might co-exist; and where this love for it is absent, the mind is open to assaults and hesitations, and is self-prepared for falling a victim to such astute frauds as are so artfully practised by the Lawless one. Εἰς τό, the infinitive of purpose, in order to their being saved. The love of the truth had salvation for its object, but that they disregarded. In their indifference to the means they rejected the end; or rather being careless about the end, they neglected the means.

(Ver. 11.) καὶ διὰ τοῦτο πέμπει αὐτοῖς ὁ Θεὸς ἐνέργειαν πλάνης, εἰς τὸ πιστεῦσαι αὐτοὺς τῷ ψεύδει—" and on this account God is sending them an inworking error that they should believe a lie." The Received Text reads πέμψει with D³ K L ℵ⁴ and very many versions, with several of the fathers, but the present has in its favour A B D¹ F ℵ¹; besides, the change would be naturally suggested by the occurrence of the clause in a prophecy. Καί has virtually a consecutive force—"and so," for this reason, that is, because they received not the love of the truth. Ἐνέργεια πλάνης is not a "strong delusion," for the phrase refers not to the passive result, but to the active cause, καὶ πλανῆσαι ἰσχύουσαν (Œcumenius). Nor is it πλάνην ἐνεργόν, but ἐνέργεια is an activity which deepens and circulates the πλάνη—on this last word see under 1 Thess. ii, 3. The genitive may again be that of the point of view, or of characterization—the inworking is marked by error, and is moulded by it, πλάνης corresponding to the ψεύδους of verse 9. Εἰς τό points out the final purpose, and not the mere result, *mit dem Erfolge* (Baumgarten-Crusius), or, "so as they will believe a lie" (Macknight); *non meram sequelam, sed consilium indicat* (Schott). Hofmann's connection with εἰς τό is *gewaltsam*, strained, as Lünemann calls it. Τῷ ψεύδει is "the lie," not falsehood in the abstract, or falsehood generally, but the falsehood just detailed, and involved in the phrases, the coming of the Lawless one, working of Satan—the liar, power and signs and wonders of falsehood, deceit of iniquity—all this complex array and network of imposture which belongs to the open manifestation of the Man of Sin, and by which they are entangled and taken. "The lie" is opposed to the truth the love of which they did not receive, and the want of which left their minds an easy prey to this machinery of deception. They believe the pretensions of this wretched mimic and dethroner of God; his false wonders they take as genuine miracles; they believe the lie. This unparalleled hallucination indicates a mysterious state of mind and of society—antichristian, antitheistic, credulous, with a fatal facility of being imposed upon by hellish mastery and subtlety; and the apostle expressly says—

πέμπει αὐτοῖς ὁ Θεός—"God is sending them this inworking of error to the end that they may believe the lie." The present is used probably as a species of doctrinal present, connecting itself continuously or contemporaneously with the process which the apostle is describing. Lünemann, Ellicott, and others regard it as a direct present, the mystery of iniquity being even now at work. True; but the decided development of the mystery is laid in that far future, to which belongs God's action of sending the inworking of error. This infliction directly ascribed to God is glossed over by not a few commentators, as the Greek fathers, and many after them, as if the verb "He is sending" only meant "He permits to be sent." As a specimen, Œcumenius explains, Τὸ πέμψει, μὴ οὕτω δέξῃ, ὡς τοῦ Θεοῦ πέμποντος, ἀλλὰ τὴν ἀπὸ τοῦ Θεοῦ συγχώρησιν, οὕτως ἔθος καλεῖν τῷ Παύλῳ. Joannes Damascenus writes, Τὸ δὲ ἀποστελεῖ αὐτοῖς ὁ Θεὸς, συγχωρήσει ἀποσταλῆναι, quoting as analogous Rom. i, 26. Schott explains, *haud raro, quae Deum sapienter permittere dicamus, ejusmodi formulis enuntiari, quae Deum hanc perversitatem summam immittentem . . . describant.* The Eastern church had less profound views of divine relations and acts than the Western church. The wilful and persistent rejection of the truth God punishes with judicial blindness, so that the power of discernment is blunted, and error comes to be accepted as truth—nay, the perversity becomes sometimes so morbid that men bring on them the woe pronounced against such as "call evil good, and good evil; that put darkness for light, and light for darkness; that put bitter for sweet, and sweet for bitter" (Is. v, 20). Sin often receives its chastisement in a deeper load of sin; is punished by the sinner's sinking into worse enormities. Indifference to the truth gets its divine recompense in its facile seduction into gross and grosser errors. It indeed, by its own spiritual callousness, lays itself open to such awful retribution; but this punitive infliction is in itself God's own act, according to His own fixed procedure as Moral Governor. The Scripture ever recognizes His immediate agency in such penal visitations, whatever instrumentality may be employed. Compare 1 Kings xxii, 20; 2 Sam. xxiv, 1; Job. xii, 16; Is. lxvi, 3, 4; Ezek. xiv, 9.

(Ver. 12.) ἵνα κριθῶσιν ἅπαντες οἱ μὴ πιστεύσαντες τῇ ἀληθείᾳ, ἀλλ' εὐδοκήσαντες (ἐν) τῇ ἀδικίᾳ—"in order that they all might be judged who believed not the truth, but had pleasure in unrighteousness." The readings ἅπαντες and πάντες are pretty nearly balanced, the former having in its favour A F ℵ, and the latter B D E L, mss., and many of the fathers. The authorities for and against ἐν are pretty nearly balanced—it is bracketed by Lachmann, and rejected by Tischendorf in his first edition. The preposition may have been omitted to balance the clauses, as in B D F ℵ[3], but it is found in A D³ K L ℵ¹, and the construction with the simple dative does not occur in the New Testament, though the accusative of the object is found. The first clause (ἵνα) develops, not the result (Koppe, Pelt, Schott), but the final purpose, a purpose more remote than that expressed by εἰς τὸ of the previous clause, though connected with it as a step in the fatal progress, and connected too with πέμπει, indicating a more distant divine act, which leads εἰς τὸ πιστεῦσαι. The simple verb κριθῶσιν does not of itself here or elsewhere express the idea of condemned, "damned," but the context plainly implies it. The sin is heinous, and the judgment is according to truth. The aorist, πιστεύσαντες, glances back at the period which has passed before the judgment, and the object of this denied belief is τῇ ἀληθείᾳ, the love of which they had not received, and faith in which, therefore, they did not possess—their faith being given in judicial infatuation to the lie. This clause expresses negatively what the clause beginning with εἰς τὸ affirms, and the next clause expresses positively what the clause commencing with ἀνθ' ὧν puts into a negative form. For εὐδοκέω see i, 11. To have delight in unrighteousness, in what is opposed to the divine character and law, must from its nature foster unbelief, and suffocate all love of the truth. There is thus a moral reason for want of faith in the truth, and that is delight in unrighteousness, which is wholly incompatible with it.

The apostle now thanks God for their election, and their realization of it, exhorts them to adhere to sound teaching, and asks for them divine comfort and confirmation.

(Ver. 13.) Ἡμεῖς δὲ ὀφείλομεν εὐχαριστεῖν τῷ Θεῷ πάντοτε περὶ ὑμῶν—" But we are bound to give thanks to God always for you." By δὲ he passes to another and different subject. They are judged who believe not the truth, but for you we are bound to give thanks. By ἡμεῖς he does not mean himself alone (Jowett, Conybeare), but includes his colleagues Silvanus and Timothy. For the form of the phrase, &c., see under i, 3. We not only do it; we cannot help doing it. It is an obligation to which we gladly bow. Riggenbach approves of Hofmann's connection—that over against the antichristian deception which God will send, and which has already begun we, the preachers of the gospel, give thanks for what He is now doing by us to save you from the coming judgment. Such a connection is rather laboured.

ἀδελφοὶ ἠγαπημένοι ὑπὸ Κυρίου—" brethren beloved by the Lord." See under 1 Thess. 1, 4. There it is Θεοῦ, here Κυρίου, meaning Christ, the prevailing reference in the epistles and especially here; for though love in this aspect is usually ascribed to the Father, yet as τῷ Θεῷ precedes and ὁ Θεός follows, Κυρίου must have a different personal allusion. Rom. viii, 37; Gal. ii, 20; Ephes. v, 2, 25. See under Ephes. 1, 2. The ground or theme of thanksgiving is now given—

ὅτι εἵλατο ὑμᾶς ὁ Θεὸς ἀπ' ἀρχῆς εἰς σωτηρίαν—" that God chose you from the beginning unto salvation." The Received Text reads εἵλετο, with K and many mss., but the Alexandrian form, εἵλατο, has the overwhelming authority of A B D F L ℵ. Compare 1 Thess. 1, 4. Ὅτι, "to wit, that," is expository in nature, and introduces the matter of the thanksgiving. Donaldson, *Gr. Gr.*, § 5, 84; Winer, § 53, 9. Only in this place does the apostle use αἱρεῖσθαι of the divine election, ἐκλέγεσθαι being employed by him in 1 Cor. i, 27, 28.; Ephes. i, 4. But the word is employed in the Septuagint in the compound verb, Deut. vii, 6, 7; x, 15, and the simple verb, xxvi, 18. Compare Philip. i, 22; Heb. xi. 25. See under Ephes. i, 4. The purpose, the divine choice, was εἰς σωτηρίαν, "unto salvation," as if in contrast to that awful κρίσις, which falls on those who believe not the truth. See under 1 Thess. v, 9. The epoch of the divine choice is—

ἀπ' ἀρχῆς, " from the beginning."

(1) There is a reading ἀπαρχήν, supported by B F, a very few mss, the Vulgate which has *primitias*, and Joannes Damascenus who reads in his commentary ὥσπερ ἀπαρχήν. The reading is also found in Cyril, Ambrosiaster, and Pelagius, and is accepted by Lachmann, Jowett, and Riggenbach; but the common reading has in its favour A D K L ℵ, the Claromontane Latin which has *ab initio*, and similarly many Greek and Latin fathers. Lünemann alleges that the assertion would not be historically true, as the Thessalonians were not the first believers in Macedonia, and that, therefore, the word cannot be used as in Rom. xvi, 5, "firstfruits of Asia "; 1 Cor.

xvi, 15, "The house of Stephanas, firstfruits of Achaia." But Riggenbach and Hofmann find only this vague idea—"firstfruits in comparison with the rest of the world"—the mass of the profane. To this there are two objections—first, where James (i, 18) uses the term with such a reference he qualifies it by τις; and second, in the two places referred to, "firstfruits of Asia," "firstfruits of Achaia," the reference is to an individual and to a household. Rev. xiv, 4 explains itself—" being firstfruits to God and the Lamb." But apart from such reasonings the reading is on good grounds to be rejected. (2) Some give ἀπ' ἀρχῆς a relative or a temporal signification, "from the beginning" of the gospel among you. Thus Zuingli—*ab initio praedicationis;* similarly Vorstius, Krause, Michaelis. Such a sense would have required some notifying addition, as in Philip. iv, 15, "in the beginning of the gospel," and the connection of the phrase with ὁ Θεὸς εἵλατο is wholly different from its use and position in Luke i, 2, and in 1 John ii, 7, 24. Schrader opines from this alleged signification that the writer of the epistle supposes that a long time had elapsed since the gospel was first preached in Thessalonica, and could not, therefore, be the apostle Paul. (3) The phrase is to be taken in an absolute, though in a popular sense, from eternity. Compare 1 John i, 1; ii, 13, and also John i, 1; Isaiah xliii, 13—Κύριος ὁ Θεὸς ἔτι ἀπ' ἀρχῆς. The phrase, with this meaning, is unique in the apostle's writings, his modes of expression being πρὸ τῶν αἰώνων, 1 Cor. ii, 7; πρὸ καταβολῆς κόσμου, Eph. 1, 4; ἀπὸ τῶν αἰώνων, Eph. iii, 9; similarly, Col. i, 26; πρὸ χρόνων αἰωνίων, 2 Tim. i. 9. The choice of God is, from its nature, an eternal choice, though His call takes place in time, and through the preaching of the gospel. This divine and ultimate aspect and origin of human salvation the apostle rejoices to contemplate, as, rising above all human instrumentalities, weakness, and failures, it carries all back to His blessed sovereignty and His gracious self-formed purpose, and gives Him all the glory.

ἐν ἁγιασμῷ πνεύματος—" in sanctification of the Spirit." Two erroneous views of this clause have been given; first, that of De Wette that ἐν, directly connected with εἵλατο, is virtually εἰς, chosen to sanctification, the nearest object of the divine election. But ἐν bears its common signification, and to give it the sense of εἰς would obscure εἰς σωτηρίαν. Nor can ἐν here mean *sub conditione* (Pelt). Secondly, some understand by πνεῦμα the human spirit—as Koppe and Schott. The absence of the article does not necessitate such a meaning, as its omission may be accounted for by what Middleton calls the principle of correlation, *i.e.*, where the noun governing is indefinite, the governed becomes anarthrous (*Greek Article*, p. 36, and the modifying explanation in the note.) The connection of the clause has been variously understood. (1) Some connect it immediately with σωτηρίαν, as Schott, Baumgarten-Crusius, Hofmann, Riggenbach. The meaning then is, salvation by means of sanctification, &c., ἐν being regarded as instrumental, as in Theophylact's explanation, ἔσωσεν ὑμᾶς ἁγιάσας διὰ τοῦ πνεύματος, and Chrysostom says expressly that ἐν is used for διά—'Ἰδοὺ τὸ, ἐν, πάλιν διὰ ἐστιν. (2) It is better to connect the last clauses of the verse with εἵλατο εἰς σωτηρίαν, and then ἐν may be taken in its more ordinary signification, pointing to the sphere in which the choice to salvation realized itself. Lünemann takes ἐν as instrumental, pointing to the means by which this election works its gracious end. Hofmann and Riggenbach object to the connection of ἐν with εἵλατο, simply because the election cannot be conditioned by any subjective process, and they object equally to its connection—εἵλατο εἰς σωτηρίαν, because it is not the election but the being saved that is brought about by sanctification—Hofmann adding *das Wählen keines Mittels bedarf*, the choice needed no means. The objection is one-sided, for election to salvation does not realize itself immediately; the chariot of fire does not come down and snatch away one after another to glory. The election of God, though it be independent or unconditioned, works through a certain process, or in a certain element it attains its end. Two combined elements are specified here—first, in sanctification of the Spirit, the genitive being that of efficient cause. Winer, § 30, 1; Scheuerlein, § 17. The meaning of the phrase is not ἁγιασμὸς πνευματικός (Pelt). This sanctification is inwrought by the Spirit in the elect and to prepare them for this σωτηρία, which involves not only the pardon of their sins, but also that spiritual change of nature which makes them meet for the inheritance of the saints in light. The second element is—

καὶ πίστει ἀληθείας—" and faith in the truth," the genitive being that of object. Winer, § 30, 1; Philip. i, 27. The phrase does not mean πίστιν ἀληθινήν (Pelt), nor πίστεως ἀληθοῦς (Chrysostom). Compare 1 Peter i, 12. The truth is Christian truth (John xiv, 6; xviii, 37), there being an implied contrast to the previous πιστεῦσαι τῷ ψεύδει. There are thus two aspects or sides of the element in which the divine choice realizes itself—the divine or objective aspect, sanctification by the Spirit; and the human or subjective aspect, believing reception of the truth. The two things are closely associated. Chrysostom asks, διὰ τί οὐ πρότερον εἶπε τὴν πίστιν, ἀλλὰ τὸν ἁγιασμόν; and his answer is, "because even after sanctification we have need of much faith that we may not be shaken. Seest thou how he shows that nothing is of themselves, but the whole of God?" It is hard to say what stress is to be laid on the order of the clauses as indicating order or temporal connection in the blessings. Olshausen says, "it seems that belief in the truth of the gospel must precede sanctification by the Holy Spirit, as the cause precedes the effect. The interpreters pass over this difficulty, which is not a slight one." His solution is, "that by faith the apostle means faith perfected in insight, and not the quite general faith which is given with the very first elements." But there cannot be faith without the Spirit's work, nor can the Spirit's work be without faith in such a case. The Spirit brings home the truth to the heart, and the heart under His blessing consciously and cordially accepts it—Himself the agent, and His truth the organ of our sanctification. This work of the Spirit done in them, this faith possessed by them, and the destiny to which these lead are comprehended in the divine choice as really as the ὑμᾶς are included in it.

(Ver. 14.) εἰς ὃ ἐκάλεσεν ὑμᾶς διὰ τοῦ εὐαγγελίου ἡμῶν— "whereunto He called you by our gospel." F ℵ, the Vulgate, and Philoxenian Syriac insert καί after εἰς ὅ, and for ὑμᾶς, A B D¹ read ἡμᾶς with the Claromontane Latin, &c. It might be said, indeed, that ὑμᾶς is a correction to correspond with the ὑμᾶς of the previous verse, but ἡμᾶς wants uncial authority. What is the antecedent to εἰς ὅ, which cannot mean "*deshalb*"? (Olshausen.) Some propose the last clauses of the previous verse, "sanctification of the Spirit, and belief of the truth"—the final end of salvation to which these belong being the obtainment of glory (Fromond, Schott, De Wette, Hofmann). The reference, however, is better taken, not merely to the sphere, but to salvation along with its means. Aretius, indeed, theologically confines the reference to πίστις, but then it might have been εἰς ἥν—*plenius explicat causam organicam.* (2) Pelt explains, *ad electionem atque animum quo eadem digni evadimus*, an explanation away from the point; for the election was a divine eternal act. (3) The reference then is to the complex statement of the previous verse, and not to any of its separate parts, "to which," that is, "to being saved in sanctification of the Spirit and belief of the truth." God who chose them to this also called them to it. The election takes effect in and through the call. So Theophylact.

διὰ τοῦ εὐαγγελίου ἡμῶν—"by our gospel." See under 1 Thess. i, 5. The divine call evinced itself through the preaching of the gospel by the apostle and his colleagues, and ἀκοή precedes πίστις as the historic condition (Rom. x, 17). And the end is—

εἰς περιποίησιν δόξης τοῦ Κυρίου ἡμῶν Ἰησοῦ Χριστοῦ—"unto the obtaining of the glory of our Lord Jesus Christ." The clause is in apposition with εἰς ὅ and its antecedents, and is perhaps not a mere exact specification of εἰς σωτηρίαν, or a giving of the final aspect and consummation of σωτηρία. For περιποίησις see under 1 Thess. v, 9, and more fully under Ephes. i, 14. The genitive in the proper names is that of possession, not of origin (Pelt). John xvii, 4; Rom. viii, 17. Those who are saved obtain a share in that glory which the Lord Jesus possesses—the sense given by the body of expositors. Other interpretations have been proposed, but without any basis. (1) Some take περιποίησις in a passive sense, and give δόξης the sense of an adjective or epithet, in order to be a glorious possession of the Lord Jesus Christ, *zum herrlichen Eigenthum* (Luther, so also Menochius, Harduin, and Estius—*alius sensus, haudquaquam improbandus, ut ejus essent gloriosa possessio*). But this exegesis is against the distinct use and meaning of περιποίησις in the first epistle, and it would assign the glory fully as much to Christ as to the Thessalonian believers; whereas it is their condition specially which the apostle describes, and puts as the basis of the counsel which follows. (2) Others, giving περιποίησις an active sense, connect it with Θεός as the nominative to ἐκάλεσεν, and give it this peculiar signification, ἵνα δόξαν περιποιήσῃ τῷ υἱῷ αὑτοῦ, "that He might obtain glory for His Son." So Œcumenius, and virtually Chrysostom, Theophylact, Vatablus, a-Lapide, and the Syriac version. Calvin, as one explanation, (*qui sensus melius convenit*), *vel quod eos Christus acquisierit in suam gloriam*. Ambrosiaster—*acquiruntur ad augmentum gloriae corporis Christi*. But this sense would certainly require the dative τῷ Κυρίῳ; and the apostle has expressed one aspect of that idea otherwise, and very distinctly, in i, 10. The ultimate destiny to which the divine choice leads them by the sure steps detailed is participation in Christ's glory—the saved in the Saviour's glory—rich, ennobling, and eternal, the divine plan and purpose stretching from eternity (ἀπ' ἀρχῆς), and leading onward to περιποίησιν δόξης τοῦ Κυρίου ἡμῶν in a coming eternity. Compare Rom. viii, 30.

(Ver. 15.) Ἄρα οὖν, ἀδελφοί, στήκετε—" accordingly, then, brethren, stand firm." Ἄρα illative, and οὖν collective. See 1 Thess. v, 6; Gal. vi, 10. The counsel is thus based on the previous statement. Such being the divine eternal interest in you; such your condition, believing and sanctified; such the reality and the end of your divine call—glory with Christ, "stand firm;" στήκετε being in contrast to σαλευθῆναι of the second verse. See under 1 Thess. iii, 8; Gal. vi, 1; Philip. i, 27. Firmness, in the midst of agitations, defections, and unsound novelties, is enjoined.

καὶ κρατεῖτε τὰς παραδόσεις ἃς ἐδιδάχθητε—"and hold fast the instructions which ye were taught" (1 Cor. xi, 2). Παράδοσις is employed in the gospels to signify traditional doctrines and usages (Matt. xv, 2; Mark vii, 3). See under Gal. i, 14; Col. ii, 8. It signifies here apostolical doctrines taught or delivered orally as in iii, 6; Joseph., *Antiq.*, x, 4, 1; Polybius, xi, 8, 2. More distinctly it is added—

ἃς ἐδιδάχθητε—"which ye were taught." The passive governs the accusative of object, the active governing both that and the accusative of person. Winer, § 32, 5. The

παράδοσις is not at all something handed down, but something handed over to these Thessalonians—
εἴτε διὰ λόγου εἴτε δι' ἐπιστολῆς ἡμῶν—" whether by word or by our epistle." Ἐἴτε ... εἴτε—whether ... whether, whether ... or, specifying and yet connecting the two ways by which the action of the verb is usually done, oral and written communication (1 Cor. xii, 26; xiii, 8). The phrase, our epistle, in connection with the aorist, refers to the first epistle, and not also to the one under hand or to epistolary communication generally (Riggenbach). It has been noticed that the apostle does not say here, as in ii, 2, ἐπιστολῆς ὡς δι' ἡμῶν. The inferential remark of Chrysostom is away from the true meaning altogether; "therefore let us think the traditions of the church also worthy of credit" (Damascenus in Riggenbach).

(Ver. 16.) Αὐτὸς δὲ ὁ Κύριος ἡμῶν Ἰησοῦς Χριστὸς καὶ ὁ Θεὸς ὁ πατὴρ ἡμῶν—" But may our Lord Jesus Christ and God our Father." There are minor differences in the order of the names and the insertion of the definite article. The Received Text has καὶ instead of ὁ before πατήρ, with A D³ K L, the Vulgate and Claromontane Latin versions, and several of the fathers, but the ὁ is found in B D¹ F ℵ¹, and in the Peshito; and it is difficult to say which on the whole is the better supported reading—perhaps the latter. The δὲ indicates a transitional contrast, hearty prayer for them in contrast with earnest counsel tendered to them. See under 1 Thess. iii, 11; v, 23. Αὐτὸς in itself and in its position has a solemn emphasis on it —Himself standing out in His own grace and majesty from us —ἡμῶν—the last word. Again, a prayer after an admonition, τοῦτο γάρ ἐστιν ὄντως βοηθεῖν, "I indeed have spoken thus; but the whole is of God, to strengthen, to confirm" (Chrysostom). The order is peculiar, though it occurs in the benediction (2 Cor. xiii, 14). The Lord Jesus Christ is placed first, contrary to the apostle's habit in so many places. This order may have been adopted, not simply "because Christ is mediator between men and God" (Lünemann), for in that case the order might have been God, Christ, you—the order of spiritual bestowment, God through Christ, or God and Christ, the ultimate Source and the Medium. If, as Alford says, a climax is intended, is there an anti-climax in the reverse order? But perhaps the preference arose thus—Christ and the Father are so one that a singular verb is employed in this benediction, which is really a prayer to both divine persons as equally givers, and the Son is named first as being so recently referred to in the words, the glory of our Lord Jesus Christ—the ultimate and indescribable inheritance of believers. Naturally in offering this prayer the apostle first mentions Him for whose glory they are set apart, as he asks comfort and strength to guard them on their way to that glory, and to prepare them for it. For ὁ Θεὸς ὁ πατὴρ ἡμῶν see Gal. i, 4. God the Father is the ultimate source of all spiritual blessing. Both, as the one object of prayer, are to the apostle divine, for Divinity alone is the living object of adoration. The Greek fathers naturally refer to this order of naming the divine persons—Theodoret especially as against Arius and Eunomius —the argument being, that the honour of the Son is not less than that of the Father though He is usually mentioned second, as in the Baptismal service—the order of the names not involving difference of dignity.

ὁ ἀγαπήσας ἡμᾶς καὶ δοὺς—"who loved us and gave us." The aorist does not mean *qui nos amat et quovis tempore amavit*, but refers to a past act, and is no doubt the love manifested in the mission of the only begotten Son (John iii, 16; 1 John iv, 10; Ephes. ii, 4). It seems probable that ὁ Θεὸς ὁ πατήρ is specially characterized by the participle, for ἀγάπη is usually ascribed to Him (Riggenbach, Lünemann). Others incline to include Jesus also, and to this the singular participle can be no objection, for a singular verb follows, and as Alford remarks, the apostle could not have written ἀγαπήσαντες—the unity of Father and Son being so distinctly recognized. It is impossible to decide, and it would be profane to be dogmatic on the point, yet we rather incline to the single reference to the Father, whose spontaneous, gracious, sovereign, and intense love is the source of all spiritual blessing. It is, however, quite capricious in Baumgarten-Crusius to refer the first participle to Christ, and the second, δοὺς, to the Father.

καὶ δοὺς παράκλησιν αἰωνίαν καὶ ἐλπίδα ἀγαθὴν ἐν χάριτι— " and gave us everlasting consolation and good hope in grace."

This second aorist is in historical reference or similar parallel to the first—loved us, and in that act of love gave us, when the gift of His love came into the world and died. Παράκλησις is here consolation, as in Luke ii, 25 ; vi, 24; xvi, 25 ; 2 Cor. i, 3; Heb. vi, 18. The feminine form αἰωνίαν occurs only here and in Heb. ix, 12. The phrase does not of itself mean or characterize eternal blessedness (Chrysostom, Estius, Grotius, Fromond). For the consolation is enjoyed in the present, and it is everlasting as compared with any comfort which time or the world can present and which from its nature is transitory and imperfect, for it suffices for all time and for eternity. There are evils, trials, changes, and struggles around believers —" without fightings, within fears"; so many temptations to harass them; so much indwelling sin to oppress them; so much, in short, to create sorrow and lassitude, that they have pressing need of comfort. Such comfort they have in the conscious enjoyment of their Father's love, and in the conviction that what they suffer is for their good, that what is laid on them is less than they deserve, and that grace is given them to bear it so that "where afflictions abound, consolations much more abound." This is true of all time, and such assurances and enjoyments last for ever. Along with this also—

καὶ ἐλπίδα ἀγαθήν—" and good hope." That hope regards the future, and is good not only in its basis, but in its cheering power, and in the blessed object which it contemplates (Titus ii, 13 ; Col. i, 5 ; Heb. vii, 19 ; 1 Peter i, 3, 4). The last words, ἐν χάριτι, are best connected with the participle δούς, ἐν marking the element in which the double gift of consolation and hope takes place. Some connect the phrase with both participles, as Estius, Lünemann, De Wette; for the grace is always included in the first participle, and, as has been remarked, when applied to God in Christ it usually stands absolute (Alford). Rom. viii, 37; Gal. ii, 20; Ephes. v, 2. Others would connect the words with ἐλπίδα, a hope resting on grace, but some fuller expression would be required to sustain this sense. The gift of God in its combined aspect of consolation and hope takes effect in His grace, that grace being opposed to necessity on His part, and to any merit on ours. The prayer is that our Lord Jesus Christ and God—

(Ver. 17.) παρακαλέσαι ὑμῶν τὰς καρδίας—"comfort your hearts." The verb παρακαλέσαι is singular, and in the aorist optative. The two nominatives, "our Lord Jesus Christ Himself and God our Father," are both so much regarded by the apostle in his prayer as one that a singular is employed. If the prayer to both express unity of operation, that unity implies oneness of essence, and both so appealed to in prayer are regarded by the apostle as of equal divinity. See under 1 Thess. iii, 11. They had been troubled about the Second Advent, and the apostle prays that they may be comforted, with no self-created consolation, and by no human sympathizer, but by our Lord Jesus Christ and God our Father, who knows all hearts, and has all access to them. The apostle had written to comfort them, but he implores comfort from a higher source.

καὶ στηρίξαι ἐν παντὶ ἔργῳ καὶ λόγῳ ἀγαθῷ—"and stablish you in every good work and word." The Received Text has ὑμᾶς after the verb, with D³ K L, but it is omitted in A B D¹ F ℵ, both Latin and both Syriac versions, and many Greek and Latin fathers. The Received Text reads also λόγῳ καὶ ἔργῳ, with F K, but the reverse order has in its favour A B D L ℵ. For an accusative to στηρίξαι, singular like the previous optatives, some would supply καρδίας, and others more rightly ὑμᾶς, from the previous ὑμῶν. The apostle prays for strength to them, ἐν pointing out the element in which that strength was to evince itself. It does not mean "for," εἰς (Grotius), nor can it signify "by means of," διά, as Chrysostom renders it, followed by Theophylact and Bengel. The sense in that case would be, "may God strengthen you by His work and word"; but with such a meaning παντὶ and ἀγαθῷ are both superfluous and inapplicable. Nor can λόγος in this position mean doctrine, τὰ ὀρθὰ δόγματα (Œcumenius, Theophylact); *sana doctrina* (Calvin). Work and word so placed have a meaning easily understood—in every good work and word, in all you do and say, may He strengthen you (Rom. xvi, 25, and Fritzsche *in loc.*). Spiritual stability so conferred in answer to such a prayer would ward off that risk of σαλευθῆναι spoken of in the second verse.

CHAPTER III

(Ver. 1.) Τὸ λοιπὸν προσεύχεσθε, ἀδελφοί, περὶ ἡμῶν—"Finally pray, brethren, for us." For τὸ λοιπὸν, as to what remains to be written, or what I have yet to say, see under 1 Thess. iv, 1; and compare under Gal. vi, 17. For περὶ ἡμῶν, see under Ephes. vi, 19.

He had been offering prayer for them, and now he asks them to offer prayer for himself and his colleagues. The prayer which he directed them to present for him was not for any personal end, but for himself and colleagues in connection with their necessary labours, and the end which such toil and self-denial had in view. These are two collateral aspects, each introduced by ἵνα, which in such a connection contains the purport of the prayer with its purpose. The first is more general and impersonal—

ἵνα ὁ λόγος τοῦ Κυρίου τρέχῃ καὶ δοξάζηται καθὼς καὶ πρὸς ὑμᾶς—"that the word of the Lord may run and be glorified even as it is also with you." By ὁ λόγος is meant the gospel, 1 Thess. i, 8; ii, 13—the genitive being that of subject. The first verb τρέχῃ expresses free and unimpeded diffusion, that it may speed its way everywhere without hindrance, all barriers of every kind being removed. Comp. Ps. cxlvii, 15; 2 Tim. ii, 9. Mere rapid spread is not enough, but the prayer comprehends "that it may be glorified," that is in its cordial reception everywhere among Jews and Gentiles, when the Saviour whom it reveals is savingly embraced; when its divine power is felt unto salvation, and all its ennobling influences are seen to mould the character into spiritual symmetry. When it thus realizes its great purpose, its glory as a divine message is manifested, Rom. xi, 13. The verb is not middle as Pelt supposes, *laudem sibi paret*, for that is not the usage of the New Testament, nor is that meaning at all sustained by the following πρὸς, which simply denotes locality. The glorification of the gospel has no allusion to any miracles wrought in its attestation. Καθὼς καὶ πρὸς ὑμᾶς—"even as it also is with you"—connected closely with the second verb, though Hoffman connects with both. But it is the glorifying of the word in its saving virtue that the apostle brings up; its diffusion was momentous to him only as a means to this end. For πρὸς, see 1 Thes. iii, 4. It had been glorified "among them," not specially in them or by them, but among them it had been accepted; and in their turning from idols and waiting for His Son from heaven, in their faith's work, their love's labour, and their hope's patience (1 Thess. i, 3), in the growth of all Christian graces in the midst of peril and persecution, the word of the Lord had been glorified also with them as in other cities. Prayer for the success of the gospel was prayer for us—περὶ ἡμῶν; he and his colleagues were so identified with the enterprise.

(Ver. 2.) καὶ ἵνα ῥυσθῶμεν ἀπὸ τῶν ἀτόπων καὶ πονηρῶν ἀνθρώπων—"and that we may be delivered from perverse and wicked men." This portion of the prayer is closely connected with the first—that the gospel may have free course and be glorified, and that we may be at liberty unhampered by ungodly adversaries to take our part in the great work of preaching and diffusing it. The present verbs of the former verse seem to denote a continuous theme and purpose, but the aorist in this clause may denote an act of deliverance from a danger really impending, ἵνα again combining the subject and the design of the prayer.

The epithet ἄτοπος is peculiar, meaning literally placeless, or not in the right place, or what is out of the way; applied to ἡδονή (Euripides, *Iph. Taur.*, 842); to ὄρνις (Aristoph., *Aves*, 276); to opinion, δοῦλοι ὄντες τῶν ἀτόπων, slaves always to novelties or paradoxes (Thucyd., iii, 30). As applied to persons, it means one who says or does what is inappropriate or out of place, *ineptus, absurdus* (Cicero *De Oratore*, ii, 4); and so often in Plato, ἐξ ἀτόπου καὶ ἀήθους (*Leg.*, i, 646 B), τοῦ θαυμαστοῦ τε καὶ ἀτόπου, (*Ep.* vii, 333 C; Ast., *Lex. Platon. sub voce*). But the word passes into a darker signification— what is unnatural or disgusting—a person who is wrongful or wicked. Thus οὐδὲν ἄτοπον, Luke xxiii, 41; Acts xxviii, 6. The anomalous easily passed into the unlawful, οὔτ' ἄτοπος ἦν ἂν οὔτε μοιχὸς οὐδὲ εἷς (Athenæus, vii, 279 c, p. 18, vol. III, ed. Schweigh.); and so μηδὲν ἄτοπον, *nihil damni* (Joseph., *Antiq.*,vi, 14; 2 Macc. xiv, 23, &c.; Kypke *in Acta*, xxviii, 6). Suidas explains ἀτοπίας, as descriptive of water, by κακίας, and renders it by such epithets as ξένον, κακόν, μοχθηρόν (*sub voce*). Philo explains in reference to the divine summons to Adam, Where art thou? that the proper answer to the question would be "nowhere." τόπον γὰρ οὐδένα ἔχει ἡ τοῦ φαύλου ψυχὴ, ᾧ ἐπιβήσεται . . . παρ' ὃ καὶ ἄτοπος λέγεται εἶναι ὁ φαῦλος . . . ἄτοπον δὲ ἐστι κακὸν δύσθετον (*Allegor.*, iii, p. 274, vol. I, ed. Mangey). Hesychius defines the term by πονηρός, αἰσχρός. See Loesner *in loc.* It represents in the Septuagint the Hebrew אָוֶן, iniquity, falsehood, (Job xi, 11; xxxvi, 21; Prov. xxx, 20); also שָׁוְא, vanity, (Job xxxv, 13); the Hiphil of רָשַׁע is expressed by ἄτοπα ποιήσειν, (Job xxxiv, 12), "surely God will not do wickedly." Compare Job xxvii, 6, οὐ γὰρ σύνοιδα ἐμαυτῷ ἄτοπα πράξας. The Vulgate here renders by *importunis*, the Claromontane by *iniquis*, and the English version in the margin by *absurd*. Macknight renders *brutish*, that is, according to the etymology, "men who have, or deserve to have, no place in society." Erasmus—*qui nulli loco convenientes quales sunt haeretici*. Estius—*forsan et ad etymon vocabuli allusit—loco nusquam consistebant*. Doddridge—those "whom no topics can work on." Different opinions have been held as to who these perverse and wicked men were. The answer will depend on the sense assigned to the next clause—

οὐ γὰρ πάντων ἡ πίστις—"for the faith does not belong to all." This use of the possessive genitive is common—Acts i, 7; 1 Cor. iii, 21; 1 Cor. vi, 19. Winer, § 30, 5. Πάντων is not to be softened into ὀλίγων (Pelt). Πίστις is most naturally the Christian faith, the want of which led such men to thwart and persecute the apostle. It cannot signify probity, as Schoettgen, Bullinger, Krause, Flatt, as if the meaning were—there are few good men whom we can safely trust. Nor can it mean true faith, as Schott, Jowett. Jowett bases on this misinterpretation the notion that the persons referred to were false brethren, apparent friends, secret enemies; so partly Calvin, Zuingli, and Flatt. The clause is meant to show why perverse and wicked men were so hostile to him, and the cause that he asked the Thessalonians to pray for his deliverance from them. It is pressing the words to give them this meaning—all men have not the capacity of faith—"have no receptivity for it," (Alford); *fidei non sunt omnes capaces*, (Crellius); similarly Pelt, De Wette, Lünemann. But the apostle does not allude to this point at all; his simple assertion refers to the fact that all men have not faith, and not to the moral or spiritual grounds of its absence. So that it is wrong to base on the clause any doctrine about divine sovereignty, or the withholding of divine grace, as is done by some. The men so referred to are described generally, and Chrysostom and Theophylact are wrong in confining the reference to heretics as Hymenaeus and Philetus. Such a class would have been named with a more specific designation. Those opponents were probably Jews; Jews in Corinth who opposed themselves and blasphemed, who in their malignity broke out in insurrection with one accord against Paul and brought him to the judgment seat of Gallio (Acts xviii, 12).

(Ver. 3.) Πιστὸς δέ ἐστιν ὁ Κύριος, ὃς στηρίξει ὑμᾶς—" but faithful is the Lord who shall establish you." Codices A D¹ F, with the Latin versions, read Θεός for Κύριος, doubtless an alteration to the more common phrase, as found in 1 Cor. i, 9; xi, 13; 2 Cor. i, 18. But Κύριος has preponderant authority in B D³ K L ℵ, the Syriac versions, &c. By Κύριος is naturally meant the Lord Jesus, and not the Father, as Schrader, Schott, Olshausen, Hilgenfeld. See under ii, 13; 1 Thess. iii, 11, 13. The Lord is the object of that faith which all men have not. Men are faithless, but (δέ) He is faithful. The paronomasia is suggestive. Winer, § 68, 2. Faithful is He, and He so faithful will confirm you, in answer to the prayer offered for them in ii, 17—a prayer suggested by the spiritual perplexities occasioned by the errors which he has been exposing.

καὶ φυλάξει ἀπὸ τοῦ πονηροῦ—" and will preserve you from the evil one." The reference in πονηροῦ is difficult, though certainly it is not a kind of collective substitute for the πονηρῶν ἀνθρώπων of the previous verse. Compare Koppe, Rosenmüller, Flatt. The word, however, may be either masculine or neuter, either the evil one, or evil in the abstract (Rom. xii, 9; 1 Thess. v, 22). Lünemann contends for the latter, because the clause is but a negative resumption of στηρίξαι ἐν παντὶ ἔργῳ καὶ λόγῳ ἀγαθῷ. But (1) the resumption is not very distinct, and it is at best but fragmentary, for it is broken by the formal τὸ λοιπὸν, and by the use of φυλάξει, introducing a new idea—preservation from evil—scarcely the full negative form of being confirmed in every good word and work. The epithet, similarly used in other parts of Scripture, seems to have a personal reference (Matt. xiii, 19; Ephes. vi, 16; 1 John iii, 12). Compare Matt. v, 37; vi, 13; 1 John v, 18 (if not a quotation). (2) The clause seems to be an echo of the clause in the Lord's prayer, and in that petition the masculine is preferable. (3) Satan is specially referred to in the previous chapter in connection with that awful development described—the personal counterpart of God. (4) The acceptance of the neuter form would be a kind of anti-climax—stablish you in every good work and word; stablish you and keep you from evil—a bare and unemphatic conclusion, implied also in the previous positive prayers. But it is impossible to decide the question—

(Ver. 4.) Πεποίθαμεν δὲ ἐν Κυρίῳ ἐφ' ὑμᾶς—"but we have confidence in the Lord as regards you." Δέ introduces an additional thought somewhat in contrast to what has been just expressed. Not only is our reliance on the Lord who is faithful, but we have also confidence towards you in the Lord. The ἐν and the ἐφ' are thus distinguished, the first with Κυρίῳ, marking the inner element or sphere in which this trust is felt, for "the Lord is faithful," and ἐφ' ὑμᾶς pointing out the objects of it, towards and on you, the personal direction. Winer, § 49 *l*; Gal. v, 10; Philip. ii, 24; Rom. xiv, 14. This relation is often expressed by the dative in classical writers. 2 Cor. i, 9. No trust could be satisfactory to him but one ἐν Κυρίῳ, especially when it concerned the future obedience of believers, His grace being so requisite to bring about the desired result. The confidence referred to the following—

ὅτι ἃ παραγγέλλομεν ὑμῖν καὶ ποιεῖτε καὶ ποιήσετε—"that the things which we command ye are both doing and will do." There are several various readings. The Received Text has ὑμῖν after παραγγέλλομεν with A D³ F K L, but it is omitted in B D¹ ℵ, two mss., the Vulgate, and some of the fathers. It is probably a correction from the 6th verse. A D¹ ℵ¹ omit καὶ before ποιεῖτε, and so does the Peshito; but perhaps it should be retained. There are other and not probable readings in B F G, B and F having καὶ ἐποιήσατε, while F omits καὶ ποιήσετε, the longer reading being preferred by Lachmann. Ὅτι introduces the matter of the apostle's confidence. The verb is not in the past tense, *quæ praecepimus*, but signifies what we are now enjoining, a transition to the commands in the following verses. What we command you is the protasis, not what we command and ye do (Erasmus), but the sense is, what we command—that ye both do and will do. The thoughts are linked together. They are prayed for that they may be stablished in every good work and word; they are established and kept from the evil one by the faithful Lord; and the apostle's confidence, resting on the same Lord, is that they, so confirmed and preserved, are obeying and will obey his mandates, which rest on Christ's authority, and are observed only through His imparted grace. He thus takes it for granted that they will act up to his anticipations, and the confidence so expressed implies a charge that they will do so. The two verbs καὶ ποιεῖτε καὶ ποιήσετε are placed in simultaneous or co-ordinate connection. Winer, § 53, 4. The verb παραγγέλλω is almost peculiar to these Thessalonian epistles, being found besides only once in 1 Tim. vi, 13, and twice in first Corinthians (1 Cor. vii, 10 ; xi, 17).

(Ver. 5.) Ὁ δὲ Κύριος κατευθύναι ὑμῶν τὰς καρδίας—"but may the Lord direct your hearts." By δέ this prayer is somewhat in contrast to the previous assertion—"we have confidence toward you that ye are doing, but over and above may He direct your hearts." For the verb see under 1 Thess. iii, 11— "We need," says Theodoret, "both good purpose and co-operation from above." The heart, "the reservoir of the entire life power," is the centre of the spiritual nature also, with its impulses, energies, resolves, and cognitions. Delitzsch, *Bib. Psych.*, iv, 12. That heart is capricious and wayward, and needs to have the way pointed out to it, and to be kept in that way by Him who alone knows it. Κύριος here is undoubtedly again the Saviour, as in the other previous verses, and not God (Hilgenfeld), nor the Holy Spirit, as the Greek fathers, Basil, Theodoret, Theophylact, Œcumenius. Basil's argument is, εἴτε γὰρ περὶ τοῦ Θεοῦ καὶ Πατρὸς ὁ λόγος πάντως ἂν εἴρητο, ὁ δὲ

Κύριος ὑμᾶς κατευθύναι εἰς τὴν ἑαυτοῦ ἀγάπην, εἴτε περὶ τοῦ Υἱοῦ, προσέκειτο ἂν εἰς τὴν ἑαυτοῦ ὑπομονήν (*De Spiritu Sancto*, xxi, pp. 60, 61, *Opera*, tom. III, Gaume, Paris). The argument of the Greek fathers who follow Basil is similar— the Lord cannot be Christ, for He is asked to direct them into the patience of Christ, as if He were a different person. But this is not the usage of the New Testament, and Χριστοῦ is repeated as being at the end of the verse, and as being in contrast with the intervening Θεοῦ. The direction of the heart is His work, who is Saviour and Lord, who by His grace and His Spirit guides and blesses His people. Self-led hearts are usually misled hearts. He prays that their hearts be directed—

εἰς τὴν ἀγάπην τοῦ Θεοῦ καὶ εἰς τὴν ὑπομονὴν τοῦ Χριστοῦ—" into the love of God and into the patience of Christ." The Received Text omits τήν before ὑπομονήν, but all MSS. have it. The words ἡ ἀγάπη τοῦ Θεοῦ may mean by themselves either God's love to us, or our love to God. To take the genitive as that of object is more in harmony with the context, love to God, τὸ ἀγαπῆσαι αὐτόν (Theophylact). So De Wette, Lünemann, &c. The other signification would not be at all suitable. The phrase is to be taken, therefore, not as meaning love enjoined by God (Clericus) nor infused by God (Pelt), nor is the sense, to imitate the love which God has shown to mankind (Macknight), nor can it be the love which God has to us, and has especially manifested in the work of redemption (Riggenbach, Olshausen). The love of God is the source of all true spiritual power, and the grand motive to all acceptable obedience. The entire decalogue is summed up into love. God, robed in perfection, is altogether lovely, and every one knowing Him and trusting Him will love Him and study to please Him. Yet the wayward heart needs to be directed by a higher power into this love—

καὶ εἰς τὴν ὑπομονὴν τοῦ Χριστοῦ—" and into the patience of Christ." For the noun see under 1 Thess. i, 3. The clause is somewhat difficult.

I. Very many understand it as the Authorized Version— "patient waiting for Christ." So Chrysostom in one of his interpretations, Œcumenius, Ambrosiaster, Erasmus, Vatablus, a-Lapide, Calvin, Benson, Hofmann. (1) But ὑπομονή never bears such a meaning. It is found thirty-four times, and has always the sense of patience, patient endurance. (2) The word used to signify, to wait for Christ, is another compound, ἀναμένειν, and its substantive might have been expected here if such were the meaning. (3) Hofmann's examples will not sustain him. In Jeremiah xiv, 8, God is called ὑπομονὴ Ἰσραήλ, a different form of expression altogether. The genitive is, therefore, not of object, nor does the similarity of the two clauses require it.

II. It is regarded by some as signifying patience on account of Christ—*patientia propter Christum praestita* (Bengel); or as De Wette—steadfastness in the cause of Christ. Such a meaning would require more than the simple genitive.

III. Nor is the genitive that of source or author—the patience which Christ bestows (Grotius, Pelt).

IV. The phrase means "the patience of Christ"—such patience as characterized Christ—the genitive being generally that of possession, or as Chrysostom distinctly puts it in one of his explanations—ἵνα ὑπομένωμεν ὡς ἐκεῖνος ὑπέμεινεν. Compare 2 Cor. i, 5. Patience under suffering characterized Christ—perfect subordination to the divine will—and such steadfastness and unmurmuring acquiescence should mark all who are Christ's. The Thessalonian believers were subjected to persecution, and they needed this patient endurance, and therefore the apostle implores Christ to lead them into this grace, which distinguished Himself with prominent fulness—no suffering like His in depth and severity, and no patience like His in its serene and self-supporting power. The apostle in the first epistle had given several warnings and premonitions about social disorders creeping into the church from the impression that the day of the Lord was on them (1 Thess. iv, 11, 12). But the restlessness and irregularities had been growing, and the wrong impression had been deepened by forged revelations, utterances, and letters. Idleness and habits of gossip and aimless gadding about had been perilously increasing. The jeopardy was imminent, the credit of Christianity was at stake, and the apostle is the more earnest and severe in his dissuasives and rebukes. The church itself in its centre was sound, but there were attached to it those busybodies whom the apostle marks as he exhorts the better portion to withdraw from fellowship with them.

(Ver. 6.) Παραγγέλλομεν δὲ ὑμῖν, ἀδελφοί, ἐν ὀνόματι τοῦ Κυρίου (ἡμῶν) Ἰησοῦ Χριστοῦ—" Now we command you, brethren, in the name of the Lord Jesus Christ." The Received Text has ἡμῶν after A D³ F K L ℵ and the Vulgate, but the pronoun is wanting in B D¹ E¹, and in the Claromontane and Sangerm. Latin. It has good authority, but it may be an interpolation from common usage. By παραγγέλλομεν δὲ the apostle resumes the ἃ παραγγέλλομεν of verse 4, and puts it as a distinct and special injunction, in the confidence that the body of the people were obeying, and would obey them, the ἀδελφοί being not the office-bearers (Olshausen), but the believing community. The charge is given solemnly—in the name of our Lord Jesus Christ, under His commission, by His authority—ἃ γὰρ ἐγὼ λέγω ἐκεῖνος λέγει (Theophylact). 1 Cor. v, 4. The charge is—

στέλλεσθαι ὑμᾶς ἀπὸ παντὸς ἀδελφοῦ ἀτάκτως περιπατοῦντος —"that ye withdraw yourselves from every brother walking disorderly." The verb is the object infinitive, the duty contained in παραγγέλλομεν. Στέλλω is properly to set or place, as an army; and figuratively, to fit out, to prepare, and then to send or despatch—the common signification. Examples of those meanings need not be given. As a nautical term it denotes to send in sail, ἱστία (*Iliad*, i, 433; *Od.*, iii, 11), and thence to draw in or to repress (Joseph., *Antiq.*, v, 8, 3), or to restrain from, ἀπὸ (Philo *De Spec. Leg.*) Polybius thus employs it, ἐκ συνηθείας καταξίωσιν στέλλεσθαι (viii, 22, 4). In the middle voice the reflexive meaning is *se subtrahere*. The idea of fear is sometimes implied, to shrink away for fear (Mal. ii, 5). Hesychius says στέλλεται, φοβεῖται. No idea of tremor can find place here. Theodoret explains it τὸ στέλλεσθαι ἀντὶ τοῦ χωρίζεσθαι; and the Vulgate, *ut subtrahatis vos;* the Syriac, ܬܬܦܪܩܘܢ ܐܢܬܘܢ. See 2 Cor. viii, 20; Heb. x, 38; and under Gal. ii, 12. See the notes of Loesner, Kypke, Elsner. For ἀτάκτως see under 1 Thess. v, 14. The adverb is explained in the context—working not at all, busybodies—in flagrant contrast to the example of industry and independence set by the apostle himself during his stay in Thessalonica.

καὶ μὴ κατὰ τὴν παράδοσιν ἣν παρελάβοσαν παρ' ἡμῶν—"and not according to the instruction which they received from us." There are difficulties about the reading of the verb. The Received Text has παρέλαβε, which has almost no authority, and is probably a grammatical correction of the plural παρελάβετε, adopted by Lachmann after B F, the Philoxenian Syriac, and some of the fathers—a reading suggested by the syntactic difficulty; παρέλαβον has D³ K L ℵ³, with several of the Greek fathers; and παρελάβοσαν is found in A ℵ¹; ἐλάβοσαν being found in D¹. The two last are different forms of the third person plural. The form in οσαν is unusual, and may have been corrected, but it is found in the Sept., Exod. xv, 27; xvi, 24; xviii, 26; Josh. v, 11; and among the Byzantine writers. Winer, § 13, 2*f;* Phavorinus, *sub voce* ἤχθοσαν, p. 228, ed. Dindorf; Lobeck, *Phrynichus*, p. 349. The third person plural has the highest authority of MSS. and versions, though the peculiar form cannot be satisfactorily decided. Only, the less common Alexandrian form would be more likely to be altered than to be inserted. The plural is a construction as to sense, παντός having a collective force. Jelf, § 378 *a*. For παράδοσις see under ii, 15. It signifies instruction, given by the apostle either orally or in writing (1 Thess. iv, 11, 12), both being implied, as we learn from the following verse. Παράδοσις is here not instruction by example, as the Greek fathers and Hofmann, for that would be an anticipation of what follows, but the instruction given so distinctly, παρ' ἡμῶν, was illustrated and fortified by example, as is afterwards shown. From every one walking in this lawless way—indolent, fanatical, and self-duped—they were to separate themselves. Nothing like excommunication is spoken of—they were to avoid all intercourse with these disorderly neighbours. They are not bidden to thrust them out of church fellowship, but they were to avoid all fellowship with them, and to show in this way their decided disapproval of their inconsistencies which were bringing dishonour on the faith.

(Ver. 7.) αὐτοὶ γὰρ οἴδατε πῶς δεῖ μιμεῖσθαι ἡμᾶς—"for ye

yourselves know how ye ought to follow us." Γάρ, confirmatory and illustrative of the wisdom and necessity of the previous injunction—"yourselves know it," we need not tell you now. For μιμεῖσθαι see under 1 Thess. i, 6. Yourselves know how ye ought to live, in imitation of us. Our life lays you under obligation to copy it. On this point the reference is not the general imitation of Christian graces, but this special aspect of the apostle's conduct.

ὅτι οὐκ ἠτακτήσαμεν ἐν ὑμῖν—"for we behaved not disorderly among you." Ὅτι is causal, or "secondary causal," as Ellicott expresses it, meaning not so much because, as seeing that—an argument and an example. Ἀτακτεῖν, a verb occurring only here, is the same in meaning as ἀτάκτως περιπατεῖν. The adjective occurs only in 1 Thess. v, 14, and the adverb in verses 6 and 11. See under 1 Thess. v, 14; Kypke, *in loc.* The disorder is specified immediately. Hofmann artificially takes ὅτι with οἴδατε—ye know how ye ought to follow us, and, as a parallel clause, ye know that we were not disorderly, bringing verse 9 under the same vinculum. The apostle appeals to his own conduct and to their estimate of it. He asserts about it what he felt assured they would unanimously affirm—

(Ver. 8.) οὐδὲ δωρεὰν ἄρτον ἐφάγομεν παρά τινος—"neither did we eat bread for nought from any one." Ἄρτον φαγεῖν, in imitation of אכל לחם, means to take food, bread being the staff of life (Gen. xliii, 25; 2 Sam. ix, 7; Prov. xxiii, 6; Mark vi, 36) = ἐσθίειν in ver. 10. Δωρεὰν, emphatic in position, is like μακράν, an adverbial accusative; *gratis,* Vulgate. See under Gal. ii, 21. Παρά τινος is a familiar idiom—"off any one"—that is, at any one's expense. This food was not a gift from any body; he earned it for himself. In the highest sense his sustenance would not have been δωρεάν, "for the labourer is worthy of his meat" (1 Cor. ix); but his meaning is that he set an example of honest industry, and maintained himself by manual toil.

ἀλλ' ἐν κόπῳ καὶ μόχθῳ νύκτα καὶ ἡμέραν ἐργαζόμενοι—"but in toil and travel, day and night working." The genitive reading νυκτὸς καὶ ἡμέρας has B F ℵ in its favour. It may, however, be an assimilation to 1 Thess. ii, 9; iii, 10.

There is no need to regard the participle as irregularly used for the finite verb, or to supply ἦμεν. Winer, 45, 8. The words may be understood in two ways: (1) Ἐργαζόμενοι, as a modal participle, may belong to ἄρτον ἐφάγομεν, as in contrast to δωρεάν—but we ate bread, working night and day, not δωρεάν (Alford, Riggenbach, Lünemann). (2) Or ἐν κόπῳ καὶ μόχθῳ may be the positive complement, in opposition to δωρεάν, of ἄρτον ἐφάγομεν, and νύκτα καὶ ἡμέραν ἐργαζόμενοι, an explanatory parallel; that is, we did not eat bread for nought, but we ate it in toil and labour, as we wrought night and day (De Wette, Winer, Conybeare, Lillie, Ellicott, Hofmann). The emphatic position, Ellicott remarks, requires the sharper antithesis. There is in either way a full antithesis. We did not eat bread (δωρεάν) at any one's expense; on the contrary (ἀλλά), we ate it in toil and travel, working day and night. Δωρεάν is denied by the severity of the toil, and denied also by its continuity; it was heavy and unintermitted. For the two pairs of nouns see under 1 Thess. ii, 9; iii, 10.

Μόχθος in the New Testament occurs only in connection with κόπος—a terse and familiar idiom—toil to weariness, labour to utter exhaustion.

πρὸς τὸ μὴ ἐπιβαρῆσαί τινα ὑμῶν—"that we might not be burdensome to any of you." See under 1 Thess. ii, 9, where the same words occur with the very same inference.

(Ver. 9.) The next clause is a qualifying limitation—οὐχ ὅτι οὐκ ἔχομεν ἐξουσίαν—"not that we have not power." The clause is a restriction of the previous utterance to prevent misunderstanding. 2 Cor. i, 24; iii, 5; Philip. iii, 12; iv, 11, 17; and examples in Hartung, II, p. 153. The sense is—we did this, not because we have not power τοῦ μὴ ἐργάζεσθαι (1 Cor. ix, 6), or τοῦ δωρεὰν φαγεῖν ἄρτον; the apostle reserved his right of ministerial support, though he might occasionally waive it, as in this instance. See the long argument in 1 Cor. ix. What he did in Thessalonica and what he was doing at Corinth was not to be regarded as any surrender of his claim. His purpose was—

ἀλλ' ἵνα ἑαυτοὺς τύπον δῶμεν ὑμῖν εἰς τὸ μιμεῖσθαι ἡμᾶς— "but in order that we should give ourselves as an example

Ver. 10.] SECOND EPISTLE TO THE THESSALONIANS 313

to you that ye should imitate us;" that is, but foregoing our right we wrought and earned our bread, to set you an example. The pronoun ἑαυτούς, originally belonging to the third person, is used here for ἡμᾶς αὐτούς. Winer, § 22, 5; Bernhardy, p. 272; Rom. viii, 23; and for the second person, John xii, 8; Philip. ii, 12. The purpose, τύπον δῶμεν, is prefaced by the telic ἵνα, and its farther connected object, εἰς τό, was that you should imitate us. He abstained from his right in order that he might set an example, and he set that example in order that it might be followed. A practical purpose, one of immediate moment and utility, was ever before him in all his actions. There needed an example of honest, unashamed industry in that church, some members of which were prone to idleness, and the apostle in self-denying care set it, working to utter weariness, and toiling at hours when other people rested, "day and night." He was in no way ashamed of his handicraft labour, or of the special form of it to which he had been trained.

(Ver. 10.) Καὶ γὰρ ὅτε ἦμεν πρὸς ὑμᾶς τοῦτο παρηγγέλλομεν ὑμῖν—"for also when we were with you, this we charged you." Γὰρ is apparently co-ordinate with γὰρ in verse 7—"a second confirmation of the wisdom and pertinence of the preceding warning" (Ellicott). He takes καὶ simply as connective, serving to connect the two verses. Lünemann and Alford give καὶ an ascensive force, referring it to the following τοῦτο, as bringing out an additional element in the reminiscence. Winer, § 53, 8. Hofmann thus understands it—for even when we were with you, already at that time we commanded you. This is virtually the view of Theodoret—οὐδὲν καινὸν ὑμῖν γράφομεν—but what from the beginning we taught you. But καὶ is not related to the record of the sojourn which underlies the previous verses; it rather belongs to τοῦτο παραγγέλλομεν—we laboured and earned our bread, foregoing our just claim; that was our example, and this also was our familiar command—we were commanding you, the verb being in the imperfect.

For πρὸς ὑμᾶς, see under 1 Thess. iii, 4. Τοῦτο refers to what follows—

ὅτι εἴ τις οὐ θέλει ἐργάζεσθαι μηδὲ ἐσθιέτω—"that if any one will not work, neither let him eat." For the use of εἰ οὐ, as distinct from εἰ μή, except in the New Testament—the negative coalescing with εἰ to express a single idea—see Winer, 55, 2 c; Gayler, p. 99, &c. The phrase is an oratorical enthymeme warranting its converse; but every one does eat, therefore let every one labour. 1 Cor. xi, 6. There is an allusion to Gen. iii, 19—" In the sweat of thy face shalt thou eat bread till thou return unto the ground." The form of the saying is proverbial as the expression of a universal law. If one can work and will not, or if he cannot dig, and is ashamed to beg, then he must starve or steal. Of course there are exceptions, when there is physical inability or work cannot be had—*nolle vitium est* (Bengel)—but as a general principle, eating presupposes working according to divine arrangement, and strength to earn food and health to enjoy it are comprised in the petition, "Give us this day our daily bread." The idlers referred to had no right to "sorn" on their friends or burden the funds of the church. There does not appear to have been such a common table, such a fraternal community of goods as Ewald supposes. Similar sentiments are found in Jewish authors.

(Ver. 11.) Ἀκούομεν γὰρ τινας περιπατοῦντας ἐν ὑμῖν ἀτάκτως—"For we hear of some walking among you disorderly." Γὰρ assigns the reason for the repetition of the παραγγελία, and does not, as in Hofmann's view, refer to the whole section, verses 6-10. The participle marks or asserts the state as now in existence, and so far differs from the infinitive. Winer, § 45, 4; Scheuerlein, § 45, 5; Kühner, §§ 657-664. Only a small portion of the church is thus characterized, τινας; and for the adverb see under verse 6, and under 1 Thess. v, 14. What the disorderliness consisted in is now stated—

μηδὲν ἐργαζομένους ἀλλὰ περιεργαζομένους—"doing no business, but being busybodies." The verb περιεργάζομαι occurs only here. It signified originally to work round a thing, or with great pains. Thus it was said of Theon the painter, καὶ πλέον οὐδὲν περιείργασται τῷ Θέωνι. Æl. *Var. Hist.*, ii, 44, and the note of Perizonius on the verb. The accusation of Diogenes against Socrates was περιειργάσθαι γὰρ καὶ τῷ οἰκιδίῳ (Do., iv, 12). Then it signifies to overdo—to be a busybody.

Ἐν τοῖς περισσοῖς τῶν ἔργων σου μὴ περιεργάζου (Sirach, iii, 23.) Σωκράτης ἀδικεῖ καὶ περιεργάζεται ζητῶν τὰ τε ὑπὸ γῆς καὶ τὰ ἐπουράνια (Plato, *Apol.*, 19, B). Περίεργος is similarly employed in 1 Tim. v, 13. Compare Titus i, 10. Hesychius gives it quaintly, ποιητὸν ἐποίησα—*factum feci*. Theophylact explains it as idleness, carried away to useless things, curiously inquiring into other people's lives, and thence falling εἰς καταλαλίας, ἀργολογίας, εὐτραπελίας, Theodoret says the characteristics of the idle are ἀδολεσχία καὶ φλυαρία καὶ ἡ ἀνόνητος πολυπραγμοσύνη. It is difficult to imitate in a translation the paronomasia. Demosthenes has ἐξ ὧν ἐργάζῃ καὶ περιεργάζῃ (*Philip.*, iv, p. 96, vol. I, *Opera*, ed. Schaefer); and Quintilian has *non agere sed satagere* (*Institut.*, vi, 3, 54, p. 257, vol. I, *Opera*, ed. Gernhard). The phrase has been variously translated—*nihil facientes, sed curiose agentes* (Erasmus); *nihil operantes, sed circumoperantes* (Estius); *nihil operis agentes, sed curiose satagentes* (Calvin); *thund nüt und thund zevil*—"they do nothing and do too much"— (Zuingli in his old German); *ne travaillant point, mais se travaillant pour rien* (French version); *nicht arbeit treibend sondern sich herumtreibend*; "working nothing, but overworking" (Webster and Wilkinson); "doing nothing, but overdoing" (Robinson). The lines of Phædrus come to mind—

"*Trepide concursans, occupata in otio,
Gratis anhelans, multa agendo nihil agens.*"

Phædrus, II, 5. See under 1 Thess. iii, 11, 12.

(Ver. 12.) Τοῖς δὲ τοιούτοις παραγγέλλομεν καὶ παρακαλοῦμεν ἐν Κυρίῳ Ἰησοῦ Χριστῷ—"Now them who are such we charge and exhort in the Lord Jesus Christ." The Received Text has διὰ τοῦ Κυρίου ἡμῶν Ἰησοῦ Χριστοῦ, on the authority of D³ K L ℵ³, many mss., and the Greek fathers; but our text is supported by the higher authority of A B D¹ F ℵ¹, with the Latin versions and fathers, the Received Text being probably a correction to the more usual formula. The phrase τοῖς τοιούτοις takes in the whole class who have been so characterized (Krüger, § 50, 4, 6); *de toto genere eorum, qui tales sunt usurpatur* (Kühner *in Xen. Mem.*, i, 5, 2). The dative belongs specially to the first verb, as the second verb governs the accusative—αὐτούς—understood. Both verbs "we command and exhort" the one strengthening the other—authority and earnestness combined—are connected with "in the Lord Jesus Christ," as the sphere in which they realize themselves. The matter was of no small moment to the welfare of the church and the progress of the gospel, and therefore the charge is given in this solemn and authoritative form. See under 1 Thess. iv, 1. The purpose and matter of the charge was—

ἵνα μετὰ ἡσυχίας ἐργαζόμενοι τὸν ἑαυτῶν ἄρτον ἐσθίωσιν—"that working with quietness they eat their own bread." They were to work and no longer to go "loafing" about—intermeddling disturbers—doing everything but what they ought to do; but they were to give themselves to their proper occupation, and that with quietness, μετὰ denoting the accompaniment of their industry. Winer, § 47 h. The phrase stands opposed to ἀτάκτως . . . περιεργαζόμενοι. Their life and conduct were to be in contrast to what they had been. So far from idling they were to work; so far from overworking themselves in laborious trifling, they were to toil with quietness—with a tranquil mind and without any unnecessary bustle. And working in this way they were to eat—

τὸν ἑαυτῶν ἄρτον—"their own bread"—special moment on ἑαυτῶν—what is theirs as having quietly and honestly earned it, according to the repeated injunction and after the example of the apostle who did not eat any man's bread for nought, but wrought with labour and travail night and day, that he might not be chargeable to any of them.

(Ver. 13.) Ὑμεῖς δὲ, ἀδελφοὶ, μὴ ἐνκακήσητε καλοποιοῦντες—"But ye, brethren, be not dispirited in well-doing." The Received Text has εκκ, but ενκ is found in A B D¹ ℵ. For the forms and the meaning of the verb, see under Gal. vi, 9. For the use and meaning of the participle, see under verse 11.

Ye, brethren, on the other hand (δὲ), who have maintained the true course, unaffected by these examples of pernicious and fanatical idleness; "brethren," the sound portion of the church, who obeyed the precept and followed the example of the apostle.

The Greek fathers give to καλοποιοῦντες a restricted meaning suggested by the context. Chrysostom says, "withdraw yourselves from them and reprove them, do not, however, suffer them to perish with hunger;" the well-doing being confined in that case to almsgiving or beneficence. He is followed by Theophylact, Œcumenius, and Theodoret who says expressly μὴ νικήσῃ τὴν ὑμετέραν φιλοτιμίαν ἡ ἐκείνων μοχθηρία. This view has also been adopted by Calvin, Estius, Flatt, Pelt, De Wette, Ewald, Bisping, Bloomfield, and, to some extent, Olshausen. The meaning in that case might be that, while they had seen examples of kindness abused on the part of the slothful, their hearts were not to be shut against cases deserving of pity and support; they were to make a distinction between the lazy poor and the really poor. This is Koppe's view virtually, which implies greatly more than the apostle has expressed. But this interpretation restricts unnecessarily the meaning of the participle. The compound verb, which occurs only here, is a later term for τὸ καλὸν ποιεῖν. In Lev. v, 4 (Codex A), we have καλῶς ποιῆσαι as opposed to κακοποιεῖν, (Lobeck, *Phryn.*, p. 200). The meaning is to do well, *so handeln wie es gut und recht ist*—the contrast in καλο being to the loose and dishonourable lives of the persons reprobated in the previous verses. Lünemann's restriction is too narrow and negative, *persist in* not allowing yourselves to be tainted by their evil example. It is better to take the word in its wide or general sense, and as explained also by the context. They were not to weary in acting fairly and honourably on all occasions, in doing all that was right and good in all spheres of life and duty, more especially in whatever these previous warnings and charges implied, and there was the more need of their consistent perseverance, as others had deflected from the honest and blameless course.

(Ver. 14.) Εἰ δέ τις οὐχ ὑπακούει τῷ λόγῳ ἡμῶν διὰ τῆς ἐπιστολῆς, τοῦτον σημειοῦσθε—"But if any man obey not our word by the epistle, that man mark." The connection of διὰ τῆς ἐπιστολῆς has been disputed, whether it should be joined to what precedes or to what comes after it.

I. The phrase has been connected with the verb σημειοῦσθε in two ways. First, ἡ ἐπιστολή has been taken to mean this Second Epistle, and the meaning assigned is—"by means of this epistle mark him;" that is, as Pelt says, *eum hac epistola freti severius tractate et a consortio vestro secludite;* or as Bengel, *notate, notâ censoria; hanc epistolam, ejus admonendi causa, adhibentes, eique inculcantes ut, aliorum judicio perspecto, se demittat.* But this interpretation gives the verb a meaning which cannot be sustained.

II. Secondly, with the same verbal connection, some regard ἡ ἐπιστολή as a letter to be sent by the Thessalonians to the apostle, the sense then being, mark such an one by means of a letter sent to me about him. This has been a common interpretation, held by Luther, Calvin, Musculus, Hemming, Balduin, Grotius, Zachariae, Koppe. Winer allows its possibility (§ 18, 9, 3), and it is found in the margin of the Authorized Version, "signify that man by an epistle." "Yf eny man obey not our sayinges, send us word of him by a letter."—*Tyndale* followed by *Cranmer* and *Genevan*. "If any obey not our word, note him by an epistle."—*Rheims*. "If any man obey not our doctrine, signifie him by an epistle."—*Bishops'*. But there are strong objections to such an interpretation. (1) In the phrase διὰ τῆς ἐπιστολῆς the article cannot specify a letter still to be written, nor is there any probability in the explanation of Winer, "in the letter which you have then to write and which I then hope to receive from you." Neither can it mean your answer to this letter, for it is not implied in the context. The article τῆς would denote either this or an earlier one, were there any allusion to it in the previous verses. (2) The phrase διὰ τῆς ἐπιστολῆς would with this interpretation have from its position an unaccountable emphasis upon it. (3) The present order of the words is against this view, and the expected order would be τοῦτον διὰ τῆς ἐπιστολῆς σημειοῦσθε. (4) Nor does the middle σημειοῦσθε agree well with the notion of a letter sent by them to the apostle, it would rather be "mark out for us," ἡμῖν. (5) It can scarcely be supposed, that after what he has said on the subject in verse 6, the apostle should ask or expect any communication on the subject of those persons, the treatment of whom he has thus described and enjoined. There is nothing leading us to suppose that the churches could not note such an one without consulting the apostle. Such a correspondence must have been precarious from Paul's frequent change of residence, and as Riggenbach says, "what a paralysis of all self-dependence would it have involved!" And therefore the other interpretation is to be preferred which connects διὰ τῆς ἐπιστολῆς with the immediately preceding word, τῷ λόγῳ ἡμῶν, our word or deliverance conveyed to you by this letter; the λόγος supposed to be disobeyed being found in verse 12, and ἡ ἐπιστολή, meaning the letter under hand, as in Rom. xvi, 22; Col. iv, 16; 1 Thess. v, 27. Compare 1 Cor. v, 9. Chrysostom's comment implies this construction; Œcumenius has τῷ διὰ τῆς ἐπιστολῆς ἀποσταλέντι. The view has been held by Estius, Piscator, Aretius, a-Lapide, Beza, Fromond, Hammond, Schott, Olshausen, De Wette, Baumgarten-Crusius, Bisping, Ewald, Hofmann, Riggenbach, Ellicott, and Alford. A. Buttmann, p. 80. It is no objection to this construction that τῷ is not repeated after ἡμῶν—τῷ λόγῳ ἡμῶν τῷ διὰ—for τῷ λόγῳ ἡμῶν διὰ τῆς ἐπιστολῆς is one idea—a written injunction. Winer, § 20, 2; Fritzsche's note *ad Rom.* iii, 25. The Syriac reads—if any one hearken not to these our words in the epistle, ܒܐܓܪܬܐ; and the Vulgate follows the Greek order, *verbo nostro per epistolam*. If any one obey not our word or utterance conveyed by this letter which I am now writing, note such an one.

τοῦτον σημειοῦσθε καὶ μὴ συναναμίγνεσθε αὐτῷ, or, μὴ συναναμίγνυσθαι αὐτῷ.—The Received Text inserts καὶ, as in the first reading, on the authority of D¹ F K L, the Vulgate and Syriac versions, with Basil, Ambrosiaster, and Augustine; but καὶ is omitted in A B D³ ℵ 17, the Claromont. and Sangerm. Latin, the Gothic version, with Chrysostom. The infinitive, again, is read in A B D¹ ℵ, in the Claromont. and Sangerm. Latin, the Gothic versions, with Chrysostom. Ellicott, however, remarks that the reading of the last syllable cannot well be decided by the reading of MSS., as there is a constant interchange of ε and αι by itacism. Perhaps the infinitive is, from the omission of the καὶ, the older reading—compare 1 Cor. v, 9, which yet may have suggested the infinitive here. The meaning is the same whichever reading may be adopted. Τοῦτον—that man, held up and emphasized. The verb σημειοῦσθε occurs only here in the New Testament. It denotes in the active to put a mark on, or to distinguish by means of a σημεῖον, verbs in οω having this factitive meaning. It is used in the passive of a road marked in its distances by milestones (Polyb., iii, 398), also of letters, σεσημειώμενας τῇ τοῦ πατρὸς σφραγῖδι (Dion Halicar., iv, 57). In the middle it denotes to mark for oneself (Polybius, xxii, 11, 12; compare Sept., Ps. iv, 6). Thomas Magister, quoting Aristophanes, says that ἀποσημαίνεσθαι is the proper term (p. 337, 7th ed., Ritschl). The middle has its dynamic force (Krüger, § 52, 8, 4). They were to put a σημεῖον on such an one—to note him that they might avoid him. The double compound infinitive is a characteristic of the later Greek. 1 Cor. v, 9, 11; compare Sept., Hosea vii, 8 (Codex A). It occurs in Athenæus, οἱ μὲν Γεργῖνοι συναναμιγνύμενοι τοῖς κατὰ τὴν πόλιν (vi, 68, p. 481, *Opera*, vol. II, ed. Schweigh.; Plutarch, *Philopœm.*, 21). They were to have no fraternal intercourse with such an one—much the same advice as that given already in v. 6. How much is implied in this withdrawal from intercourse it is impossible to say. The object is—

ἵνα ἐντραπῇ—"that he may be shamed." The verb is passive, not middle, as Pelt takes it, *intus converti, ad se ipsum quasi redire;* so Grotius. 1 Cor. iv, 14; Titus ii, 8. The middle with the accusative occurs in Luke xviii, 2, and the noun in 1 Cor. vi, 5; xv, 34. This shame, produced by the withdrawal of his brethren from fellowship with him, was meant to induce thought, contrition, and reform.

(Ver. 15.) καὶ μὴ ὡς ἐχθρὸν ἡγεῖσθε—"and regard him not as an enemy." Καὶ is not for ἀλλά (Jowett, De Wette), but is simply connective—joining a command, not opposed to the previous one, but in harmony with it, and showing the spirit in which it is to be carried out. For ὡς see under ii, 2; it qualifies ἐχθρόν. He is not to be regarded in the light of an enemy. Compare ὥσπερ with the same verb in Job xix, 11; xxxiii, 10, representing חָשַׁב; Col. iii, 23. He was not, as an enemy, to be repelled and battled with. He had indeed become inconsistent; a false impression about the Second Advent had led him sadly astray; he was neglecting immediate secular duty, and had fallen into perilous habits of indolent dissipation of time; but he was still to be counted a brother, as he had not forsaken the faith, or cut himself off from communion by notorious immorality, or by a relapse into heathen creed and profligacy.

ἀλλὰ νουθετεῖτε ὡς ἀδελφόν — "but admonish him as a brother," the one ὡς corresponding to the other. Νουθετεῖν, to correct by word and then deed. See under 1 Thess. v, 12. Theophylact says, νουθετεῖν προσέταξεν, οὐκ ὀνειδίζειν; still as a brother, though an erring one, was he to be kindly dealt with; undue severity was to be avoided, the purpose being not to frown him away, but to win him back.

(Ver. 16.) Αὐτὸς δὲ ὁ Κύριος τῆς εἰρήνης δῴη ὑμῖν τὴν εἰρήνην διὰ παντὸς ἐν παντὶ τρόπῳ—"Now may the Lord of peace Himself give you peace by all means, evermore and in every way." The reading τρόπῳ is well supported, having in its favour A^2 B D^3 K L $\aleph$, almost all mss., with the Syriac and Coptic versions, Theodoret and Damascenus. On the other hand τόπῳ is found in A^1 D^1 F, two mss., in the Vulgate and Claromontane Latin versions, in the Gothic version, and in Chrysostom. The unusual phrase ἐν παντὶ τρόπῳ is thus well authenticated; the other, ἐν παντὶ τόπῳ, was somewhat familiar, being found in 1 Cor. i, 2; 2 Cor. ii, 14; 1 Tim. ii, 8. As Bouman remarks, the reference to time in διὰ παντὸς would naturally suggest to the copyist a reference to place— ἐν παντὶ τόπῳ. By δέ he passes to a prayer, as in contrast to the previous injunction, as in 1 Thess. v, 23, the αὐτός being emphatic. See also under ii, 16. By ὁ Κύριος Christ is to be understood, and we have ὁ Θεός similarly, Rom. xv, 33; xvi, 20; 2 Cor. xiii, 11; Philip. iv. 9; Heb. xiii, 20. For the relation expressed by the genitive, see under 1 Thess. v, 23—God of peace, characterized by peace, and especially the giver of it. The Greek fathers unnecessarily and unwarrantably restrict this peace to concord—to peace among themselves, and their view is followed by Estius, Calovius, Pelt—Schott including both outer and inner peace— and Calvin, "the bridling of the refractory." But there is nothing in the epistle to imply that the peace had been broken, or that alienation and disunion were afflicting the Thessalonian church. The peace—τῆς εἰρήνης, τὴν εἰρήνην—is peace in its widest and profoundest sense, the peace of God that passes all understanding, blessed confidence, conscious acceptance, joyous anticipation; and that διὰ παντός, "always," without intermission, not periodically (Matt. xviii, 10; Acts ii, 25; Rom. xi, 10); "and in every way," ἐν παντὶ τρόπῳ—in every possible form and mode in which God can give it and you accept it—for time, for eternity, for earth, for heaven. The stress is on ὑμῖν, "on you," that you may realize this peace, and be kept from all spiritual disturbance—all disquietude such as that felt by those who imagined that the day of Christ was at hand. This wish or prayer is, as Lünemann remarks, the apostolic way of saying *valete* or ἔρρωσθε—as the classic writers employ *salutem* or εὖ πράττειν.

ὁ Κύριος μετὰ πάντων ὑμῶν—"the Lord be with you all." A brief but all-inclusive benediction, invoking the presence of Christ to be with them in its benign and cheering influences, in its guiding and sustaining power. With you all—πάντων, not pleonastic (Jowett), but comprehensive; the brother walking disorderly and to be admonished, if he be not contumacious, is not excluded.

(Ver. 17.) Ὁ ἀσπασμὸς τῇ ἐμῇ χειρὶ Παύλου, ὅ ἐστι σημεῖον ἐν πάσῃ ἐπιστολῇ· οὕτως γράφω—"The salutation by the hand of me, Paul, which is a token in every epistle: so I write." The Authorized Version renders the first clause in three ways—"the salutation of me, Paul, with mine own hand," (1 Cor. xvi, 21); "the salutation by the hand of me, Paul," (Col. iv, 18); and here "the salutation of Paul, with mine own hand." Παύλου is a species of appositional genitive with ἐμῇ. Jelf, § 467. The neuter ὅ is not in attraction with σημεῖον (Winer, § 24, 3), instead of ὅς, the antecedent being ἀσπασμός, but refers to the fact of the previous clause—which circumstance, which salutation in mine own hand is a token or mark of authorship or genuineness in every epistle. Up till this verse the epistle had been dictated by the apostle and written by an amanuensis. But verses 17, 18 are autographic, and are meant to authenticate the letter as his own composition, and to show in contrast that it was not ὡς δι' ἡμῶν, ii, 2. His own handwriting was the voucher, σημεῖον. It is apparently wrong to suppose that the apostle wrote only the last verse. Chrysostom says ἀσπασμὸν καλεῖ τὴν εὐχήν, an opinion repeated by Theophylact—Theodoret saying more explicitly ἀσπασμὸν ἐκάλεσε τὴν ἐν τῷ τέλει κειμένην εὐλογίαν, and the view is adopted by Estius, Piscator, a-Lapide, Beza, Bengel, Baur, Hofmann, and Riggenbach. But the mere benediction in itself can scarcely be called a salutation while the salutation implies and is naturally followed by the benediction. The words which express the salutation and its character are in his own hand, and he naturally writes also the brief benediction which follows the saluting words. And this autographic σημεῖον was to be ἐν πάσῃ ἐπιστολῇ, "in every epistle." Theophylact in his first explanation, τῇ ἴσως πεμφθησομένῃ πρὸς ὑμᾶς, and Lünemann, restrict the reference too much when they suppose the meaning to be, in every epistle which he might purpose to send to the Thessalonian church. For we find at least that he adopted the practice in writing to other churches; though, in consequence of the letter forged in his name and circulated in Thessalonica (ii, 2), he began this mode of authentication in writing to the church in that city. Lünemann objects that the authentication is not found in all the epistles written after this date, and that therefore the phrase must be taken in a relative, not in an absolute sense. It is found, however, in all that seem to require it. It does not occur in first Thessalonians, for circumstances had not then arisen to necessitate it; but it is found in Colossians, and the first epistle to the Corinthians. The circumstances in which the other epistles were sent might make such authentication superfluous. In the epistle to the Romans, the last three or four verses were probably autographic; the epistle to the Galatians was, contrary to his usual custom, written wholly with his own hand; the second epistle to the Corinthians was sent by Titus, and the greeting and benediction may have been autographic; the epistle to the Ephesians was sent by Tychicus, who himself could vouch for it, but the apostle may have written the last verse; that to the Philippians was carried by Epaphroditus, though the apostle again, probably without saying it, added the last verse; the epistle to Philemon was apparently a holograph; so in all likelihood were those sent to individuals, as Timothy and Titus. It was, not, however, what the apostle wrote, but his handwriting that proved the genuineness of the letter, and his handwriting being so different from that of the copyist, he did not always need formally to call attention to it. Grotius wrongly infers from this verse that this epistle was the first sent to Thessalonica. See Introduction. The words οὕτως γράφω are to be taken in the simplest signification, "so I write," "witness my hand," referring to the manner and form of letters in which verses 17, 18 were written. See his own account of it, πηλίκα γράμματα, under Gal. vi, 11. The clause refers, therefore, simply to the manner—not ταῦτα but only οὕτως, this is my handwriting—so that it is wrong to suppose that the apostle added anything as a specimen, such as his name or signature; *certum quendam nexum literarum, quo nomen suum scribebat* (Grotius); or, as a-Lapide describes it— *sicut jam multi signum manus ut vocant, per certos gyros, quos non facile sit imitari;* or some ingenious monogram— *nomen Pauli monogrammate aliquo expressum ab ipso fuisse, conjunctis scilicet apte literis* Π *and* A, *posteriori hoc elemento paulo altius evecto, ut* A *simul referret;* and for this opinion Zeltner adduces seven reasons, one example being that the Emperor Charles employed such a signature. But, as Wolf argues, the apostle refers to no occult or inimitable signature, and though the custom referred to may have been common among the later rabbis, it cannot be ascribed certainly to the apostolic age. The conjecture is too artificial, the apostle often naming himself in the simplest manner possible, as 2 Cor. x, 1; Gal. v, 2; Ephes. iii, 3; Col. i, 23; 1 Thess. ii, 18; Philemon 19. Bengel's notion is similar—*Paulum singulari et inimitabili pictura et ductu literarum expressisse illud, gratia, &c.*, verse 18. The view of Œcumenius is liable to the same objection—that the apostle wrote down some words, οἷον τὸ ἀσπάζομαι ὑμᾶς ἢ τὸ Ἔρρωσθε, ἢ τι τοιοῦτον. To say with Lünemann that the apostle's use of the phrase for the first time would imply that his handwriting was unknown to the Thessalonians, is an inference balanced by the conjecture that he may have written the salutation of the first epistle without calling attention to it—

(Ver. 18.) ἡ χάρις τοῦ Κυρίου ἡμῶν Ἰησοῦ Χριστοῦ μετὰ πάντων ὑμῶν—"the grace of our Lord Jesus Christ be with you all." The concluding benediction is the same as that of the first epistle (see under 1 Thess. v, 28), with the exception of πάντων here—not a word of course, but showing that those were not excluded who had incurred his rebuke. His full heart includes in his parting blessing the entire church without exception, and the epistle, like the first one, would be "read unto all the holy brethren." The 'Αμήν is usually bracketed or omitted. Though it is found in A D F K L ℵ³, it is most probably a liturgical conclusion. The subscription ἀπὸ 'Αθηνῶν, with its variation, is certainly to be rejected.

ΠΡΟΣ ΘΕΣΣΑΛΟΝΙΚΕΙΣ, Β.

ESSAY

ON

THE MAN OF SIN

THE MAN OF SIN

2 THESS. II, 3-10.

THE various points in this paragraph are: that prior to the Advent, which had been regarded as come, there are to be the apostacy and the revelation of the Man of Sin; that he opposes God, and exalts himself above God and every object of worship; that he seats himself in God's temple, exhibiting himself as God; that the Mystery of Iniquity had already begun to work, but was retarded by some mightier influence, on the removal of which the Lawless one should be revealed; that his power and craft should be Satanic in character and result; and that he shall be destroyed by the Lord at His second and personal coming at the end of the present dispensation.

(1) The first question is, Is this utterance a prophecy in the true sense of the term? (2) If it is a prophecy, has it been already fulfilled, or has there been any person or any system verifying the description given? (3) But if history presents no one so audacious as to displace God, usurp His seat, and arrogate His worship, does the oracle remain to be fulfilled, and may we or can we form any conjecture about the time and region of its fulfilment, its ominous antecedents, its development, and its dark and malignant consolidation?

I

IS IT A PROPHECY?

(1) Some deny it to be a prophecy. Tychsen thought that the passage was a quotation, clause by clause, from a

letter which the Thessalonians had sent to the apostle, a hypothesis that has not even ingenuity to recommend it. (2) Others, admitting its prophetic form and features, so idealize it that it ceases to be in any true sense a prediction. According to this view it presents a vivid lesson, the minuter features of which are not meant to be separately considered, for they contribute only to the general impression—are a kind of sombre drapery, or a dark background to the portrait. The apostle simply gives a vivid view of his own forebodings, many of them created by his own personal history, so that the futurity does not stretch beyond his own horizon. Thus Schneckenburger regards the paragraph as merely the personification of evil, the climax of antagonism to the Gospel, a general defection prior to its great triumphs—the ὁ κατέχων being the imperial power of Rome, and the μυστήριον, Jewish sorcery penetrating into heathendom, as in the case of Elymas. Koppe says, that the apostle has only bodied forth the general prophetic creed of the Jews, which they gathered from the prophecies of Daniel—an awful outbreak of ungodliness after the apostle's own time, he himself in his apostolical energy and earnestness being the restraining power (ὁ κατέχων), taken away at his death. The view advocated by Pelt is somewhat similar, that the "Adversary" is the consummation of spiritual evil, which *in Pontificiorum Romanorum operibus ac serie luculentissime sese prodiit;* that the mystery already working was the tendency to fall back to the Jewish legalism, false γνῶσις and angelolatry; that the restraining power is the will of God, holding back the kingdom of Satan; that the instrumentality is the *imperii Romani vis;* and that the coming of the Lord is but *regni divini victoria,* thus denying personality to the Man of Sin and also the Second Advent. Storr holds a like opinion—that the verses forebode the outbreak of a virulent and powerful opposition to God and all religion at some future and unknown period, and that by τὸ κατέχον is meant *copia hominum verissimo amore inflammatorum in Christianam religionem.* This last opinion as to the meaning of τὸ κατέχον is virtually held by Heydenreich, Schott, and Grimm; and, as the apostle, himself one of this band of devoted believers, thought that he should survive until the Second

Coming, the taking the restraining power out of the way cannot be his death, but only his imprisonment. Jowett's view is not very different—that the language about the apostacy was suggested to the apostle by what he saw around him among his own converts—"grievous wolves" entering into the church at Ephesus, the "turning away of all them of Asia." But it is enough to say that all this happened at a posterior time. Jowett adds, that four elements enter into the conception of the Man of Sin. (1) "The traditional imagery of the elder prophets"—But the prophecy is bare and plain in language. (2) "The style of the apostle and his age"—A mere assumption. (3) "The impression of recent historical events which supply the form"—A vague and unsupported statement. (4) "The state of the world and of the church, and the consciousness that, where good is, evil must ever be in aggravated proportions, which supply the matter of the prophecy"—An hypothesis which really means that the prophecy is only an assertion that what is and has been will be in all time coming. Out of such hints Jowett could construct a prophecy equally with the apostle, for such a prophecy is only a moody reflection thrown into the style of an ancient Hebrew oracle without its imagery. Such a theory also takes away all prophetic authority from the passage, which becomes only a reflex of the apostle's own experience stated in general terms—the individual and sectional pictured as the universal, his own little sphere in its trials and struggles assuming the aspect of world-wide history and doom. That is to say, the verses are a gloomy meditation on present scenes, not any unveiling of things to come—a morbid subjectivity so intensified that it personates its thoughts, and throws its difficulties and discouragements into a dramatic form. But surely this is to deny the inspiration of the apostle, and it takes all reality out of his pictorial words, leaving behind but a weak delusive residuum, which only projects into the future an image of the present and the past. Accepting the prophetic form, however, we feel bound to believe in the underlying truth. The apostle opens up the time far off, and we receive the disclosure of subsequent crises as the proof of a divine gift, and a fulfilment of the Saviour's promise. Prophecy is to Him as history, the future and the past being undivided and uncontrasted in His divine existence and duration. The paragraph is given to us as an avowed prediction, whatever be its true meaning and interpretation; and we are not to explain it away as a mere portraiture of present combinations and antagonisms, seen and measured in the light of the apostle's own life and trials—nay, exaggerated in the working of his earnest and mighty spirit. De Wette and Lünemann propound a similar hypothesis. They, however, do not hold the opinion that the paragraph is a vague and abstract picture, but rightly interpret "the Man of Sin" of a person, though with this sound exegesis they deny the objective reality and divine authority of the prediction. De Wette says, "Whoever finds more than a subjective outlook into the future of the church from his own historical position falls into error. Such foreknowledge is beyond human reach, and the apostle paid a tribute to human weakness, *der menschlichen Schwachheit einen Zoll*, since he wished to know too much beforehand, as is apparent from 1 Thess. iv, 17; 1 Cor. xv, 51; Rom. xi, 25. The personification of Antichrist is a misinterpretation of the prophecies of Daniel, *phantastische Auslegung*, mingled with some speculation of his own in connection with the dogma of the Divine Wisdom and Logos." He adds, "An incarnation of God in Christ we believe; but an incarnation of Satan, such as the apostle accidentally points out, is not to be thought of, for the honour of humanity." These assertions of the impossibility of prophecy in general, and the falseness of this one in the matter of it, betoken a philosophical unbelief, which would, if carried to its ultimate sweep, root out the basis of all divine revelation. De Wette goes so far, indeed, as to assert that the limitation of human knowledge by time and space, *durch Zeit und Raum*, to which Jesus Christ Himself was subject, makes prophecy as containing objective truth an impossibility to the apostle and to every man. Nay, he advances and affirms that the prediction is in itself untrue, for this antagonism to God, connected with Satan's imposture, is a contradiction to the reflective understanding as well as to the pious feeling—*ebenso sehr dem denkenden Verstande als dem frommen Gefühle*. Lünemann ascribes the prophetic form to the apostle's Jewish education, and to the current *Jüdischen Apokalyptik*, based on the picture of Antiochus, and of Gog and Magog, in the prophecies of Daniel and Ezekiel. What the apostle wished to paint of the future was impossible. "The exact conclusion about the course of events and their historical foretokens was a knowledge not granted to him or to any man, even though he be filled with the spirit of Christ"—the proof adduced being Matt. xxiv, 35; Mark xiii, 32; Acts i, 7. The events of this prophecy, however, were so near in his supposition, that he hoped to outlive them, for he believed that he was to survive till the Second Coming. "The prophecy was not fulfilled in the apostolic age, and it is capricious to look for its fulfilment in a remote future." These declarations not only eliminate from prophecy all that really gives it value, but also, undermining its possibility, remove it entirely from the Word of God, spiritual influence being too feeble to produce it; while they brand it either as daring conjecture, or as a romantic and forbidden attempt to uncover what God has so surely veiled from mortal vision. Such opinions are at once to be rejected, and there is no common ground between us and those who hold them. Our creed is that expressed by the apostle, "No prophecy of the Scripture is of any private interpretation, for prophecy came not in old time by the will of man, but holy men of God spake as they were moved by the Holy Ghost" (2 Peter i, 20, 21).

II

IF THE PARAGRAPH BE A PROPHECY, HAS IT BEEN FULFILLED?

Many maintain that it has long since come to pass, and they understand by the παρουσία of verse 8, the coming of Christ at the destruction of Jerusalem. These "praeterist" interpretations are very discordant. Some of them being political in nature fall far short of the full sense of the prophecy. One class of such expounders associates the fulfilment with the Roman emperors, another with the Jewish people and their leaders, and a third with some ecclesiastical system.

First Class.—Associating fulfilment with Roman Emperors.

1. The theory of Grotius is that Caligula was the Anti-

christ, inasmuch as he ordered prayers to be universally presented to him, and wished a colossal statue of himself to be erected in the temple at Jerusalem—an attempt which Herod Agrippa I. succeeded in putting aside—the ὁ κατέχων being the proconsul Vitellius who strongly opposed the project, and the ὁ ἄνομος of verse 8 being Simon Magus, who is consumed by the ministry of the apostle Peter. But (1) this last distinction is certainly wrong—"the Adversary" and the "Lawless one" are the same person, and the ministry of Peter cannot be called the coming of Christ, ἡ παρουσία τοῦ Κυρίου. (2) After Vitellius was "taken out of the way," the project was not carried out, and this is opposed to the spirit and words of the oracle, which affirms that after he that letteth has been taken out of the way, then the "Lawless one" shall be revealed. The reply of Grotius in reference to the erection of the idol-statue, that before God the will is as the deed, serves no purpose in this exegesis. (3) There is an extraordinary anachronism in the interpretation, for Caligula had been more than ten years dead before this epistle was written.

2. Wetstein finds Antichrist in Titus, because, after the temple had been burnt down, his army brought their standards into it, and setting them over against the eastern gate, offered sacrifice to them, and proclaimed Titus αὐτοκράτωρ (Joseph., *Bell. Jud.*, vi, 6, 1). The restraining power is in that case Nero, who must die before Titus can reign, the "falling away" referring to the struggle of Galba, Otho, and Vitellius, and their deaths, which opened the way for the ascendency of the Flavian House. But the character of Titus will not suit the epithet "man of sin," nor Nero that of the restraining one, and the homage done by his victorious troops to their military ensigns was not in any sense homage to himself as affecting divinity.

3. Döllinger is more precise, for he holds that the youthful Nero is Antichrist, and the stupid Claudius still reigning his ὁ κατέχων, rendering the participle "who is now in possession." The reasons are, that Nero was addicted to magical arts, and that he commenced that war in Judaea which led to the desecration of the temple, the previous "falling away" being the wretched imposture of the Gnostic heresy. But there is a

want of reality about these hypotheses and all similar political speculations, and they do not fit in to the bold and awful language of the paragraph.

4. Kern, Bauer, and Hilgenfeld, who maintain that the expectation expressed by the apostle in this paragraph has long ago found its refutation in history, imagine that the Antichrist is Nero, who was long supposed to be about to return to earth, ὁ κατέχων in that case being Vespasian possessing the throne—the "falling away" being the profligacy of the Jews, and the mystery of iniquity, the Gnostic heresy.

Mariana found Antichrist in Nero, Bossuet in Diocletian and in Julian, and Maurice discovers him in the Emperor Vitellius. Noack finds the man of sin and the restraining power alike in Simon Magus and his *Treiben*. Some saw Antichrist in the first Napoleon, as Faber, who found him typified in the wilful king of Daniel. When he was shut up in St. Helena, some thought that the Atlantic was the sea out of which the beast was to emerge.[1]

5. Some similar vague opinions may be noted. Victorinus conjectures the man of sin to be a revivified hero or chieftain; Lactantius, that he will be a Syrian sovereign, sprung from an evil spirit; Cyril, that he will be a dragon, who by his sorcery will raise himself to the mastery of the Roman Empire. Theophylact portrays him as a man who will carry Satan along with him. Andreas believes that he will be a king inspired by Satan, who will reconsolidate the old empire of Rome and reign in Jerusalem. Aretius asserts that he will be a king of the Romans, who will reign over the Saracens at Bagdad. The schoolmen, such as Albert and Hugo, have a view not unlike: Aquinas saying more definitely, that he will be born at Babylon, be initiated into Magianism, and that his life and works will be a caricature of those of Christ. There is a *Libellus de Antichristo*, once ascribed to Augustine, to Alcuin, and to Rabanus Maurus, and printed in their works, but now believed to be written by Adso (A.D. 950), Abbas Monasterii Dervensis (Montier-en-Der), in which he says that the devil will descend on the mother of Antichrist, as did the

[1] Frere's *Combined View of the Prophecies*, p. 468; Hoblyn *On the Numbers of Daniel*, p. 142.

Divine Spirit on the Virgin, *et totam eam replebit, et totam eam circumdabit, totamque tenebit, et totam interius exteriusque possidebit eam, ut diabolo per hominem cooperante concipiat, et quod natum fuerit totum sit iniquum, totum malum, totum perditum.* He is to be born at Babylon, and brought up at Chorazin and Bethsaida. A king of the Franks is to reunite the empire, and after a faithful reign he shall retire to Jerusalem, and there lay down his royal power—*sceptrum et coronam suam deponet.* Then Antichrist will assume the supremacy and saying to the Jews, "I am Christ," will slay all his adversaries, Enoch and Elijah among them, rebuild Solomon's temple, and take his seat in it, feigning that he is the Son of Almighty God, and doing many false wonders, &c. Augustine, *Opera*, p. 1649, vol. VI, Gaume, Paris; Alcuini *Opera*, vol. II, 1291, Migne.

Second Class.—Others, again, who understand by the "Coming" the destruction of Jerusalem, find the Man of Sin in some element or aspect of the Jewish people prior to that terrible catastrophe. Thus—

1. Whitby regards the entire nation as Antichrist, and as the Man of Sin, quoting Josephus who records, "It is impossible to recount severally the particulars of their wickedness, nor was there any generation since the memory of man more fruitful in iniquity." That nation is also well called the Adversary of Christ, as the gospels and epistles abundantly show. They, by their Sanhedrim, sat in the temple of God—enacting laws, and elevating tradition above the divine statues, and led away into sedition by jugglers and impostors. The ὁ κατέχων is the Emperor Claudius, who made two edicts in favour of the Jews, and whose mild government kept back the final national outbreak, and he was at length taken out of the way. The phrase ἐκ μέσου γίνεσθαι imports death, often a violent death, and Claudius, according to Suetonius, was poisoned. But this scheme is devoid of all probability The apostacy, he says, is the revolt of the Jews from the Roman Empire, or from the faith. The first notion ascribes an unlikely meaning to ἀποστασία, and how could the Jews revolt from a faith which they never embraced ? Nor did the Sanhedrim, a body so strictly monotheistic in creed, ever sit in the temple

and assume itself, or any member of it, to be God either in prerogative or in name.

2. Schöttgen on the other hand supposes that by the Man of Sin is meant the Pharisees, the Rabbis, and the doctors of the law, who not only sinned themselves, but caused others to sin, nay, committed the sin against the Holy Ghost in ascribing Christ's miracles to connivance with Beelzebub. The chief priests sit in the temple of God and so far fulfil the prophecy, the falling off being their rebellion against the authority of Rome, and the restraining power being perhaps (*fortasse*) the prayers of the Christians which warded off the catastrophe till they left the city and retired to Pella in safety. Somewhat similarly Le Clerc takes the Man of Sin to be the rebellious Jews with their leader Simon, the son of Gioras, whose atrocities are related by Josephus. The mystery of iniquity is their insurrectionary turbulence under pretence of national independence and zealous attachment to the law of Moses, and the restraining power is the Emperor and the political leaders who sought to dissuade them from the rebellion, *rex Agrippa et pontifices plurimi*.

3. Nösselt and Krause understand by Antichrist the Jewish zealots, and by the restraining power the Emperor Claudius.

4. Harduin holds that the falling away is the defection of the Jews into paganism, that the Man of Sin is the High Priest Ananias—his ὁ κατέχων being his predecessor, whose removal by death was necessary to his elevation. From the beginning of his high-priesthood he was a prophet of lies, and he was destroyed at the capture of Jerusalem by Titus.

5. Baumgarten thinks that the prophecy was suggested by the apostle's own experience in Europe, and his interpretation of it in the light of old prophecy; the Jewish population being so malignantly hostile to him, and the Gentiles being brought into wicked league with them. This union of Israel with the secular power had led to the crucifixion of the Son of God, and had given to that atrocity the aspect of legality and zeal for God, and such a union will consummate the final development of evil, "those who have the care of the sanctuary having a part in it." The apostacy of the Jews from Him who was the promised Messiah, their king and head, had already

shown itself in Thessalonica, but the restraining power was still at work, that power being the imperial authority; for when the apostle affirmed in Philippi that he was a Roman citizen, he was dismissed in peace. This power "withheld the outbreak of extreme corruption" and the apostle could not look for the Man of Sin anywhere but within the limits of the secular power, "for it is to the empires of this world that all the visions and prophecies of Daniel refer."

6. Hammond, differing from these political and Jewish hypotheses, argues that the Man of Sin is Simon Magus, who, as the head of the Gnostics, professed himself the "supreme Father of all, who had created the God of the Jews"; the "falling away" being a lapse into Gnosticism; ὁ κατέχων being ὁ νόμος; τὸ κατέχον being the union still subsisting between Christians and Jews so long as those Christians conformed to the Jewish law, but which soon came to an end, when Gnosticism was revealed in its true colours, as a system of deadly antipathy to the gospel; and the mystery of iniquity being "the wicked lives of these unbelieving persecutors." Simon "did miracles by the help of devils, and was taken for a god—nay, was owned in Samaria for a god, and had a statue erected to him on the banks of the Tiber with the inscription *Simoni sancto Deo*." The eighth verse is explained by him thus—that as the chariot and fiery horses of Simon, with which this magician undertook a voyage in the air, were blown away by Peter's mouth and vanished at the name of Christ, and so the impostor fell down and brake his legs, and soon ended his miserable and shameful days by suicide—the "breath of his mouth" is thus the power of the Gospel in the mouths of Peter and Paul, and the "brightness of his coming" the vengeance that befell the Jews by the Roman armies, at which time the Gnostics that sided with them were destroyed also.

7. Wieseler regards the Man of Sin as no abstract idea *keine collectiv Person*, but an actual individual in whom the power of sin should be embodied, in whom the apostacy should culminate—the godless self-deifying ruler of a worldly empire—that Christ who was expected to come in Paul's own day is to be his immediate destroyer; the restraining power being the pious in Jerusalem viewed collectively, or if an individual

is meant, then he is James the Just, who was named the bulwark of the people. Jerusalem fell, James was slain, but Antichrist did not make his appearance. What then comes of the truth of this oracle?

To all these opinions there are insuperable objections, and each of them is beset with special difficulties. None of them realizes to the full or exhausts the prophetic delineation, but each comes greatly short of it. Some features of it may appear in them, but not in complete combination. None of them forms a portrait of which the prediction might be taken as a faithful description. Neither Caligula, nor Nero, nor any emperor, nor Simon Magus realizes the epithet—the Man of Sin, the Adversary, the Lawless one displacing God in His own Temple and claiming the homage due to Him, and beguiling the world "with lying wonders and all deceivableness of unrighteousness." The ferocity and sensuality of those emperors and the imposture of Simon—whatever in short stood out in characterizing prominence in their lives—could not be described as in these clauses. The resemblance is very faint and fragmentary and the interpretation is only guess-work. The other conjectures as to the Jews, their Rabbis, their zealots, their priests or political leaders, are as improbable, for the Man of Sin is an individual and not a company or succession of wild or wicked men. Lastly, the $\pi\alpha\rho o\upsilon\sigma\acute{\iota}\alpha$ cannot be the destruction of the Jewish capital, for, as the general usage of the New Testament indicates, and as these Epistles unmistakeably prove, the term denotes *the second and personal* coming of the Lord Jesus.

Third Class.—Looking into a more remote future, a third and larger party of interpreters identify the Man of Sin with some ecclesiastical system. Some even look to the Mohammedan imposture—its name-father being the Man of Sin; "the falling away," the defection of so many in the Oriental and Greek Churches from Christian truth; and the Roman Empire being the restraining power. Pope Innocent III stirred anew the zeal of the Crusaders by pronouncing Mohammed to be the Man of Sin. That the apostacy was to precede the revelation of the Man of Sin is so far true in this case, yet Mohammed was the means of increasing and extending the defection. Nor did he ever put forward any claim to be God;

nor did he sit in the temple of God, for the phrase means something more than the conversion of churches into mosques; and certainly he never professed to work miracles and signs—nay, he expressly disavowed the possession of such a power. So much probability, however, was attached to this opinion that some have imagined a double Antichrist—an Eastern one in Mohammed and the Turkish power, and a Western one in the Pope and his spiritual despotism. So Melancthon, Bucer, Piscator, Musculus, and Vorstius. Bishop Bale says that Antichrist in Europe is the Pope, but Mohammed in Africa; and Montague, a chaplain under the Stuart dynasty, pleaded that the characteristics of the prophecy belong rather to the Turk than the Pope (Newton, p. 467. Compare also Fell's *Annotations*). But the notion is baseless as an interpretation of this passage.

The prevailing Protestant interpretation has been that the Man of Sin is Popery, gathered up into the person of the Pope; or the Papal hierarchy, the head of which is the occupant of the Papal chair,—the falling away being a defection from inspired truth to human tradition; the "restraining power" being the old Roman Empire, out of the ruins of which the Papacy rose. There is no little verisimilitude in this opinion, and it arose before the period of the Reformation and among men belonging to the Church of Rome. Gregory I, toward the end of the sixth century, had foreshadowed the opinion in asserting theoretically that any one possessing the kind and amount of power, which the Pope claimed soon after his time, would be the forerunner of Antichrist. His words are, *Ego autem fidenter dico quia quisquis se universalem sacerdotem vocat, vel vocari desiderat, in elatione sua Antichristum præcurrit, quia superbiendo se cæteris præponit.*[1] He calls the title of Universal Priest *erroris nomen, stultum ac superbum vocabulum, perversum, nefandum, scelestum vocabulum, nomen blasphemiae;* and in one of his letters he asks, *Sed in hac ejus superbia quid aliud nisi propinqua jam Antichristi esse tempora designatur;*[2] and these were his utterances when John, Bishop of Constantinople, first assumed

---

[1] Ep. XXXIII, lib. vii, p. 891, *Opera*, vol. III, Migne.
[2] Ep. XXI, lib. v, p. 749.

the title of Universal Bishop. Arnulphus, Bishop of Orleans about A.D. 991, spoke in the Synod of Rheims against Pope John XV, summing up by saying that if he had not charity and was puffed up with knowledge, he was Antichrist.[1] Joachim, of the twelfth century, in his *Commentary on the Apocalypse*, describes the second Beast as ruled by some great prelate who will be like Simon Magus, and as it were Universalis Pontifex —the very Antichrist of whom the apostle speaks. In the famous interview with King Richard on his way to Palestine, Joachim is said to have maintained that Antichrist was shortly to come, was born already in Rome, and was soon to be raised to the apostolic see. But the Franciscans, in self-defence, may have interpolated Joachim's works. At the end of the same century Amalric, professor of logic and divinity, more than hinted that the Pope was Antichrist; and the idea pleased two classes especially—those who abhorred the lax morality of the Papal court, like the Franciscans; and those political Imperialists who were battling against the Papacy and its pretensions: men, on the one hand, like Peter John of Olivi, Ubertinus, and Grostête who, on being excommunicated, appealed from the court of the Pope to the tribunal of Christ; and on the other, like Eberhard, who accuses Hildebrand of laying the foundation of Antichrist's kingdom 170 years before his time; and identifies him with the little horn of Daniel.[2] So also Petrus de Vineis, chancellor to Frederick II, and his defender against the Pope; Marsilius of Padua, a famous jurist; Roger Bacon, &c. Some of these men were writing under strong natural feeling against the Pope as a personal antagonist, and therefore they denounced him in bitter terms intended to wound and humble him; so that their denunciations of him were not suggested by sober and careful interpretation of this prophecy, and they would have shrunk from applying to him all its terms.

If such license of language was taken occasionally by persons within the pale of the Romish Church, it is not to be wondered at that those who were in separation from it came to hold similar views, such as the Waldensians, the Hussites, and the followers of Wycliffe. The Waldensian document belonging to

[1] Zanchius, 488.   [2] Ibid, p. 489.

the thirteenth century—Treatise of Antichrist—identifies the Man of Sin with Antichrist, Babylon, the fourth Beast, the harlot; but La Nobla Leyczon, "the noble lesson," of over 470 lines written in the Provençal dialect in the latter part of the twelfth century, speaks more doubtfully. "The people are to be well advised when Antichrist comes that we give no credence to his doings or his sayings. But according to Scripture there are many Antichrists, for all who are contrary to Christ are Antichrist." Those documents are of great antiquity, though Leger has certainly exaggerated the early origin of the Waldenses; and the date referred to in the poem is doubtful, as the point of commencement cannot be exactly ascertained.[1] Men like Lord Cobham and like Walter Brute, who suffered under Papal tyranny, naturally felt that the Pope as a spiritual despot must be the Antichrist. The Reformers as a body held the same view—Luther, Melancthon, Calvin, Zuingli, Bucer, Beza, Bullinger, &c.; Cranmer, Ridley, Latimer, Jewell, Hooper, Hooker, &c. It is embodied in the articles of the Smalcald Confession. King James put forth the same view in his *Apologia pro Juram. Fidel.*; and for this publication he is complimented by our translators in their dedication, "that it hath given such a blow unto that Man of Sin as will not be healed." Hosts of English divines and commentators have given the same interpretation, such as Bishop Andrews, Sanderson, Napier of Merchiston, Mede, Bishop Newton, Faber, &c. Many find the Papacy in the first or second Apocalyptic Beast; and some identify the system with both Beasts, as Pareus, Vitringa, Croly, Elliott. This view represents also the popular belief, at least in Scotland, and it is often brought forward in times of anti-Papal agitation. The points of similarity between the Pope or Popery and the description of this paragraph have been elaborated by Bishop Jewel in his *Exposition*, and the commentary of Bishop Wordsworth puts them in a more precise and definite form. The same identification may be found in Bishop Newton, in Faber's *Sacred Calendar of Prophecy*, and in many current and popular works.

The points of identification are the following:—Many of the

[1] Gieseler, III, 418; Elliott, II, 686; Mosheim, 428; Hallam, I, 28.

Roman Pontiffs were men of sin, characterized by debauchery, sensuality, cruelty, and bloody ambition. Popish writers describe the vileness of many Popes in the blackest terms. About the tenth century, from John VIII to Leo IX fifty Popes are said, by Genebrard, to be *apostatici potius quam apostolici*. Baronius shrinks not from depicting those of the tenth century as being guilty of robbery, assassination, simony, dissipation, tyranny, sacrilege, perjury, and all kinds of wickedness. Two courtesans, mother and daughter, dispensed the Papal patronage of the period. During the pontificate of John XII, women were afraid of going to St. Peter's tomb, lest they should be violated by Peter's successor. Cardinal Bellarmine admits that he was nearly the most wicked of the Popes. Boniface VII is declared by Cardinal Baronius to have been a thief, a miscreant, and a murderer. John XXIII was found guilty by the Council of Constance of forty species of vices, including incest and unnatural lust. Sixtus IV established brothels in Rome, and was the "Vicar General of God and Venus." Alexander VI was a monster of depravity. His vices and crimes were so base that they are unfit for description, and he was poisoned with a cup which he had treacherously prepared for others. It is needless to extend the list. There have been, certainly, many exceptions—many good men in the Papal chair; but so many have been notorious for sins and profligacies that they are held by many to give the Papal succession the aspect and character of "The Man of Sin."

Then, on the same hypothesis, the "falling away," $\dot{\alpha}\pi o\sigma\tau\alpha\sigma\acute{\iota}\alpha$, is the declension from the pure and primitive faith of the early centuries, and no system of apostasy can be compared with Popery in long continuity of time and wide extent of place. Among the elements of such apostasy may be reckoned false doctrine, idolatry, or worship of images, and the gradual assumption of a universal pontificate in the person of St. Peter's successor. The Second Council of Nice, in A.D. 787, authorized many previous errors and practices which had been growing for centuries.

The "mystery of iniquity" is so called from its early and secret working: what at first was harmless grew by degrees into sin and degradation. Jewel instances celibacy, single communion, the power of the keys, purgatory, pre-eminence of the Romish Bishop—all which things came in gradually and with no evil purpose, acquired strength without being observed, and at length obtained an extreme form, a virulent predominance.

Bishop Wordsworth says, "It may be asked how could this power be said to be at work in St. Paul's age," and his reply is "St. Paul was inspired by the Holy Ghost. The Holy Ghost can see what man cannot see;" and he adds, "no wonder we should not be able to discern it." But the germs were to some extent visible even then to human sight. The quick eye of the apostle discerned them, as may be learned from various indications in his epistles.

This word, in its Latin form *mysterium*, was formally inscribed in letters of gold on the front of the Pope's tiara, and is said to have been removed by Pope Julius II, who reigned from A.D. 1503 to 1513.[1] But such an ostentatious use of the word differs from the meaning of the clause. From the word mystery the Popish expositor Estius has an argument against the identification of the Man of Sin with the Pope. The mystery of iniquity was already working in secret attempts to oppress the church in the apostle's own times. *Si enim uti contendunt Romanus Pontifex Antichristus est, extitit autem Antichristus Apostolorum tempore, nec alius tunc Romanus Pontifex fuit, nisi beatus Petrus, igitur Petrus erat Antichristus.*

Again, the description of the fourth verse is said to be realized in Popery. The Man of Sin is the opposer, ὁ ἀντικείμενος, in nearly every sense. Christ is the Rock, and the Pope says "I am the Rock," "a rival foundation." The Pope exalts himself above all gods, such as Elohim or civil rulers, for every Pope on being crowned with the tiara is saluted as *Pater Principum et Regum, Rector orbis*.[2] On his coins the legend runs, *omnes reges servient ei*. It is his prerogative to cancel an oath of allegiance; and he declares that oaths of allegiance to persons excommunicated are void, for the kingly power is subject to the pontifical and is bound to obey it. Bulls for these purposes have often been issued, as by Hildebrand against the Emperor Henry IV, by Gregory IX and Innocent IV against the Emperor Frederick

[1] Newton, 642; Wordsworth's *Letters*, p. 41.
[2] The full form is in Wordsworth's *Letters*, p. 317.

II, by Paul III against Henry VIII of England, by Pius V against Queen Elizabeth—a sentence repeated by Gregory XIII and Sixtus V.

Then as to the session in the Temple of God, showing himself as God, the Pope on his election and proclamation is carried into St. Peter's and seated on the high altar, where he is saluted by the kneeling cardinals—*osculo pedis, manus, et oris*. The Church calls this ceremony the adoration—the princes of the Roman church kiss "the profane feet which trample on the altar of the Most High." The medals of Martin V have the legend *Quem creant, adorant*.

Next, the restraining power is with this interpretation said to be the old Roman Empire—*Romanus status*, as Tertullian calls it, who also says, "that Christians had special need to pray for the empire, since on its removal some terrible violence would come."[1] That is to say, when the Roman Empire was dismembered, the Man of Sin would grow in daringness—for he was curbed and kept down by the civil power, which brooked no rival and tolerated no upstart. Paul had spoken of this when he was with the Thessalonians, and therefore he does not repeat it in writing, and for another reason too, as Jerome alleges, "if St. Paul had written openly, and boldly said that the Man of Sin would not come until the Roman Empire was destroyed, a just cause of persecution would then appear to have been afforded against the church in her infancy."[2] Chrysostom (*in loc.*) repeats the same assertion, and also Augustine.[3] So that the reserve of the apostle is taken as a proof that he must have meant the imperial power. It is true that when the court and government were transferred to Constantinople, Rome was left as a prey to the ecclesiastical power. Odoacer in A.D. 476 deposed and exiled Romulus Augustulus, and with his removal the Roman Empire in the West came to an end. De Maistre says, "a secret hand chased the emperors from the Eternal City to give it to the head of the Eternal Church." In A.D. 755, the Pope obtained the exarchate of Ravenna, and in 774 got possession of the kingdom of the Lombards, and having at

---

[1] *Apologia*, xxxii, p. 236, vol. I, *Opera*, ed. Œhler.
[2] *Epist. ad Algasiam*, lib. 121, p. 888, vol. I, *Opera*, ed. Vallar.
[3] *De Civitate Dei*, lib. xx, cap. 19, p. 958, vol. VII. *Opera*, Gaume.

length accepted the territory of the Vandals, Ostrogoths, and Lombards, he formally assumed the *triregno*,[1] the triple tiara, the super-imperial crown—*extra ecclesiam*—the symbol of his political prerogative as opposed to the mitre, the symbol of his ecclesiastical dignity *intra ecclesiam*.

The "miracles and signs and lying wonders" which the Lawless one is to perform find, it is averred, a fulfilment in the Church of Rome, where miracles of various kinds are recorded in every century, such as those wrought at the tomb of the Abbé Paris and at many other tombs, as told in the Roman Breviary: the annual liquefaction of the blood of St. Januarius at Naples; the wonders done by sacred images moving, speaking, weeping, bleeding; supernatural visitations from the Virgin and the saints; and great prodigies done by holy relics.

Now, many of these resemblances are very striking, and Popery is a system in many of its features quite opposed to the spirit and the letter of the inspired volume—a dark system of spiritual slavery, the iron of which enters into the soul. The Inquisition on the one side was balanced by indulgences on the other side. Its cruelties have been ferocious in their outbreaks: *Te Deum* was sung in the church of St. Louis in Rome for the Massacre of St. Bartholomew, and a medal with the words *Pietas excitavit justitiam* was struck in commemoration of it. Its arrogance is blasphemous; its sacerdotal prerogatives in confession, absolution, and transubstantiation are quite superhuman in pretension. The devotion it inculcates to the Papal chair, as by the creed of Pius IV and the Bull *in Cœna Domini*, is inconsistent with personal freedom and civil liberty. It claims toleration, but yields none save under necessity. Its people are, in the mass of them, as firm believers in legend and tradition as in the Word of God. Popery is a system of baleful intervention between heaven and earth: the priest stands between the sinner and God, auricular confession between him and the footstool of mercy, penance between him and godly sorrow, the mass between him and the righteousness of Christ, indulgences between him and a self-denying and earnest life, tradition between him and holy Scripture, and purgatory between him and the heavenly world.

[1] Elliott, vol. II, p. 901.

This identification of the Pope with the Man of Sin was not very popular in the days of the Stuarts. Mede, the famous writer on prophecy, says in one of his letters that "some of his opinions would have made another man a Dean, Prebend, or something else ere this, but the point of the Pope's being Antichrist as a dead fly marred the savour of that ointment."

It is scarcely to be wondered at that some Popish writers retaliated on Protestant commentators and polemics. Estius says that Protestants, *primo auctore Luthero*, have formed an apostacy from the true faith and worship, and paved the way for Antichrist—*ut hodie insigniter facit Jacobus rex Angliae*.[1] Compare a-Lapide and Fromond. Archbishop Bramhall brings the matter nearer home, for at the conclusion of his "Fair Warning of Scottish Discipline," a tract which is a plea for the lowest Erastianism, he says, "it were worth the enquiry whether the marks of Antichrist do not agree as eminently to the General Assembly of Scotland as either to the Pope or to the Turk."[2] The king of France, with the advice of his council, forbad that any one should call the Pope Antichrist; and Grotius, at the time Swedish ambassador in Paris, composed a treatise on Antichrist, minimizing the difference between Protestantism and Popery in the vain hope of effecting some reconciliation.[3] Baxter attacked the "Grotian theory," accused Grotius of a design to reconcile Papists and Protestants in a Cassandrian Popery, and, believing that the scheme had been regarded with favour in England, among others attacked Bramhall. Bramhall in his reply shrank from avowing his belief that the Pope is Antichrist, and makes so many distinctions and limitations as to show that he did not heartily concur in the views of the Reformers.[4]

For very different reasons from any of the preceding ones, the Polish Socinians regarded the Pope as Antichrist, since he was the main supporter of Trinitarian doctrine; and Schlichting explains the clause, "a strong delusion that they should

---

[1] Estius, p. 79.
[2] *Works*, p. 287, vol. III, Oxford, 1844.
[3] See Bochart's reply, *Examen Libelli de Antichristo, Opera*, vol. I, p. 1044.
[4] Bramhall's *Works*, vol. III, p. 500.

believe a lie," by saying, "they refused to believe that the man Jesus is a God made by the one God; therefore let them believe that He is the one very God himself" (*in loc.*).

But while the resemblance is so close between the Papacy and this prophetic description, the Papacy does not by any means exhaust it. The oracle harmonizes with it on many points, but goes greatly beyond it. Popery embodies no small portion of it, but does not comprehend all of it. The Man of Sin has not yet appeared. No one so daring, so defiant, so Antichristic, so successful in imposture, has yet appeared among men or in the Popish community. The arguments against identification are—

1. The phrases and epithets, "the Man of Sin," the "Son of Perdition," the "Lawless One," naturally represent a single individual, not a polity or system. Had the apostle wished to portray a system, he could have used an abstract term like ἡ ἀποστασία. The terse personal language forepictures one man, one human being, as really as the phrase "son of perdition" described from the Lord's lips the fate of Judas the traitor. In 1 Tim. iv, 1, when the apostle portrays a coming defection, he uses the plural number—"some shall depart from the faith," &c.; and in 2 Tim. iii, 2 the plural is again employed —"men shall be lovers of themselves," &c., Jannes and Jambres being a specimen of them. The "falling away" consists of those who have fallen away—the apostacy, of apostates; but the apostacy as a fact or as a system is not to be identified with the "Man of Sin," for it precedes him and is the condition of his appearance. He is then one human being, and is not to be identified with a complicated system such as Popery. On the other hand, the Apocalyptic Beast plainly represents a polity, and the second Beast seems to correspond to the little horn of the fourth Beast of Daniel.

2. Nor can these individualistic phrases mean a succession of men, *series et successio hominum*, or the line of nearly three hundred Popes. The instances adduced by Bishop Newton in favour of that view will not sustain him.[1] Thus he argues, "a king is often used for a succession of kings, as in Dan. vii, viii"; but in these chapters there are no parallel instances.

[1] *Dissertations on the Prophecies*, p. 440, 16th edition (London, 1832).

In the seventh chapter it is said distinctly, "the four beasts are four kings," in explanation of the symbols; and in the eighth chapter "the kings of Media and Persia" are spoken of in the plural number; "a king of fierce countenance" is foretold, but he is evidently one individual. The declaration "the rough goat is the king of Greece, and the great horn that is between his eyes is the first king," implies by the terms a succession of individuals. Bishop Newton refers again to the phrase, Heb. ix, 7, "into the second went the high priest alone once every year," a clause he expounds as "denoting the series and order of high priests." But the high priest means in this sentence the one for the time being, and a definition of hereditary sacerdotal function in this way is wholly different in terms from a prediction delivered in the singular number. Other instances adduced in proof have nothing analogous in them, for they are symbols with their interpretation. Bishop Newton adds, "No commentator ever conceived the whore of Babylon to be meant of a single woman, and why then should the 'Man of Sin' be taken for a single man?" But the statement involves a strange confusion of ideas about the sign and the thing signified. The woman, as an hieroglyph, is most certainly a single woman, but she may symbolize a variety of malign and seductive influences, for she is "that great city which reigneth over the kings of the earth." On the other hand, in the paragraph before us, there is no imagery or symbolism—all is as plain and prosaic as if it were a mere historical statement of fact. The arguments of Elliott for a plural sense are similar, and their refutation is of equal facility. He says that "ὁ κατέχων in the masculine singular is used synonymously with τὸ κατέχον in the neuter, as of a power—referring to the then existing line, succession, or government of the Roman emperors." He adds as to this example, "It at once annihilates all the arguments of those who would contend on the ground of this phraseology for a personal individual Antichrist."[1] But as we deny the meaning which he assigns to the two participles, his whole argument falls to the ground. His other proofs are like those of Bishop Newton, such as the reference to the high priest (Lev. xxi, 10), "the high priest among his

[1] *Horæ Apocalypticæ*, p. 833.

brethren shall not rend his clothes," where the official designation means each high priest for the time, in order to define his office. So with regard to the Jewish king (Deut. xvii, 15): the king, an official epithet, warrants its application to each one who holds the office and who is to be guided by the law. But when a phrase portrays a man by his character, it only includes himself, unless a class is specified or an assertion is made bringing others under the same category. Nothing of the kind occurs in the verses under consideration. A succession of priests and kings is contemplated in these verses quoted, and is therefore naturally presupposed, but there is no such idea asserted or implied in this passage. The words are therefore to be taken in their simple and current significance, as if they formed part of a narrative. One individual is distinctly pointed out under the awful epithets. There is no hint that one is to be taken as a symbol of many. Thrice the emphatic singular is employed. The ὁ κατέχων becomes τὸ κατέχον— a significant change; but it is ὁ ἄνθρωπος τῆς ἁμαρτίας, ὁ υἱὸς τῆς ἀπωλείας, ὁ ἀντικείμενος, direct and individual unity; and then, after an inserted appeal to previous conversations, a return to him is made by the singular αὐτὸν = ὁ ἄνομος, and the relatives ὅν . . . . οὗ —plain immediate matter of fact, a single personality without figure or disguise or anything to suggest a plurality or succession.

3. And this natural interpretation of the phrases is the earliest one. The first fathers took the Man of Sin to be a single person, and since they regarded the prophecy as unfulfilled in their day, they did not attempt to interpret its language by bringing it into harmony with any supposed accomplishment. Thus Irenæus describes him as *diabolicam apostasiam in se recapitulans;* . . . *se autem extollens unum idolum.* . . . *habens in semetipso reliquorum idolorum varium errorem.*[1] Justin Martyr uses the words ὁ τῆς ἀποστασίας ἄνθρωπος, his quotations, references, and explanations being all in the singular number.[2] Origen in his references to the prophecy also employs the singular, and understands one individual opposed κατὰ διάμετρον to the

---

[1] *Advers. Hæres.*, lib. v, c. 25, p. 783, vol. I, *Opera*, ed. Stieren.
[2] *Dial. cum Tryph.*, c. 110, p. 364, vol. II, *Opera*, ed. Otto.

Christ, υἱὸν τοῦ πονηροῦ δαίμονος καὶ Σατανᾶ καὶ διαβόλου.[1] Hippolytus affirms that Antichrist is to be born in Dan, as the Christ was in Judah, calling him the son of the devil, . . . that tyrant and shameless one and enemy of God.[2] In a paragraph the genuineness of which has been doubted, he says, "that deceiver seeks to make himself like to the Son of God," with numerous other allusions. Tertullian holds the same view;[3] and Chrysostom, *in loc.*, more expressly writes ἄνθρωπός τις πᾶσαν αὐτοῦ (Σατανᾶ) δεχόμενος τὴν ἐνέργειαν. Cyril of Jerusalem does not differ,[4] nor Augustine, who styles him *adversarius ejus Antichristus*, though he indicates the other view. Lactantius describes Antichrist as one person—*hic est autem, qui appellatur Antichristus; orietur ex Syria, malo spiritu genitus.*[5] Jerome's own view is precise—*qui adversatur Christo et ideo vocatur Antichristus.*[6]

That the Man of Sin was to be one human being—one man so terribly signalized in character, energy, and perdition—was the first and prevailing interpretation, for it was suggested by the terse simplicity and the unambiguous singular unity of the terms. The long line of Popes is therefore not intended by the phrases under discussion. Nay, so many schisms have raged among Popes and in the Popedom, that they could scarcely be represented by a unity. Baronius himself admits twenty-six schisms, and others make thirty. The claim of Liberius to the Papal chair was denied by the fathers, and Athanasius called him a monster. Silverius was in A.D. 536 elected by simony, and Julius II pronounced the election void. Stephen flung the corpse of his predecessor into the Tiber, and his rescission of the dead man's acts was reversed by his own successor John X. Sergius III called a council and nullified the acts of John. Sylvester, John, and Benedict fought fiercely in the eleventh century against one another for the tiara, but agreed at length to divide the revenues. To expel this "three-headed

---

[1] *Contra Celsum*, p. 307, ed. Spencer.
[2] *De Christo et Antichristo*, xv., *Opera*, ed. De Lagarde, pp. 7, 8.
[3] *De Resurrect.*, xxiv, p. 497, vol. II, *Opera*, ed. Œhler.
[4] *Cateches.* xv, 7, p. 212, *Opera*, ed. Miller.
[5] *Divin. Institut.*, lib. vii, c. 17-19.
[6] *Epist. ad Algas.*, already quoted.

monster," Gratian bought the Papacy and became Gregory VI. In the twelfth century happened the great schism, which lasted seventy years, one Pope reigning in Avignon and another in Rome, Urban and Clement dividing Christendom, and thundering anathemas at one another. The succession was uncertain, and none could tell who was rightful pontiff. At a later period Eugenius and the Council of Florence excommunicated Felix, and the Council of Basle and the latter heartily reciprocated the anathema. There are various theories on the nature of the Papal supremacy and infallibility, and on many tenets of its theology. Pope Gelasius in the fifth century condemned communion in one kind; his successors strictly command it. Gregory the Great branded the title of Universal Bishop as impious; his successors glory in it. Pope Vigilius fell into the heresy of Eutychianism, Pope Liberius into that of Arianism. Pope Honorius was condemned as a Monothelite by Pope Leo II. The infallibility meant to secure unity has often showed itself in suicidal weakness. Pope Sixtus in 1589 completed an authorized edition of the Latin Vulgate, which had been begun by Pope Pius IV, continued by Pope Pius V, and announced by a bull of date 1st March, 1589; and the preface threatens from the chair every one with excommunication who shall dare to alter the text in the smallest way. But in spite of this fence, the book was found to be full of blunders. The successor of Pope Sixtus V (Gregory XIV) was so sensible of this, and so little afraid of the Papal thunder, that he made preparations for a new edition, which was finished by Pope Clement VIII three years afterwards in 1592, and it was similarly defended with threats of highest curses on every one who should presume in any way to change it. Cardinal Bellarmine, to save the Papal infallibility, laid the blame on the printer, and this poor and unworthy defence—an awkward attempt to escape from a dilemma—is said to have secured the cardinal's canonization. Baldwin the Jesuit went so far as to affirm that the edition of Sixtus was never published! Thus the two literary infallibilities clashed, and in the contradiction throw one another into mutual destruction.

4. Nor is the description of the 4th verse exhausted in its

application to the Pope as the head of the Papal hierarchy, "who opposeth and exalteth himself above all that is called God or that is worshipped;" that is, every one called God, and every object of divine homage, for σέβασμα is not used in Scripture of objects of human veneration, such as rulers and magistrates. Two features very strongly marked are given—opposition to every God, true or false, and self-elevation above every God, true or false. Now, there is no little idolatry in the Romish Church; but these words are not a charge of idolatry, but of utter antagonism to God. The Pope holds the three creeds and owns himself to be a worshipper and servant of God. He professes to identify himself with God's cause, and he offers adoration to Father, Son, and Spirit. He blesses the people, not in his own name, but in the blessed triune name. So far from being the antagonist of God avowedly, as is the Man of Sin, he claims to be only a humble vassal in spiritual fellowship with the Divine Master, and his hymnal prayer for grace to do God's work is *Veni Creator Spiritus*. So far from exalting himself above God, he proclaims himself "servant of servants to the Most High," and craves from God divine grace and direction. In all he does—even in the burning of heretics, in organizing crusades against unbelievers, in crooked and unscrupulous diplomacy, in tampering with oaths and civil allegiance, in acts of ferocious cruelty and wildest ambition, or in doing ungodly and wicked deeds at which most men shudder—he ever acknowledges the divine authority and avows submission to the divine guidance. Nor can it be properly said that the Roman Pontiff "opposes and exalts himself above every object of worship," for his sin lies quite in an opposite direction. He is not opposed to the σεβάσματα, for he is ever multiplying them; nor does he exalt himself above them, for after he has made them they are objects of veneration to him really as much as to any of his vassals. He puts himself under them, and exalts them over himself, for he does them homage along with the poorest of his flock. By virtue of a commission as Christ's first minister, as he alleges, he ordains σεβάσματα, but at once he prostrates himself beneath them as their inferior, and in no way opposes or lifts his head above them. So that the clause does not distinctly and formally characterize either him or the

Papal system ; for it describes a frightful antitheism—open, fanatical, malignant, and haughty antagonism to God, and every object of divine worship—"he opposes, and exalts himself."

5. Nor does the next clause verify itself fully in the Popedom : " So that he sitteth in the temple of God, showing himself that he is God." There is no question that the Pope arrogates central dominion and does many things with so high a hand that he resembles this description and almost fixes it upon himself. One very close approach to this verification takes place at his installation, when he is carried into St. Peter's and seated by the cardinals on the high altar as his throne. This, considering the Romish belief about the altar and the uses to which it is applied, is an act of daring profanation, making a footstool of that on which in Popish conviction is done the most awful work of the priest on earth, and on which is offered the most solemn religious service. This is Bishop Wordsworth's great proof and position. But (1) can St. Peter's at Rome be called, or has it any claim to be called, the Temple of God ; or can the designation be given to the earlier church of the Lateran, which is the Pope's church as Bishop of Rome, and loftily called *Ecclesiarum urbis et orbis Mater et Caput?* (2) If the temple of God means the Christian church, how can he be said in literal palpability to go and take his seat in that temple, so wholly an ideal structure ? (3) When we reflect on the myriads of Protestants in all parts of the earth, we cannot hold that the centre and capital of Christ's church in the world is the city of Rome, and though Rome be truly the centre and capital of Papalism, yet we should refuse to call the Popish church by the solemn and exclusive title of the temple of God. Though the seating of the Pope on the high altar might even on Popish premises be branded as an act of consummate impiety, it does not come up to the charge, " showing himself that he is God." The Pope's seat on the high altar is professedly the symbol of his being the one vicar and representative of the Lord Jesus on earth. But no Pope ever did show himself that he was God. No one has ever been guilty of such gross self-deification. Blasphemous titles may be given him ; he has not assumed them. The adoration paid to him on the high altar is gross in itself, and may be a kind of idolatry ; but

it professes to be only the adoration of Christ's presence and power in him. The claim of infallibility on the part of the Pope looks like a shadow of divine omniscience and immutability, and his theocratic government exalts him to a divine altitude as its anointed head. It is a power like to God's which he assumes over the consciences of men and the destinies of nations, as if he were sovereign and unchallenged disposer; or when he has claimed the impious prerogative of authenticating the books of Scripture to invest them with canonical authority,[1] as Pope Gregory VII said, "Not a single book of scripture shall be held canonical without the Pope's authority." But in all these things he does not show himself that he is God, for the formal acknowledgement of God prefaces all his decrees and sanctifies, as his adherents call it, all his deeds, even the worst of them. In his loftiest and most daring claims he shows himself only as God's viceroy. Hildebrand, in building up and compacting this marvellous complication of spiritual tyranny, believed himself to be only God's chosen instrument for the work. The Council of Trent gives the Pope simply the supreme power in the universal church, though Cardillus said to the Council " the Pope holds as a mortal god the place of Christ on earth." "The Pope," says the gloss on the canon law, " is not a man." Bernard said, " None except God is like the Pope." Turrecrema and Barclay tell us *Doctorculi volunt adulando eos quasi aequiparare Deo*. The canon law declares that he occupies "the place not of a mere man, but of God;" he is called " our Lord God;" some affirming that the Pope and the Lord form the same tribunal. " The Pope is above right, and can change the substantial nature of things;" can, according to Bellarmine, change duty into sin, and sin into duty.[2] Some

---

[1] Another Pope, Sixtus V, in 1590, authorized a Latin Bible as an authentic infallible standard, in the place of the Hebrew and Greek original; and in this Latin Bible several books are called canonical which were never regarded as such by the Christian Church for fifteen hundred years! and in 1592 behold another development! Clement VIII comes forth with another Latin Bible to supersede the infallible Bible of his predecessor, and differing from it in several thousand places! Wordsworth, pp. 108, 109.

[2] For the authorities, see Edgar's *Variations of Popery*, p. 129, London.

of these epithets and assertions, as *Dominus Deus, Noster Papa*, given and made by canons, divines, and councils had no small authority surrounding them, but for the most part they were the extravagance of adulation, and were generally met by some opposition.[1] Those wild and wanton blasphemies, while they come amazingly close to the words of this verse, do not satisfy them. No Pope has ever arrogated those names to himself, nor would his arrogation of them have been tolerated. No Pope has ever really deified himself and ventured to supersede God in His own temple. What he has said, or done, or assumed, does almost by inference imply it; but cannot be fully identified with it. No Pope has so acted out antitheism as to thrust aside God formally and put himself in His place; but the Man of Sin is openly and avowedly to take God's seat within His own house, and so to displace its divine occupant as to be not God's rival merely but God's substitute, " showing himself that he is God."

6. The prediction of false miracles in verse 9 suits the Papacy, which abounds with them—not only in transubstantiation, but in a great variety of shapes.[2] Some of the miracles have been already referred to. A curious illustration is given by Athanasius. Among other reasons why the Son said of the time of the last days οὐδὲ ὁ υἱὸς οἶδε, one was that he might confute future impostors, angelic or human, who might pretend to know it. If Antichrist will say, I am Christ, pretend to a supernatural knowledge of the last times, and work in confirmation miraculous signs, let him be confronted with this utterance, that is, If the true Christ did not know it, how shall a false Christ reach the possession of such knowledge?[3]

The wonder of transubstantiation has been told in frightful words. "He that created me," says one cardinal, "if it be lawful to say it, gave me power to create Himself." "Her ladyship once conceived the Son of God, while the priest daily calls into existence the same Son in a corporeal form."[4]

---

[1] Jewel's *Works*, vol. II, p. 195.
[2] Jewel, VII, 187.
[3] III *Orat. contra Arianos*, p. 426, vol. II, Migne.
[4] Edgar's *Variations of Popery*, p. 384.

But as we have said, the prophecy under consideration portrays a single human being, not a system or polity. In a word, Popery is characterized by many bad features, in direct opposition to the letter and spirit of Scripture; the primacy of the Bishop of Rome rests on no true foundation; many of the earlier Decretals are spurious; the so-called Donation by Constantine of Italy and Rome and the provinces of the West to Sylvester, in A.D. 324, was a downright forgery, yet, as Gibbon says, by it the Popes "were invested with the purple and prerogatives of the Cæsars." But idolatry, superstition, will-worship, injustice, lust of power, lordship over men's consciences, and utter disregard of equity in pursuit of its ends, though they so sadly and sinfully characterize the Papal system everywhere, are not found in this prophetic sketch. Nor is there any allusion to images, worship of saints and angels, faith in relics, or the intense and absorbing adoration of the virgin; to the invention of purgatory, the sale of indulgences, priestly absolution, the power assumed over the world of spirits—symbolized in his badge of the two cross-keys, the one that of purgatory, the other that of heaven. The apostle portrays the apostacy, out of which springs a man in whom evil holds a defiant supremacy; who shall rage with hellish hostility against God, and trample on every object of worship; who takes his seat in God's temple and claims for himself as God all adoration; the Lawless one who seduces the world by prodigies and lying wonders and all deceivableness of unrighteousness, for he is all but an incarnation of Satan—the Man of Sin, and therefore also the Son of Perdition. No one has yet appeared in whom all these elements are concentrated; but Popery, as certainly a signal and continued defection from the true faith, and as embodying many of these features, seems to typify him; or it may be the apostacy preceding and preparing for his advent.

Whatever truth may be in the statements of Tertullian, Lactantius, Jerome and others, that there was among the churches a secret understanding about the speedy doom of the Roman Empire, this esoteric knowledge was soon thrown into open circulation—as in the Sibylline verses. Tertullian and Lactantius refer to these oracles and quote them. They are of different ages, but many of them belong to the period of the Antonines, and the so-called second book of Esdras is written in a similar spirit. Bishop Jewel quotes the Sibyl for the identification of Antichrist with the Pope—"Sibylla saith that this king shall be πολιόκρανος, that is, that he shall have a white head, and be called by a name much like to *Pontus*,"—a prophecy according to the Bishop fulfilled in the white mitre of silver worn by the Pope, while in Latin he is named *Pontifex*. The reference is to the lines—

"Εσσετ' ἄναξ πολιόκρανος ἔχων πέλας οὔνομα πόντου.

But the epithet means silver-helmed, the allusion being to a warrior and not to a priest; and the name resembling the sea is Hadrian, as the context plainly shows, and the reference in the name is to the Hadriatic sea. The terrible enemy and destroyer who occupies such prominence in the Sibylline verses is Nero returned to life. The vaticination says—

ἵν', ὅταν γ' ἐπανέλθῃ
Ἐκ περάτων γαίης ὁ φυγὰς μητροκτόνος ἐλθών.[1]

The return of the revivified Nero from the East as Antichrist haunted men's minds for a very long period, and by writers of the period it is often alluded to. Not a few supposed him to be Antichrist, as is told by Augustine, though he stigmatizes it as *tanta præsumptio* in his *De Civitate Dei* (lib. xx, c. xix); and it is alluded to by Chrysostom, Jerome, Cyril, and Tertullian, and in the history of Sulpicius Severus (ii. 28). This belief of Nero's return began in his lifetime, as the promise of some mathematici or astrologers, and many in Rome and the provinces firmly believed it after the tyrant's death. Compare Suetonius, *Nero*, 40; Tacitus, ii. 8; Dio Chrysostom, xxi. *Orat. de Pulchr.*, p. 314, vol. I, *Opera*, ed. Emperius.

The Man of Sin is to appear immediately before the Second Advent. He is to be in the world when Christ comes, and the "appearance of His coming" destroys him. His manifestation

[1] 142, also 144, *Oracula Sibyllina*, ed. Friedlieb. The lines preceding and following the first we have quoted are a spirited description of the downfall of the Roman power, and of the helplessness of its wealth and its gods to save it.

as an individual is therefore confined to a single lifetime, so that again in this view he cannot be identified with Popery, which has endured for ages. It is no objection to say that the apostle does not profess to fix the time of the Second Advent; he simply says that the apostacy and the Man of Sin precede it. The apostacy may require centuries for its development, the mystery of lawlessness may work through ages, but the Advent finds the Man of Sin in existence, and acting out his predicted character, and him at once it consumes, and then he realizes his name as the Son of Perdition. In the opinion of the fathers, as Barnabas and Irenaeus, his reign is to be short.

The Jewish tradition about Antichrist needs not be gone into at length, but it regarded Antichrist as an individual whose advent is preceded by twelve signs—such as a grievous oppression of the Jews on the part of the Romans for nine months When the Messiah Ben-Joseph, named Nehemiah, will appear and defeat the persecuting despot, then shall come the Antichrist, called by the Jews Armillus, who is to be born of a marble statue in one of the churches in Rome. To the Romans he will give himself out as their Messiah, and they will accept him as God for king. Subduing the world and proving from Scripture that he is God, Nehemiah, with a guard of thirty thousand soldiers, shall herald him with the proclamation, I am the Lord thy God; thou shalt have none other gods but me. But Armillus will deny that any such statement is found in the law, and will order the Jews to act as the other nations and adore him as their god. This challenge produces a great battle, in which the Messiah Ben-Joseph is slain, and terrible affliction shall fall on the Jews for forty-five days. But Michael shall blow three peals of his trumpet; at the first peal shall come the true Messiah, Ben David, with the prophet Elijah, and all Jews in the world will joyfully flock to Jerusalem. Armillus, who has an army of Idumeans, that is Christians, shall besiege Jerusalem, and he himself and his army shall perish. The name Armillus is taken from the last clause of Isaiah xi, 4. The Hebrew reads, וּבְרוּחַ שְׂפָתָיו יָמִית רָשָׁע, "and with the breath of his lips will he slay the wicked;" but the Chaldee version has מְמִית אַרְמִילוֹס רַשִׁיעָא, "shall slay the wicked Armillus" (Eisenmenger's

Entdekt. Juden., ii, 705 ; Buxtorf, *Synagoga Judaica*, p. 717). The legend has also spread among Mahometans. Their Antichrist, Messiah Ben David as he is named by the Jews, shall come and devastate the world with the exception of Mecca and Medina. But Jesus shall descend on the white tower at the east of Damascus and destroy him. Pocock, *Porta Mosis*, p. 221, 222.

Lastly, I enter not into the question whether the Babylon of the Apocalypse be Papal or Pagan Rome. Lacunza, a Spanish Jesuit under the name of Ben Ezra, identifies Babylon with the existing Church of Rome, and argues for a future personal infidel Antichrist, in whose affairs the infidel Spanish clergy will take a prominent part.[1] But granting it to be Papal Rome, it seems to present many features of contrast to Antichrist, or the Man of Sin, especially if the typical Antichrist of the book of Daniel be combined in the delineation. Babylon is a feminine, shameless, and seductive influence throned on the seven hills; has seven kings, and then ten kings, which at length hate her, make her desolate and naked, eat her flesh and burn her with fire. Then she is lamented by all her royal accomplices standing afar off and saying, "Alas, alas, that great city, that mighty city." Babylon contains to the close some genuine believers, who are exhorted to come out of her. On the other hand, the Man of Sin is a masculine and individual power, warlike and truculent, springs out of a great apostacy, and is put down with none to lament his fall, and all his followers are involved in perdition, his locality being apparently in Jerusalem and certainly not in Rome. Nay, after Babylon is destroyed, as is told in the 18th chapter of the Apocalypse, there remains an antichristian power, which is overthrown, as is told in the 19th chapter of the same book. The striking features of this antithesis certainly forbid any identification of these two wicked forms of antagonism to God and His Son Jesus Christ. But there is in the last confederacy, destroyed after Babylon is overthrown, a person constantly described in the singular form as the false prophet (Rev. xvi, 13; xix, 20). He is allied to the second beast, and is its minister, and he works miracles and deceives men, as does the Man of Sin. The false prophet is thus

[1] *Coming of the Messiah*, translated by the late Edward Irving.

different from the second beast, which may represent the Papal system; it revives all the old tyranny, deals in miracles and idolatry, refuses civil rights—as to buy and sell—to all who refuse to wear its symbols or will not bow to its supremacy, and it persecutes to the death all who are opposed to its system. What is ascribed to the second beast is also ascribed to the false prophet as its minister and guardian, so that if this false prophet be the Man of Sin, the inference is that he, though unbelieving and atheistical, will take advantage of the Papal tyranny or some similar spiritual system to revivify it into some darker shape and convert it into the means of his own aggrandisement. Such a revival, in a form of political and spiritual intolerance combined with a special irreligious defection and the shaking of all social order, may be the falling away which the Man of Sin lays hold of as the step to his terrible antitheistic pre-eminence, uniting "superstition and unbelief in a combined attack on liberty and religion, the embodiment of Satanic as distinct from brutal wickedness." Having attained his throne of blasphemy, his power shall be fatal to the apostacy, out of which he sprung; yet we find commentators on the Apocalypse discovering Antichrist in it in various ways and identifying him with the Papal power. Thus the angel clothed with a cloud, a rainbow on his head and his face as the sun, is said to be Jesus, who is counterfeited by Pope Leo X, his name being recognized in the phrase "as when a lion roareth."[1]

Gualterus thought the wild boar of the forest, in Psalm lxxx, a type of the Pope, and at once selected Bocca di Porco (hog's snout), the name of Pope Sergius II. Antichrist, a name so accursed, proved a good weapon to use in a controversy, and so the rival Popes branded each other as Antichrist, and St. Bernard hurls the same terms against the Anti-Pope Anacletus. The little horn had eyes as a man, and it symbolizes the Pope; the eyes, being the organ of vision, refer to the overseer or bishop—*oculus pastoralis*—and by necessity of inference to the Pope—*speculator super omnia*.[2]

A special question still is—what is meant by this power that holds back and delays the appearance of the Man of Sin? It

[1] Elliot, *Horae Apocalypticae*, p. 388.
[2] Elliot, p. 900.

must be something mighty and beneficent, for it checks and retards a great and malignant evil. The old fathers believed it to be the Roman Empire and Emperor, but these have passed away, and the Man of Sin has not come. Some thought of the German Empire restored by Charlemagne, but Napoleon dissolved it in 1806, and neither yet has the Man of Sin come.

Were the "Man of Sin" the Popedom, it might be said that the civil power has been always restraining it, and the two have been often in deadly conflict, not only in mediæval but in more recent times. The gross pretensions of the Papal power have been generally repressed by statesmen, who were alarmed at its stealthy encroachments and its wary and watchful ambition. This withholding power is connected by Ewald with the expected return of Elijah, who, when he comes, will confront the Antichrist, till he be removed again to heaven. Such an opinion is a peculiar dream, which there is nothing in the passage to suggest. Hofmann regards the restraining power as supernatural, and it may therefore be expressed in either a masculine or a neuter form, ὁ κατέχων, τὸ κατέχον. Its type is the good angel who withstood the evil genius that sought to infuse sinister purposes into the heart of the king of Persia. The same author, looking back to the prophecies of Daniel, believes in the actual return of Antiochus, the inveterate persecutor of the covenant people, who on his personal remanifestation shall, as more thoroughly demonized by the long interval, begin his ancient work in deadlier energy—shall, in fact, eclipse his former self in godlessness and ferocity. Such a revivification is not suggested by this prophecy.

This restraining power, in fine, may be, as Alford expresses it, "the fabric of human polity and those who rule that polity, by which the great upbursting of godlessness is kept down and hindered." Similarly Ellicott. Whatever thwarts personal ambition or suppresses atheistic impulses growing to a head, whatever counteracts the growth of that mystery which dethrones God and enslaves man, be it civil rule or evangelical influence, may be the withholding power, given first in the abstract—τὶ κατέχον—then to be embodied in some eminent individual—ὁ κατέχων; he will be removed, and then, the dam having burst, evil will deluge the earth—

that evil finding its living centre and impersonation in the Lawless one, who gathers in to himself all power, secular and sacred, and fulfils his course by this wanton self-created apotheosis.

Already, in the apostle's day was this proud impiety of apotheosis beginning to prevail, this mystery of insane superstition was unfolding itself. The term Augustus itself implied divineness, and the step toward deification was easy. The Emperor Augustus had allowed a temple to be dedicated to him in Pergamus, and the imperial god and his deified capital shared a joint worship. The statue of the Cæsar had ever a special sacredness attached to it. The living Caligula was worshipped on the Capitoline hill, and Domitian styled himself "Lord and God." Trajan, according to Pliny, made a god of Nerva; his predecessor, from a sincere conviction of his divinity. Antinous, a debased favourite of Hadrian, was similarly exalted, and the fane of Isis at Rome celebrated him on one of its tablets "as the temple associate of the Egyptian gods." During the Roman occupation, a temple was built at Colchester to the divine Emperor Claudius. The living when deified assumed the name of some deity, but the dead on receiving the honour were simply admitted into the Pantheon. The custom spread through the empire, and was not confined to Rome and the imperial dynasty. An approach to this folly is found in the Acts of the Apostles, when the people shouted aloud at Herod's oration, "It is the voice of a god and not of a man" (xii, 22). The boldest part of this daring and self-glorifying profanity is adopted by the "Man of Sin"—he makes himself a god, and enters not into any Pantheon as the rival or colleague of other divinities, but into God's own Temple and seats himself as God without equal or superior. At any common epoch no one would venture on this blasphemous vanity—it would find no response, and the profane and rash impertinence would be speedily blasted and shivered to atoms—"Men would clap their hands at him and hiss him from his place." The character of his period may therefore be inferred from his successful adventure, as he is borne on the tide of the time to the highest pinnacle, even to the earthly throne of God —an altitude to which common ambition never looked up, and from which ordinary insolence would shrink back in dismay and terror. He shall be, as usually happens, the creature of his age, realizing its godlessness, and giving it palpability in himself—his colossal genius towering above all his contemporaries by means of their encouragement and hero-worship—for they see themselves reflected and glorified in him, as he grasps, with sublime audacity, the divine prerogative, and wields it as a native and unchallenged right.

Had not France, as a nation, become so audacious and atheistic, had not society been so altered, wrecked, and thrown into anarchy, Paris would never have witnessed the spectacle of a prostitute throned on the high altar of Notre Dame, saluted and worshipped under the title of the "Goddess of Reason." The act was the fruit and crown of the national insanity, and had one of the revolutionary leaders proclaimed himself the "god of reason," and maintained and exercised his godship, he would have been, in some respects, a type and illustration of the Man of Sin. That God had become man is the old belief, that man has become God is the new phantasm; that *Être Suprême* being, according to positivism, humanity or the collective life of all human beings, the Infinite being ignored. When men take home to them the old falsehood, "ye are gods," they are only opening a way for one of themselves, of greater courage and dexterity, to assert "I am God." Humanity in the last times finding its divinity within itself, shall at length bow down to its apotheosis in the Man of Sin as its collective image and representative. Wearied of a God of love who gives it everything, and to whom all thanks are ever due, it sets up this god of power, and its worship of humanity enthroned in him, so near itself and so like itself, is but a new form of self-adulation. Throwing off all faith in the Saviour, it places a wretched confidence in a self-deifying usurper, whose tyranny is equalled only by his blasphemy. Flinging all former beliefs to the winds, losing all confidence in God's truth, and superseding it by some new revelation of self-evolved speculations—gratifying to a proud, daring, and pantheistic intellect—it becomes the victim of delusion and a lie, for it has not received the love of the truth. The Man of Sin will be but the living reflection of the godless apostacies and impieties of his period, the power of the god of this world inspiring and stimulating him. What Satan could be, were he permitted to assume humanity, that will his organ be—showing pre-eminence, not in immorality, or brutishness, or any inordinate lusts and orgies, but lifted above all in pride and insolence, and flinging out his contemptuous challenge to all power in heaven, and all authority and law on earth. And his kingdom shall be confirmed with all miracles, and signs, and wonders, and with all deceivableness of unrighteousness, so that it can accumulate evidences, to doubt which may be branded as unreasonable and unnatural scepticism.

Antichrist has been often described as made up in the style of the expositor's own age. Some of the early fathers—believers in magic and occult powers—portrayed him as Simon Magus, endowed with vaster craft and energy. Mediæval schoolmen regarded him as the boldest and subtlest of disputants, able to confound, by his scholastic shrewdness, every opponent. Men of monastic seclusion thought of him as awing the world by his austerities. Malvenda pictures him as possessed of rare and victorious eloquence, so cunning and overpowering that he will succeed in proving, beyond a doubt, that the Lord Jesus was an impostor. Maitland seems to ascribe to him, not the knowledge and employment of science, but imagination and pantheistic eloquence. It is difficult to conjecture that subversal of the divine administration and erasure of the divine existence in idea and purpose—that union of reckless disbelief on the one hand and of credulousness on the other—which the possibility of the ascendency of the Man of Sin presupposes. It may be that his transcendent intellect shall not only take advantage of all circumstances propitious to his lawless audacity, but that he shall cunningly arrange and combine human passions, policy, and events, to further his enterprise; or that he shall, by force of will, originality of conception, and sublimity of godless daringness, at once create the crisis which lifts him to his awful pinnacle. Bede imagines that he shall spread abroad a report —" Lo, Christ is here!" " Lo, he is there!"—that men may be accustomed to the expectation of a new Christ, and that then he shall openly and impiously assume the blessed name. It is the last struggle of sin and Satan, inspired and envenomed by a thousand memories of defeat, the concentrated malice and rage of centuries, intensified into frenzied and furious antitheism. It is the devil's final effort, so wisely and warily conducted, so long and cunningly prepared for by the apostacy, as to augur success; and it may be that ordinary defences and strategy would be unequal to the contest. There has ever been opposition to God in the world, sometimes rising into virulent eminence—as in Balaam and Antiochus, and in many blasphemers and persecutors; this, however, is its last and loftiest culmination. But Satan's ministers, and his vice-devil organ encounter an irresistible doom—he is consumed by the breath of Christ's mouth. The prospect is a dark one, but it is the apostle's picture. This terrible monstrosity may be connected with the apocalyptic conspiracy of Gog and Magog —a great and appalling reaction after the revival, or so-called millenium, has passed away (Rev. xx, 7, 8, &c.). The Lord himself puts the startling question, "When the Son of Man cometh, shall he find faith on the earth?" (Luke xviii, 8). This opinion is in the core of it similar to that of Olshausen, Ellicott, Alford, Riggenbach, Lacunza, Lillie, Lange,[1] though the last takes a limited and secular view, tinged perhaps with the political combinations and prospects of the European continent, when he writes of Antichristianism, that while Ultramontane absolutists see it in the consummation of Radicalism, and Radical literati look on Jesuitism as the incarnation of this evil principle, his supposition is that these extremes may be reconciled, and "the last form of Antichristianism may proceed from a coalition between completed absolutism and completed Radicalism." We should be disposed to say that such a coalition—destroying all rule, trampling on all right, and breaking all social bonds—would prepare that anarchy, in the midst of which, and taking advantage of it, the daring power of the Man of Sin shall climb to this solitary eminence, stand out as the supplanter of God, and crown himself as the personal concentration, or the organ and representative, of all secular and spiritual despotism.

[1] Article, "Antichrist" in Herzog, *Real. Encyclopädie*, Gotha, 1863.

What the temple of God is, in which the Man of Sin is to take his seat, it is difficult to say. The ναός, as we have seen, may be an image, and may mean the church of Christ. But the sense is not supported by analogy, for, as we have also seen, in all the places in which the word is used in a symbolic sense, the clause explains the metaphor, or contains the assertion that believers form the temple—" Know ye not that ye are the temple of God,"—"which temple ye are" (1 Cor. iii, 16, 17; vi, 19). Compare Ephes. ii, 20, 21, 22. The somewhat similar phrase, "temple of my God," in Rev. iii, 12, does not refer to the church of Christ on earth, but to the heavenly edifice. Besides, what idea would the first readers of that epistle associate with the "temple of God" when there was only one structure bearing the name of it, and it was in the city of Jerusalem? Shall that temple be rebuilt, or shall some central sanctuary of the latter day, the metropolitan church of the world, bear the hallowed appellation; or shall it be some place of honour hitherto unreached by any one, which the Man of Sin shall stealthily climb to, and in which, throwing off his disguise, he shall begin by word and deed· to act out his predicted career? The realistic view seems most in harmony with the meaning of the terms, which suppose some locality in which this profane parade of himself as God shall take place (Elliott, p. 835).

To conclude, I question if the term Antichrist, so commonly given to the Man of Sin, be properly applied to him. True, indeed, as the Man of Sin does a work so opposite to Christ's in relation both to God and man, in its nature and purpose—dishonouring the Father and enveloping the world in awful peril—he may be called Antichrist. The meaning of the word may be disputed, as ἀντί may signify either "instead of" or "against." Thus ἀντιβασιλεύς, "a viceroy"; ἀνθύπατος, a "pro-consul": but ἀντιφιλοσοφέω, "to hold opposite tenets"; ἀντειπεῖν, "to speak against"; ἀντίθεσις, "opposition"; ἀντιλογία, "contradiction"; ἀντίταγμα, "the opposite army"; ἀνταγωνιστής, an "opponent." Thus we have the term "antipope," and this seems to be the common meaning of ἀντί in composition. With the former meaning it would not differ much from ψευδόχριστος, as in Matt. xxiv, 24, a pretender or a

vice-Christ, whom, according to Jerome, the Jews will accept
as the true Messiah, and, as in the words of Irenaeus, *tentans
semetipsum Christum ostendere*, one giving himself out to be
the Christ. But the word means, opposed to Christ. Irenaeus
seems to have combined both views, for the previous clause is
in quo adversarius sedebit.[1] Musculus says that Antichrist
means Christ's vicar, and this the Pope pretends to be; but
a-Lapide replies that, on that theory, Peter and Paul and all
the apostles were antichrists, for they acted as vicars of Christ.
The word is used only by John, and that no less than five
times; three times, 1 John ii, 18, 22; iv, 3; 2 Ep. 7. The
apostle also explains the meaning of the term, which is
peculiar to him. In iv, 3, he writes, "and every spirit that con-
fesseth not that Jesus Christ is come in the flesh is not of God,
and this is the spirit of antichrist." In the 2nd epistle, verse 7,
"many deceivers are entered into the world who confess not
that Jesus Christ is come in the flesh." This is a "deceiver
and an antichrist." (1) The stress in those definitions lies in
the words "in the flesh," not in the denial of the Messiahship
or of His coming (for such an error would comprehend all the
Jews), but in the denial of the true humanity, of His coming in
the flesh. (2) The persons to whom the name is given had once
been in visible fellowship with the church "among us, but not
of us"—a statement that could not be made of unbelieving Jews.
(3) The language also implies that these persons still made a
Christian profession, and under its guise they are deceivers,
for it is not want of faith altogether or infidelity, but a defective faith, or the denial of a primary and distinctive truth, that
characterizes them. They were $\pi o\lambda\lambda o\grave{i}$ $\pi\lambda\acute{a}\nu o\iota$, each of them
was $\acute{o}$ $\psi\epsilon\acute{v}\sigma\tau\eta s$ and $\acute{o}$ $\pi\lambda\acute{a}\nu os$, beguiling men, and teaching
fatal heresy under the guise of Christian discipleship. (4) In
ii, 22, the apostle says, "he is antichrist that denieth the
Father and the Son," the sense probably being that the denial
of the Son necessarily involves denial of the Father, since
Father and Son are correlative terms, and the Father without
the Son is not the true God—"whosoever denieth the Son
the same hath not the Father." (5) The word is also used in the
plural—ii, 18, "even now there are many antichrists," $\pi o\lambda\lambda o\grave{i}$

[1] *Advers. Haeres.*, v. 25; a-Lapide; Maitland, p. 385.

ἀντίχριστοι, many persons holding and propagating those views which are so radically antichristian in nature and result. (6) The Antichrist is therefore in John no special individual marked out, for there were many deceivers. There is no hint that these numerous antichrists are precursors of the Antichrist, identifying him with "the Man of Sin," as De Wette, Lücke, and Düsterdieck. (7) These antichrists of John's epistles were already in the world doing their work, and that work was deception, but the Man of Sin is to appear at a future period. (8) The form of error promulgated by these men seems to have been incipient Gnosticism, obscuring the true doctrine of the incarnation and of the person of Christ. The error was soon to ripen into Doketism, and the theory of Æons and Emanations, as held by Cerinthus, and many heresiarchs after him. It impugned Christ's real humanity, made him a mere phantom, and thus destroyed the reality of His sympathy and His teaching; and as He was not a partaker of their flesh and blood, He had no kinship with men, and could in no way represent them in atonement or example. This system of error and enmity is wholly different from that portrayed in 2 Thess., and it has been only by importing descriptions from Daniel and the Apocalypse that any identification has been attempted. The antichrist or antichrists were "deceivers," "liars," apostates from the church, busy and malignant in their zeal at the moment, not forepictured to come at some future epoch. They were in existence "even now," so that as all vital error is antichristian, and leads to yet lower depths, they were preparing the way for the apostacy. With all its antichristian elements, Popery has never held the false doctrine defined in John's epistles, but has ever protested against it, and its error lies in the opposite direction, for it abounds in realistic symbols of Christ, and fabricates representations of the babe and the manger, the cross and the nails, the five wounds and the sepulchre. The fathers indeed as a body identified the predicted Man of Sin with Antichrist, and usually so named him. But, in the first place, as we have seen, the definitions of Antichrist in John, both of his error and his time, and the use of the plural antichrists, πολλοί, fairly preclude such an identification; secondly, it is not warranted by this prediction,

Christ is not mentioned in this description till His Second Coming is referred to. The antagonism of the Man of Sin is directly, specially, and immediately against God; he opposeth and exalteth himself above every one called God; takes his seat in the temple of God, showing himself that he is God. He is thus not a false Christ, but a false God; and he is characterized not by infidelity, but by atheism, or rather scornful antitheism—a counter-God rather than a counter-Christ. Of course, it is implied that a denial of Christ must have preceded as an intermediate step in the blasphemous process of self-deification, but the spirit and letter of the entire paragraph portray not unbelief in Christ, but fierce and ultimate hostility to God—not a ψευδόχριστος, but a ψευδόθεος.

INDEX OF GREEK WORDS MORE PARTICULARLY REFERRED TO

ἀγαθόν, 204.
ἀγαθωσύνη, 252.
ἀγάπη, 36, 187, 230, 307.
ἁγιασμός, 126.
ἅγιοι, 120, 246.
ἁγιωσύνη, 120.
ἀγῶνι, 57.
ἀδιαλείπτως, 206.
ἀθετέω, 135.
αἰφνίδιος, 178.
αἰώνιος, 298.
ἀκαθαρσία, 135.
ἀκοή, 77.
ἀκριβῶς, 174.
ἀληθινός, 53.
ἅμα, 192.
ἄμεμπτος, 71, 120.
ἀναγινώσκω, 220.
ἀνάγκη, 110.
ἀναιρέω, 281.
ἀναμένειν, 52.
ἀνάστασις, 167.
ἀναπληρῶσαι, 89.
ἄνεσις, 238.
ἀνέχεσθε, 233.
ἀνταποδοῦναι, 113.
ἀντικείμενος, 268.
ἀξίως, 74.

ἀπάντησιν, 169.
ἅπαξ καὶ δίς, 96.
ἀποδείκνυμι, 273.
ἀποκαλύπτω, 266.
ἀποκαλύψει (ἐν), 230.
ἀπορφανίζω, 92.
ἀποστασία, 265.
ἀπώλεια, 267.
ἁρπάζω, 169.
ἄρτι, 108.
ἀρχάγγελος, 162.
ἀσθενής, 203.
ἀσφάλεια, 178.
ἄτακτος, 201.
ἀτακτέω, 311.
ἄτοπος, 302.

βάρος, 63, 64.
βασιλεία (τοῦ Θεοῦ), 74, 235.
βούλομαι and θέλω, 95.

γάρ, 54, 57, 98.
γρηγορέω, 183, 190.

δέχομαι, 45, 76.
δίκην τίνειν, 243.
διωγμός, 233.
δοκιμάζειν, 59, 211.

δόλος, 58.
δόξα, 74, 245.
δύναμις, 41, 240.

εἰδέναι, 198.
εἶδος, 212.
εἰρήνη, 177, 321.
ἐκδίκησις, 242.
ἔκδικος, 134.
ἐκδιώκω, 85.
ἐκκλησία, 30, 31.
ἐκλογή, 39.
ἐλπίς, 37, 96, 299.
ἔμπροσθεν, 37.
ἔνδειγμα, 234.
ἐνδοξασθῆναι, 246.
ἐνέστηκεν, 259.
ἐνεργεῖται, 79, 276.
ἐνορκίζω, 220.
ἐπιθυμία, 95, 130.
ἐπιποθέω, 109.
ἐπιστρέφω, 51.
ἐπισυναγωγή, 255.
ἐπιφάνεια, 282.
ἐξαπατάω, 264.
ἐξήχηται, 47.
ἐξουθενέω, 209.
ἔξω (οἱ), 144.
ἐρωτάω, 123.
εὐδοκέω 100.
εὐδοκία, 251.
εὐσχημόνως, 144.

ζῶμεν, 112.
ζῶν, 52.

ἢ οὐχί, 97.
ἤπιοι, 65.
ἡσυχάζειν, 142.

θάλπω, 66.

θαυμασθῆναι, 247.
θεοδίδακτοι, 139.
θροεῖσθαι, 256.
θλῖψις, 233.
θώραξ, 187.

καθεύδω, 184.
καιρός, 92, 173.
καλόν, 211.
καλοποιέω, 317.
καλῶν (ὁ), 217.
καταργεῖν, 282.
καταρτίζω, 115.
κατευθύναι, 117, 306.
κατέχον, 274.
κεῖμαι, 106.
κέλευσμα, 161.
κενή, 55.
κλέπτης, 176.
κοιμωμένοι, 146, 147.
κολακεία, 61.
κοπιάω, 196.
κόπος, 36, 68, 312.
κτάομαι, 128.

λόγῳ (ἐν) Κυρίου, 154.
λοιπὸν (τὸ), 122.
λυπῆσθε, 147.

μακροθυμέω, 203.
μαρτύρομαι, 73.
μεθύσκομαι, 185.
μέλλω, 106.
μεταδοῦναι, 67.
μόχθος, 68, 312.
μυστήριον, 276.

ναός, 270.
νήφω, 183.
νουθετέω, 198, 321.
νοῦς, 256.

νυκτὸς καὶ ἡμέρας, 68, 311.
νῦν, 274.

οἵτινες, 243.
ὄλεθρος, 169.
ὀλιγόψυχος, 202.
ὁλόκληρος, 216.
ὁλοτελής, 215.
ὁμείρομαι, 66.
ὀργὴ, 89, 189.

πάθος, 130.
παραγγέλλω, 306.
παράδοσις, 296, 310.
παρακαλέω, 73, 103, 194.
παράκλησις, 58, 299.
παραλαμβάνω, 76.
παραμυθέω, 73.
παρουσία, 98, 255, 283.
παρρησία, 56.
πειράζων, 108.
περιεργάζομαι, 314.
περικεφαλαία, 187.
περιλειπόμενοι, 156.
περιποίησις, 189, 295.
περισσεύω, 118.
περισσοτέρως, 93.
πίστις, 232.
πλάνη, 58,
πλεονάζω, 118, 230.
πλεονεκτεῖν, 133.
πλεονεξία, 61.
πληροφορία, 42.
πρᾶγμα, 132.
προιστάμενοι, 197.]

πρόφασις, 61.

ῥυόμενον, 53.

σαίνεσθαι, 104.
σαλευθῆναι, 255.
σβέννυμι, 208.
σέβασμα, 269.
σημεῖον, 285.
σημειόω, 319.
σκεῦος, 128.
στέγειν, 100.
συμφυλέτης, 81.
συνεργός, 102.

τίθημι, 189.
τοιγαροῦν, 135.
τόπος, 46.
τρέχω, 301.
τροφός, 66.

ὑβρισθέντες, 56.
ὑπεραυξάνει, 229.
ὑπερβαίνειν, 131.
ὑπερεκπερισσοῦ, 114.
ὑπομονή, 37, 232, 308.

φθάνειν, 89, 160.
φιλαδελφία, 137.
φίλημα, 218.
φιλοτιμεῖσθαι, 141.

χαρά, 45, 96, 113.
χρόνος, 173.

www.ingramcontent.com/pod-product-compliance
Lightning Source LLC
Chambersburg PA
CBHW071225230426
43668CB00011B/1313